Professor Emeritus of Music History
at the University of Louisville,
Gerhard Herz was the first elected
chairman of the American chapter of
the Neue Bach Gesellschaft. His work
has become well known in this country
through his editions of Bach's Cantatas
4 and 140 in the Norton Critical
Scores series. His recently completed
Bach Sources in America now offers
scholars a comprehensive catalog of
American Bach manuscripts.

Essays on
J.S. Bach

Studies in Musicology, No. 73

George Buelow, Series Editor

Professor of Music
Indiana University

Other Titles in This Series

Essays on J.S. Bach

by
Gerhard Herz

Emeritus Professor of Music History
University of Louisville
Louisville, Kentucky

UMI RESEARCH PRESS
Ann Arbor, Michigan

Produced and distributed by
UMI Research Press
an imprint of
University Microfilms International
A Xerox Information Resources Company
Ann Arbor, Michigan 48106

Library of Congress Cataloging in Publication Data

Herz, Gerhard, 1911-
Essays on J.S. Bach.

(Studies in musicology ; no. 73)
In part a translation, with new introd., of the
author's dissertation, Johann Sebastian Bach im
Zeitalter des Rationalismus und der Frühromantik
(University of Zurich, 1934)
Bibliography: p.
1. Bach, Johann Sebastian , 1685-1750. I. Herz,
Gerhard, 1911- . Johann Sebastian Bach im
Zeitalter des Rationalismus und der Frühromantik.
English. 1985. II. Title. III. Series.

ML410.B1H348   1985   780'.92'4   84-22222
ISBN 0-8357-1475-6 (alk. paper)

Frontispiece.   Johann Sebastian Bach.
Portrait by Elias Gottlieb Haussmann, 1748
Reproduced by kind permission of
William H. Scheide, Princeton, N.J.

Contents

Part III

Part IV

Part V

Part VI

Part VII

Foreword

In the introduction to this book of collected writings on Johann Sebastian Bach, Gerhard Herz tells with poignancy how the German political tragedy of the 1930s affected both his personal and professional life and forced his career as a musicologist to be anchored in the United States. Herz was, of course, only one of many Germans of Jewish origins to emigrate to the United States during that tragic decade. But for the development of musicology, his story explains in part how a whole generation of young American students of music history would be enriched by the presence of such distinguished scholars in our country, and it was a unique moment in the growth of music studies in American higher education.

He devoted his entire teaching career to the University of Louisville, and in his typically modest and unselfish way contributed until his retirement to a legacy of great teaching in music at that institution. It is astonishing, given his devotion to teaching (as well as to community musical life), that Herz has produced so many distinguished works of scholarship.

Most American students of J.S. Bach will remember Herz for his two basic studies of Bach cantatas: BWV 4: *Christ lag in Todesbanden,* and BWV 140: *Wachet auf ruft uns die Stimme.* The latter work includes what has become the essential means by which the revolutionary new dating of Bach's cantatas, the so-called "new chronology" of Alfred Dürr and Georg von Dadelsen, has been disseminated throughout much of the English-speaking world. The organization into English of the complexities of the extraordinary research achievements of Dürr and Dadelsen reflects Herz's sustained commitment over a lifetime to spreading his knowledge of new Bach scholarship to students and other lovers of Bach's music.

The essays in this volume, including his important doctoral dissertation, never before appearing in English translation, of course represent only a small part of Herz's accomplishments. In addition to the two editions of Bach cantatas in the Norton Critical Scores series, these essays (the larger part in English for the first time), represent many of his other writings that have appeared in various forms over the decades. For example, the essay on the first movement of Bach's Cantata BWV 77 originally served as a program note for a performance of the work during a meeting of the AMS South-Central Chapter (Louisville, 1974). For an extensive list of Herz's writings, see the bibliography in *Essays on the Music of J.S. Bach and Other Divers Subjects, A Tribute to Gerhard Herz* (Louisville, 1981).

Herz was the first chairman of the new American Chapter of the Neue Bach Gesellschaft. His recently completed *Bach Sources in America* achieves for the first time a comprehensive catalog of Bach manuscripts found in America. From every viewpoint Herz has given of himself to his chosen life's work as a teacher and scholar, whose greatest passion has been and remains the music of Bach. To know Herz is to know a man who lives in the spirit of Bach's music, its humanism, its craftsmanship, and its ethical goodness. UMI Research Press is honored, especially in the tricentennial year of Bach's birth, to make available this volume which includes some of Herz's most important and valuable thoughts about Bach and his music.

GEORGE J. BUELOW

Part I

Johann Sebastian Bach in the Age of Rationalism and Early Romanticism

Aspects of the History of the Bach Movement from
Its Inception to the Revival of the
Matthew Passion in the Year
1829

Preface

This book, written half a century ago, has been superseded by two indispensable works: Hans Theodor David's and Arthur Mendel's *Bach Reader* (1945) and Werner Neumann's and Hans-Joachim Schulze's *Bach-Dokumente* (1963, 1969 and 1972). In the meantime a number of special studies in the ever growing Bach literature have scrutinized particular subjects or phases of the period I had dealt with, and explored them in depth and far greater detail. Since the English translation leaves this book unchanged, it will have to be regarded as an already-historical document of the music-conception that Wilibald Gurlitt inspired and as an interpretation of music history typical of the early 1930s. Because this book appears not as a new edition brought up-to-date but rather as a reprint in translation, published here for the first time, I felt that an Introduction was appropriate. In this Introduction I have described not only the story of its origin but also the politically turbulent history of its publication and finally the role that this publication was to play in my career as a musicologist in America.

Introduction

Fifty years ago no one could have predicted that one day I would sit at the water's edge on the Florida coast of the Gulf of Mexico and write the story of my doctoral dissertation. In the spring of 1930, I graduated at the age of eighteen from the *Hindenburg Gymnasium* in Düsseldorf. I was still undecided whether to pursue a career as violinist, music critic, or music historian. These doubts vanished after a visit to Cologne to see Emanuel Feuermann, the legendary cellist, who died all too early, in 1942. After I played some Bach and Mozart for him but fumbled in sightreading the Scherzo from Beethoven's String Quartet, Opus 18 No. 6, Feuermann advised me to forego the strenuous life of a professional violinist and to become a music critic or musicologist.

Already the first two semesters (1930-31) at the University of Freiburg/Br. proved that Feuermann's judgment had been sound. Immediately I fell under the spell of Professor Wilibald Gurlitt. My former uncertainty began to give way to the possibility of a life devoted to the then still young discipline of musicology, which was not yet taught in the United States as one of the components of the Humanities leading to the Ph.D. degree. The contagious enthusiasm and singlemindedness of purpose of Gurlitt's lectures, translated into living sound in the Collegium Musicum in which I participated as violinist, were new and deep impressions that overwhelmed the nineteen-year-old student. The frequent presence of the sound of the first Freiburg Praetorius organ increased the feeling that historical truth lay at the center of all endeavors undertaken at the musicological institute of the University of Freiburg. Thanks to Gurlitt, who like the Pied Piper of Hamelin gathered his disciples around him, musicology had become by semester's end a no longer avoidable vocation.

In the second semester Gurlitt offered a course on the history of the Bach movement. The first lecture, in which Gurlitt ranged from Luther and Veit Bach to Hindemith, struck me like a flash of light. I vowed that some day I would participate in the exploration of this subject. I worked like one possessed on a paper about Schumann's piano accompaniment to Bach's sonatas and partitas for unaccompanied violin. It was this report that attracted Gurlitt's attention. He thought I could develop it more fully and perhaps make it publishable, a suggestion I failed to follow. The dependable violinist of the Collegium Musicum, who used to amuse the professor with Rhenish jokes in the beer-tavern to which we went customarily after rehearsals, finally dared ask the question—could he perhaps choose a certain phase of the Bach movement as subject for his still-far-off dissertation. Gurlitt's answer was: "Do not start with Schumann but rather with Scheibe." With this response my goal was defined and with Gurlitt's concurrence Berlin was chosen as the most logical place for my research.

I spent the summer semester of 1931, however, at the University of Vienna where Bach research and musicological studies were neglected in spite of stimulating lectures by Alfred Orel on Brahms and by Egon Wellesz on modern music. Although Rudolf von Ficker's way of speaking was dry and unemotional, I gained valuable insights into Beethoven's late style. Robert Lach, fluent pianist that he was, ended his lectures habitually with the playing of long stretches from Wagner's *Ring des Nibelungen*. Robert Haas used to sit motionless at his desk and read from his *Aufführungspraxis der Musik* without interrupting the monotonous flow of his words by a single example on the piano or phonograph. Gurlitt's fiery musicological zeal was not at home in the Vienna of 1931. In its stead the Department of Musicology at the University of Vienna granted its students the privilege of obtaining free admission to the standing room section on the top balcony of the Staatsoper.

What I remember most about these three months in Vienna, are the thirty-nine felicitous evenings I spent at the opera house. They started with Richard Strauss conducting Mozart's *Idomeneo* and Beethoven's *Fidelio,* the latter in breakneck tempo. This, I learned, was due to a card game Strauss had scheduled after the performance. The great singers were Leo Slezak, Lotte Lehmann, Elisabeth Schumann and Richard Mayr, the first Ochs von Lerchenau at the *Rosenkavalier's* première in Vienna in 1911. I heard Lehmann, Schumann and Mayr three times in that opera. Such casts, mainly in Strauss and Wagner operas, conducted by Strauss's friend Clemens Krauss and staged superbly by Lothar Wallerstein, made my study of music history take a back seat to the history that was being made at the opera house. *Götterdämmerung* and *Tristan und Isolde* (with Lauritz Melchior) were about the last performances conducted by Franz Schalk (1863—Sept. 3, 1931), the Bruckner disciple who during Gustav Mahler's directorship had been appointed to the Vienna Court Opera. After a performance of Strauss' *Ariadne auf Naxos,* Schalk wanted no part of the heated ovation contest between the supporters of Lotte Lehmann and Maria Jeritza. Jeritza preferred to have the stage to herself in *Cavalleria Rusticana* or as Puccini's horse riding *Girl of the Golden West.*

Towards the end of this summer an event occurred which cast a shadow over this harmonious semester and became a harbinger of more drastic events to follow. A march, organized by the Nazis along the Vienna *Ring* boulevard, spread to and engulfed the University. I was present when some of these rowdies stormed into the lecture room in which Egon Wellesz was discussing Mussorgsky's original version of *Boris Godunov*. They threatened Wellesz and prevented the continuation of the lecture. Similar violent actions also interfered with the lectures of other chiefly Jewish professors. This riot led to the first interruption of the academic function of the University of Vienna which had to close its doors for several days.

In spite of this ominous conclusion to my days in Vienna, the next three semesters (fall 1931—spring 1933) at the University of Berlin became a productive working period for me, clouded by political events only at its very end. Perhaps subconsciously seeking a mentor whom I could venerate as I had venerated Gurlitt, I soon fell under the spell of that wonderful combination of charm and wisdom that was Curt Sachs. His course on the history of musical instruments as a world encompassing field was entirely new to me. Sachs lectured informally, always without notes, yet always in a most fascinating and illuminating manner. The young Friedrich Blume impressed me with his impeccably prepared lectures. Their convincing logic gave me a new sense of the methodical way in which musicological problems could be organized. After I had delivered a paper on Schütz's *Psalmen Davids* on which I had worked very hard, I was admitted to his Collegium Musicum. However, Sachs and Blume exhausted my unreserved enthusiasm for the Berlin musicologists. The main seminar of Arnold Schering produced from time to time stimulating ideas and discussions. This was particularly noticeable if one compared them to the dryly presented though factually solid lectures of Erich M. von Hornbostel and Johannes Wolf. The courses given by the almost eighty-year-old Max Friedländer and by Hans Joachim Moser, who was to compromise himself so completely during the Nazi era, were certainly livelier but less profound.

In the meantime I had selected art history as my principal minor field of specialization. I accumulated a fair amount of knowledge from Professor Brinckmann's courses; but it was Professor Fischel's humanistic approach, resembling that of Sachs, that made regular attendance at his lectures an esthetic pleasure not to be missed, especially since they were given before selected paintings at the *Kaiser Friedrich-Museum*. It is revealing that the great teachers, the true humanists among these scholars, Sachs, Fischel and later also Gurlitt, were the ones who would be deprived of their academic positions by the Nazi regime. In spite of the many courses in which I had enrolled and to which I should add history of journalism, my second minor field of specialization, I spent most of my time during these three Berlin semesters in the Music Division of the Staatsbibliothek. There I collected, bit by bit, the material for my dissertation.

Gurlitt's trust in me, which I tried to live up to, helped me maintain a certain mental distance from the riots and ever increasing political confrontations. On January 30, 1933, the day on which Hindenburg named Hitler Chancellor of Germany, the swastika was raised in the courtyard of the University. While a mass of students intoned the Nazi anthem, the *Horst Wessel-Lied,* I stood in the midst of a sea of outstretched arms, my fists clenched in my pockets in rage. One month later, on February 28, I saw the Reichstag building in flames as the elevated railroad took me from the Staatsbibliothek to my rented room in Berlin-Wilmersdorf.

In 1932 one could still hear the child prodigy Yehudi Menuhin as soloist with the Berlin Philharmonic Orchestra or Arthur Schnabel in one of his recitals of Beethoven's piano sonatas. But early in 1933 Bruno Walter was no longer allowed to conduct the scheduled concert by the Berlin Philharmonic Orchestra of Mozart's G minor Symphony and Mahler's Fourth. Richard Strauss substituted for Walter, but I resold my ticket. I went instead to one of the large Berlin synagogues where Albert Einstein almost succeeded in making his theory of relativity intelligible to a vast audience of laymen. As the political situation became increasingly hopeless, my ability to concentrate on my work began to suffer. In March an occasion arose to return to Düsseldorf in the car of a relative. I accepted the offer even though this meant sacrificing my dearly bought ticket to the Civic Opera's new staging of *Don Giovanni,* conducted by Furtwängler.

My family spent the summer vacation in the Thuringian Forest in a country inn owned by a Jewish lady, other hotels no longer being accessible to us. There and in Düsseldorf I organized and supplemented the material collected in Berlin so that I could submit it to Professor Gurlitt. In fall I travelled to Freiburg where Gurlitt had just been named Dean of the philosophical faculty. He interpreted it not so much as an honor bestowed upon him but rather upon the still young discipline of musicology. He received me with his old Freiburg friendliness and approved what I presented to him. At the same time he seemed deeply concerned about the recent political events and how they could affect the academic freedom of German universities. His extreme pessimism with regard to the future caused him to suggest that it probably would be wiser to complete my doctoral work in the "free air" of Switzerland. The manner in which he conveyed his feelings raised no doubts in my mind as to the honesty of his advice. In contrast to his most gifted disciple, Professor Heinrich Besseler, Gurlitt remained untouched by the Nazi ideology. In fact, in 1937 he was removed from his academic position.

The question whether I should pursue my doctor's degree under Ernst Kurth in Bern or go to Zurich where I had relatives, was decided in favor of Zurich. I had reason to doubt that Professor Kurth would accept my rather far advanced research in the form in which it was gathered and prepared for Gurlitt. At the University of Zurich, on the other hand, it became apparent that Professor Antoine-Elisée Cherbuliez accepted the subject of the dissertation without hesitation. The Zurich Collegium Musicum, led by Cherbuliez who was a capable cellist, gave me many joyous hours of music making. However, Gurlitt's inspired quest for authentic performance of old music was not the avowed aim of Cherbuliez's Collegium Musicum.

While we music history majors attended the lectures of the Zurich music critic, Professor Gysi, out of a sense of duty, we went to the elegant lectures of the young, cultured Basel art historian, Joseph Gantner, out of interest. In Gantner's seminar I read a paper about "Das Problem der Generation," the book of the musical Munich art historian Wilhelm Pinder which had appeared in 1926 and created quite a stir. The purpose of my paper was to examine whether Pinder's thesis was applicable to music history. The Zurich art historian, Professor Konrad Escher, agreed with my suggestion that Netherland painting from the van Eycks to Rembrandt constituted a suitable field of specialization for my doctoral examination a year hence. Attending the public lectures by Heinrich Wölfflin, the almost seventy-year-old patriarch among Swiss art historians, was a profound experience. In contrast to Escher who in my oral doctoral exam did not get beyond the predecessors of the van Eycks, Wölfflin dealt with the great masters of the Renaissance, with Raphael and Michelangelo, rather than with those who paved the way for them.

Two weeks before Wölfflin was to give his final public lecture in the *Auditorium Maximum* of the University, four music students (Ingolf Dahl as harpsichordist, I, another violinist, and a cellist) were asked to introduce the occasion with the playing of some baroque trio sonatas. Hug and Co., the renowned Zurich House of Music, lent us three Italian string instruments for this purpose. I shall never forget the week during which I drew the bow across the strings of "my" Pietro Guarneri violin, effortlessly producing tones of organ-like sumptuousness or beguiling delicacy. After the performance Wölfflin invited the four of us to his home where we were entertained like Renaissance princes.

Ingolf Dahl, who later at the University of Southern California in Los Angeles was to make a name for himself as composer, pianist, conductor, and also as Stravinsky's collaborator, became a close friend of mine. Almost every weekend we went into the mountains to ski, a sport I had already learned during my Freiburg winter in the Black Forest. On New Year's Day 1934 I skied from Lenzerheide to Chur. During this run, an effortless gliding in the gently downwards leading tracks of the road, I could not help but sing out of joy, taking off my skis only at the Chur railroad station. In its way this experience has remained as vivid to me as my first Toscanini record (Rossini's Overture to *The Barber of Seville* on 78 rpm!). The beauty of the snowy Swiss mountains was an ideal counterbalance to the intensive work at the Zurich *Zentralbibliothek* where I pressed forward with my studies for two semesters until the manuscript seemed finally ready for the typewriter.

The next month spent at home in Düsseldorf and the summer spent in Zurich belonged to the completion and typing of my dissertation. The doctoral examinations took place in July 1934. "Netherland landscape painting in the first half of the 16th century" was the subject of the paper in art history which was to be completed within three days during which one was permitted to make full use of the library. Dictated at midnight of the third day to a graduate student and expert typist, the finished paper was handed in on the next morning by the sleepwalking candidate sprouting a three-day beard. Three hours were set aside for the paper in music history during which time one was locked into a conference room without access to any bibliographical aids. The subject, "The Variation Principle in the Music of the Age of Baroque," was so broad and rich that I became hardly aware of being left to my own resources.

The oral examinations took place on July 14, 1934, which I did not look forward to as a *jour de gloire*. The half hour examination testing my knowledge of the history of journalism proceeded quite satisfactorily. Professor Escher's oral examination in art history hardly went beyond the first decade of the two and a half centuries of my field of concentration. I had prepared myself for it by more than a year of reading and a ten-day trip to the chief museums of Holland and Belgium. As I learned later, I was much unhappier about this oral ordeal than the examining professor. Professors Gysi and Cherbuliez each took one hour for the oral examination in musicology which was "limited" to the music of Western civilization. Along general lines I felt sufficiently well prepared so that this crucial test turned into two long and animated conversations which I found interesting rather than painful or embarrassing. In the late afternoon I was presented with the unofficial diploma which stated that I had passed my examinations and received the degree of Doctor of Philosophy with the distinction *magna cum laude*. Only a few hours later I went to the railroad station to meet my parents and my brother Hans, who later in America as the political scientist and author, John H. Herz, made a respected name for himself. A splendid supper, to which three of my ever-helpful Zurich friends were also invited, ended the day.

After my return from the month-long vacation in the Swiss mountains, my music theory teacher, Hans W. David, the music critic of the Düsseldorf Jewish weekly paper, allowed me to write occasional concert reviews. The concerts of the Düsseldorf *Kulturbund* had to be held in the city's main synagogue that on

November 9, 1938 was set on fire. These concerts competed in quality though not in quantity with those of the Düsseldorf symphony orchestra and the performances at the opera house which Jews were no longer allowed to attend. The Budapest Quartet played among other works Hindemith's String Quartet, Opus 22, which the Nazis considered to be "degenerate art." Emanuel Feuermann and Wilhelm (William) Steinberg gave an evening of cello sonatas. Alexander Kipnis sang Schubert's *Winterreise* while many of his listeners were overcome by tears.

In 1935 the music critic of the *Frankfurter Zeitung* had the courage and decency to ask me to report on the *Maggio Musicale* in Florence. I was also invited to send reviews about this Florentine event to the *Jüdische Rundschau* in Berlin. I owed this opportunity to serve as music critic to the Italian historian Nello Rosselli, who had invited me towards the end of 1934 to spend a few months with him and his family in Florence.

Because the Rossellis had engaged a German-speaking governess for their two young daughters, Nello Rosselli was anxious to gain an insight into the German language and literature from a German refugee. In the beautiful house on the Via Giuseppe Giusti in Florence which Nello's mother Amelia shared with her son's family, I met a number of sympathetic, cultured, consistently antifascist artists and university professors. Of course, the latter were, like Rosselli, no longer allowed to teach. From the composer Mario Castelnuovo Tedesco, for instance, I received a lovely note of recommendation that I was able to use to good advantage after my emigration to America.

Nello's socialist brother Carlo was frequently mentioned at more intimate conversations. I learned that after a number of astonishing, partly clandestine, partly provocative political actions, Carlo Rosselli had been banished to the Lipari Islands in the Gulf of Naples. From there he had succeeded in escaping to North Africa by way of a waiting motorboat. After this escapade Carlo settled in Paris where he founded the paper *Giustizia e Libertà* and became the center of the Italian antifascist movement abroad. When Nello spoke of his brother, his admiration and pride seemed always dampened by worry.

In Florence as in Düsseldorf and Zurich the playing of chamber music was one of my chief diversions. Among those who joined us occasionally was Thomas Mann's daughter Monika who played piano. After I had been Nello Rosselli's guest for about three months, I moved, just one block from his house, to the *Pensione Aschaffenburg* established by three of my cousins from Cologne. It was a most interesting time because artists used to stop over there. Among them was Edwin Fischer who played Mozart's Piano Concerto in D minor with the superb Florentine orchestra, and later the members of Adolf Busch's chamber orchestra whose performance of Bach's Brandenburg Concertos in the Palazzo Pitti may well have been the first time that these concertos were played publicly by a small ensemble of Bachian size.

Despite being under surveillance by the Italian secret police, I became a correspondent of two newspapers. During the *Maggio Musicale* I became a *persona grata.* As such I had to endure official receptions and dinners, most of them staged with great pomp in the Palazzo Vecchio. When, at summer's end, the Italians invaded Ethiopia, my long simmering disgust and loathing of Mussolini's policies reached their boiling point. I left his heavenly beautiful country in September 1935 and returned to my homeland which had become politically even more repulsive.

A year earlier, at the time I received my Ph.D., Professor Cherbuliez had urged me to send an abstract of my dissertation to Albert Schweitzer. Schweitzer was at that time in Guensbach, Alsace, in the house that he built when he received the Goethe prize in 1932. In my letter to him I used Gurlitt and Cherbuliez as references, added the table of contents of my dissertation and mentioned that I had no longer any future in Germany because I was Jewish. Schweitzer's warm-hearted answer of September 26, 1934 speaks for itself:

> Dear Dr. Gerhard Herz.
> In the waiting room in Colmar. Fatigued and pressed for time. Your subject is *very interesting.* How many *words* will the work contain? I would suggest a Swiss publisher. Perhaps, Paul Haupt, Bern, Falkenplatz 14, who is also the publisher of the works of Prof. Kurth (and who is also my publisher). I go now to England and Scotland. But December back to Guensbach. Send there a typed copy of your manuscript if it is all right with you. Cordially, pardon the hurry—Ah, how sad is all this! Day in and day out I must think of those people who, like you, have been hit by such an incomprehensible fate.
> Yours sincerely, Albert Schweitzer.

One year later my dissertation was published by the Bärenreiter-Verlag in Kassel. I sent a copy to Albert Schweitzer. At the time that my article "Zur Geschichte der Bachbewegung" appeared in the *Schweizerische Musikzeitung* (Zurich, November 1935) I received a questionnaire from Bärenreiter. The answers to its questions showed of course that the author of the published dissertation was "non-Aryan." Thereupon Karl Vötterle, the founder of the Bärenreiter-Verlag, wrote that for reasons certainly known to me he was worried about the book's future and that he thought it advisable to try to find another publisher abroad. I believed then and still believe that Vötterle's letter in which he appeared visibly embarrassed, was forced upon him by new "guidelines" of the Nazi party. In my predicament I turned again to Schweitzer whose advice regarding his Bern publisher I had failed to heed in 1934. Schweitzer responded on November 26, 1935 from Edinburgh where he was concertizing:

> I am writing to you, drowning in work and fatigue—Therefore the brevity. Your book has turned out fine. Best congratulations. I am writing now, recommending it highly, to Haupt in Bern. Get directly in touch with him. Ah, how I worry about you. Most cordially—yours treu ergebener
>
>   Albert Schweitzer.

I wrote immediately to Paul Haupt who agreed without hesitation to the takeover as publisher. From then on the dissertation appeared, merely its title page and cardboard cover reprinted, with "Paul Haupt-Verlag/Bern-Leipzig/1936."

Early in 1936 my parents and I received a letter from my Zurich uncle, a cousin of my father. He and his family were American citizens who had lived in Zurich for years at a time. It was there that I got to know them well. They had recently returned to New York. My uncle asked in his letter whether I would like to come to the United States and try to make a living there. My reply was of course an enthusiastic and most grateful yes. Upon receiving my answer my uncle sent the affidavit needed for my emigration to the United States. I now began to move heaven and earth to prepare myself for the momentous one-way trip. Above all, I tried to improve the little English I had learned at the *Gymnasium* where Latin and Greek had been stressed at the expense of modern languages.

Six months after my application, I was informed by the American consulate in Stuttgart that I could pick up my immigration visa. I informed Schweitzer who had requested that I do so, and received the following kind invitation:

> I am in Guensbach all of July. I am glad to see you. If possible, please announce the day of your arrival. Ihr herzlichst ergebener Albert Schweitzer.

After I had received my visa in Stuttgart I took the train to Colmar and the local train to Guensbach where I hoped to see and talk to Schweitzer for perhaps ten to fifteen minutes. Instead he kept me for the whole day although five or six other visitors had come to see him. When Mme Emmy Martin, Schweitzer's Guensbach housekeeper, introduced me to him he said with an unexpectedly high voice, "Stay for luncheon. Then we will talk about your book and your future."

During the big midday meal I was so nervous and overcome by awe that I had little appetite and could not take any second helpings. When Schweitzer became aware of this, he said with sarcasm in his voice: "Der Jüngling" (that is what he called me throughout the day) "has no appetite." After lunch Schweitzer himself poured the coffee in an adjoining room. When my turn came he asked mockingly: "I take it, Jüngling, no cream, no sugar." I felt I simply had to rise to the challenge and answered "On the contrary, plenty of cream and three lumps of sugar please." And he, with a twinkle in his eyes that made him look like Mark Twain, turned to Mme Martin and said "If we keep the Jüngling here for another week, he'll yet be all right."

He sent me to his second floor study while he chatted and bade farewell to the other guests downstairs. When Schweitzer joined me, he began with specific questions that centered on the efforts Bach's disciples had made to keep their

Master's keyboard music alive. He asked these questions with a concentration on the moment at hand such as I had never experienced before, except possibly from Gurlitt. He was apparently quite satisfied with the conclusions I had drawn from my source material. Then the talk turned to my emigration to America, and the warmth of his compassion touched me especially because it was in such soothing contrast to the outspokenness I had come to know during luncheon. Then he said, "Stay for supper. But now I must work. Take a walk and come back in two hours." He retreated to his downstairs study. As I started, my Leica camera in hand, through the peaceful landscape of the Münster Valley I looked back and saw Schweitzer sitting at his desk. The window was open and he was writing busily, as if nothing had ever interrupted the train of his thoughts that were then shaping his philosophy of culture. Punctually at four o'clock I returned. Schweitzer emerged from his study and said, "Jüngling, come along, I must practice now." We walked to the village church the door of which Schweitzer opened with an old fashioned enormous key. We climbed the steep, wooden steps to the organ loft where Schweitzer asked me to sit next to him, to pull the stops and turn pages for him. He began with Bach's Fantasia and Fugue in G minor. After the playing of more Bach he berated me for not knowing César Franck's organ chorales, and launched into one of them, and then ... it happened. In my eagerness to turn the page in time, I stepped on the lowest pedal ... boom! Schweitzer, startled, threw up his hands and with a sigh that understood all, exclaimed "Ach ja, these musicologists!"

On our homeward walk Schweitzer stopped often and talked in Alsatian dialect to the villagers—men with berets, baggy trousers and wooden shoes and women in colorful aprons, accompanied by their children. He knew them all and all their problems, and they called him "Monsieur Albert." At home, two students from the nearby University of Freiburg—my beloved former Freiburg—had arrived from across the Rhine. To the dismay of Mme Martin Schweitzer invited them to stay for dinner. These two were now as nervous and submissive as I had been at lunch time. I still can see Schweitzer's amused expression, how he chuckled with almost fiendish delight, as I anticipated the timid "no thank yous" for the two Freiburg novices while, a moment later, I heaped big second helpings on my own plate; for by now I felt at home and was hungry. After dinner Schweitzer insisted on walking the three of us to the station. When the Freiburg students started to rave about the new Germany and its Nazi ideology, he made short shrift of them. He put his bear-like arms protectively around my shoulders and said, "Your German 'Wave of the Future' is the sad reason that I must now think of the future of this youngster." Two obviously bewildered students and one transfigured grateful one bade

Schweitzer good-bye on that August evening in 1936. Schweitzer did not again set foot on German soil until the Nazi nightmare had passed.

Three months later I received my exit visa. I could not have left Germany without it. At the end of November 1936 I was the first of my family to embark on the trip to America. Many musicians and some musicologists who wished me well had written letters of recommendation for me. Also Schweitzer had promised to do so. He had asked me to let him know the day of my departure. The evenings of November 5, 6, 8, and 9 he must have spent writing not one, but fifteen partly very long letters, all but one handwritten. They were addressed to his friends and colleagues in the United States and reached me in four installments. His personal farewell letter to me ends with the words "Best wishes for the journey. God be with you. I will not forget you. Most cordially yours Albert Schweitzer."

In the meantime my book about the early phases of the Bach movement was passed over in silence in Germany. At least I did not see any reviews written in my country. However, I must admit that I did not search for them. One can hardly imagine today what occupied the mind of a German Jew at that time. What was on one's mind to the exclusion of practically everything else was survival; the thought of how to escape the country whose language one spoke and whose culture one had absorbed, and how to start life over again in a foreign country.

I had not even tried to find out whether my book was perhaps reviewed in a Swiss or Austrian paper or journal. But later I was most grateful to find some appreciative words about it when I read Georg Kinsky's pioneering study: *Die Originalausgaben der Werke Johann Sebastian Bachs* (Vienna, Leipzig, Zurich, 1937). A longer review appeared in the *Rivista Musicale Italiana* (XL, p. 160/1). After World War II it was Friedrich Blume who in *J.S. Bach im Wandel der Geschichte* of 1947 (English edition, *Two Centuries of Bach,* London, 1950) pointed out that my dissertation had been ignored at the time of its publication and thus had not been given its proper place in the Bach literature.

After my arrival in America nothing was more helpful than Schweitzer's letters. They opened the doors to musicians, musicologists and music publishers. Schweitzer's letter to Carl Engel, the head of the music publishing house of G. Schirmer and editor of *The Musical Quarterly,* had the effect that I was invited to read a paper at the fall (1937) meeting of the New York Chapter of the American Musicological Society. This paper, *Certain Aspects of the Bach Movement,* the English of which still left much to be desired, appeared a year later in the October 1938 issue of *The Musical Quarterly.* The first part of Schweitzer's letter to Edward Nies-Berger, his colleague and collaborator in the edition of Bach's organ works, may serve as an example of the warmth with which the great humanitarian recommended me to his friends. He wrote on November 6, 1936:

> Dear Mr. Nies-Berger.
> Permit me that I recommend Dr. Gerhard Herz to you who emigrates to the USA. He has lived up to now in Düsseldorf and is an excellent music scholar. He has written a very interesting work on the "History of the Bach movement" (that is, on what Bach's disciples at the end of the 18th and beginning of the 19th century have done to make known the works of their Master). This book has been published by Paul Haupt in Berne and has won much recognition.
>
> Because of his descent Dr. Herz has no future in Germany and goes therefore to America where he has relatives. I know him personally as an able and likable person and therefore dare to beg you to be of help to him as far as this lies in your power so that he may come into contact with musicians and music journals. If you can render a service to him I thank you for it as though you had done it for myself....

During the year 1937, which, like most refugee musicians and musicologists from Nazi Germany, I spent in New York City, I enjoyed the friendly help of Carleton Sprague Smith, the head of the Music Division of the New York Public Library. When pursuing my own research there, I frequently sat across the table from Arthur Mendel and Hans Theodor David. The latter had also just recently come to America. It thus appears that their collaboration on *The Bach Reader* began already at that early time. I also received helpful and benevolent advice from Paul Henry Lang whom I visited at Columbia University and with whom I still entertain a warm friendship. Later in 1937 Curt Sachs arrived in New York City. When he began lecturing with no accent and in fluent English at the Music Division of the New York Public Library, his old Berlin disciple was again among his listeners. At that time it was my most fervent wish to work for Sachs, perhaps as his assistant. Sachs, talking to me like a father, urged me, however, to rid myself of my inferiority complexes and to spare no effort in trying to find a college or university position outside the State of New York where every refugee seemed to get stuck. Towards the end of 1937 Sachs' advice was to bear fruit.

When the Metropolitan Museum of Art announced a guest lecture by Professor Krautheimer, the art historian of the University of Louisville, I used the occasion to meet him. He gave me valuable information about his university and told me that a nice elderly lady offered courses there in music appreciation; but that her classes seemed to lack the methodical scholarship and historical background that were obligatory in the field of art history. Krautheimer was of the opinion that, once this lady reached retirement age, the University of Louisville could well use a trained and properly qualified musicologist.

I was at that time not yet in a hurry because my most urgent goal was to master the English language. To achieve this, I took English classes for foreigners which President Roosevelt's *Works Project Administration* (WPA) had inaugurated. After nine months in America it happened that I dreamed for the first time in English.

That Louisville was eventually to become my American home, is the indirect result of a monstrous act of violence. On June 10, 1937 both Nello and Carlo Rosselli were murdered at Mussolini's (it was later said, Gaetano Ciano's) instigation. Carlo, who commanded the *colonna italiana* on the loyalist side in the Spanish Civil War, had been wounded and gone to France to recuperate. When Nello learned of this through the underground, he immediately went to visit his brother. The speed with which he received his exit visa should have made him suspicious. As it was, his visit betrayed to his political enemies Carlo's whereabouts in Bagnoles de l'Orne. There, on a remote side road, the car in which both brothers were riding was stopped by two women who pretended to need help with a flat tire. Out of the bushes leaped a number of French *Cagoulards,* a terrorist group the Italian secret police had hired to commit the crime. The two brothers were not shot but in the most brutal manner stabbed to death. This cruel death of my friend and benefactor had a shattering impact on me. I first read the news on the front page of the *New York Times.* Now I could no longer postpone a duty I had neglected because my formerly fairly fluent Italian had given way to English. I sent the warm letter Nello Rosselli had written in my behalf to his friend, Max Ascoli. Ascoli, who had left Italy in 1931, was Professor of Political Science at the *New School for Social Research* in New York and later the editor of the liberal political journal, *The Reporter.*

As an "amico di Nello" I was received literally with open arms and introduced to other Italian antifascist intellectuals who lived in New York. A young couple let me read all the terrible details about this tragedy in the issues of *Giustizia e Libertà* that appeared after Carlo's and Nello's murder. Such contacts helped me emotionally to come to terms with the stern fact that this tragedy was irreversible. Max Ascoli and his first wife were also in a most touching manner concerned about my future in America. When they learned that a vague contact with the University of Louisville had been initiated, their eyes lit up. They said almost simultaneously, "We must introduce you to Uncle Ben." Uncle Ben was Bernard Flexner, one of the three renowned Flexner brothers who had come from Louisville. Bernard, who was obviously one of the Ascolis' most intimate friends, headed the *Emergency Committee in Aid of Displaced German Scholars.* Thanks to the Ascolis' efforts I almost immediately received an invitation to come to his home on Park Avenue where he lived with his sister Mary. There, too, Schweitzer's letters made the impression Schweitzer had hoped for. Mr. Flexner promised to write to Dr.

Raymond A. Kent, President of the University of Louisville; but nothing happened for several months. Finally, in the fall of 1937, I received a phone call from Charles Kent, the University President's son. Charles, an excellent pianist who later became Dean of the Peabody School of Music in Baltimore, Maryland, invited himself over to my room near the Metropolitan Museum of Art. There we spent a most enjoyable afternoon and evening during which we played a whole repertory of violin sonatas from Bach to Brahms and Reger. This pleasant informal contact apparently took the place of the duties that today's search committees are expected to perform.

Less than a month later I received a letter from Dwight Anderson, Dean of the School of Music, inviting me to come to Louisville in early December. Mr. Flexner, extremely pleased, suggested that on my railroad trip to Louisville I stop over in Washington, D.C., and call on Supreme Court Justice Louis D. Brandeis who like Flexner had been born in Louisville. During the half hour interview with the eighty-one-year-old Justice who had known Gurlitt's father, the art historian Cornelius Gurlitt, I felt that I was in the presence of a great man.

During the four days of interviews in Louisville, I was introduced to President Kent, Dean Anderson and to the chairman of the Humanities Division, Dr. Ernest C. Hassold. I also met Professor Krautheimer's successor, Justus Bier, the well known art historian and Riemenschneider specialist. Dr. Bier, who had also recently come to America as a refugee from Nazi Germany, was present at a luncheon with the Dean and some colleagues of the College of Liberal Arts. With a heavy South-German accent, yet with carefree humor, Professor Bier conversed quite nonchalantly in anything but faultless English. Observing this, my inferiority complex, due to my own still imperfect English, turned abruptly into a superiority complex. I am thus indebted to Dr. Bier, who became a lifelong friend, for having been the source of my natural and uninhibited behavior during those crucial days in Louisville.

Shortly after Christmas I received the not unexpected offer to join the faculty of the University of Louisville in early February 1938.

During the first year of my employment Mr. Flexner's *Emergency Committee in Aid of Displaced German Scholars* funded one half of my salary of $2,000. Dwight Anderson later referred to this salary humorously as the best business deal of his entire career as Dean. In spite of this admittedly low compensation I succeeded with the help of relatives in paving the way for the increasingly urgent immigration of my two brothers, Hans (of Geneva) and Werner (of Cologne). They arrived in New York in 1938, shortly after I had completed my first semester in Louisville. After the ominous *Kristallnacht* of November 9, 1938, during which the furniture and everything else in my parents' house on the Goethestrasse in Düsseldorf was reduced to rubble—our two Bechstein grand pianos included—the emigration of my parents became a *sine qua non.* They arrived in New York together with my eighteen-year-old sister Lore in the spring of 1939, less than half a year before the outbreak of World War II. They spent their first months in the New World with my brother Hans who was then working, also aided by Bernard Flexner's Committee, at the *Institute for Advanced Study* in Princeton. In July they arrived in Louisville where my parents spent the rest of their lives, both reaching a ripe old age.

Thus Schweitzer's appreciation of my dissertation and his subsequent concern about my academic future contributed indirectly to the saving of all members of my immediate family, though we were not spared the heartbreaking news of deaths and "disappearances" of family members in the years that were to come.

This seems to be the appropriate point to break off my academic memoirs, which centered on the role my dissertation has played in my life. The German book of 1935 was dedicated to "My Parents," to my father, a judge in Düsseldorf, who funded my studies, and to my mother from whom I inherited my love of music. My most recent book, entitled *Bach Sources in America,* bears the inscription: "To America with gratitude." It is dedicated to the country that received me as an equal in 1936 when I had to leave my homeland, gave me freedom, citizenship, and the right and opportunity to work, and thus became my new home.

1

J.S. Bach's Impact on the World Around Him

Bach must have known that he was the greatest organ virtuoso in the world. It was all too evident and admitted everywhere.[1]

The Bach movement is as old as Bach's appearance in history. Not only with the master's death did his work and personality become debatable and a source of misunderstanding. During his lifetime controversy began to envelope him: a stranger in his own time. The gap between Bach's philosophy and that of his contemporaries was such that they could no longer immediately relate to his work. Despite their admiration for his sheer boundless craftsmanship they rejected his creative work because of its historical orientation and "backwardness." They had to reject it, for as modern and progressive individuals they felt responsible for the continuing existence of their art. They could not, therefore, celebrate in Bach the great culmination of an era, for the emergence of their new artistic ideal was predicated on the breakdown of this era. Bach "is a terminal point. Nothing goes out from him; everything merely leads up to him."[2]

Schweitzer recognized this terminal characteristic historically, while Bach's contemporaries must have felt its direct effect. Because he was the last link in a chain, it was inevitable that Bach be misunderstood by his own time, which like all ages tended to move ahead. Biographers concentrating on his immense oeuvre have tended to deny the truth of this historical fact. The idea that the time was not yet ripe for Bach is a dilettantic approach. Bach was not ahead of his time—rather, his time was ahead of him. Bach, looking back to the Middle Ages, summarized what the centuries before him had seen and thought. In his art the creative endeavors of the past flowed together into a reservoir to receive their final filtering and clarification.

J.S. Bach's personality stands apart from our contemporary concepts. The modern concept of genius is not yet applicable to him. We note the remarkable fact that he was apparently not aware of his own genius and value. His impact on the future musical development, his present fame, our performance practice of his works—all this would probably have been totally inconceivable to the master. "I was obliged to be industrious. Whoever is equally industrious will succeed equally well."[3] Genius and diligence were the same to him. He did not consider the divine spark which inspired work after work a unique gift of nature. Like a medieval artist he seems modestly to have signed his works "I did what I could."[4] Worldly success could become no problem for him. Because the bulk of his works had a liturgical function, even the greatest of them such as the *St. Matthew Passion,* passed without echo. Because of this purely functional purpose, one can understand why Bach had no interest in making his cantatas and passion music known through publication. They were an integral part of the divine service, fulfilling their mission as church music which did not need to be made public. His church music is *Gebrauchsmusik* for his own rather than for later ages, for which he would have had to set down a score complete in every detail. He knew from the way music was being performed around him that the traditions on which he still counted were disappearing. Yet he made not the slightest effort to preserve the valuable treasure of his works for posterity. He has certainly not contributed to the fact that at least a goodly portion of his oeuvre has survived.

Bach's Religion

Bach was no musician for future generations. He certainly did not see his mission there. What mattered much more to him was to preserve the heritage of the past and to protect the traditions coming under attack by his own time. Bach was firmly rooted in orthodox Lutheranism, whose musical language is heard in the hymn tunes of the cantatas. Throughout his life Johann Sebastian remained true to the religious heritage of the old Thuringian Bach family. In no way did he wish to differ from his forebears in the service of the church. He was truly pious. For him the old Lutheran faith was so good and sacred that Pietism could not become a serious problem. This firmness of conviction is reflected in both his life and his artistic work.

Bach grew up in an orthodox environment. He was reared as an orthodox Lutheran and reared his own children as strict Lutherans. In Mühlhausen (1707-08) he sided with the orthodox minister, Eilmar, who was carrying on a feud with Bach's own pastor, the Pietist Frohne. Frohne[5] is supposed to have been by far the more sympathetic person; yet it was the zealot, the fanatic to the letter, Eilmar, who stood godfather to Bach's first child. These religious controversies eventually caused Bach to submit his resignation.[6]

When he was Chapelmaster (1717-23) at the *reformed* Court of Cöthen, Bach sent his children to the newly founded Lutheran, rather than to the reformed, school. The *Clavier Büchlein vor A.M. Bachin (Anno 1722)* carries on its titlepage a warning against Calvinism,[7] even though it was written in *reformed* Cöthen in 1772. In Leipzig (1723-50), whose university was a stronghold of orthodox Lutheranism, he composed almost exclusively for the church. For the Leipzig period we also have sufficient evidence of his unshakable clinging to dogmatic Lutheranism, into which, towards the end of his life, he withdrew more and more in heroic isolation. In a dispute in 1728 over the introduction of a new hymnbook, Bach took a conservative, Lutheran stand, and in the end the Council conceded that he was right.[8] The "Clavierübung 3. Teil" (1739) containing the organ Chorale Preludes to Luther's well known catechism chorales[9] gives further testimony to his adherence to Lutheran dogma.

Even more revealing and significant are the contents of the library[10] Bach left at his death. There, in addition to Luther's complete works, were found above all, the writings of his followers in the next centuries (Heinrich Müller, Rostock, August Pfeiffer, Leipzig and many others). August Hermann Francke and Philipp Jacob Spener were the only Pietists represented, each with only one volume. Much certainly was missing from his library (for example, the cantata poets were not listed in the inventory). However, what remained is sufficient to show Bach as a strict and deeply religious Lutheran whose library contained only theological works.

Bach represented orthodox Lutheranism at a time when the old world of guilds and social classes, of Baroque forms of life and faith, were already beginning to weaken. A process of disintegration of the old forms of worship had set in—a process in which the new religious movement of Pietism, that began around 1700, participated. Bach could not ignore Pietism. He had, somehow, to take a stand. In his middle years he was even occasionally inspired by Pietism; but he was never shaken in his basic, old orthodox conviction. Pietism sought the enlargement and broadening of the *congregation,* not the preservation of the congregational nucleus in the strict Lutheran sense. The missionary character that the Pietistic religious service assumed, the pedagogical intent of the preacher to convince, the personal searching for God—all this contradicted the basic meaning of the *Gemeinde* and led to a dangerous spiritual isolation and individualization of its members. Bach must have seen these possibilities. As a man who felt at home in the old world of guilds, "the disintegration of the guilds and the good old order"[11] must have been a thorn in the eye. After all, he saw how his Lutheran congregation was threatened in its foundations and how, through the new liturgical functions of edification and conversion, the old, deep-rooted *de tempore,* the special meaning of each Sunday was also certain to disappear. Most essential is the fact that in Bach the Lutheran Church was still alive in its old vigor and freshness, thanks to his sense of responsibility and ever-present loyalty to his long family tradition. Furthermore, his cantata texts alone demonstrate that for Bach the dogmatic writings and ritual had not yet died and become meaningless;[12] but that for him the symbolic world of the church was still there to be experienced.

In him true Lutheranism was once more embodied, free of superficiality and not yet sunk to the level of mere routine and formula. Bach remained true to the *old* because it had not yet become old for him.

The Pietistic attitude towards church music sheds further light on Bach's steadfast Lutheranism. Orthodox Lutherans consistently defended the elaborate polyphonic style of church music[13] so close to Bach's heart. Pietism, through the introduction of the song form into the church, sought to undermine the symbolic world of the polyphonic style. For Bach, art does not stand in the service of subjective edification and conversion, as it did for the Pietists. The words *"der Anti Melancholicus"* written on the title page of the *Clavierbüchlein for A.M. Bach* reflect a healthy and uncomplicated kind of house music which as yet knows nothing of Pietistic escapism and self-absorption. By warning on the same page against Calvinism, Bach also expressed his opposition to the position of the reformed church, which was extremely inimical to art, equating art with worldliness and accepting only the chorale as the focus of the church service, while banishing from its service the artistic elaboration of the hymn-tune as well as the Latin text. Bach saw in Pietism and Calvinism adversaries of the polyphonic style whose last guardian and greatest exponent he was destined to be. Doubts as to whether his music was sacred or not existed for him as little as they did for Luther and his church. For both of them there existed only one music which became sacred or profane through the spirit in which it was performed.

Bach's Position in Society

Bach's position in society was as much determined by tradition as was his attitude towards religion.[14] He was free from ambition and the search for fame. Unlike other artists, Bach did not travel. He never visited Italy. He remained in the land of his ancestors and did not seek a position commensurate with his genius. Bach accepted the orders of society as he found them, taking his assigned place within them as best he could with God's help. Bach remained in music loving Thuringia and Saxony all his life. When he felt the need to leave for a short time, he travelled north. The Catholic south never interested him. As a *"secret listener"*[15] he learned the craft of organ playing from the classical representatives of North German Protestant organ music. He trained himself as a composer by laboriously copying the works of his most outstanding predecessors. Bach did not step beyond the bounds of tradition set by his century. When Bach, Chapelmaster at the court of Cöthen, accepted the appointment as Cantor at St. Thomas and *Director chori musici* in Leipzig, he returned of his own free will to the world of time-honored tradition. That Bach spent 27 years—the main part of his life—in Leipzig which, aside from Hamburg, was the most important bourgeois-ecclesiastical center in Germany, speaks for itself. The courts of Dresden and Berlin did not attract him, even though he was not spared all sorts of irritations and disagreements in Leipzig.

During the term of office of Bach's predecessor, Johann Kuhnau,[16] a change had already begun to undermine the authoritative position of the Thomas Cantor. The social structure of the medieval world was being replaced by the new Rationalistic order. At first, musicians still retained the rights and privileges they had enjoyed from the time of Absolutism, but they now had to fight to preserve them. Attempts to circumvent and infringe upon these privileges became increasingly frequent. These disputes paved the way for the change from guild-member to independent musician. The discords to which the musician was now exposed and the struggle for his rights he was forced to lead were the first signs of a change in his heretofore firmly established social position. A new generation railed against medieval traditions and vested class rights. One could foresee that democratic terms like "freedom of trade" and "equal rights for all" would follow in the wake of the new concept of the world.

What mattered to Bach was to retain the old world order within his sphere of influence and, if necessary, to champion it. He jealously saw to it that the old privileged position of music in the school curriculum was maintained.[17] Up to Bach's time, academic life in the Latin School was completely permeated by music. Originally, the principal function of these schools was to train a capable chorus for church services and festive secular occasions. The close relationship between music life and school made the Latin School a springboard for many professional musicians. For a long time this source satisfied the demand of Saxony and Thuringia for organists and cantors.

According to tradition, students and teachers were housed together in the *Alumneum.* To be a Thomas pupil of Bach meant more than our present day idea of a teacher-student relationship. It meant being taken into the master's home and life, entering a true community of living and learning. In addition to his Thomas school choir, Johann Sebastian Bach as *Director chori musici* had at his disposal the organizations of town musicians for the performance of his churchly duties, as well as for town-council and academic festivities.[18] His permanent church orchestra consisted of the four *townpipers* and their journeyman, the three *Art-fiddlers* and the *Beer-fiddlers,* who not until later were considered social equals. These orchestral forces were usually supplemented by university students whose Collegium Musicum Bach directed from 1729 on. These performance conditions were far from ideal. Despite the technically probably quite reliable groups of musicians and the regular cooperation of some students on whose help he depended, Bach was forced to lead a continuous struggle in his pursuit of a *"well-appointed church-music."* He never attained this goal because the number of those who neither wished to hear an orchestra in church nor appreciated the polyphonic style was already so large in Leipzig that the Council felt encouraged to refuse such *unnecessary* expenditures.

During Kuhnau's time the vested interests of the Cantor were already being threatened by competitive musical forces. Telemann, who was a student in Leipzig from 1701-04, took the musical directorship of the *New Church* away from Kuhnau, and enticed the students away from assisting the cantor by introducing them to the opera. These insulting encroachments upon the old privileges of the cantor were explicitly approved by the Town Council.[19] Social change had progressed to such an extent that the council, regarding the written laws as outdated, could dare to circumvent them because public opinion no longer endorsed them. Besides, Kuhnau was not the man to assert himself against these trends. He was not strong enough to face up to the conflicts of the time into which he was born. It needed the strong personality of a Bach to assert himself vigorously by opposing the progressive innovators of his time and embodying the ideal of a *Soli-Deo-gloria* music making once again amidst all the worldliness around him.

That the opera, the most dangerous rival of church music, was discontinued[20] shortly before Bach's arrival in Leipzig (in 1723) seems almost symbolic. Thanks to the fact that Bach knew his rights, the old legal status of the cantorship was restored. A rift developed only when Johann August Ernesti, who belonged to a younger generation than Bach, became director of the school in 1734. Ernesti, modern and humanistically oriented, opposed the (as he thought) much too strict tradition and the privileged position of music in the curriculum. What ensued was the well known fight over the *First Prefect,* Krause,[21] which actually was about the Cantor's right to appoint the Prefect. Here we see Bach, like Michael Kohlhaas, headstrong, fighting for his rights. He "fought the fight, less for himself than for his art and position."[22] After a long series of complaints and appeals Bach received personal satisfaction from the Elector of Saxony. The fundamental significance of this quarrel lies in the fact that these developments mark the beginning of a general indifference towards church music, whose central position in the life of the times was already shaken. In his letter of August 13, 1736, to the Town Council, Bach expressed his fears that "the services may be disturbed and the church music fall into the most serious decay, and the school, too, within a short time, suffer such deterioration as shall make it impossible for many years to bring it back to its former estate."[23] From his point of view as guardian of the God-given rights of church music, Bach was undoubtedly right. On the other hand, there must have been a reason if the Council and Consistory could not bring themselves to side with their Cantor. Bach's time felt unable to continue to recognize the old privileged position still enjoyed by church music. Public opinion was against it.

Bach the Musician, as Seen by His Contemporaries

The world of religious struggles and social reorganization, in the midst of which Bach stood as preserver of the old, explains the isolation of the master in his own time and the impression his personality made on his fellowmen. If one tries to comprehend Bach merely by looking at his environment, a gap remains which does not explain Bach's spiritual orientation towards the past. The cultural soil in which Bach was rooted was fundamentally different from that of his contemporaries. The culminating nature of his music as well as of his personality can be found neither in the theory nor in the practice of the music of his time. Bach shared the fate of all those in whom the discrepancy between *Zeitgeist* and their own creative spirit was unbridgeable, with the only difference that Bach in his piety did not perceive its tragic nature. Throughout his life he had no friend, nor member of his family, who understood him completely, so that nothing about the true inner Bach has come down to us. Still today we see Bach chiefly through the eyes of Forkel, who received his information from Bach's oldest sons. They, as true children of their times, also did not fully understand the inner workings of their father's mind. Bach belonged to a different world. His artistic aim differed from that of his time. For this reason Bach never became *fashionable.* In him still lived something of the Middle Ages which caused this alienation from his time. Contrary to the progressive Handel, Bach, with time, increasingly moved away from the current style. The *Art of the Fugue,* his most conservative and his boldest work, was written in the midst of the era of *gallant music.*

Bach expected only a few of his works to have a lasting impact. We should see his musical legacy in the works which he revised again during the last years of his life, and which he wanted to leave to his sons and pupils in impeccable form. These were some of his organ compositions which he took up and scrutinized once more. Bach, the teacher of harpsichordists and above all organists, entrusted his musical legacy to his pupils. In them he wished to live on. Bach must have known only too well that his church cantatas and passion music were lost to posterity. After the master's death, the Bach movement retreated into the circle of his pupils, the organists and harpsichordists whom he had reared. This is what these revisions meant.

Revisions and parodies in connection with repeated performances—as shown by the different versions of the St. Matthew Passion[24]—are not significant in this context. Just as little does the plundering of old works for the creation of new ones necessarily indicate particular favorites of the master. *Contrafactur* as well as *Parody* were recognized working techniques for the entire Baroque age. They are also characteristic of Bach's entire oeuvre and thus tend to destroy the image of the subjective tone-painter which Mosevius and Schweitzer have created.

A meaning similar to that drawn from the revisions can be deduced from the works printed during Bach's lifetime. Printed music was a precious rarity until well into the eighteenth century.[25] Until the Thirty Years War it was the obligation to society of every good composer to see that his principal compositions appeared in print. (See Schein and Schütz.) After the war, however, music printing declined sharply, so that the printing and engraving of a work became an exception and a luxury. The result was that Bach's era as well as the preceding period are shrouded in darkness. Musicology can hardly expect enlightenment from the discovery of new manuscripts. The lack of music printing explains the function of Baroque music as occasional music. This dependence on the manuscript prevented a significant circulation of Bach's works during his lifetime and immediately after his death. Only those who made an effort by copying his works, as did some of his pupils, could remain in contact with the master. What was printed was not sufficient to engender a close relationship.

Aside from the Ratswahl Cantata of 1708,[26] which, according to old custom, had to be printed for the city of Mühlhausen, and Schemelli's *Musical Song Book* for whose compilation Bach's valuable help had been won, the following works by Bach appeared in print: the *Ode of Mourning* upon the death of the Electress of Saxony (1727), the *Musical Offering* dedicated to the King of Prussia, and the *Canonic Variations* on the Christmas hymn *Vom Himmel hoch da komm ich her,* the test piece Bach submitted upon becoming a member of Mizler's Society of the Musical Sciences. They were all works engraved in copper for a specific, extramusical, representative purpose. The compositions which Bach on his own initiative selected and had printed show again the great pedagogue and counterpoint instructor of his sons and pupils. They are the four parts of his *Clavier-Übung,* six chorale preludes (the so-called *Schübler Chorales*) and the *Art of the Fugue.* Didactic in purpose, they were intended for the circle in which he hoped his art would live on. With his musical legacy left to his pupils and their pupils, the master himself not only anticipated but also paved the way for the Bach movement until Forkel.

The *"Jesus Juva"* and the *"Soli Deo Gloria"* with which Bach began and closed all his works, had not become an empty formula, but represented his innermost religious feelings that could not be passed on. His contemporaries could not see Bach the craftsman in God's service, whose art was not affected by personal problems. Yet his fellowmen noted with amazement that Bach did not lead the life of an artist of genius, that he did not seek his fortune in the world. ("In general he did not have the most brilliant good fortune because he did not do what it requires, namely, roam the world over," said C.P.E. Bach of his father.[27]) And Mizler's obituary (compiled in 1754 by C.P.E. Bach and J. Fr. Agricola)[28] speaks with a touch of amazement of Bach's strong attachment to his native soil. Bach remained in the country of his ancestors and did nothing to advance his fame and the success of his works. The feeling of being a tool, the feeling of being a *genius* could not have occurred to Bach. Like his contemporaries, Bach looked up to Handel, as a man of genius in the modern sense. He tried twice in his lifetime to meet Handel, while the latter avoided him.[29] How highly Bach thought of Handel and how eager he was to get to know him is also shown by the characteristic fact that Bach, with Anna Magdalena, laboriously copied Handel's St. John Passion (after Brockes). In addition, he copied in his own hand the parts of a 7-movement Concerto Grosso in F minor, as well as a solo cantata of his famous contemporary.[30] On the other hand, Handel's interest in the composer Bach was not great enough that he would ever have copied one of his works. He also never owned one of Bach's works copied by another. Bach still practiced the method of copying as an organic way of making works his own. By copying he took possession of the specific styles of other masters. A man of progress, such as Handel, preferred to depend on the uniqueness of his own genius; therefore, copying as a learning process had lost its meaning for him.

According to C.P.E. Bach's testimony, Bach not only respected Handel, but also Hasse, the brothers Graun, Telemann, Zelenka and Benda—all of whom he knew personally—as well as Fux, Caldara, and Keiser, "and in general everything that was worthy of esteem in Berlin and Dresden,"[31] even though his remark about the "little Dresden ditties," directed at Hasse's operas, revealed his less than enthusiastic liking for Hasse's nonpolyphonic style. Bach was, after all, too great a master of counterpoint. As such he was also seen by his contemporaries.

His musical contemporaries recognized in Bach the craftsman to whom, as master of every kind of technique, polyphonic composition had become second nature. They recognized in him the master of musical workmanship, but above all, Bach the harpsichordist and organist was celebrated in the annals of his time. His virtuosity on manual and pedal alike was admired by all.[32] He also was respected as one of the greatest authorities on keyboard instruments, organ as well as harpsichord, which he tuned and furnished with quills himself.[33] This unusual patriarchal relationship to his instruments, these bonds between creative artist and his tools represented something extraordinary for his time. Because most of his contemporaries had already lost this understanding of their craft, C.P.E. Bach writes at great length about this trait of his father.[34] J.S. Bach still considered the maintenance of his instruments, the tuning and quilling, a part of his creative activity. We also learn from C.P.E. Bach that his father composed at his desk, away from any instrument. Only later did he listen to his new compositions, testing the creations conceived in his mind for their acoustic effect. Furthermore, C.P.E. Bach portrayed his father as the respected pedagogue in his workshop, training organ and keyboard virtuosos. He described his father's method of teaching composition which began with four-part thorough-bass and harmonization of chorales. This in turn shows that Bach introduced his pupils from the very beginning to this basic treasure of church music. This same awareness of the importance of the *cantus firmus* caused Bach to use the chorale time and again as an inexhaustible source for his own compositions.

His contemporaries saw one more thing, and here their criticism sets in. They saw the *uneducated* and *outdated* master, the self-taught Bach who had trained himself into becoming a "strong fugue writer" merely through "his own study and reflection."[35] It is the picture of a composer who, except for the first practical instructions from his older brother in Ohrdruf, had not required a personal teacher, for whom the musical atmosphere of the Lüneburg St. Michael's school sufficed to develop his knowledge and who, thanks to his intellectual independence and his exceptional ear, acquired through the technique of copying and listening what he lacked. It is the picture of a composer who grasped everything by himself, who learned everything either by listening or by looking at the music and therefore had no need for scholarship—in short, who had an aversion towards all theorizing. We don't have a single word from Bach himself about the sound of his music, quite in contrast to C.P.E. Bach, a typical representative of the next generation. It was J.S. Bach who as a stranger to his time, looked backward; the great master of a past art who drew his knowledge from the works of Kerll, Pachelbel, Frescobaldi, Fischer, Strunck, Buxtehude, Reinken, Bruhns and Böhm—all strong fugue writers.[36]

Adlung said, "The late Leipzig Bach also held Froberger in high esteem, even though he was somewhat old fashioned."[37] "Somewhat old fashioned," these words sum up the entire criticism Bach received from his contemporaries. Bach educated himself from *outmoded* and already *obsolete* masters. He stood on the shoulders of past generations instead of participating in building the present and future of music. Stylistically Bach was closer to his predecessors than to his contemporaries. He drew his compositional strength directly from the works of the German past, and did so without teacher. Yet he was not exclusively influenced by these masters, but was devoted to the French Overture and Suite with which he became acquainted in Celle. He also had the highest admiration for the sense of form of the Italians. This attracted him especially in the works of Vivaldi, and impelled him time and again to infuse into these Italian forms the German style of polyphony. In contrast to some of his contemporaries, Bach did not blindly imitate, but transformed the Italian style.

The Bach picture sketched by his own generation shows the sovereign master of all the technical laws of music, composing at his desk. It shows the celebrated harpsichord and organ virtuoso with a fundamental knowledge of the construction of these instruments. It shows the self-taught composer carrying on the tradition of German organ music. It shows him loyal to his Saxon homeland, free of the restless ambition of the artist for glory and success. But one feature is missing in this portrait of the master—his piety. It failed to include the devout Bach. This profoundest trait of Bach's nature, which actually provides an answer to the *why* of his stylistic attitude, could not be recognized by the Age of Rationalism that surrounded him. The deeper content of his works thus remained necessarily hidden from his contemporaries who were only able to admire the formal and artistic components of his creations. Since Bach's philosophy of life had become foreign to his time, the deeper content of his works could no longer be understood intuitively as a meaningful language. The Age of Reason understood the forms of the master. Yet, once stripped of their deeper significance, their intricate design had to appear to his contemporaries as an end in itself which transcended the natural. Here lie the roots for the criticism which his time meted out to Bach, the composer. His compact, massive, polyphonic style received more disapproval than praise. Musicologists will have to try to understand this criticism if the first phase of the Bach movement is to appear in its true light.

Contemporary Criticism of the Composer Bach

It seems that musicology will have to revise its judgment of Johann Adolph Scheibe and his famous criticism of Bach the composer. Until now Bach biographers have sided in this controversy too much with the master, whom they found in need of defense. Yet the historic greatness of Bach is not well served by a subjectively colored view, of which in this case, neither Spitta nor Schweitzer is free. In our discussion Scheibe's accusations will be interpreted as a valid expression of his time and its attitude towards Bach. It will further be shown that in the course of history Scheibe's critical statements are repeated time and again whenever an attempt is made to attack what is hard to understand in Bach's compositions.

Scheibe must first of all be viewed without prejudice as a historical figure. He was one of the most eminent German music estheticians during the Age of Rationalism. He was a scholar to whom even Lessing paid the greatest attention. Gerber, who certainly was a great admirer of Bach, said of Scheibe, "there is no doubt that he belongs among the principal theorists and musical aestheticians."[38] In his chief work, *Der Critische Musicus,*[39] Scheibe made a magnificent attempt to create a system of musical sciences. He strove to erect a system of music with no religious superstructure, but constructed according to the concepts of reason. Scheibe's historical merit lies in his determination to arrive at a reorganization of music. Scheibe was on the side of progress. As a Rationalist and champion of the *doctrine of the affections* he disapproved of contrapuntal *artifices* as exaggerated music for the eye that ran counter to true feeling. In Scheibe's view, the true purpose of music, like that of every art, was the "imitation of nature."[40] This was the fundamental attitude of the entire era. The *"Gothic Barbarism"* of the polyphonic style which intertwines chains of melodies and sounds them simultaneously, ought to be eradicated, while the individual line should be freed from the many-voiced web. The Age of Netherlands polyphony appeared to this period as the low point in the history of western music. It was said that melody was drowned in a swamp of simultaneously sounding melodic lines. What mattered now was to let the "sweet amenity of melody"[41] rise again. Hasse and Graun were, in Scheibe's opinion, the masters with whom "a new musical epoch begins."[42] They had, according to Scheibe, rediscovered the beauty of good taste and, in the realm of music "they have reached the final purpose which had been the aim of all efforts of their predecessors."[43] The art of the two opera composers at the courts of Dresden and Berlin represented for Scheibe a *non plus ultra*. This point of view was quite typical of the Age of Reason which—bound by its normative narrowing vision to *one* ideal of beauty—introduced the idea of progress as an integral part of historical development.

Before this forum, whose spokesman was Scheibe, Bach could not hold his own untainted as a composer. Scheibe called him an "extraordinary artist,"[44] the "most eminent of the *Musikanten*"[45] whose "dexterity"[46] he greatly admired, yet whose music was lacking in "amenity."[47] Since Bach judged "according to his own fingers,"[48] thinking and composing with the keyboard instrument in mind, his vocal and instrumental parts are not only extremely difficult to execute, but they also lose their naturalness. This "turgid way of writing"[49] which, according to Scheibe, is caused by the "constant employment of voices of equal value,"[50] that is, the polyphonic style, in which the individual voices "permanently quarrel with each other,"[51] brings Bach from the "natural" to the "artificial," from the "lofty" to the "obscure."[52] For Bach's "excess of art darkens its beauty."[53] "One admires the onerous labor which, however, is vainly employed, since it conflicts with Nature."[54] A composer who "does not think reasonably and methodically may, through his laborious efforts, arouse admiration, but by no means will he touch his listeners and make an impression that will move them."[55] Here then, we find the inner meaning of Bach's style uncomprehended, and the content of his music faced in a state of bewilderment. In addition to the master of the polyphonic style, the musician Bach is further censured for lacking the appropriate relation to the work in terms of the rationalistic doctrine of the affections. (The Bach, for example, who wrote the "Herr unser Herrscher" chorus of the *St. John Passion*.)

Music demands the approval of the ear as well as that of the intellect.[56] In Scheibe's opinion Bach's failings lie in his preference for polyphony and the wealth of dissonance in his compositions.[57] Furthermore, his melodies are embellished by far too many (mostly written out) ornaments.[58] All this adds up to a "turgid and confused style"[59] and to an obscuring of the text[60] which causes the listener literally to "lose his mind." Bach employs too many means to achieve his musical goal. By using too much Art he transcends Nature. The result is that Art prevails over Nature. This irritated Scheibe. He saw Bach still anchored in a stylistic world exceeding the bounds of nature. For Scheibe, a piece of music composed in the old style must necessarily be obsolete; art created with effort is necessarily unnatural, extravagant, that is, bad. Art is Nature's gift to man. To create and shape art on one's own is like putting on "make-up."[61] Bach's work is in vain bacause his goal is false (i.e., out-dated). Bach does not think about the "future" of music.[62] He put himself into this position because he lacked artistic self-discipline and academic training. Bach is not conversant with Rationalistic thinking. "This great man has not acquainted himself to any degree with the sciences,"[63] said Scheibe. Time and again Scheibe expresses his resentment at the self-taught Bach. He reproaches him for having learned everything by himself, for never having attended a university to learn about "Rationalism," as Handel and Telemann had done. Since Bach did not possess Reason, the true *ratio* as his time understood it, his compositions do not demonstrate the reasoned reflection which distinguishes the works of Telemann or Graun. Scheibe saw that Bach as non-Rationalist was unable to arrive at the new artistic ideal. In turn, Scheibe, the Rationalist, could not see the world manifested in Bach's creations. Scheibe knew that the Germany of his time was in the process of a true renaissance of music and that to attain this new ideal the Gothic relics that were still alive had to be eradicated. Scheibe's criticism of Bach is thus identical with the judgment that the Age of Rationalism passed on the polyphonic style.[64] It is therefore not justifiable to interpret this controversy as a purely personal argument. This would obliterate its deeper meaning for the entire history of the misunderstanding of Bach during the Rationalistic age.

Had Scheibe been totally wrong, Bach probably would have found a better defender than Magister Birnbaum, who, in his reply to Scheibe's criticism of Bach, missed the very essence of Bach's nature. Birnbaum objects only to superficialities. He did not dare to refute Scheibe's grave reproaches against Bach's compositional style. Instead of defending Bach's polyphonic style, which is so rich in ideas, he called it easily accessible and natural.[65] He failed to see Bach's profundity, his links with the Middle Ages and his ties to the symbolic world of thought of the Lutheran Church. Because he criticized Bach for his retrospective attitude, Scheibe had a better understanding of the master. Birnbaum said of Scheibe,[66] "Undoubtedly he [Scheibe] was too hasty, and perhaps he did not really know the Honorable Court Composer. If he had known him, I am convinced that he would have bestowed upon him the same praise which in this letter he awarded to the famous Mr. Graun." (See above.) This statement proves that Birnbaum failed to recognize the two worlds that faced each other here. Whoever recommends measuring Bach's artistic ideal against that of Graun, has misunderstood the true Bach. Thus Scheibe's document constitutes the most realistic expression of the attitude of Bach's contemporaries towards his work.

After Bach's death several important comments were made that add some new features to this picture of Bach. First of all, the obituary written by Telemann for his great colleague has come down to us.[67] It closes with these lines:

> Departed Bach! Long since thy splendid organ playing
> Alone brought thee the noble cognomen "the Great,"
> And what thy pen had writ, the highest art displaying,
> Did some with joy and some with envy contemplate.
>
> Then sleep! The candle of thy fame ne'er low will burn;
> The pupils thou has trained, and those they train in turn
> Prepare thy future crown of glory brightly glowing.
> Thy children's hands adorn it with its jewels bright,
> But what shall cause thy true worth to be judged aright
> Berlin to us now in a worthy son is showing.

The Bach picture sketched in this chapter is found again in these lines which, compared to other Baroque poesy, are rather simple and beautiful. The *great* Bach is the splendid organ player, the virtuoso, beside whom the composer, though respected, fades. Telemann sees Bach's significance for *posterity* mainly in the effect of his teaching, in the *school* he had created and which had produced many a notable artist, first among them his great son, Carl Philipp Emanuel.

This interesting document by Telemann who, in spite of his admiration for Johann Sebastian Bach, sides with Carl Philipp Emanuel, that is, with his time, is supplemented by the news of the master's death published in the *Spenersche Zeitung*.[68] There one reads, "The loss of this uncommonly skillful man is profoundly mourned by all true connoisseurs of music." The loss of the "skillful" Bach, of the able artist, the craftsman, is lamented, not the death of the devout Bach, nor that of the composer. Only the "true connoisseurs of music" mourn his death, that is, his colleagues who understand his craft. They lost in him their greatest organ and clavier virtuoso. The Town Council of Leipzig seems even to have rejoiced inwardly about the loss of this one-sided musician and poor schoolmaster. It declared after the master's death, "The School needed a Cantor and not a Capellmeister."[69]

One among Bach's contemporaries and colleagues saw a greater loss in Bach's death than the rest. Friedrich Wilhelm Marpurg had perhaps the clearest vision of what Bach could have meant to his time. His preface to the 1752 edition of the *Art of the Fugue,* written at Philipp Emanuel's request, sounds like the defense of one who had not been attacked. What Marpurg has to say[70] shows that he was conscious of the risk involved in introducing a work of such spiritual depth and so remote from sensuality as the *Art of the Fugue* to the era of *Empfindsamkeit* and the *style galant*. He knew the danger in offering this unique creation of mirror forms and higher mathematics to those for whom the fugue had already become a relic. Marpurg said in his Preface that no one surpassed Bach "in the deep and thoughtful execution of unusual, ingenious ideas, far removed from the ordinary run, and yet spontaneous and natural." He continued, "A melody which agrees only with canons of taste obtaining at a particular time and place has value only so long as that taste prevails." On the other hand "natural and cogent thoughts maintain their worth in all times and places."[71] Marpurg was thus aware of Bach's being behind the times, but—and this is the essential point—he believed in the lasting value of Bach's art. The expert master and theorist of the fugue, Marpurg predicts, will outlive his time precisely because he does not conform to its taste. Marpurg did not see in Bach the last representative of an outmoded epoch that Scheibe and the other contemporaries saw, but a master of timeless validity. As such, Marpurg presented Bach to the reader. To the composers, however, he said, "It is to be hoped that the present work may inspire some emulation, and assist the living examples of so many righteous people whom one sees now and then at the head of a musical body, and in its ranks, to restore in some measure, in the face of the hoppity melodification of so many present day composers, the dignity of Harmony"[72] (that is, polyphony). Here Bach is portrayed as the restorer of good taste who would assist in overcoming the shallowness of the existing "hoppity melodification." Bach is seen as the possible initiator of a musical renaissance. He is called upon to revise the existing musical taste. The study of his works is seen as a possible source for the regaining of a new spiritualized style of music. Bach's systematic and orderly mentality as well as his alienation from his own time have not found a more explicit definition in the entire eighteenth century. The seriousness of Bach's style was, however, not seen as flowing from his religious personality, but as an artistic fact. Bach, it was hoped, would change the public taste of the people, but not its outlook on life. That a change of taste can occur only in the wake of a change in ideology was not yet seen by Marpurg. Neither did he come to grips with Bach's deep religious conviction. Like Scheibe he recognized that Bach was out of step with his time; but beyond that, he saw in the profundity of Bach's style the seed of a continuing life in history. This Preface to Bach's last work is like a lingering echo of the composer's great personality. It strikes one as a moving eulogy for the just-deceased master, as a warning to society not to forget that the last and greatest of an epoch that had come to an end with him, had been laid to rest.

The existing documents pertaining to the early history of the Bach movement lead eventually to the fundamental conclusion that Bach was no longer adequately understood in his lifetime. The misunderstanding of the composer Bach arose less from his artwork or his stylistic position than from the discord that existed between his artistic goals and those which his contemporaries considered their highest ideal. It stemmed from the incongruity between artist and *Zeitgeist*, between the master and the masses. Bach's artwork did not meet society's expectations in a satisfactory way that was up to date. Since Bach turned his face to the past and appeared in his outlook on life and art consciously as the guardian of tradition, his time was justified in rejecting him as a reactionary, swimming against the tide.

Notes

I am most grateful to my wife, Dr. Mary Jo Fink Herz, for her help in establishing the final form of the translation and for typing chapters 1-3. The translation has not succumbed to the temptation of correcting errors or of avoiding the repetitiousness of this work of my youth. The footnotes are identical with those of the original dissertation. Quotations from Bach and a number of other documents, however, have made grateful use of the translations appearing in H. Th. David's and A. Mendel's *Bach Reader* (1945).

1.   Friedrich Rochlitz, *Für Freunde der Tonkunst*, vol. IV, Leipzig, 1832, p. 159.

2.   Albert Schweitzer, *J.S. Bach*, 4th and 5th edition, Leipzig, 1922, p. 3.

3.   Johann Nikolaus Forkel, *Über Johann Sebastian Bachs Leben, Kunst und Kunstwerke*, new edition, Augsburg, 1925, p. 66.

4.   Jan van Eyck's motto: *as I can*=as well as I can.

5.   Philipp Spitta, *Johann Sebastian Bach*, Leipzig, 1873, 1880, vol. I, p. 354ff.

6.   Charles Sanford Terry, *Johann Sebastian Bach, eine Biographie*, Leipzig, 1929, p. 93.

7.   *"Anti Calvinismus und Christen Schule item Anti Melancholicus."*

8.   Terry, *Bach*, pp. 226-28.

9.   Concerning Bach's understanding of the Lutheran dogma, see Spitta, *Bach*, vol. II, p. 692ff. In this collection of organ chorales Spitta saw the basic dogmas of the Lutheran faith glorified in the form of a complete worship service.

10. Listed completely in Terry, *Bach*, pp. 330-33.

11. This is the title of a well known orthodox book by Valentin Ernst Löscher (1673-1749), published in 1711.

12. Cf. D. Fr. Hashagen, *J.S. Bach als Sänger und Musiker des Evangeliums und der Lutherischen Reformation*, Wismar, 1901.

13. Herein he was supported by Luther's own attitude toward music.

14. Professor Gurlitt's lectures in Freiburg/ Br. stimulated the author to examine these sources.

15. Forkel, *Bachs Leben*, p. 22.

16. 1701-22.

17. Cf. Franz Kemmerling, *Die Thomasschule zu Leipzig*, Leipzig, 1927, and Spitta, *Bach*, vol. II, p. 13.

18. Regarding what follows, cf. the documents in Arnold Schering's *Musikgeschichte Leipzigs*, vol. II, 1650/1723, Leipzig, 1926, p. 257ff.

19. Schering, *Musikgeschichte*, p. 195f.

20. Ibid., p. 470.

21. Which lasted from 1736-38.

22. Terry, *Bach*, p. 291.

23. Ibid., p. 273.

24. See B. Fr. Richter, *"Zur Geschichte der Passionsaufführungen in Leipzig,"* Bach-Jahrbuch, 1911, pp. 50-59, as well as Friedrich Smend, *Bachs Matthäus-Passion, Bach-Jahrbuch*, 1928, p. 73ff.

25. Schering, *Musikgeschichte*, p. 435f.

26. *"Gott ist mein König"* (No. 71).

27. In his second letter to Forkel, dated Jan. 13, 1775.

28. Reprinted in *Bach-Jahrbuch*, 1920.

29. Cf. *Allgemeine deutsche Bibliothek* (ed. by Nicolai), section I, of vol. 81 (1788), p. 295ff.; further, Friedrich Wilhelm Marpurg, *Beiträge zur Geschichte der Musik*, vol. I, p. 450.

30. Spitta, *Bach*, vol. I, pp. 621-23.

31. Second letter to Forkel, Jan. 13, 1775.

32. One may recall here the scheduled contest which the French clavier virtuoso Marchand avoided.

33. See C.P.E. Bach's first letter to Forkel (written at the turn of the year 1774-75).

34. Ibid.

35. C.P.E. Bach's second letter to Forkel of Jan. 13, 1775.

36. Ibid.

37. Jacob Adlung, *Anleitung zur musikalischen Gelahrtheit*, 1758, p. 711.

38. Cf. *Lexikon der Tonkünstler*, vol. II, Leipzig, 1792, p. 414.

39. The following quotations were taken from the new, enlarged and revised edition of Scheibe's *Critischer Musicus* of 1745 (Leipzig, Breitkopf & Härtel).

40. Scheibe, *Critischer Musicus*, pp. 773, 890.

41. Ibid., pp. 41-45, 578f.

42. Ibid., p. 766.

43. Ibid.

44. Ibid., p. 839.

45. Ibid.

46. Ibid.

47. Ibid., p. 840.

48. Ibid.

49. Ibid., p. 132.

50. Ibid., p. 896.

51. Ibid., p. 132.

52. Ibid., p. 840.

53. Ibid.

54. Ibid.

55. Ibid., p. 880.

56. Ibid., p. 885.

57. Ibid., p. 883.

58. Ibid., p. 840.

59. Ibid.

60. Ibid.

61. Ibid., p. 890.

62. Schweitzer, *J.S. Bach*, p. 166.

63. Scheibe, *Critischer Musicus*, p. 879.

64. For instance, Mattheson's criticism of Bach's cantata "Ich hatte viel Bekümmernis" was written in a style quite similar to that of Scheibe. See also Schweitzer, *J.S. Bach*, p. 163f.

65. Scheibe, *Critischer Musicus*, p. 851.

66. Ibid., p. 857.

67. Published in Marpurg's *Historisch-kritische Beiträge zur Aufnahme der Musik*, vol. I, 1754-55, p. 561. Reprinted in Schweitzer, *J.S. Bach*, p. 207f.

68. Of August 3, 1750.

69. Terry, *Bach*, p. 321f.

70. Reprinted in BG 25 (1875), pp. xv-xvi.

71. Ibid., p. xv.

72. Ibid., p. xvi.

2

Sebastian Bach's Survival in the Age of Rationalism

Rationalism

With the master's death in 1750 a new phase of the Bach movement began. The figure of Bach disappeared from history with his last breath. Bach the man and artist had ceased to shape the problematic nature of his earthly existence. From now on it was left to posterity to deal with the phenomenon Bach. His personality became a matter of remembrance, its continuing existence depending on the consciousness of his fellowmen. We must bear in mind that Germany was at that time not yet used to the re-creative type of artist. Because the travelling virtuoso and the church musician ordinarily presented their own works exclusively, the performance of a composition other than one's own constituted an exception. The survival of Bach's works thus became uncertain. The phenomenon Bach became a problem for others on whose grace his historic existence henceforth depended. The circle of individuals which from then on would guard Bach's legacy took the place that Bach himself had held. A look at the posterity on whose mercy Bach's afterlife now depended will explain why this new phase of the Bach movement could prosper only far away from all that was socially representative. That is, it lived on in almost rural seclusion, subterraneously, so to speak, below the stream of historically visible daily events.

The New Attitude towards the World

The cause of the enormous revolutionary process which brought about the Age of Rationalism lay essentially in the fact that the *ratio,* man's innate common sense, freed the organized world of guilds and classes from all tradition. There was no sphere into which human reason did not intrude, sweeping away old prejudices. The world of traditional privilege and convention fell apart. The Enlightenment of mankind originated in France, where it replaced religious thinking with philosophical thinking. The moral philosophy of the Age of Enlightenment took possession of the time-honored impregnable fortress of theology. With this, the preeminent position of religion was broken. In the wake of this tradition-destroying movement music was taken out of the comprehensive structure of theology and turned over to an enlightened mankind as an independent art. Removed from its limited yet useful position, the function of instrumental music, devoid of word and sect, became problematic. When, in the course of the eighteenth century, the princely courts, second home to music besides the church, decayed and vanished as art centers, music lost its environment, that is, its very meaning and purpose. With the vanishing power of church and court, music lost its true reason to exist and function. "Sonate, que me veux-tu?"[1] said Fontenelle, a nephew of the great Corneille, highlighting with this sentence the whole problem of *l'art pour l'art.* What purpose has a liberated music in a world ruled by reason, existing only for its own sake?

The new aspect of this cultural turning point, symbolically coinciding with Bach's death, is that the musical artwork was now transferred into the realms of purely sensual sounds and feelings. "It is even the prime goal of music, that it be pleasing to the ear," said Scheibe.[2] This means that for the new generation the musical artwork comes into existence only during its tonal realization; it becomes uniquely the "possession of the sense of hearing."[3] To indulge exclusively in the sensual pleasure of listening to music was something new that had to be learned. From now on music could be oriented solely towards euphony and perfection of form. Once the autonomy of the musical world had been established, the musical aspect of the independent artwork could now be judged from the standpoint of purely tonal experience. This is an esthetic approach which always does some harm, if it is applied to a composition by Bach. Only when music became totally autonomous did the basic conditions exist for the discovery of tone color as an end in itself. This has to be seen in contrast to Bach's use of D major trumpets and kettle drums,—so to speak, as the old traditional golden background—when he had something to say *ad majorem Dei gloriam.* After Bach, the Baroque orchestra, in which the rigid and impersonal sound of the winds was prominent, disintegrated and gave way to the soulful basic sound of the more flexible strings. The terraced dynamics of the Baroque orchestra were superseded by dynamics of flowing transitions, which the individual musician could stop or reinitiate at any time. Thus a new world of sound came into being. The wind instruments which remained, such as transverse flute and horn, adapted themselves to the new *cantabile* ideal of sound. The time had come for the clarinet, that most soulful and flexible woodwind instrument, to be invented. Whenever the necessity arises in history, art always finds the means to express its intentions.

Everywhere the old musical traditions disappeared and new concepts and laws took their place. It is, however, characteristic of times that break with traditional norms, to think and judge only from their own point of view.

Hitherto valid rights and customs can the more easily be replaced, because any new era is convinced of the progress inherent in its new world order. For the Age of Rationalism this is true to an exceptional degree. "Since history is held together entirely by the idea of continuous progress, the evaluation of former periods from the point of view of the present is a necessary consequence. From this consciousness of the present, history in its entirety is once again reinterpreted. The present therefore becomes climax and measure of all former phenomena. With this, historiography adopts a standardized principle of evaluation."[4] This way of thinking can in its justified egocentricity only determine that what is up to date is necessarily superior and that the more recent artwork is therefore closer to the ideal of the time. Rationalism did not reflect on compositions and musical styles of the past. "The Age of Rationalism has been the most unhistorical time in history,"[5] making its own world-understanding and cosmopolitan artistic ideal the measure of art in general. The egocentricity of this time without tradition also created a new concept of genius which stressed the subjective, the unique and was therefore incomparable. The sketchbook began to capture the unique ideas of the composer. Wealth of invention became essential. One was supposed to say something personal. Borrowings or adaptations of preexisting musical material were now severely criticized. Using themes that were common property in the Age of Baroque or the technique of *Parody* was now interpreted as a sign of mental poverty. Moritz Hauptmann, Bach authority and Thomas Cantor, still thought "that because of the very respectable constant workman-like activity of the composers of that time, genius could not possibly have been so constantly at their side."[6] It was historically no longer understood that "S. Bach, so richly endowed with creative faculty, would rob his own earlier works of exquisite pieces in order to supplement later ones."[7]

The break which the Age of Reason executed (in 1789 radically) with regard to the old world order based on vested interests, this invalidation of the old order which brought with it the emancipation of music and musician from traditional ties, and, consequently, the rise of a music that was free and of the musician who was independent—these were the chief results of the Rationalistic revolution.

Music Esthetics of Rationalism

The esthetics of music in the Age of Rationalism do not yet represent a separate discipline in the structural framework of philosophy. Music esthetics is a special field, created by musicians and directly derived from the practice of their art. The esthetic views of this time must be gathered from the works of men such as Kuhnau, Werckmeister, Rameau, Quantz or C.P.E. Bach.[8] Sebastian Bach never used his pen to define or defend his artistic ideal. He, who became hot-tempered and active only when his inner world, his service to God, was attacked,[9] was close to the artistic ideal of a man such as Andreas Werckmeister, whose writings strongly opposed the Rationalism of the French Aesthetes. Also Kuhnau's writings on music still reflected the idea that music is a gift of God. In the anti-Rationalistic thoughts of both men the essence of Protestant church music was once more affirmed. In Gerhard Pietzsch's words[10] "the musician appears [in Protestant church music] as servant of the word and the work surpasses itself by its symbolic character, as it did in the late Middle Ages, and becomes a revelation of an idea transcending the aesthetic." Or as Luther put it: "After theology I give to music the nearest place and highest honor."[11]

In Germany it was Mattheson who, in contrast to Bach, kept pace with his time by embracing Rationalism. In his later writings he formulated a pure *doctrine of affections* interpreting music as "speech in sound," whose final goal no longer lay in glorifying God or serving his church, but in arousing or mollifying human passions. The emotional element, formerly no problem in music, now acquired its rightful place in the music esthetics of the time. Musical writings became saturated with words from the realm of sentiment. What mattered now was the emotional content of music, to which one wanted to get as close as possible. The emotions conjured up by music were actually perceived as being real *(Realaffekte)*. One experienced and suffered them. One might think in this context of the literary parallel, Goethe's *Werther* (published in 1774). The doctrine of affections was indeed the proper music esthetics of the *Wertherzeit*. Music was able to affect and move the listener physically. The musician did not, however, dwell on a single affect, but alternated them, falling from one emotional state into another. He placed himself into these moods and experienced them like an actor on the stage. In this period the content of art became absolutely real. The danger point was reached when esthetics developed into a *doctrine* of these affects. In the writings of Mattheson, Scheibe, Kirnberger and Marpurg actual recipes for the writing of music were given, and the attempt was made to establish a clear-cut vocabulary, a teachable language of affects. Kirnberger disclosed a method of how "to shake sonatas out of one's sleeve" ("Sonaten aus'm Ermel zu schüddeln"),[12] and Marpurg speaks of creating affects by themes and motifs "whose success had been justified by experience."[13] He recommended them for musical use as though they were technical means and tools of which anyone could avail himself. As representative of the doctrine of affections he disregarded the fact that subjectively created themes, musical inventions and ideas, are not teachable.[14] The phrase *doctrine of affections* is already a misnomer. The borderline had to be reached once the Rationalistic doctrine of affections was pushed to its last consequences. The source of error lay in the attempt to rationalize the content of music, *that* aspect of music which depends upon something uniquely personal, on inspiration, on the *genius* of the artist, in short, on something irrational, i.e., antirational. Rationalization of the structural aspect of music, on the other hand, is quite possible, since the world of musical forms, style and technique is a social, collective property, and thus intellectually comprehensible. This aspect of music can be taught and inherited through tradition and *schooling.* The other side of music is at best trainable and can be improved only if one is born with talent and genius. The uniquely personal quality of an artwork, that which gives it in the last analysis its individual character, exceeds the potential of rational scientific studies. Here lie also the limits of musical *hermeneutics.*

Since all questions of esthetics were to be answered now by sound human perception and common sense, it became important that, besides expert knowledge, a certain level of education was required. The mere musician lacked the necessary qualifications to express himself on the *Art of Imitation.* His education must go beyond the realm of music. In the moment in which the musician began to lose his social footing, he sought characteristically to reach a balance in social refinement and erudition. Only he who by virtue of his profession was socially well entrenched could afford to be one-sided. With the breaking away of the musical profession from general society (Scheibe already spoke of the small group of people, a *"Völkchen,"* that was beginning to detach itself from the others), the fear of one-sidedness set in. Because the musician did not want to remain outside of society, he acquired knowledge beyond the scope of his own art. By trying to become intellectually and esthetically the equal of others, he thought to conceal the break with society, and to compensate for it by his learning and middle class outlook. On the other hand, he opened the formerly closed circle of the guilds and offered the hitherto protected profession of the musician to all who were willing to practice it. The knowledge of performance practice, of the technical mastery of the instruments that until now had been passed on only by the training of the townpipers, like a trade, was now conveyed to the whole world by textbooks.[15] These books disclosed the rules, the professional secrets, known up to now only to the musicians in the guilds, to all who chose to learn them, thus making the playing of music accessible to everyone. In his *Essay on the True Manner of Playing the Clavier,* Carl Philipp Emanuel Bach shared all technical and spiritual details of this instrument with the general public. By doing so, he gave away the old German secrets of his Bachian training, just like Kirnberger who, in his *Kunst des reinen Satzes,* tried to preserve for posterity the fundamental principles of Bach's manner of composition and teaching.

J.S. Bach in the Rationalistic Historiography of Music

The gradual dissolution of the guilds of musicians was accompanied by the decline of church music, and the choirs of the cantorates of most German towns had to struggle for their existence. Signs of this disintegration began as early as 1715 when Mattheson allowed three female Hamburg opera singers to perform in church. At about the same time he also admitted and used females as choir members in church music.[16] Simultaneously, as a result of the reduced role of music in the *Latin Schools,* the supply of boy sopranos diminished. In 1728, female singers made their first appearance in the church music of Frankfurt.[17] Public concerts, given in church and concert hall, originated at about the same time. While large mixed choirs did not yet exist, history was soon to demand them in the course of the eighteenth century. During this period Bach's cantatas were bound to be completely forgotten, and that not only because of their orthodox texts. Able to survive was the religious music of a composer such as Graun which, with its sentimental text, was effective in opera and church concerts. Bach spoke disparagingly of this music of the era of *Empfindsamkeit* and its representation by the *style galant* because its paucity of polyphony seemed not sufficiently artistic to him. This bourgeois art, accepted by the aristocracy, reflected the social class of the *homme galant* and thus remained reserved for this section of society. No longer associated with church and theology and freed from metaphysical powers, music, now on its own and for the first time in history completely earthly, was therefore also relieved of all higher responsibility. Profundity and transcendental forms disappeared and made way for a music which only had to sing to fulfill the *cantabile* ideal of the time. Rationalism was neither able nor willing to comprehend that Bach's work was rooted in something transcendental that surpassed experience. Bach's works stem from a way of thinking whose models are not found in the real world and nature. For Bach another world still existed that was independent of the real world, and thus closed to Rationalism and its worldly art.

Divested of content and theme, the music of the Age of Reason had to substitute a new secular content, full of *Empfindsamkeit* and feeling, burdened with emotions, which at the same time simplified music and gave it a bourgeois quality that corresponded to the general sociological change. Only now did the problem of expression in music begin to play a major role. Only now did subjective involvement in style and mood of a piece of music become essential. Only now did flexible bowing, full of nuances, and the vibrato of the string player, as well as the touch of the pianist become important, while the transverse flute replaced the old recorder that lacked expressiveness.

C.P.E. Bach's request that the artist show his deep feelings outwardly so that one could read the emotions in his face as well as hear them, has to be understood in this context. "A player cannot move others unless he himself is moved," said the great son of Sebastian Bach.[18] He then continued, "that this cannot be done without corresponding gestures is denied only by the one who is forced by his insensitiveness to sit like a wooden statue in front of his instrument."[19] This is the son's judgment of his father. The old Bach had no feelings, was no master of affects, could not transmit emotions and show affects because he sat motionless when he played.[20] Bach's immobility had dissolved in his son into constant fluctuation and motion.

Even plainer and clearer than Philipp Emanuel's comments were the remarks which Quantz in his *Versuch einer Anweisung die Flöte traversiere zu spielen*[21] made about the old German scholastic style and the change of taste to the *cantabile*. The teacher and theorist Quantz did not speak only for his own time. With this work he left to posterity a document which, as far as Bach is concerned, represents a still unexplored source of information on the philosophy of music during the time of Rationalism. Quantz belonged ideologically to the Rationalistic Berlin circle in which C.P.E. Bach was also at home. When Quantz spoke of music he always meant the effect which music made. In his opinion, the affect must actually be felt. Therefore he could not make friends with the "old ones" who "have become too deeply absorbed in musical artifices and have gone too far in this respect so that they have almost neglected the most essential part of music, namely that which is intended to touch and please."[22]

It sounds like Scheibe's criticism of Bach when Quantz takes the field against the all too richly ornamented and embellished melodies of the Baroque era:

> Some persons believe that they will appear learned if they crowd an Adagio with many graces, and twist them around in such fashion that all too often hardly one note among ten harmonizes with the bass, and little of the principal air can be perceived. Yet in this they err greatly, and show their lack of true feeling for good taste. . . . Finally, they are ignorant that there is more art in saying much with little, than little with much.[23]

The old reproach remains—what is too artistically contrived conflicts with natural feeling and does violence to the text. Therefore one should not "obscure a good piece and make the melody incomprehensible by elaborating and disrupting the notes too much."[24] This sentence which, from the linguistic aspect also could have been written by Scheibe, proves to what extent Scheibe had been a spokesman for his time. Of his German predecessors, Quantz said, "Their compositions were, as mentioned, harmonious and many-voiced, but neither melodious nor charming. They sought to compose in a more artful rather than in a comprehensible and pleasing manner. They composed more for the eye than for the ear."[25] In the art of "harmonically correct composition" as well as "on many instruments" they have "brought it very far." "Yet one finds . . . few signs of good taste and beautiful melodies; rather one finds that their taste as well as their tunes remained quite trivial, dry, meager and naïve for a longer time than those of their neighbors." This is the same observation made by Scheibe—namely that the Gothic-medieval, many-voiced style kept its hold on German music while other countries had already achieved a classical stage. It is the realization that the various European countries entered the classical era at different times, that they followed one another; that England, France and Italy reached the ideal of the *cantabile* style earlier than Germany hence the mocking remarks about the Baroque *"ruins and remnants"* in central and north Germany. The Enlightenment could no longer comprehend the *"scholasticism of the Age of the Organ."* Bach was thus not only the last guardian of a past art in Germany, but also the last nonclassicist in Europe. As Nietzsche said, "In Bach there is still too much of crude Christianity, of the crude German character, of crude scholasticism."[26]

A few other remarks by Quantz are perfectly applicable to Bach's musical style. For example, Quantz said of the Germans,

> Thus as a rule they sing with a uniform volume of tone, without light and shade.... They have little feeling for Italian flattery, which is effected by slurred notes and by diminishing and strengthening the tone. Their disagreeable, forced, and exceedingly noisy chest attacks, in which they make vigorous use of the faculty of the Germans for pronouncing the h, singing ha-ha-ha-ha for each note, make all the passage-work sound hacked up, and are far removed from the Italian manner of executing passage-work with the chest voice.[27]

In their instrumental music "the Germans valued difficult pieces more than easy ones and sought to amaze rather than to please."[28] "On the violin they played more harmonically [i.e., polyphonically, with double and triple stops] than melodically."[29] "The Allegro [one may think, for instance, of Bach's Prelude of the E major Partita for unaccompanied violin] consisted frequently from beginning to end of nothing but passage-work in which nearly every measure was similar to the next and was repeated, transposed from one key to another, which in the end necessarily had to produce revulsion."[30] The infinite flow of Baroque music was thus something to guard against. To spin off a single melodic motif was now perceived as a sign of lack of emotion, causing boredom. The length of a piece of music thus became a problem. Quantz said, "In order to keep an eye on the proper length of a concerto, one might even consult a clock.... In general it is more advantageous, if the audience finds a piece too short rather than too long."[31]

Furthermore, "many instruments of which we hardly know the names nowadays,"[32] were still being used by the Germans. This, too, applied to Bach's old fashioned orchestra, in which one still meets with the viola da gamba, the viola d'amore, the viola pomposa, the violino piccolo, the violoncello piccolo and lutes. Bach also used the recorder, the oboes d'amore and da caccia, the cornetto and corni da caccia as well as several other instruments of the German Baroque orchestra.

Quantz was the typical representative of his time when, at the end of his book, *Register der vornehmsten Sachen*, in the Index of the principal subjects, he praised Handel as "a famous German composer," while he said of Bach, "he has brought the art of organ playing to perfection." It is always the same—Bach had the reputation of being the greatest master of his time on the organ, but was not counted among the leading composers. Reichardt, the Prussian Court Capellmeister and well-known Lieder composer, said of Bach, "If Bach had possessed the truthfulness and the deep feeling for expression which inspired Handel he would be much greater than Handel; but as it is, he is only more learned and more diligent."[33] Johann Adam Hiller, who was both master of the German Singspiel and cantor of the Thomas Church, remarked that "the church music [Bach] had composed does honor to his profound mind but wants to have its special admirers."[34] Hiller, however, did not belong to these *special admirers*. As third successor to Bach in the Thomas cantorate he worked mainly for his teacher Hasse, and for Handel, while doing nothing for his great predecessor. On the contrary, he tried to fill "the mother's boys at the Thomas School with loathing for the crudities"[35] of Sebastian Bach.

Thus Bach historiography was esthetically still at the same point as in Bach's lifetime. The posthumous fame of the organ virtuoso continued, while the composer, now as before, had to seek his *special admirers*. Carl Philipp Emanuel was the *great* Bach for the eighteenth century. His fame, praised to the skies by the English music historian Burney, obscured that of his father. Bach's sons had brought it farther. They were younger, knew the new taste of their time, and therefore, could make the greater claim to be in the right with their art.

The Cultivation of Bach's Music during the Age of Rationalism

The Afterlife of Bach in the Circle of His Sons

The practical cultivation of Bach's music—no matter how sparsely it may have been carried out, sometimes even out of glaring misunderstanding—now becomes the focus of our investigation. We now concern ourselves with Bach's survival in his work, with the afterlife of his old artistic ideal in spite of the prevailing taste. Where did Bach's music survive and who performed works of the master?

Let us begin with those who doubtlessly had been closest to Bach and were the principal heirs of his music—his sons. Of these only Wilhelm Friedemann, Carl Philipp Emanuel and Johann Christoph Friedrich, the *Bückeburg Bach*, performed compositions by their father, while Johann Christian, who called his father an *old wig*, broke off all relations to the world of Sebastian Bach. He was the first of the Bach clan to go to Italy[36] to learn his craft, and there became a Roman Catholic. "*Inter nos,* he did things differently from the honest Veit," Philipp Emanuel wrote in the genealogy of the Bach family. With these words he may have intended to express "the sorrow he felt over the abandoning of the faith of his forefathers, and chose as an appropriate counterpart Veit Bach who left his country during a time of religious struggles so that he could remain true to his faith."[37] Bach's youngest son, now a Catholic, became organist at the cathedral of Milan, and migrated later to England, the most bourgeois and most progressive country in Europe, where he led the typical restless life of a basically homeless artist.

Thus J.S. Bach's survival among his sons depended on Friedemann, Philipp Emanuel and the Bückeburg Bach, that is, mainly on the two oldest sons who were in possession of their father's manuscripts and who, with a smaller generation gap, were better able to relate to their father's world. And so Forkel, who still knew where to look for Bach traditions, relied solely on their information.

Johann Christoph Friedrich Bach who, according to Friedemann, was technically the most skilled clavier player among the brothers,[38] kept alive—at least in the circle at the Bückeburg court—the memory of the keyboard composer J.S. Bach, whose harpsichord works he is said to have performed with greatest perfection. Among all the keyboard virtuosi his father had trained and, with the help of his compositions, had turned into masters of their instruments, he was most qualified to bestow upon Sebastian's harpsichord works a new lease on life. He also occasionally incorporated choral movements of his father into his own works and thus familiarized the Bückeburg court with them.[39] This is all we know about the afterlife of J.S. Bach's works as far as the artistic activities of his Bückeburg son are concerned.

The way Friedemann and Philipp Emanuel have dealt with their father's work is richer, multi-faceted, and, because it was so varied, also more afflicted by misinterpretations. Martin Falck, the most thorough biographer Friedemann Bach has found so far, informed us of the following works by Sebastian that his son performed. A performance of Cantata 149, "Man singet mit Freuden vom Sieg," is documented by the preserved textbook for October 3, 1756. The cantata was presented during the divine service at the main church *Zu unser lieben Frauen* in Halle.[40] It is further known that during his time in Halle, where he succeeded men like Zachow and Scheidt as organist at the main church, he performed several more of his father's cantatas, of which he possessed perhaps as many as three out of five annual sets. They were the cantatas "Nimm von uns, Herr, du treuer Gott," (No. 101); "Herz und Mund und Tat und Leben" (No. 147); "Vergnügte Ruh', beliebte Seelenlust" (No. 170); (these four cantatas cited so far have been preserved in copies by Friedemann), and, finally, the cantata "Es ist das Heil uns kommen her" (No. 9).[41] Preserved textbooks point moreover to several cantatas, whose music is lost, but which were perhaps works by Sebastian Bach. They are the cantatas performed on November 21, 1756, "Wertes Zion sei getrost" and on June 6, 1762 (in the morning) "Gott ist unsere Zuversicht und Stärke." These were attributed by Martin Falck[42] to Sebastian Bach, not with certainty, yet presumably. Since the church music performed at the divine services was recorded only incompletely, it does not follow that this is a complete index of the performances of Bach cantatas in Halle at this time. It is safe to assume that Friedemann's own cantatas were quite frequently replaced by church music of his father. As a consequence the strange fact must be recorded that in the Pietistic town of Halle Bach's cantatas were granted a first, though modest, afterlife.

The historic image of J.S. Bach's oldest son became completely distorted in the course of time by overemphasis on and falsification of anecdotes that portrayed him as having been a poor guardian of his father's legacy. This was a myth already dispelled by Falck.

Friedemann Bach suffered the tragic fate of having to live at the time of the Mannheim School of composers while being burdened by the old Bachian tradition. The latter committed him to the organ whose last master he was after his father's death. As the oldest of the family he could not evade his hereditary duty which dictated that he too ought to become an organist and compose cantatas. This happened, however, at a time when the deterioration of Protestant church music had already progressed so rapidly that there was no longer any sense in opposing it. In this context it must be understood that Friedemann, who talked about the gallant pieces of his brother Philipp Emanuel as "pretty little things" (the way Sebastian had talked about Hasse), improvised his own fantasies and fugues. The writing down had by now lost its meaning, even for didactic purposes. Friedemann's art of improvisation must have been extraordinary. In Zelter's view he was "the most perfect organ player" he had ever known,[43] although he had "never heard him play a single note of his father's music though everyone wished him to do so."[44] Except for Sebastian Bach "no one had mastered the art of pedal playing with such power as he."[45] Friedemann Bach brought the history of German organ music to a close. Handel and C.P.E. Bach had already left the age of the organ behind them. In 1773 Carl Philipp Emanuel had to admit to Burney with regard to the Hamburg organs that he "had not played the organ for such a long time that he no longer knew what to do with the pedal."[46]

Friedemann's social position was thus even more that of a last link to the past than that of his father. His own time abandoned him and allowed him to become destitute. With this in mind one should try to understand that it was the unemployed artist who perpetrated falsifications of some of his father's works in times of bitterest need towards the end of his life in Berlin. (Friedemann published under his own name his father's transcription for organ of Vivaldi's

D minor concerto. On the other hand, he claimed that a *Kyrie* and a choral movement, "Dienet dem Herren," both of which were compositions of his own, had been written by his father.[47] This happened at a time of need when he no longer possessed any of his father's manuscripts.) These falsifications were the acts of a destitute person, not those of an artist thirsting for fame. Already in 1774, after ten years without position, he tried to sell by auction the collection of autograph manuscripts which were his paternal heritage. Until then he had guarded this treasure carefully. During his time in Halle[48] he had, however, given away a few things to pupils (the French Suites to Rust, and the "Clavier-Büchlein vor Wilhelm Friedemann Bach" to J.C. Bach, the *Halle Bach).*[49] Later he gave to the organist Müller, his landlord in Brunswick, his manuscript of the "Well-Tempered Clavier" as well as that of the Inventions and Sinfonias. (Müller was the uncle of the Thomas Cantor of the same name who was to become an important figure in the later Bach movement.)

During this time of unemployment in Brunswick (1771-74) Friedemann depended on the hospitality and kindness of his friends. It was there that the sales of manuscripts increased. Forkel acquired from his friend Friedemann, whose organ playing filled him with "tremors of awe,"[50] among other manuscripts the Chromatic Fantasy which, along with the Goldberg Variations, he praised as unequaled. The main portion of Friedemann's paternal collection, however, went in 1774 to Eschenburg with the request to sell it. In a communication to the latter, dated July 4, 1778, Friedemann wrote,

> My departure from Brunswick was so hasty that I was unable to compile a list of the music and books I left behind. I do remember my father's *Art of the Fugue* and Quantz's Instructions on the Flute. You promised me to sell the annual sets of cantatas and other church music as well as books for cash.[51]

It is not fair to interpret this as frivolous dissipation. Friedemann held on to the works of his father until need forced him to sell his possessions. He should not be blamed for the dispersal of his paternal manuscripts, but rather his time which let him starve and thus forced him to part with the great legacy of his father. Forkel, commenting on the unsuccessful edition of several of Friedemann's Clavier Polonaises, said,

> The saddest part of this is that such misfortunes must necessarily discourage young artists of outstanding talent to strive for the acquisition of superior skills. For they see daily with their own eyes that the highly acclaimed art goes hungry and does in no way partake of the fortune heaped upon mediocre skill.[52]

Friedemann Bach's fate reflects the tragedy of the artist who was not willing to make concessions to the prevailing public taste. Society no longer provided an opportunity for him to make a living. It let him die in misery, yet lamented the "irreplaceable loss" of its "foremost organ player."[53]

As director of church music in Hamburg,[54] Philipp Emanuel also repeatedly fell back upon the rich treasure of manuscripts he had inherited from his father. Yet in his case it is not as easy to find valid excuses for the occasional false impressions he created as it was in Friedemann Bach's case. It may be practical to begin with a look at the patchwork of C.P.E. Bach's *St. Matthew Passion* of 1769, which is the passion music with which he introduced himself in Hamburg. For this performance he appropriated portions from the Passion for double chorus by his father.[55] Of Sebastian Bach's *St. Matthew Passion*, Philipp Emanuel's work contained the chorales "Was mein Gott will," "Wer hat Dich so geschlagen," "O Haupt voll Blut und Wunden," as well as the choruses "Er hat gesagt: Ich kann den Tempel Gottes abbrechen," "Wahrlich, Du bist auch einer von denen," "Barrabam," (in Philipp Emanuel's setting sung twice), "Lasst ihn kreuzigen" (both choruses), "Sein Blut komme über uns," "Es taugt nicht dass wir es in den Gotteskasten legen," "Der du den Tempel Gottes zerbrichst," "Andern hat er geholfen," "Der rufet den Elias," "Halt, lass sehen ob Elias komme." Furthermore, the introductory chorus "Christus, der uns selig macht" stemmed from his father's *St. John Passion*, the third chorale "Ich will hier bei dir stehen" from Cantata 153, "Schau lieber Gott," (however, transposed a fourth upwards from Sebastian's version, "Und ob gleich alle Teufel"). Finally, Philipp Emanuel took the chorus "Gott, über alle Götter" from Sebastian's Cantata 39, "Brich dem Hungrigen dein Brot," where it appears as the chorus "Selig sind, die aus Erbarmen" (there a fourth higher), while the chorale "O Jesu hilf zur selben Zeit" is found in Sebastian's Christmas Oratorio as "Ich steh an deiner Krippe hier." In addition, Philipp Emanuel's Passion music presumably contained movements composed by Telemann.

C.P.E. Bach's various Passions according to the three other Evangelists borrow nothing from J.S. Bach, but all the more from Telemann, who was then considered *the* composer of Passion music in Hamburg. But Philipp Emanuel's six performances of his *St. Matthew Passion* in the years 1769, 1773, 1777, 1781, 1785 and 1787 contained consistently the above-listed chorales and choruses by his father. These movements Philipp Emanuel contrasted with recitatives and arias of his own composition. Since they were, however, completely different, being written rather in the fluent operatic style of his time, the composition as a whole turned out to be a stylistic mixture. Important is the fact that Philipp Emanuel used only *chorales* and *dramatic choruses* by his father. This indicates that he seemed to acknowledge his father's superiority in the harmonization of the old church hymns as well as in the composition of the brief but massive choruses of the people. In the lyrical, meditative and contemplative movements, however, he felt, in agreement with his time, superior to J.S. Bach. He did not consider his father's recitatives, solo arias and arias set for chorus worth borrowing. In these categories the time had gone beyond Sebastian Bach. It is not known whether Philipp Emanuel openly admitted his borrowings by drawing attention to his father's choruses at any one of the six performances of his *St. Matthew Passion*. If one accepts the fact of borrowing from works of others, which at the time of his father was an accepted technique—but Sebastian Bach never copied, always revising what he borrowed—Philipp Emanuel may even be thanked for having exposed the people of Hamburg on six occasions to parts of this unequaled work by his father.

In addition to the above, Philipp Emanuel presented to his Hamburg congregation two of his father's cantatas, both in revised form[56] (No. 102 "Herr, deine Augen sehen nach dem Glauben" and No. 25 "Es ist nichts Gesundes an meinem Leibe"). Furthermore, he concluded his early Easter Cantata for the year 1756, written in Berlin, with Sebastian Bach's chorale setting "Heut' triumphiret Gottes Sohn." This again bears witness to the admiration Emanuel had for the chorale harmonizations of his father. His own chorale settings were, however, entirely homophonic in the style of a composer such as Graun. When one encounters intricate and dense polyphony in Emanuel's compositions, one may look for the *original* in the works of his father.

Towards the end of his life, C.P.E. Bach presented the *Credo* from the B minor Mass of his father to the Hamburg citizens. The performance did not take place in church, but in the concert hall, although it was given there for a charitable purpose. Since Handel had established himself in Hamburg fourteen years earlier with the magnificent choral style of his *Messiah*, Philipp Emanuel finally dared in 1786 to perform a section of his father's great Mass. In addition to compositions by Handel and Philipp Emanuel himself, movements 12-19 of the B minor Mass, to which Emanuel had written an orchestral introduction of his own (!), were heard in Hamburg for the first time. The review in the *Hamburger Correspondent*[57] especially lauded the work by Sebastian Bach, "which is one of the most excellent pieces that has ever been heard, but which must be executed by a sufficient number of voices if it is to produce its full effect." Important here is the wish for a large chorus so that the piece may produce the desired *effect!* The size and volume of sound of Handel's choruses began now to have a direct influence on Bach interpretation. The Halle master's ideal of sound, so full of pathos, began to gain a foothold in Germany. The appearance of bourgeois choral societies could not much longer be delayed. The *Hamburger Correspondent* further admired "the skill" with which the singers mastered the difficult passages, but said nothing about the impression the *et incarnatus est*, the *crucifixus*, or the *et resurrexit* made at their first performance. Here, in the concert hall, religious awe does not seem to have been felt. One merely expressed amazement at J.S. Bach the artist, who had composed everything so well, but access to the religious Bach was still lacking. This applies also to Emanuel who ignored the symbolic meaning of his father's art by himself writing church music in a style that was devoid of any transcendental and super-musical content.

This is all that is known about Bach performances in Hamburg.[58] However, since Emanuel was in possession of about half of his father's cantatas, it can be assumed from his indolence in composing for the church and his frequent borrowings from others, that in the course of his time as cantor in Hamburg he used many a cantata by his father. This can only be documented when Philipp Emanuel took the trouble to revise or transpose works by his father, or when he incorporated them, movement by movement, into his own compositions—i.e., only when he made visible changes. When, on the other hand, lack of time forced him to perform some of the *antiquated* works in their original version and neither textbooks nor official records have come down to us, no way is left to verify this probable phenomenon, so important for J.S. Bach's afterlife in Hamburg. How completely the *true* Bach was misunderstood is made evident by the fact that he enjoyed a quiet afterlife through the indolence of others who, like his sons, happened to own his works, and not because of an esthetic affirmation of his creative work. Bach was one among many good church musicians whose works it was thought well to revise for the sake of the prevailing taste; for Bach was no Telemann whose compositions needed no revision in order to satisfy demands for an up-to-date style.

Bach Performances by the Leipzig Thomas Choir

Bach's sons left their father's principal place of activity, but Bach tradition lived on in Leipzig. The library of the Thomas School owned, in addition to the parts of the motets, a number of other scores of the master. In the course of time these were increased by more manuscripts which Anna Magdalena had owned.[59] Sebastian Bach's wife shared the fate of her husband's creations. She too was forgotten by the world. Destitute and in need, she was forced to offer to the city the manuscripts of her late husband that were in her possession. Just as no gravestone marked the place where Bach's remains had been laid to rest, so did the musical companion of his life depart this world quietly in 1760, "a pauper," as the cemetery register coldly and unfeelingly stated. The Thomas School, however, survived, and the voices of the Thomas pupils still rang out in the principal churches of the city. There, the memory of Bach was never totally abandoned.

In September 1775, Bach's cantata "Erhalt uns Herr bei deinem Wort" was performed[60] in celebration of the bicentenary of the Religious Peace of Augsburg. Bach's successor, Harrer, had just died, so Penzel, the first Prefect of the choir, directed the performance. By diligently copying Bach's cantatas, the parts of which were to a considerable extent at the Thomas School, Penzel proved to be a loyal follower of the master. He either copied or compiled in score form twenty-four of Sebastian's cantatas, seventeen of them during his time in Leipzig while he was the temporary director of the choir.[61] Since these copies were frequently made just 8-14 days ahead of the Sunday to which the cantata belonged,[62] it may be assumed that at least *these* cantatas were performed in the divine service. The solidly documented festive cantata performance of September 1755, is noteworthy insofar as it constituted the only officially recorded Thomas choir performance of a Bach cantata for the next half century; that is, until the arrival of A.E. Müller, the Thomas Cantor at the time of Forkel. Some of the few copies of cantata scores that Harrer as well as Doles made during their terms in office,[63] may of course also have served practical purposes.[64] There is, however, no concrete proof that Bach's pupil Doles performed cantatas of his great teacher in the church services of the Thomas School. Also Rochlitz mentioned no cantata performances in which he participated as a young Thomas pupil (1781-88) under Doles.

Performances of Bach's motets, on the other hand, seem to have been continued by the Thomas Choir as a matter of tradition. Rochlitz, the first great Bach esthetician of the early nineteenth century, reported that he often had to join in the singing (of the motets) under Doles, although he had not yet become responsive to Bach's music. On Palm Sunday in 1776 a Bach Passion was even presented under Doles. Neefe, Beethoven's music teacher in Bonn, reported in a letter from Leipzig, dated March 27, 1776, to his friend Schubart in Ulm,[65] "Next Sunday a Passion music by Bach will be performed in the main church." It is thus possible that even before Mendelssohn's courageous achievement in 1829, a performance of Bach's *St. Matthew Passion* might have taken place. Needless to say, this may not necessarily have been a Passion by Sebastian, since in his letter Neefe omitted Bach's first name, thereby leaving the question open as to whether a Passion by Sebastian or one of his great Hamburg son was performed.

Gerber in his *New Lexikon*[66] mentioned that he had heard a motet for double chorus by Bach sung on Christmas Day, 1767, at the Thomas Church. A motet by the master was also sung at the Thomas Church on the occasion of Mozart's visit to Leipzig in 1789. It seems that whenever the choir wanted to impress and demonstrate its ability it turned to these difficult a cappella works by Bach. The Thomas Choir apparently considered Bach's motets the *Hohe Schule* of its vocal art. As Bernhard Friedrich Richter put it,[67] "The Thomas Choir may well have been the only church choir which... since Bach's death has performed his motets again and again, quite unconcerned about the trends of taste of the times. This proves that the greatness of Bach's art, even though perhaps not fully understood by the Thomas Choir, was at least sensed and felt at a very early time." This statement reiterates that whenever Bach's church music was used for the purpose of a practical performances during the Age of Rationalism, such performances went against the prevailing taste. The afterlife of Bach's art thus continued at various places within the music life of Germany, but it did so in defiance of the great musical events of the day.

The Berlin Bach Movement in the Age of Rationalism

Bach cantatas appeared a few times as rare exceptions in church services of Leipzig, Halle, and Hamburg while his motets gradually became a permanent possession of the Thomas Choir. The motets were understood esthetically and intuitively because no problems of an orchestra existed for them. However, in Bach's own time, they may now and then have been performed, not a cappella, but supported by instruments.[68] This predilection for those vocal works of Bach which had no independent orchestral parts was already apparent in Philipp Emanuel's preference for his father's chorales with which he did not mind adorning his own compositions. In this context it also becomes comprehensible that only one new edition of Bach's total creative work was published in the eighteenth century after his death—namely two collections of 4-part chorales. They were published by Birnstiel in Berlin in 1765-69. To replace this faulty and not quite accurate edition, Breitkopf in Leipzig published a second edition, in 1784, 1785 and 1786, meticulously prepared by Kirnberger, but edited by Philipp Emanuel after Kirnberger's death in 1783. The correspondence between Kirnberger and Breitkopf, edited by Arnold Schering,[69] reveals that, since 1777, Kirnberger had fought like a lion for the publication of Bach's chorales which he owned. Bach was, however, still too big a risk commercially. Since the fiasco of the *Art of the Fugue*[70] which Philipp Emanuel disposed of in 1756 for the price of old copper,[71] after no more than 30 copies had been sold, the publishers seem to have become skeptical.

Berlin and its Bach disciples, Kirnberger, Marpurg and C.P.E. Bach, at least took up the cause in behalf of their great teacher's afterlife, while Leipzig with its circle of publishers responded to their efforts with silence. The Berlin theorists of the learned style were opposed to the modern Leipzig composers such as Doles and Hiller. In Berlin a strangely rationalistic Bach cult flourished, a preoccupation with Bach's works for the sake of their strict style. In the musical circle of Berlin which Princess Amalia of Prussia, the sister of Frederick the Great, had gathered around her, Sebastian Bach came to life again as a teacher. This was, however, not the teacher who provided future organists and cantors with the technical tools of their profession, but the teacher of the learned style and the higher forms of counterpoint which, because of their inherent artful craftsmanship, required laborious training. Bach, the master of forms, it was hoped, would revise the superficial taste of the time. This kind of language had already been heard in Marpurg's Preface to the *Art of the Fugue.* Also the compilation of Bach's chorales of different provenance into Kirnberger's and Emanuel Bach's chorale collection was not intended to be more than a guidepost to learning the art of pure and strict composition. However, the individual chorales lost their spiritual function once they were lifted out of the context of the work to which they belonged musically, textually, and in respect to their liturgical position in the church year. The circle of Princess Amalia constituted the very center of this rationalistic interpretation and preoccupation with Bach's work.[72]

Anna Amalia[73] was herself a competent musician. Besides playing the harpsichord, later in life she turned more and more to the organ. In 1755, she even had an organ built into her home, although she made herself quite ridiculous in society, since a woman playing the organ was a picture from times long past. During the years 1758-83 Kirnberger was Amalia's teacher of composition. With him she studied the strict style in the true sense of the word. Under his watchful eye she composed her best works, her chorales, which she harmonized, not out of inner compulsion for use in church, but for the purely artistic pleasure she took in the art of part-writing. Only old composers served as her models. She studied Hassler and other old masters, actually rejecting everything in music that was called modern. This contrapuntal prejudice accepted as models only works of the old school, perceiving of them, however, merely the external skeleton, the good workmanship, but not the inner spirit which alone could have produced them. This restriction of vision to the contrapuntal scaffolding was the chief characteristic of Amalia's art and her attitude to it. The music theories of her great Berlin colleagues Kirnberger and Marpurg must have encouraged her in her purely form-oriented musical activities. Their treatises on counterpoint had become abstract instructions in composition, lifeless books of rules, since there was no longer a creative force like that of Sebastian Bach to back them up. With effort and pride one conquered the *Art of Pure Composition (Die Kunst des reinen Satzes)*[74] but was not able to change the existing taste and create a new style. During the Age of Rationalism Kirnberger was a great defender of Bach's art and teaching method, whether it was for him an innermost experience or not. He saw in Bach's art a most powerful anchor in the midst of the increasing shallowness of the musical style. But he fought for Bach's artistic ideal not merely as a theorist but also as pedagogue and teacher, showing thereby that the two years he had spent as Bach's pupil in Leipzig (from 1739 to 1741) had not been spent in vain.[75]

The members of Amalia's and Kirnberger's circle were historically minded, training themselves through an art of the past. By establishing and acquiring a comprehensive library of manuscripts of old music, they made an enormous contribution to the later Bach movement. Amalia's musical circle, which strongly opposed the deliberate simplicity of the *Berlin Liederschule,* was the only place of refuge for Bach's method of *teaching.* It became the collecting place for his works. Amalia's library, bequeathed upon the death of the Princess to the *Joachimsthal Gymnasium* in Berlin, became one of the principal sources for Forkel's Bach book,[76] as well as for Zelter's early Bach cult. The records of the practice sessions of the Berlin Singakademie show that the music of its first Bach performances was almost exclusively based on Bach manuscripts from the *Amalienbibliothek*. The latter harbored the largest Bach collection of the time,[77] consisting for the most part of copies made by the indefatigable Kirnberger. A cursory survey shows the following of Sebastian's main works: the *St. Matthew Passion*, the *B minor Mass*, several of the smaller Masses and Sanctus, 45 cantatas (three of them autograph) and five motets. Of Bach's chamber music and orchestral works, the Library had the six Brandenburg Concertos, the C Major Overture, the major part of the clavier concertos for 1, 2, 3 and 4 solo instruments, and a good deal more of Bach's chamber music. Plain labor performed an invaluable service for Bach scholarship in this Library. Though it did not immediately serve performances of Bach's music, it nevertheless later became an indispensable source, not only for the Berlin Bach movement under Zelter, but also for the great work of the complete edition of Bach's works. Aside from Friedemann's and Philipp Emanuel's possessions and the many original performing parts which had remained in Leipzig, the *Amalienbibliothek* in Berlin became the central point for the collecting of Bach manuscripts after Sebastian's death.

Copies and Copyists of Bach Compositions

This is not the place to present a history of Bach manuscripts and copies, and how they were scattered to the four winds once they were no longer in the hands of Bach's sons. To scrutinize the individual Bach collectors who now begin to appear must be the task of a future history of Bach manuscripts. This survey can the more easily be omitted as much of the material is already contained in the forewords to the respective volumes of the *Bach-Gesellschaft* edition. In the present study only those Bach collectors will be mentioned who, like Forkel, Schicht, Pölchau, Zelter and Hauser, let the performing Bach movement benefit from their possessions.

The variety of copies of Bach manuscripts made by his sons and pupils, as well as the copies of Bach compositions printed during the composer's lifetime, had in the time of Rationalism (from 1750 until about 1790) become so great that it is difficult to assess their effectiveness. The engraved works were actually sold in such small numbers that their distribution was no larger than that of those works which during Bach's lifetime, as well as after his death, "circulated only in handwritten copies."[78]

It would thus be wrong to assume that only the engraved copies of the four sections of the *Clavierübung*, or the *Schübler Chorales* and the *Art of the Fugue* kept the memory of Bach alive. The catalogues of publishers which listed not only the printed, but also the handwritten music in circulation, tell a different story. Max Schneider has already ferreted out what was most essential with regard to Bach's afterlife.[79] Most important were the Leipzig catalogues of Breitkopf (1761) and those of Breitkopf & Son of the years 1764, 1767, 1770 and 1774; in Hamburg, the catalogue of the publisher Westphal (1782); in Berlin, that of J.K. Fr. Rellstab (1790); and finally, the catalogue of the Viennese publisher Traeg of 1799. These catalogues listed numerous works of Bach which were for sale or loan in handwritten copies. A major role was played by the *Well-Tempered Clavier,* which was available in handwritten copies from 1764 on. Also frequently listed were the Chromatic Fantasy and Fugue, the Inventions, the Clavier Suites, several of the Clavier Concertos for 1, 2 and 3 solo instruments; furthermore, several compositions for organ, two large collections of chorales (announced in 1764 by Breitkopf & Son) and four motets; and finally, about 30 cantatas (among them several of the secular cantatas), the *St. Luke Passion* (!) and *The Musical Offering* as well as *The Art of the Fugue* (available in handwritten copies from the above cited publishers in Leipzig, Hamburg and Berlin).

These catalogues reveal that in the second half of the eighteenth century a remarkably large number of Bach's works, especially of his clavier works, were in circulation. What forces were responsible for this spreading of Bach's compositions? Who were the persons who, without the help of a printer, achieved such a wide dissemination of Bach's oeuvre? This, the central question of this chapter, can easily be deduced and answered from what has so far been described: Bach's modest afterlife in some church and concert performances of his sons; the beginnings of appreciation of Bach's vocal music at the Thomas School in Leipzig, particularly at the time during which Doles, and especially Penzel, copied or wrote out in score some of the cantatas, the original parts of which were in the Thomas School library; and finally, the laborious copying work of the Bach pupil Kirnberger at the Court of Princess Amalia of Prussia, which resulted in a substantial increase in the number of Bach manuscripts. With Doles, Penzel and above all, Kirnberger we have come into the presence of those individuals who worked for the survival of Bach's music not only by giving occasional performances, but also by making Bach's works their own by copying them. Bach's pupils, more than his sons, familiarized themselves with his works by copying them already during Bach's lifetime. Also after his death the circle of his pupils remained spiritually in touch with Bach's art by continuing its copying labors. Almost all of these copyists were organists whom Bach had trained, and who, from Johann Martin Schubart, Bach's first student and successor in Weimar, to Johann Christian Kittel, Bach's last important pupil,[80] were living in central Germany. In 1773, Burney wrote in his *Diary of a Musical Journey,*[81] "All living organists in Germany have been trained according to his school, just as most clavichord, harpsichord and fortepiano players have been trained according to the school of his son, the excellent Carl Philipp Emanuel Bach."[82]

In this circle of organists and harpsichordists, all of whom had at one time or another been touched by Bach's spirit, the master lived on. Some of his music sounded from organ lofts of small town churches in central Germany, and some of it was carried by his harpsichord students to places as far away as Königsberg and Riga.[83] The traditions of the organist and harpsichordist Bach were passed on by the circle of his pupils. Forkel, Rochlitz and Ernst Ludwig Gerber still knew Bach's organ and harpsichord compositions from first-hand performances by pupils or second generation pupils of Bach. What distinguished Bach's pupils from his sons was the fact that his pupils did not publish their own works. They merely remained copyists of their great teacher's works. With few exceptions, such as Homilius and Doles who were rather followers of Philipp Emanuel, they remained in their positions as organists in quiet rural communities. They continued to live and work in the spirit of their great mentor. As copyists of Bach's compositions they worked with philological faithfulness for the survival of his art.

Aside from the group of his first pupils who had the privilege of studying with Bach in Mühlhausen, Weimar and Cöthen, and who were still members of Bach's generation, Johann Ludwig Krebs and Johann Christian Kittel were especially active in the dissemination of Bach's music after the master's death. Krebs (1713-80), who rose from his position as organist in Zwickau and Zeitz to that of court organist at Altenburg, was Bach's favorite pupil. Burney said of him that he had "found in him at Altenburg the greatest organist in Germany."[84] As master of the organ he must have promoted Bach's music in Altenburg, for he owned[85] more than 40 organ chorales and 12 other organ compositions of his teacher (mostly in manuscript copies). His music collection contained, furthermore, several of Sebastian's clavier works, among them the Chromatic Fantasy and Fugue (in three copies), a Suite (in E minor) for lute, and a Fugue for violin and continuo. All these were compositions which he, an accomplished keyboard player, violinist and lutenist who "did not have to be afraid to perform,"[86] certainly played frequently.

Aside from the quiet and highly esteemed organ virtuoso Krebs, J.C. Kittel was a Bach disciple in the true pedagogical sense. His lifespan (1732-1809) extended into the nineteenth century. Spitta said,[87] "he trained a large number of the best Thuringian organists and tried to preserve the traditions of Bach's art in reverent memory of his master." Forkel observed in his *Musikalischer Almanach auf das Jahr 1782,*[88] "As far as the dignity of organ playing is concerned, he is considered the best interpreter of the late J.S. Bach. He improvises a strict obbligato movement in trio, quartet or quintet texture..., in the manner of J.S. Bach." Through his manual *Der angehende praktische Organist (The budding practical Organist)*[89] he attempted to keep Bach's method of organ instruction alive. Its subtitle *Unterweisung zum Zweckmässigen Gebrauch der Orgel bei Gottesverehrungen (Instructions for the proper use of the organ in the divine service)* indicates that Kittel, like Bach, saw the organ in the service of worship as late as 1803. In 1813, shortly after Kittel's death, Gerber reported the following characteristic story of him:[90] "He also continued, with undiminished keenness of mind and as the only living pillar of the old Bachian school, to educate many a good organist.[91] As a special form of reward and punishment for his pupils he used an oil painting of Johann Sebastian Bach—a fine likeness—which he had recently acquired and hung over his clavier. If the pupil showed industry worthy of this Father of Harmony, the curtain covering it was drawn aside. For the unworthy, on the other hand, Bach's countenance remained hidden."

Zelter told a similar anecdote about Kirnberger:[92]

> Kirnberger had a portrait of his master, Sebastian Bach; it was my constant admiration, and it hung in his room, between two windows, on the wall above the piano. A well-to-do Leipzig linen draper, who had formerly seen Kirnberger, when he was a chorister at the Thomas Schule, singing before his father's door, comes to Berlin, and it occurs to him to honor the now celebrated Kirnberger with a visit. Hardly were they seated, when the Leipziger bawls out, "Why, good Lord! you've actually got our Cantor, Bach, hanging there; we have him, too, in Leipzig, at the Thomas Schule. They say he was a rough fellow; didn't the conceited fool even go and have himself painted in a smart velvet coat?" Kirnberger gets up quietly, goes behind his chair, and lifting it up with both hands in the guest's face, exclaims, first gently, then *crescendo,* "Out, you dog! Out, you dog!" My Leipziger, mortally frightened, seizes his hat and stick, makes with all haste for the door, and bolts out into the street. Upon this, Kirnberger has the picture taken down and rubbed, the Philistine's chair washed, and the portrait, covered with a cloth, restored to its old place. When someone inquired, what was the meaning of the cloth? he answered, "Leave that alone! There's something behind it." This story was the origin of the report that Kirnberger had lost his senses.

This peculiar Bach cult reflects the sect-like seclusion of the early Bach movement, which deliberately confined itself to a small circle of pupils and second generation pupils, all of whom were determined to preserve the vanishing profession of the organist and considered it their mission to continue to work actively and effectively just as Bach would have done. Also Müthel, Bach's youngest pupil and copyist of his chorale preludes,[93] was "inflexibly opposed to the fashionable taste of his time."[94] These Bach disciples fulfilled their duty quietly, at times by making music at the organ or at the harpsichord, at other times, with quill in hand, by the mental task of copying his works. The manuscript copies of men such as Krebs, Altnickol, Kirnberger, Kittel, Penzel, Hering, Kellner, H.N. Gerber, J. Fischhof, Harrer, Forkel, Pölchau, and Zelter, are moving historical evidence of the loyal following the great teacher had inspired in his pupils and their descendants. This group of individuals guarded Bach's legacy most faithfully, preserved it in its unchanged form, and insured by its zeal of copying the dissemination of Bach's works.

With the generation of the pupils of Bach's pupils, the circulation of the master's oeuvre had already spread so far that individual facts are less and less often handed down to us, particularly because the anonymity of the workers in the Bach movement was generally still preserved. When the diligence of scholarly endeavors fails, one has to rely on luck, or on the historical chance which, now and then, makes one of the group of quiet Bach interpreters known by name.

According to Reichardt's testimony,[95] Kirnberger's pupil, Friedrich August Klügling, for instance, is said to have played some of Bach's works in an exemplary manner, and to have shown great skill in pedal playing on the organ. The autobiographic sketch of Johann Baptist Schenk tells us[96] that in his youth (1774-77) he studied Bach's preludes and fugues with Wagenseil, performing them on the harpsichord or clavichord. It is also known that the lively chamber music activities at the Court of Dresden included in the 1780s works by Bach, among which some fugues were especially mentioned.[97]

Christian Podbielski was another of those individuals who preserved the memory of Bach. That something has come down to us about this strange son from an old family of cantors and organists, who still played the viol da gamba at the end of the eighteenth century, we owe to one simple fact. Podbielski was E.T.A. Hoffmann's first music teacher in Könisberg. "All he had to do," said E.T.A. Hoffmann,[98] "was to play a lusty movement in his strong manner, and I was reconciled to him and to art. I was frequently overcome by a wonderfully strange feeling; many a movement, especially if it was by the old Sebastian Bach, almost resembled a ghostly gruesome tale and I was seized by those thrills to which one surrenders so willingly in the fantasies of one's youth." We thus hear, quite casually, as if it were a matter of course, that the old Podbielski also played compositions by Sebastian Bach, and are made aware of the unusual effect this art exerted on the young Romanticist, Hoffmann. In Hoffmann's family, Bach was still a link to the German past and instruments such as the viol da gamba and d'amore were still played.[99] Hoffmann himself was an excellent pianist who took special pleasure in playing Bach's Goldberg Variations before the not exactly delighted Königsberg society.[100]

Carl Gottlieb Richter of Königsberg,[101] a pupil of Philipp Emanuel Bach and Schaffrath, finally ought to be mentioned as still another member of the group of mostly anonymous Bach players of that time. His most distinguished pupil, Reichardt, said of Richter, who gained a certain reputation by frequent performances of Graun's *Tod Jesu,* that he performed, besides compositions of Emanuel Bach, also works by Sebastian "so purely and distinctly in their true meaning" that he heard only Forkel play them more perfectly later.[102] As director of the *Gesellschaft der Musikliebhaber,* Richter performed, in 1788, the "Great Passion" by Philipp Emanuel Bach,[103] which was conceivably that work of the Hamburg Bach which included parts of his father's *St. Matthew Passion*. This performance, too, might then have contributed to the Bach movement in the musical life of the city of Königsberg.

J.S. Bach and the Viennese Classic Composers

After having discussed those interpreters of Bach's art whose work had a more representative significance for the late eighteenth century, it is time to consider the role Sebastian Bach played in the lives of three such towering personalities as Haydn, Mozart, and Beethoven.

As a twelve year old boy, Beethoven was introduced to Bach's art by Christian Gottlob Neefe, Beethoven's teacher in Bonn. Cramer's *Magazin der Musik* reported on March 2, 1783,

> Louis van Beethoven...plays very fluently and powerfully on the clavier, reads very well at sight, and, in a word, he plays most of the *Well-Tempered Clavier* by Sebastian Bach which Herr Neefe has placed in his hands. Anyone who knows this collection of preludes and fugues in all keys—which could almost be called the *non plus ultra* of our art—knows what that means.[104]

Beethoven thus became acquainted with Bach's music at an early and receptive age. It is not surprising that in 1801 Beethoven joyously greeted the announcement of the Leipzig music firm, Hoffmeister & Kühnel, that they were publishing a complete edition of Bach's works with the words,[105] "That you wish to publish the works of Sebastian Bach rejoices my heart, which beats in unison with the high art of this forefather of harmony, and I desire soon to see the scheme in full swing. I hope that...I shall be able to be of great assistance in the matter, when you issue a subscription list."[106] Despite the enthusiasm which Beethoven felt for Bach, it is clearly documented that he placed Handel and Mozart above the Leipzig master.[107] In this Beethoven, who so deeply understood the lofty and lonely art of Bach, agreed with his contemporaries. He remained faithful, however, to the *Well-Tempered Clavier* throughout his life. It is also known that he studied the *Chromatic Fantasy* and *The Art of the Fugue* with great care.[108]

Beethoven was a frequently seen guest in the salon of the Baron van Swieten, which was of utmost importance for the Bach movement in Vienna. The dedication of Beethoven's First Symphony to van Swieten is a beautiful symbol of their friendship. At the end of the musical evenings at the Baron's house, van Swieten customarily asked Beethoven to stay on and "Beethoven was obliged to add a number of fugues by Sebastian Bach by way of an evening blessing."[109] Throughout his life, Beethoven remained in contact with the art of the great Thomas cantor. It is, of course, not our task to analyze the results which this spiritual encounter with Bach's music left in Beethoven's own works. It is sufficiently known that especially the late Beethoven, in spite of his highly individual style, was very much under the spell of Bach's polyphonic art. It should not be overlooked that Beethoven, while working on his Ninth Symphony, entered in his sketchbook, in 1822, the plan for an overture on the name B-a-c-h.[110] Finally, Beethoven's musical estate gives the best survey of the compositions by Bach which he had studied and thus made his own. He left several motets which had been performed at van Swieten's home—indeed "most of what was then known by Sebastian, namely the *Well-Tempered Clavier,* with visible signs of diligent study, three books of the Claiver-Übung, the 15 Inventions, the 15 Sinfonias, as well as the Toccata in D minor"[111] and a collection in one volume which later came into the possession of Anton Schindler. These works formed the basic stock of Bach's compositions that were known in the early nineteenth century. The motets and a certain number of the clavier works still represented the main body of Bach's compositions that were then known.

The 26-year-old Mozart encountered Bach's art in 1782, one year earlier than Beethoven. Shortly after he had moved from Salzburg to Vienna,[112] Mozart was introduced to van Swieten, the art-loving Director of the Vienna Court Library. The latter was quite possibly himself a second generation pupil of Bach. It is likely that he took piano lessons from Kirnberger[113] while he was ambassador in Berlin (from 1770-77). He had come into very close contact with the entire Bach circle in Berlin, with Amalia, Kirnberger, Marpurg and C.P.E. Bach. In 1770, on a trip to England, he became acquainted with Handel's music and the huge musical forces that were employed in performing his works.[114] Van Swieten considered it his mission to become the energetic promoter of these masters in Vienna. For Mozart this new acquaintance became of decisive significance.[115] In a letter of April 10, 1782, the young master wrote to his father, "I go every Sunday at noon to Baron van Swieten and there nothing is played but Handel and Bach. I am now making a collection of the Bach fugues (Sebastian's) and also those of Emanuel and Friedemann Bach." Ten days later, Mozart wrote to his sister (in his letter of April 20, 1782), "Baron van Swieten . . . has given me all the works of Handel and Sebastian Bach (after I had played them for him) to take home with me." Mozart became totally absorbed in the art of the old masters, to the great pleasure of his young bride, Konstanze, who encouraged him in these studies. When she "heard these fugues she fell in love with them at once. She wants to hear nothing but fugues, and particularly nothing but Handel and Bach."[116] It was she who spurred Mozart on to compose works in the old style and to write them down. She begged him to write fugues, "the most artistic and the most beautiful kind of music," and when he had created one, Mozart wrote,[117] "the reason that this fugue came into the world is really my dear Konstanze." The frequently misunderstood life companion of Mozart appears here in an entirely new light.

The study of Bach began for Mozart in 1782 with the *Well-Tempered Clavier,* from which he made several transcriptions in the same year. He arranged five fugues from Part II of this collection for string quartet (Nos. 2, 5, 7, 8, 9), adapting the E-flat minor fugue (No. 8) to the character of the string instruments by transposing it into the more suitable key of D minor. Furthermore, an arrangement of six three-part fugues for violin, viola and violoncello, each introduced by an adagio, is in all probability a work of Mozart, although no autograph manuscript has come down to us. The six fugues turn out to be transcriptions of works by Sebastian Bach, with the exception of one which belongs to Friedemann Bach. Three of these fugues stem from the *Well-Tempered Clavier.*[118] The two others were taken from the Trio Sonatas for organ and *The Art of the Fugue.* Only two of the adagios belonging to this manuscript can be traced to Sebastian Bach, while the four remaining ones represent, with some probability, creations of Mozart himself. This collection points, through its extant copies at the libraries in Berlin and Vienna, to van Swieten. It indicates further that Mozart had become acquainted not only with the *Well-Tempered Clavier* through his musical patron, but probably also with Bach's *Organ Trios* and the *Art of the Fugue.*

Mozart had gained access to Bach earlier and, above all, had come into more intensive contact with Bach's art than with that of Handel, although the style of the latter corresponded more closely to the prevailing taste. Even though Mozart was introduced to Handel's music at van Swieten's[119] at the same time that he became acquainted with Bach, he mentioned nothing of the impression Handel made upon him at that time. His actual preoccupation with Handel's works began only in 1788-89, when Mozart arranged the *Messiah, Alexander's Feast* and the *Ode for St. Cecilia's Day* for the private concerts at the Baron's home,[120] where they were presented without audience for an intimate circle of friends. Mozart substituted woodwind instruments for the organ, which van Swieten's home did not possess. Present-day performances of the *Messiah* employing both Handel's organ *and* Mozart's wind instruments misrepresent Handel's true intentions just as much as those of Mozart's arrangement.

In 1789, shortly after his involvement with Handel's choral works, Mozart also became acquainted with vocal music by Sebastian Bach. As told by Rochlitz, this famous encounter took place when the composer from Vienna visited the Thomas School in Leipzig. There, Mozart heard the showpiece of the Thomas Choir, Bach's eight-part motet *"Singet dem Herrn ein neues Lied."* Mozart, listening attentively, sat up, startled, after the first few measures, then exclaimed surprised and joyful, "What is this? Finally, here is something from which one can learn."[121] Mozart's spontaneous reaction proves that this kind of vocal music was entirely new to him and that he had not become acquainted with Bach's choral music at van Swieten's. The story is well known how, after the sounds of the motet had died away, Mozart made Doles bring him the other motets of the master, the original parts of which the Thomas School possessed. He became totally absorbed in the sheet by sheet study of the different voices and reconstructed in this manner these compositions in his mind. When he finished, he asked for and received a copy of these works.

There were, finally, two more compositions by the Thomas Cantor in Mozart's possession. They are documented by the list of the books and music Mozart left at his death. In his estate were found the so called *kleine harmonische Labyrinth* (Little Harmonic Labyrinth) for organ,[122] which goes back to Bach and the second part of the *Clavierübung*, consisting of the Italian Concerto and the French Overture. With this the facts which document Mozart's relation to Bach's work are exhausted. While this is a scanty selection compared to Bach's total output, it was rich enough to lead a musical genius such as Mozart to draw from the deepest sources of Bach's art, to stir up his creative genius at its very core and to transform his compositional style. How profoundly the experience of Bach's music changed Mozart, only his own compositions can show, which, with the year 1782, enter upon a new period in his style.[123]

It can be assumed that Haydn,[124] who was even more at home in van Swieten's musical circle than Mozart, was at least equally familiar with the art of Bach and Handel that was practiced there. Haydn's musical estate contained, in addition to the *Well-Tempered Clavier* (in Nägeli's printed edition of 1801) and two books of the motets, a handwritten score of the B minor Mass which he presumably had acquired in the last years of his life from the conscientious Viennese publisher, Johann Traeg.[125]

The Viennese Bach movement, which has been pursued in this context only with regard to Haydn, Mozart, and Beethoven, showed an amazing vitality. This is all the more thought provoking as this Catholic city in the south was rather far removed from the true boundaries of the German Bach movement. That the music publisher Johann Traeg, who compiled his catalogues with particular care, and Baron van Swieten, the patron of his active circle of musical friends, were both residents of Vienna is a facilitating factor of Bach research in Vienna. Yet, this favorable coincidence should not obscure the fact that also in the musical circles of other German cities, which were perhaps of less interest to the music historian than the Vienna of that time, Sebastian Bach had grown into a living force which was to become a determining factor in the development of music.

Notes

1. Quoted by Schering, in *Zeitschrift der internationalen Musikgesellschaft*, vol. VIII, p. 266.

2. Scheibe, *Critischer Musicus*, p. 882.

3. Cf. Gerhard Pietzsch, *Acta Musicologica*, vol. IV/3 (1932), p. 106.

4. Elisabeth Hegar, in *Sammlung musikwissenschaftlicher Abhandlungen*, vol. VII, p. 27.

5. Schweitzer, *J.S. Bach*, p. 211.

6. Moritz Hauptmann, *Briefe an Franz Hauser*, Leipzig, 1871, vol. II, p. 103. Letter of Dec. 7, 1850.

7. Said Moritz Hauptmann. Quoted by Schering in *Bach-Jahrbuch*, 1921, p. 49.

8. Concerning what follows, see Hugo Goldschmidt, *Musikästhetik des 18. Jahrhunderts*.

9. Bach did not defend himself in person against Scheibe's attacks, but against the Town Council and Ernesti he took pen in hand for two years.

10. Pietzsch, *Acta Musicologica*, vol. IV/3, p. 106.

11. Quoted by Artur Prüfer, *S. Bach und die Tonkunst des 19. Jahrhunderts*, p. 7.

12. Published in 1783 by Birnstiel in Berlin.

13. Cf. Eugen Rosenkaimer, *J.A. Scheibe als Verfasser seines "Critischen Musicus,"* Bonn, 1929, p. 43.

14. On Jan. 4, 1819 Goethe wrote to Zelter (cf. Correspondence, vol. II, p. 5): "At the same time, I studied Marperger's [sic] *Vollkommenen Capellmeister* and had to smile while I informed myself. How serious and brave that time had been and how did not such a man feel the shackles of philistinism in which he was caught."

15. Cf. the musical treatises by Altenburg (Trumpet), Quantz (Transverse Flute), C.P.E. Bach (Clavier), Leopold Mozart (Violin), Kittel (Organ) and Kirnberger *(Art of Pure Writing)*.

16. See Caroline Valentin, *Geschichte der Musik in Frankfurt/M.*, p. 241.

17. Ibid.

18. *Versuch über die wahre Art das Klavier zu spielen* (Essay on the True Manner of Playing the Clavier), 3. Hauptstück, section 13.

19. Ibid.

20. Scheibe, *Critischer Musicus*, p. 840.

21. Berlin, 1752.

22. Johann Joachim Quantz, *Flöte traversiere*, Einleitung, section 16, p. 16.

23. Ibid., XI. Hauptstück, section 6, p. 102.

24. Ibid., XVIII. Hauptstück, section 15, p. 286.

25. Ibid., section 78, p. 9.

26. *Der Wanderer und sein Schatten, Menschliches Allzumenschliches* II, 2. Abteilung, p. 149.

27. Quantz, *Flöte traversiere*, XVIII. Hauptstück, section 80.

28. Ibid., section 81.

29. Ibid., section 40, p. 300.

30. Ibid., section 81.

31. Ibid., section 40, p. 300.

32. Ibid., section 81.

33. *Musikalisches Kunstmagazin,* vol. I, p. 196. (See also Richard Hohenemser, *Welche Einflüsse hatte die Wiederbelebung der älteren Musik im 19. Jahrhundert auf die deutschen Komponisten,* p. 19.)

34. J.A. Hiller, *Wöchentliche Nachrichten und Anmerkungen die Musik betreffend,* Leipzig, 1766, p. 50.

35. Enclosure to Zelter's letter of August 10-23, 1827. See Zelter-Goethe correspondence, vol. II, p. 507.

36. In 1754.

37. These are the words of Johann Christian Bach's biographer, Max Schwarz. Cf. *Sammelbände der internationalen Musikgesellschaft,* vol. II (1900-1901), p. 408.

38. Forkel, *J.S. Bachs Leben,* p. 65.

39. See Georg Schünemann, "J.Chr.Fr. Bach," *Bach-Jahrbuch,* 1914, p. 117.

40. Martin Falck, *Wilhelm Friedemann Bach,* Leipzig, 1913, p. 141.

41. Ibid., p. 27.

42. Ibid., p. 141.

43. Letter of April 6-11, 1829, to Goethe. (Correspondence, vol. III, p. 133.)

44. See Herbert Kelletat, *Zur Geschichte der deutschen Orgelmusik in der Frühklassik,* p. 18.

45. As Schubart said in his *Ideen zu einer Aesthetik der Tonkunst,* p. 89. (Quoted by Kelletat, *Orgelmusik,* p. 21).

46. See *Tagebuch einer musikalischen Reise,* 1773, vol. III, p. 217. (Quoted by Kelletat, *Orgelmusik,* p. 114).

47. Falck, *W.F. Bach,* p. 53.

48. 1746-64 as organist; 1764-70 unemployed.

49. Falck, *W.F. Bach,* p. 54.

50. Forkel, *J.S. Bachs Leben,* p. 36.

51. Quoted by Falck, *W.F. Bach,* p. 54.

52. See Forkel, *Almanach auf das Jahr 1784,* p. 202.

53. C.F. Cramer, *Magazin für Musik,* vol. II, 1784. (Quoted after Falck, *W.F. Bach,* p. 57).

54. 1767-88.

55. Regarding this and what follows, see Heinrich Miesner, *Ph.Em. Bach in Hamburg,* Berlin, 1929, pp. 60, 63ff.

56.   A. Schweitzer (J.S. Bach, p. 635) said of these still extant arrangements, "They do not throw a very favorable light on C.P.E. Bach's understanding of the art of his father."

57.   No. 57 of April 11, 1786. Quoted by Miesner, *C.P.E. Bach*, p. 20f.

58.   Schweitzer (*J.S. Bach*, p. 550f.) mentions, however, a performance of J.S. Bach's *Magnificat* by C.P.E. Bach which is supposed to have taken place in Hamburg in 1779.

59.   See B. Fr. Richter, *Bach-Jahrbuch*, 1906, p. 47. These manuscripts came into the possession of the Town Council probably in 1752. According to Richter (p. 49) they were the parts of the second Jahrgang of Bach's chorale cantatas.

60.   Ibid., *Bach-Jahrbuch*, p. 63.

61.   Ibid., pp. 50, 56-57.

62.   Ibid.

63.   Harrer was Thomas cantor from 1750-56, Doles from 1756-89.

64.   Richter, *Bach-Jahrbuch*, 1915, p. 5.

65.   See Ludwig Schiedermair, *Eine unbekannte Leipziger Erlebnisschrift Neefes*, in *Jahrbuch der Musikbibliothek Peters* for the year 1933, p. 52.

66.   See entry J.S. Bach in vol. I.

67.   Richter, *Bach-Jahrbuch*, 1912, p. 30.

68.   Terry, *J.S. Bach*, p. 234.

69.   Cf. *Bach-Jahrbuch* 1918, p. 141ff., *Joh. Phil. Kirnberger als Herausgeber Bachscher Choräle*.

70.   Cf. the edition of 1752 with Marpurg's Foreword. (See chapter 1).

71.   Schweitzer, *J.S. Bach*, p. 216.

72.   Regarding what follows, see Curt Sachs, *Prinzessin Amalia von Preussen als Musikerin*. (*Hohenzollern-Jahrbuch*, 1910).

73.   1723-87.

74.   Title of the treatise by Johann Philipp Kirnberger, published in 1779.

75.   See. S. Borris-Zuckermann, *Kirnbergers Leben und Werk und seine Bedeutung im Berliner Musikkreis um 1750*, pp. 7, 26.

76.   Forkel, *J.S. Bachs Leben*, p. 84.

77.   See the complete listing in Robert Eitner's *Monatshefte für Musikgeschichte*, vol. XV, (1883-84), Appendix, p. 28ff.

78.   Schweitzer, *J.S. Bach*, p. 217.

79.   Schneider, *Bach-Jahrbuch*, 1906, p. 84ff., "Verzeichnis der bis zum Jahre 1851 gedruckten und der geschriebenen im Handel gewesenen Werke von Bach."

80.   Johann Gottfried Müthel, who came to the already ailing Bach in May 1750, can only have been his pupil for the shortest possible time. (See Spitta, vol. II, p. 728).

81.   Burney, *Tagebuch*, vol. III, p. 53f.

82.   Gerber worded it this way in his *Lexikon der Tonkünstler*, vol. I, 1790, p. 77: "Sebastian Bach to whom we are indebted in this century for most of our great men" [in music].

83. Goldberg and Müthel.

84. H. Löffler, "J.L. Krebs," in *Bach-Jahrbuch*, 1930, p. 124.

85. Ibid., pp. 124-27.

86. Cf. the letter of recommendation which Bach wrote in Krebs' behalf on August 24, 1735. Quoted by Spitta, *J.S. Bach*, vol. II, p. 722.

87. Ibid., p. 727.

88. Kelletat, *Orgelmusik*, p. 117.

89. Erfurt 1801-03.

90. See *Neues Lexikon* (Leipzig, 1813), Part III, p. 58.

91. Hässler, Umbreit, J.C.H. Rinck and M.G. Fischer.

92. Letter of Jan. 20-24, 1829, to Goethe. Correspondence, vol. III, p. 107.

93. Kelletat, *Orgelmusik*, p. 34.

94. Schubart, *Ideen zu einer Aesthetik der Tonkunst*, Vienna, 1808, p. 105. Quoted by Kelletat, *Orgelmusik*, p. 32.

95. *Briefe eines aufmerksamen Reisenden, die Musik betreffend*, vol. I, p. 117. Quoted by Kelletat, *Orgelmusik*, p. 116.

96. Published in *Studien zur Musikwissenschaft*, fascicle 11, Vienna 1924, p. 77f.

97. See Richard Engländer, *Dresdener Musikleben und Dresdener Instrumentalpflege in der Zeit zwischen Hasse und Weber*, in *Zeitschrift für Musikwissenschaft* 1931-32, p. 415.

98. In his *Fermate*, complete works, vol. VI, p. 59.

99. See *Kater Murr*, complete works, vol. X, p. 88f.

100. See *Kreisleriana*, complete works, vol. I, pp. 23 and 26.

101. 1728-1809. He lived from 1761 on in Königsberg.

102. Hermann Güttler, *Königsbergs Musikkultur im 18. Jahrhundert*.

103. Ibid.

104. Alexander Wheelock Thayer, *L. van Beethovens Leben*. German edition and revision by Hermann Deiters, Leipzig 1907-17, vol. I, p. 150.

105. Letter of Jan. 15, 1801 to Hoffmeister.

106. As to the failure of the planned complete edition, see chapter 4.

107. Thayer, *Beethovens Leben*, vol. II, p. 559.

108. See G. Nottebohm, *II. Beethoveniana*.

109. Anton Schindler, *Beethoven*, 3rd edition, Münster, 1860, p. 20.

110. Thayer, *Beethovens Leben*, vol. IV, p. 415.

111. Schindler, *Beethoven*, vol. II, p. 184.

112. In 1781.

113.   See *Der Bär, Jahrbuch von Breitkopf & Härtel* for the years 1929-30, p. 101f.

114.   Ibid., p. 92.

115.   Regarding what follows, see Ernst Lewicki, *Mozarts Verhältnis zu Seb. Bach,* in *Mitteilungen für die Mozart-Gemeinde in Berlin,* fascicle 15, March 1903, p. 163ff.

116.   The same letter of April 20, 1782.

117.   Ibid.

118.   The E-flat minor Fugue from Book I (transposed to D minor); the F-sharp minor Fugue from Book II (transposed to G minor) the F-sharp Major Fugue from Book II (transposed to F major).

119.   This is documented by his letter of April 10, 1782.

120.   Cf. Richard Hohenemser, *Welche Einflüsse,* pp. 28-29, 36.

121.   Lewicki, *Mozart,* p. 176.

122.   BG, vol. 38, Anhang II, p. 225.

123.   One may recall here the following compositions of the master:
        The Finale in fugal style of the G Major Quartet from the year 1782 (K. 387), the first of the six quartets dedicated to Haydn in 1785. These quartets represent a fundamental change in Mozart's conception of the *strict* style.
        The C minor Serenade for wind instruments with its canonic Minuet (K. 388), of 1782.
        The Fantasy and Fugue in C minor for pianoforte (K. 394); and, above all, the Fugue in C minor for two pianofortes (K. 426), so astonishingly rich in dissonances and in rational structure.
        These compositions date from 1782 along with the magnificent Mass in C minor with its choral fugues in the *Gloria* and *Sanctus.* During Mozart's last creative period he wrote the Overture to the *Magic Flute* and the song of the men clad in armor from the Finale of act II in which the Lutheran chorale "Wenn wir in höchsten Nöten sind" is intertwined with the orchestra in the polyphonic style of J.S. Bach.
        Finally we might think of the concluding movement of the *Jupiter Symphony* and Mozart's swan song, his *Requiem.*

124.   E.F. Schmidt, "Joseph Haydn und Philipp Emanuel Bach," in *Zeitschrift für Musikwissenschaft,* vol. XIV/6, March 1932.

125.   A copy was offered for sale in the *1. Nachtrag zum Katalog Traeg 1804.*

J.S. Bach and the Church Music of the Age of Rationalism: A Style-Critical Comparison of Bach's *St. Matthew Passion* and C.H. Graun's *Tod Jesu*

The first two chapters have contrasted the sociological, religious, and esthetic changes and new developments with the world of Johann Sebastian Bach and have presented the early history of Bach interpretation and misinterpretation resulting from these dialectics. How the tensions found in the literature of the time in general, and in Bach historiography in particular, affected the performance practice of his works, will now be investigated in the sphere of the purely musical. By means of two works, chosen to be contrasted and compared stylistically, our esthetic and factual knowledge will be enlarged and at the same time be made more precise. This investigation will reveal the same contrasts within the individual works which characterized Bach's position in the world around him.

The Reason for This Comparison

It is fortunate that history has offered two works based on the same subject matter which, on the evidence of their performance history, practically cry out for comparison: Bach's *St. Matthew Passion* and Carl Heinrich Graun's *Tod Jesu*. The success which society granted these two works had been so great that it popularized the names of their creators in the course of the centuries.

Indeed, even today the image of the religious Bach is usually limited to the musical experience of the Matthew Passion. Graun's *Tod Jesu*, on the other hand, outshone the Passion music of the eighteenth century in spite of Telemann's, Handel's and C.P.E. Bach's Passion music and thus must be accepted as the most valid expression of the religious sentiment of his time. The history of these two works thus invites comparison. For it was Graun's fame, especially that of his *Tod Jesu*, which relegated Bach's church music to the past. Graun reflected the taste of his time to an extent only rarely encountered by an artwork in history. It is this ideal balance between work and *Zeitgeist* which accounts for the fact that Graun's *Tod Jesu* became the representative piece of sacred music in the epoch of Frederick the Great. In fact, it outlasted this epoch by becoming, through the annual Good Friday performances by the Berlin Singakademie and other German choral societies, the traditional Passiontide music of the German people.

Its preeminent position was not challenged until 1829, when Mendelssohn revived Bach's *St. Matthew Passion*, augmented, however, by some traits of Graun and other Romantic features. The response was such that Graun's Passion music was gradually forced to abandon its long-established privileged position in favor of Bach's Matthew Passion.

The historical vitality which related these works to one another saves us the trouble of having to select two works, one from Bach's vast oeuvre, the other from the even richer output of his contemporaries. History has already made this choice, a choice which of course did not derive from Bach and Graun, but from the judgment of society, which had nothing but praise for these two works. They represent their creators, who may never have thought of establishing their reputations solely through these compositions. If we accept this one-sidedness of history—and, in all fairness, history's instinct for selecting works of quality ought not be disputed—we can without hesitation enter the musical world of Graun and Bach and undertake a short style-critical comparison of the two works.

C.H. Graun and His Berlin Circle

Carl Heinrich Graun[1] belonged to the musical circle of Frederick the Great. While in Rheinsberg, Graun laid the foundation for what was later to become the Royal Chapel. After the move to Berlin in 1740, C.P.E. Bach joined the old Rheinsberg musicians, the brothers Graun, Quantz, G. Benda, Schaffrath, Janitsch and Ehms. By 1744, the opera house, built by Knobelsdorff, was completed. It became a place of courtly representation and display of splendor, comparable to its models in Braunschweig and especially in Dresden. While C.P.E. Bach and Quantz were the mainstays of the royal chamber orchestra in Potsdam, Graun, as director of the opera, stood in the center of the reorganized music life of Berlin. In that capacity he may actually be considered the musical representative of Frederick the Great's Berlin. Graun, who is discussed here as the composer of a Passiontide work, was, to be sure, basically an opera composer.[2] His operas constantly had to accommodate the personal wishes of Frederick the Great, who interfered not only with the text but frequently also with the music of his works, so his *Tod Jesu* may for this very reason be considered one of Graun's most original works. Here he was able to compose as he pleased, for no one disagreed with his text or music. The king's remark, "this tastes like the church," revealed that his interest in this musical genre was not particularly keen. This attitude was quite unlike that of his sister, Amalia, and the Berlin theorists Marpurg and Kirnberger, whose propensity for old music contrasted sharply with the tendencies of the music that Frederick the Great controlled. There was a deep conflict between the Berlin theorists and the practical musicians whose basic attitude was oriented towards the new and therefore was unfavorable to J.S. Bach.

Bach's famous trip to Berlin in the year 1747 which, in terms of its effect, has often been overrated, though it gave us the *Musical Offering,* revealed to Frederick's circle only that side of Bach which the Rationalistic world was able to perceive—the great extemporizing composer, the improvising virtuoso and the incomparable artist at the organ. No doubt, the trip to Berlin contributed to Bach's fame, but it neither initiated nor achieved a revival of Bach's music in the Prussian capital. The king of the Enlightenment was too far removed from the inner world of the great Thomas cantor fully to understand Bach as a person and composer. The king's own faith, which went beyond his father's Pietism to reach a form of deism, was too different from that of Bach to be able to comprehend the functional nature of Bach's art. The king's view, sharpened by Rationalism, probably saw in Bach merely the accomplished master of musical form and texture. For he no longer shared the world of ideas which governed Bach's entire creative work nor the immediate experience of the Lutheran Bible. For him, who had so fully absorbed the literary standard of the French language, the dependence of Bach's vocal music on German Baroque texts was most probably also displeasing. Finally, it is known that the king had an aversion to genuine church music, particularly to the chorale, the very center of Bach's creative thoughts. And if, for once, the king expressed an opinion on a piece of sacred music, as he did in the case of Graun's *Tod Jesu,* he applauded specifically its operatic elements, the precariously secular arias. How much this music told him about heaven is well expressed by the king's remark that the *Tod Jesu* was Graun's "best opera."

On the basis of his position alone, Graun was, besides Hasse, the director of the Dresden opera, the most representative musician of the Germany of that time. Graun shared with Telemann, C.P.E. Bach and Hasse the historic task of carrying out the breakup of polyphonic music. They created scores in which the orchestra only functioned as an accompaniment to the vocal parts, giving the latter prominence among all the sonorities, rather than interweaving them. With this sense of mission, Graun, in cooperation with his colleagues, depleted the polyphonic style and transformed it into a homophonic style which emphasized no more than two voices—the melody and the bass—while the other voices assumed the function of harmonically filling parts. In this respect, C.P.E. Bach said of Hasse,[3] (and this also applies to Graun) "he is the most cunning deceiver in the world; for in a score of twenty written-out parts he rarely lets more than three of them do the work; but with those he is able to

achieve such heavenly effects as one never would expect of a crammed score."
This remark demonstrates again to what extent Philipp Emanuel had moved
away, in the Berlin atmosphere, from the spirit of his father's scores, of which
he still possessed a great number.

With the generation of Bach's sons, the German polyphonic texture
became outdated and was replaced by a sense of chain-like harmonically
rounded forms. Above all, "Hasse and Graun, also admired by the Italians,
have...by their imaginative, natural and moving works" pointed the way for
German music towards "good taste"[4] and a singable style. Graun was, like
Philipp Emanuel Bach, a pioneer of the German Classic style.

Passion Music at the Time of Bach and Graun

After having outlined Bach's social position, his personality and his
significance in the history of music, we now must turn to his Passion Cantata
Der Tod Jesu. (In this context reference should be made, with regard to
Graun's biography, to the works by A. Mayer-Reinach[5] and K. Mennicke,[6]
and with regard to the history of Passion music, to the thorough essay by
Walter Lott[7] and to Hermann Kretzschmar's summary presentation of the
history of Passion music in his *Führer durch den Konzertsaal.*)[8]

C.H. Graun's *Der Tod Jesu,* written in 1755, belongs to those Passiontide
compositions which no longer were based on the declamation of the words of
the Scriptures. In Graun's time, the presentation of Christ's Passion, read or
sung, had already been banished from the main worship service. "The time of
year during which one usually sings and preaches of the sufferings of Our Lord
Jesus Christ" (to use Luther's words) had, in its liturgical meaning, during the
centuries following the Reformation, taken on more and more the character of
a time of penance and introspection. Inasmuch as Good Friday and penance
became synonymous and the liturgy of the day of penance was adopted, there
was no longer any room in the main service for the story of Christ's Passion,
which was, therefore, relegated to the Vesper service (beginning at one o'clock
in the afternoon). The church musicians of the eighteenth century were faced
with these and similar changes in the liturgy. Bach, too, composed his Passions
for the vesper service. This new situation called for a new definition of the
concept of Passion music.

In Hamburg, the center of German Rationalism, the break with the old
types of Passion-presentation occurred with the Choral Passion, in which three
soloists declaimed the text in Gregorian recitation; with the Motet Passion,
which set the entire biblical text polyphonically; and with the dramatic
Passion, which combined both these elements and inserted Lutheran chorales
into the fixed scriptural text.[9] As much as these three types of Passion music
differed from one another, the story of Christ's Passion was always sung to the

unaltered words of the Evangelists. In the year 1704, the Hamburg Rationalist Hunold (Menantes) made use of poetic license by altering the hitherto sacrosanct scriptural text in his *Der blutige und sterbende Jesus.* The setting by Reinhard Keiser, the master of the Hamburg opera, was the first Passion music in the German language which was freely written in rhymed verse, lacking both Evangelist and chorale. Here one was already on the way to the church opera. Keiser the oratorio composer was exactly the same as Keiser the opera composer. With him the style of German Passion music merged with that of the classical Italian oratorio and thus sacrificed its true national character.

German sacred music lost its tradition and indigenous character during the Age of Rationalism. Telemann, Keiser's great successor in Hamburg, who created with his *Seliges Erwägen* (1727) *the* German Oratorio-Passion before Graun's *Tod Jesu* (1755), even boasted of his ability to write in any style. Telemann, who was receptive to everything, could compose with equal ease in the German, French and Italian idiom. The reason for the failure of the Hamburg Rationalist composers to write true church music lies in the eclectic nature of music that allowed artistic experimentation. Yet, like Telemann, these composers "held it [church music] in highest esteem, studied on its account most diligently the works of other composers and wrote a majority of their compositions in this genre."[10] Although the Rationalists believed that they could compose anything, they lacked the immediate and close relationship with the liturgical events that would enable them to write true church music. Their church music often makes an impression of triviality, since its composers no longer comprehended the miraculous that transcends the measure of man. A good deal more can be said about heaven than what this type of representational and pictorial Passion music had to offer. Even Handel belongs among these composers as far as his St. John Passion, written in 1704 (text after Postel), and his Passion music of the year 1716 (text after Brockes) are concerned. The only difference is that Brockes's text, entitled characteristically, *Der für die Sünden der Welt gemarterte und sterbende Jesus* (Jesus dying and tortured for the sins of the world) alleviated the theatrical nature of Hunold's Passion. Besides Handel, Brockes's text was also set to music by Keiser, Telemann, Mattheson, Stölzel and J.C. Bachofen; even Bach utilized it for some arias in his St. John Passion. Brockes's Passion libretto reinserted at least the chorale as well as the figure of the Evangelist who, however, recited the scriptural text in a freely arranged version. By overemphasizing the minute and the detailed, the text forced the music to become pictorial, depriving it of the unifying big line that characterizes all true church music.

Because it was so characteristic of its time, the first performance of Telemann's Brockes-Passion must still be mentioned. It took place—several years before the appearance of Bach's Passions—on April 2, 1716, in the

Frankfurt church in which, fifty years earlier, Spener had delivered his sermons. The performance was given in a purely concert-like manner, with famous opera singers engaged from out of town. Still more important is the fact that everyone who attended had to pay an admission fee of 30 Kreuzer for the charitable purpose of the event.[11] This was thus no longer a worship service, but a church concert in the modern sense.

The Significance of Graun's Tod Jesu for the Passion Music of Its Time

The two works by Bach and Graun must be viewed in a context in which the writing of Passion music had been secularized by Rationalism and idealized by Pietism. Graun's Passion-Cantata was the historically logical product of the development of Passion compositions described so far.

The text of *Der Tod Jesu*, which complied in its inborn musicality with the sentimental and pictorial trends of the time, was written by K.W. Ramler, a Berlin poet, extremely popular at the time. It was dedicated to Princess Amalia of Prussia, in fact written "according to her own outline in order to be set to music by her."[12] Indeed, there exists a complete compositional plan by her for this work that precedes Graun's composition. However, she seems to have completed only the opening churus, "Sein Odem ist schwach" (His breath is faint), which Kirnberger published in Part II of his *Kunst des reinen Satzes* (1779). Ramler's text won highest acclaim from many, including the linguistically eloquent Herder, who could not praise enough Ramler's "unexcelled poetic gift...his mastery of the allegorical."[13] By narrating the biblical events in the form of parables, the language attains an allegoric and pictorial quality which, in its lyrical contemplative manner takes the composer safely by the hand. The flowery text and the sound envisaged by the composer striving for *affections,* are able to blend into a unity here which became, in essence, responsible for the success of the work. In addition, Graun altered the text of some passages; but by being occasionally all too literal in his pictorial recreation of the text, he also paid his tribute to it. "The composer gives me the impression of an ever-ready mimic" a critic said of Graun in 1805,[14] intimating by this remark that the danger for the artwork lies in too close a fusion of music and poetic text. By eliminating the Evangelist from the dramatic action of the Passion, and by abandoning the scriptural text in favor of a new operatic libretto, the subject matter was transported from its historic reality into the realm of the ideal, and the dogmatic story of the Passion was lifted into the sphere of the contemplative. Not only the story, but also the congregation as such became an ideal, indefinite entity. We are no longer dealing here with the figures of the Bible, but with the "Herzensergiessungen" (outpourings of the heart) of a Christian of the year 1755 who replaced the original drama with subjective emotional reflections. Granted that these reflections were fervently felt by their creator, they could easily be misunderstood by the listener with regard to the degree of inherent honesty and truthfulness. It remained for the intuitive genius of a Haydn to take the pictorially cluttered allegorical poetry of his time out of the church and place it where it could be truly effective, in the idyllic setting of nature. He accomplished this historically unique task with his *Creation* and *The Seasons*. Because Ramler's general human sentiment had vanquished the objective liturgical facts, the orthodox realm was already abandoned by the text alone.

The Significance of the St. Matthew Passion at This Time

Measured against the degree of secularization surrounding him, Bach's Passion music represents a step back into the church. Of course, one should not expect that Bach returned Passion music to the state of the Lutheran church of 1550. It must, however, be stated explicitly that in the *St. Matthew Passion,* Bach was indebted to *his* time to a greater degree than in any other of his works. He incorporated in it what the world around him had to offer in terms of new forms, whereas little is felt of the scholasticism and dogmatic nature of his later organ and vocal style. Among Bach's works the St. Matthew Passion makes it easier for us to find in it a reflection of our own world of emotions. The Matthew Passion does not keep us from discovering in some of its passages related, Romantic features, as little as these may have been intended as such by the composer. Since the story of the Passion aroused in the dogma-conscious personality of Bach the whole range of his religious imagination, we easily become personally involved. The wealth of this work—its story and its music— is so overwhelming that it dwarfs momentarily all historical questions. The Romantic period thus had to select from Bach's vast oeuvre the St. Matthew Passion, that work of the master the broad emotional scope of which least resisted a subjective interpretation, added from without. One may see in Bach's Matthew Passion a combination of his perhaps most intense religious feelings and greatest concession to the madrigalesque and operatic forms of his time. In short, one may recognize Bach's Passion music for double chorus as the *most modern* work among his compositions for the church. With this in mind, the documentary material that will be chosen and used for comparison with Graun's music ought to have the effect of doubly strong evidence.

What Bach has done with regard to the text of the Passion alone, is already extraordinary, if it is compared to the texts of his contemporaries. Most importantly, Bach reinstated the literal text of the Gospel in place of Picander's versified biblical story.[15] Furthermore, Bach took only a relatively small portion of Picander's original libretto over into his Passion. He even changed the wording of Picander's arias, some quite drastically; but above all he divested them of their all too personal character. For example, Picander's

"Wiewohl mein Herz in Thränen schwimmt, weil Jesus von mir Abschied nimmt" (My heart is bathed in tears because Jesus does depart from me) Bach turned into "Wiewohl mein Herz in Thränen schwimmt, weil Jesus von *uns* [us] Abschied nimmt." This means that Bach intended to retain the congregational spirit of the worship service. Unlike the Hamburg composers, Bach did not like to see the Passion lowered to the level of a sacred concert. In almost all arias Bach replaced the "I" of Picander's lyric poetry by "we." A few times Bach wrote some of the texts of the arias and ariosos himself, thus asking us not to look for discrepancies between text and music. As far as his Passions are concerned, he never found a libretto that satisfied him completely. He also recast Brockes's Passion-poem thoroughly for his use in the St. John Passion. Lacking a satisfactory librettist Bach took it upon himself to relate his texts more closely to the liturgy. Also the insertion of hymn verses into his Passion text was Bach's idea alone, not that of Picander. Bach retained the text of the Gospel as well as that of the hymn, i.e., the chorale, in their traditional function, thereby leaving intact "the foundation, the core of what consistent use by the church had rendered sacrosanct."[16]

Loyal to the cantus firmus and scriptural word, Bach opposed the sacred opera as a species of music that in liturgical respect had become shallow. By preserving the biblical text and inserting Lutheran hymn verses, Bach returned to the Passion its liturgical substance. By using both the old and the new, Bach created a synthesis which, viewed solely from the textual side, wants to be regarded as religious service rather than as poetry.

A look at the texts on which Bach's and Graun's Passions are based shows that we are confronted by two different worlds. In Bach's case a connection with the Passion Play is still perceptible. The voice parts represent symbolically the clearly defined biblical characters which were previously impersonated. This trace of realism disappeared with Graun. With the replacement of the familiar biblical text with poetic paraphrase, the *presence* of the historical figures vanished. The entire reflection on Christ's Passion now takes place in the listener's imagination. The fact that Graun assigned the narration of the story alternately to the solo soprano, alto, tenor or bass shows furthermore how idealized and impersonal his Passion was meant to be.

Style-Critical Comparison of the Two Works

The dogmatic side of Bach appears in his retention of "Luther's language, this greatest transformation of Christianity achieved by a German."[17] Moreover, he assured himself of the participation of the congregation by the interpolation of chorales throughout the entire work. With Graun, who abandoned Luther's prose in favor of Ramler's poetry, the hymn tune, based on Ramler's verses, no longer had the meaning of a congregational hymn, but rather that of a sentimental edifying song, the tune of which was known to everyone from the church. The six chorales—"misunderstood signs of an earlier time"[18]—which Graun interspersed in his work and which attempt to add an element of the old German Passion to the otherwise Italianate character of his Passion cantata, create the suspicion that they were supposed to turn a nonchurchly work into a churchly one. A comparison between the opening chorale "Du dessen Augen flossen" (Thou whose eyes were weeping) and Bach's "Wenn ich einmal soll scheiden" (When I shall leave this world), both based on the melody "O Welt, ich muss dich lassen" (O World, I must leave you), will suffice to reveal the same discrepancy also in the realm of music.

In Graun's case we have the simple and pure chords of the six diatonic steps, one set next to another, rather than flowing melodic lines of individual voices. The triadic harmonization emanates clearly from the tonic center. There is no longer any connection with the old church modes. The harmony is so easy to grasp and the movement of the voices so simple that the chorale needs only the support of the continuo, i.e., that of the organ. Graun has set the chorales in a perfectly faultless a cappella style; but he also has encroached upon their form and melody. For the repetition of the first section (the *Stollen*) he used a new harmonization and even made a change in the melody, turning the repetition into a variation. Finally, Graun added to the chorale some newly composed concluding measures that were meant to reduce the emotional level and let the music fade away. This constitutes an encroachment upon the cantus firmus of which Bach was never guilty. Bach's attitude towards the chorale was entirely different. Everything in Bach's chorales flows; each voice has a life of its own. The resultant harmonic whole attains an extraordinary richness through its many dissonances, passing tones and suspensions, a harmonic complexity that, for its proper realization in sound, needs the support of instruments. This complex four-part vocal style is diametrically opposed to the pure a cappella concept.

In his dislike of a cappella music Bach even went so far as to enrich a pure vocal Mass by Palestrina, which he transcribed for his own use, with an additional orchestration of his own. Although Bach adapted here the a cappella style to his own stylistic preference, his compositional intentions are in this respect still disregarded. Out of lack of judgment and false sentimentality one can, to this very day, still hear the chorale "Wenn ich einmal soll scheiden" sung by unaccompanied chorus. The most striking feature of this chorale is its Phrygian mode. Because Bach still had access to the old church modes he could explore the whole realm of tonality in a much more comprehensive and original manner. In contrast to Graun, he left the structure of the chorale, which to him was a sacred treasure, untouched. While the chorale was for Bach the dogmatic center, it was for Graun sentimental introduction. Orthodox Lutheranism clings firmly to its sacred possession; Pietism altered it and gave it *Liedform*. In spite of the identity of the hymn tune, its four-part harmonization alone reveals two entirely different mental attitudes.

Even a superficial inspection of Graun's work reveals the large number, and especially the length, of its great da capo arias, in contrast to Bach's *St. Matthew Passion.* Stylistically they are nothing but genuine operatic arias in the style of a Handel or Hasse. Sung by a virtuoso, these melodious pieces, brimming over with coloraturas, could hardly fail to have their operatic rather than religious impact. They share with Handel's musicianship the same exuberant energy and, by contrast, the same simple singing style. Both masters sided with the style of classical Italian music. Only he who rejects Handel's oratorios is entitled to label Graun's *Tod Jesu* as antiquated. That it now has fallen into total oblivion seems just as little justified as the onesidedness of its dominance until a century ago.

Criticism of Graun's work might rather begin with his recitative style. The text, not clear in its connection with the Passion story, suffers frequently from a too extreme kind of word painting of its pictorial language. The constant change from one voice to another, which was already seen as a characteristic feature of the ideally conceived figure of the narrator, tends to obscure the true textual facts even more. Yet Graun's recitatives by no means lack *musical* effectiveness; but they do contribute to the general shortcoming of the work, the limited intelligibility of its content.

In comparison, there is total clarity in Bach's work. Through the clear distribution of the Gospel text among the bearers of the action and the narrating Evangelist, Bach could afford a much broader emotional scale and wider tonal range. There is never any doubt as to who speaks and what he speaks about. The aria, too, received another function in Bach's work. In contrast to Graun's aria, Bach's takes its spark directly from the reading of the Gospel text (from the recitative). It thus constitutes the reflection on the preceding Scriptural passage and functions as the words of the individual soul, which now may be sung by any voice in Bach's work, like a sermon within the liturgically fixed action of the Passion. Together with the ariosos and several choruses (choral arias), the arias constitute the sole contemplative element in Bach's Passion; but even this is frequently lifted above the realm of the madrigalesque by simultaneous employment of Scriptural words or by a simultaneously inserted hymn tune. (One may think for instance of the opening and final choruses of the First part, of the tenor aria "Ich will bei meinem Jesu wachen" [I want to guard my Jesus], or of the alto aria "Ach wo ist mein Jesu hin" [Ah, where has my Jesus gone.]) Bach's aria constitutes a resting point, a brief lingering and reminiscing of the soul within the inexorable course of the dramatic action. By simply reacting to the immediately preceding event which wants to be thought about and absorbed, Bach's aria always stays within the framework of the action. Graun's aria, on the other hand, is a reflection on what was already an emotional reflection (namely his recitative).

Not only the functional meaning of recitative and aria in the works of the two masters is totally different. They are worlds apart stylistically and musically. Like Handel—and Handel is always to be seen as Bach's great counterpart—Graun advocated the sparse texture of the Italians. He thinned out polyphony from within, from the inner voices. This thinness of the musical texture, which today is perhaps interpreted as lack of intellectual substance, was concealed for the listener of that time by the sentimentally saturated groundtone of his emotional world. (See C.P.E. Bach's remark about Hasse above.) Not until Wagner's time did we learn also to saturate Bach's many-voiced style with our emotions and to be able to tolerate the addition of this pathetic burden. Graun no longer concerned himself with Bach's profound spirituality, but, like Handel, with a type of music that wanted to be listened to. This means that no intellectual difficulties should interfere with the reception by the human ear and mind. Graun's music always counts on its audience and on being performable. For the sake of its classical ideal of a cantabile style the intellectual principle of polyphony had to be undermined. Clarity and relevance, required by all classic styles, interfere with the horizontal flow of Baroque music. Especially Graun's arias develop a song-like cell structure and melodic shape that seem to be generated by purely harmonic considerations. Graun's melody wants to sing. Even the themes of the two choral fugues which the work contains do not want to be building stones with which a contrapuntal structure is to be erected. They want to be the leading idea, containing the contents of the music as in a capsule, thus setting the tone for the movement as it develops. The manner by which he shaped his harmonies and melodies shows Graun on the way to classicism. He follows in the same path with his rhythms which already cling closely to the pattern established by the rule of the bar.

The orchestration of the work also follows the direction taken. The four-part chorus is joined by the string quartet and the continuo is brightened by the soft colors of the woodwind instruments (two flutes, two oboes and two bassoons). This is Handel's orchestra, Handel's instrumentation (but without Mozart's added instruments). Graun's orchestra wants to sing; its woodwinds and strings are entirely at the service of the homophonic and cantabile style. The wind instruments are rarely treated independently; they simply double the strings or the vocal parts of their respective compass. The orchestral accompaniment is thus confined almost exclusively to four staves, except for the final chorale and two of the arias in which for once the wind instruments are allowed a certain life of their own. The only special instrumental effects in the entire score that Graun indulged in are muted strings in two arias and the pizzicato of the violins in the final chorale. Otherwise the homogeneity of sound is maintained throughout. In its aim to blend, the orchestra solely serves the singing. In the five four-part choruses of the work, even the accompaniment is limited to the strings; in the two fugues[19] (the Handelian style of which is enhanced by a good measure of sentimentality) it has the mere function of doubling and thus strengthening the vocal parts. The three other choruses are nothing but four-part songs, the instrumental accompaniment of which simply enhances the sonorities. "The chorus is a simple melody, scored tutti," as Graun said quite characteristically in a letter to Telemann.[20] Also in the realm of the chorus Graun strives for song-like symmetry, simplicity and clarity. The cantabile and sentimental fugues do not interfere with the composer's determination to achieve a classical style. The entire work inhabits a uniform stylistic territory and a uniform realm of sonorities. Focusing on the basic sound of the string quartet, in which the woodwinds have the effect of occasionally "turned-on lights," Graun's orchestra is the embodiment of the cantabile ideal of sound. The dynamically rigid and often impersonal aspect of the Baroque orchestra which Bach frequently still preserved in the continuous sound of the oboes, has been overcome. Graun's orchestra melts into a perfect oneness with the chorus and is capable of an endless variety of shadings down to the smallest detail.

This must again be contrasted with Bach. Already the comparison of the two chorales had pointed out Bach's intricate harmony, rhythmic freedom and melodic independence whereas a look at recitative and aria showed their fundamentally different meaning for Bach because of the realism of the subject matter. The question of the sound of Bach's music has not yet been asked. And yet, it alone answers the question of how far Bach actually had ventured into the tonal world of the modern composers with these forms borrowed from opera and oratorio. Even here it must be stated that the aria, be it written for the solo singer or chorus, did not change Bach's concept of sound. He remained faithful to his orchestral forces that looked back to the heyday of the Baroque era. He liked to go back (especially in the arias) beyond the sound of the violin, the transverse flute and the oboe, by employing the sharp and reedy sound of the already obsolete oboe d'amore (twice in the *St. Matthew Passion*) and still more frequently, that of the oboe da caccia (five times). Also the viola da gamba, discarded by his contemporaries, lives on as the obbligato instrument in one of the arias.[21]

With its sharp contours that the dominating wind instruments create, Bach's orchestra does not serve the Italian cantabile. Rather, it highlights the clear identity of the individual parts, thus serving the polyphonic texture. Even in places where madrigalesque traits had entered into the Passion, the intellectual principle of polyphony lifted these secular elements onto a higher level. Since Bach's orchestra does not yet fuse into a homogeneous sound, but is divided by sharply separated individual sounds, just like the organ of his time, it is not yet able to be subservient to the vocal parts. It functions, rather, as an equal partner, in true consciousness of polyphonic responsibility, which does not tolerate the despotic dominance of an individual voice. His transcriptions of Italian music present the most outspoken evidence that Bach could think only in terms of part writing. The merely sentimental did not interest him. He sensed in it the early signs of decay in the church which the others called *progress;* but Bach belonged to the church. His cantatas, motets and Passion music do not belong in the concert hall. Bach's Lutheran faith based on Revelation contrasts sharply with the idealistic general piety of a person such as Graun. The place of sacred music, of the church, was abandoned only when the weight of polyphony declined, when the musical texture was thinned out and symbolism made way for and was replaced by a new *Empfindsamkeit* and a virtuosity solely for the sake of vocal agility. Graun's *Tod Jesu* is a sacred cantata which presupposes familiarity with the story of the Passion. A character—we do not know whether he represents eyewitness or historian— leads the listeners only to the emotional aspects of the events, while the authentic text of the Bible is relegated to no more than an occasional quotation. By abandoning Luther's dogma to such an extent, Graun's work can be said to have left the church. Compared to Bach's *St. Matthew Passion,* Graun's *Tod Jesu* is, with regard to its length and content, a "lyric miniature."[22] Yet, seen historically, it was the "perfect expression of the religious sentiment of a time"[23] which had its roots in the Pietism of the eighteenth century. The work and its creator alike represent an idealized Christianity. The way from Bach to Graun is the historic way of sacred music from church to concert hall.

Although for the first performance of *Der Tod Jesu,* which took place on March 26, 1755, in the cathedral at Berlin, the churchly frame was still preserved, the forces used for the performance were entirely secular. The solo parts were taken by members of the opera; the basic personnel of the orchestra came from the Chapel Royal. C.P.E. Bach was the harpsichordist, Graun's brother, Johann Gottlieb, led the violins as concertmaster, and J. Fr. Agricola, who sang the solo tenor part, indicated the beat. Characteristically enough, Graun himself was in the audience. The composer listened to the sound and the effect of his work, he no longer directed it himself. Frederick the Great missed the first performance, which would hardly have happened at the first performance of an opera. Sponsor of the performance was the *musikübende Gesellschaft* of the cathedral organist, Johann Philipp Sack.[24] This was an early, voluntary and independent bourgeois musical organization which must be considered a forerunner of the big public concerts. Just as the work gives only the appearance of a sacred work, an appearance that Handel's oratorios had already abandoned, the musical forces needed for the performance no longer came from the traditional church organizations, but from the opera and groups of musical amateurs. At first, Graun's *Tod Jesu* lived on in the Berlin patron-churches, above all in the Nikolai Church. The orchestra that was used was always that of the *Konzert der Musikliebhaber* (Concert of Musical Amateurs), that is, of music-loving citizens. The Berlin *Singakademie,* which now came into being, welcomed Graun's Passion-Cantata spiritually as well as physically into its bourgeois environment. As the townpipers had by now ceded their privileged position to the bourgeois orchestral societies, the school choirs, in a state of decline, now had to follow too, and had to be taken over by the bourgeoisie.

The historicity of Graun's *Tod Jesu* and Bach's *St. Matthew Passion* leads directly into the time of origin of our modern public concerts and choral societies. It leads into the nineteenth century which, inspired by a new religiousness and by the Romantic movement, conquered Rationalism, took Bach out of the ancestral gallery of musical heroes and awakened him to a new life.

Notes

1. Regarding what follows, cf. Georg Thouret, *Friedrich der Grosse als Musikfreund und Musiker*, Leipzig, 1898.

2. As such he was appraised in a scholarly manner by Albert Mayer-Reinach, "C.H. Graun als Opernkomponist" (C.H. Graun as opera composer), in *Sammelbände der internationalen Musikgesellschaft*, vol. I, p. 448ff.

3. As told by Charles Burney in his *Tagebuch einer musikalischen Reise*, Hamburg, 1773, vol. III, p. 192.

4. Scheibe, *Critischer Musicus*, p. 148.

5. Mayer-Reinach, "C.H. Graun," p. 448ff.

6. Mennicke, "Zur Biographie der Brüder Graun," in *Neue Zeitschrift für Musik*, No. 8 (1904) and *Hasse und die Brüder Graun als Symphoniker*, Leipzig, 1906.

7. Lott, "Zur Geschichte der Passionskomposition von 1650 bis 1800," *Archiv für Musikwissenschaft*, vol. III/3, 1921.

8. Kretzschmar, *Führer*, 2. Abteilung (Part II), vol. I, 1921, pp. 3-110.

9. This appears for the first time in Johann Sebastiani's St. Matthew Passion of 1672, the year of H. Schütz's death.

10. Quoted by Caroline Valentin in *Geschichte der Musik in Frankfurt am Main*, Frankfurt, 1906, p. 227.

11. Carl Israel, *Frankfurter Concert-Chronik von 1713 bis 1870*, (1876), p. 18.

12. K.W. Ramler, *Geistliche Kantaten* (Sacred Cantatas), 2nd ed., Berlin 1770. The dedication appears at the beginning of the book.

13. Herder about Ramler. Handwritten addition to Ramler's *Sacred Cantatas* (in the copy of the Zurich Zentralbibliothek).

14. *Leipziger allgemeine musikalische Zeitung*, vol. VII, 1805, p. 797.

15. See Friedrich Smend, "Bachs Matthäus-Passion," *Bach-Jahrbuch*, 1928.

16.   Karl von Winterfeld, *Der evangelische Kirchengesang*, vol. III. p. 364.

17.   Richard Benz, *Die Stunde der deutschen Musik*.

18.   Spitta, *J.S. Bach*, vol. II, p. 329.

19.   No. 10, *Christus hat uns ein Vorbild gelassen* (Christ has left an example to us) is a double fugue.

20.   Letter of Nov. 9, 1751; ed. by B. Kitzig in *Zeitschrift für Musikwissenschaft*, vol. IX, 1927, p. 397.

21.   In the aria *Komm, süsses Kreuz* (Come, sweet cross).

22.   K. Mennicke, *Hasse und die Brüder Graun*, p. 465.

23.   Ibid.

24.   This Society was founded in 1749 in Berlin.

4

Johann Sebastian Bach in the Early Romantic Period

What interests many persons today in Bach's church music is not their specifically churchly nature. It is partly a general musical element, and partly that aspect, also present in Bach, where the bond with secular music becomes visible.[1]

The history of the Bach movement in the Age of Reason extends to the end of the eighteenth century. At the threshold of the new century, new, powerful forces begin to change the earlier image of Bach. A reaction to Rationalism sets in. The *Storm and Stress* generation had already energetically undermined the preeminence of the mind as an objectively evaluating, critical intelligence. In the grip of the primal force of feeling, driven by the healthy human instinct that is not inclined toward reflection, the generation of the young Goethe had declared war on the timelessly unhistorical intellect. The *Storm and Stress* movement had paved the way for the German Romanticists, in whose ideas the new ideology was now to find its clear expression.

The New Sense for History

The rationalistic image of the world was no longer understood. The abstract, hierarchical system of Rationalism, which was able to judge everything by one rule, was now replaced by a new appreciation of the uniqueness of things. A new reverence and love for things both great and small arose, a solemn respect for the diversity of phenomena, such as the Age of Reason had never known. The Age of Romanticism, in fact, could not figure out the image of the world rationally, nor did it want to do so. The result was a completely new sense for history. Only when there was a will to comprehend every epoch and every artistic style both as directly related to God[2] and as phenomena by themselves, only when one attempted and learned to project oneself into past realities, could a genuine sense for history come to life. In contrast to Rationalism, this new sense for history appreciated what is individual and to a large extent irrational, but did not attempt, like Rationalism, to force it into a set scheme. History thus gained a value in and of itself. The uniqueness of the historical fact, as of personality, moved to the forefront of attention. The discovery of the historical world was one of the main achievements of this period. Only now could historical phases once again be put into a sequential order. The sense of the Romanticists for the history of the past displaced the encyclopedic knowledge of ongoing, present history in Rationalism and made room for a more genetic concept of history. A first attempt at putting the new image of history into practice was made at the University of Göttingen, the standard setter of the day, where the traditional sciences were brought into contact with the historical sciences.

This changed attitude towards history also produced a changed attitude on the part of the new age towards art. Here too an awareness awakened for the diverse, at times incompatible, forms of artistic creativity. Individual artistic styles were acknowledged to have their own characteristic values, and one strove to attain an understanding of the various types of historical artistic manifestations. The Romanticist tried to attain as intensive a capacity for empathy as possible. He did not assign fixed definitions to concepts such as *music,* as the Rationalists did. In the Romantic period the outlines of a world with a standardized structure become blurred. Concepts lose their focus and derive their meaning from the case in question, from the one-time experience.

The New Relationship to Art, Especially to Music

Music became saturated with a new spiritual content, which music criticism interpreted as religiosity. Metaphysics reentered the sphere of music. "The principal source of music lies in the heart,"[3] said Heinse; in fact, the composer is "more of a creator than any other artist."[4] What is stressed here is the freedom and originality of music, which by its nature, unlike painting, has no model. With this, the rationalistic principle of *imitation* was overcome once and for all. The new esthetic viewpoints were expressed with great clarity by Wackenroder (1773-98), who stands chronologically at the beginning of German Romanticism. He found the creative spark incomprehensible, something truly godly. He could not imagine the artist creating, except in a half-aware, ecstatic state. The act of creation thus becomes an unconscious, irrational, god-given process. "Art is higher than Man,"[5] said Wackenroder. When he spoke of the "land of music" as the "land of faith,"[6] it signified for him an escape from a detested life. Only one who surrenders to longing can share in the all-encompassing love and the beauty of faith. The sphere of longing comes to be the sphere of art. Striking in Wackenroder is the mystically enraptured language in which he clothed his words and thoughts. He also had a strong leaning toward Catholicism, to which his most intimate friend, Ludwig Tieck, and Friedrich von Schlegel later converted. The fundamental difference between Romantic religiosity and the Lutheran piety of a man such as Bach becomes obvious. The purely human, overflowing love and infatuation of the Romanticists, their faith anchored in the realm of longing, is far removed from a faith that is anchored in the realm of certainty embodied by the Lutheran gospel. For the Romanticist, faith is rapture, something fleeting, flexible, wispy, not something dogmatic that could afford a sure footing.

Thus art too is something intangible. It must be taken on faith. It cannot be grasped by the dispassionate mind. While for Bach art is only a medium through which shines the divine itself, art for the Romanticist is irrationality pure and simple, behind which nothing is hidden. Art is the goal of an escape from the world, as is faith. E.T.A. Hoffmann said,[7] "By its intrinsic, unique character, music is therefore religious in nature, and its origins can be sought and found nowhere but in religion, in the church." Furthermore, "It [music] unlocks for man an unknown realm, a world which has nothing in common with the world of the senses that surrounds him, and in which he leaves behind all feelings that can be defined by words, so that he may give himself up to what is inexpressible."[8] The inexpressible, the religious, is in fact the act of submission to art. This dichotomy of the world is typical for the spiritual posture of the entire Romantic movement. Art has its origin in a realm of imagination, a realm of dreams, which lies beyond all everyday experience.

Besides this inclination to rapture, there existed also an urge to be immersed in faraway times. Ancient, bygone cultures and artistic achievements were longed for. The German Middle Ages, with their Gothic cathedrals and town halls, the splendor of their emperors, knights and crusaders, became objects of fanatical enthusiasm. And the art of these long-lost times came to new life as well. Goethe felt its power in 1770, when he stood in amazed contemplation before the cathedral in Strasbourg. Herder collected the *"Voices of the Peoples in their Songs."* Through Brentano and Arnim, the song treasures of their own nation, *Des Knaben Wunderhorn,* saw the light of day, and the Brothers Grimm brought the ancient fairy tales of their homeland back to life. It was a time of searching for and discovering stored treasures, a German *Renaissance,* which in its longing for and awareness of the past also took powerful possession of music.

In 1804 the Leipzig *Allgemeine Musikalische Zeitung*[9] reported, "In the musical world, this is the time of the resurrection of the dead; and fortunately this resurrection extends... only to the just. Ten years ago, Sebastian Bach, Handel, Emanuel Bach, Jomelli and other great men of the past were like the deceased, of whom one spoke with reverence, but whose society one no longer enjoyed." Until the inception of this new intellectual outlook, the important figures in music history were lodged in a gallery of ancestors, as it were, a place conceded to them by the musical fraternity. The entire output of written music history in the Age of Reason concerned itself with fields of specialization. It consisted of reports that the initiates and musical scholars exchanged among themselves. Because of his reputation, Bach was honored as one of the great colleagues of the profession; his craftsmanship was praised highly and recommended as an exemplary model to posterity. But the master was not looked at in a historical light. Only now, when the historical-Romantic style of music criticism replaced the rationalistic method, could Bach become one of history's great composers, become a historical figure.

Because the guiding concept of the Romantic age was the idea of historical evolution, and all things were seen as part of an organically maturing historical process rather than as isolated phenomena as in the Age of Reason, the forgotten masters too reentered the musical consciousness of the time, and were now seen in the context of their historical styles. While self-centered Rationalism could not even conceive of reviving old music, it was the goal of Romanticism to reexperience the realities of music history. Thus in the course of this change in human consciousness the past was revived and, along with other masters, Bach was made into what he had never been—part of the national culture of the German people.

The Transformation of the Foundations of Society: The Development of Bourgeois Concert Life

In the beginning neither economic nor intellectual conditions were favorable for a revival of Bach's works. Initially, the social changes did not encourage the Bach movement. While the development of bourgeois concert life led away from Bach's type of spiritual outlook, it did not prevent Sebastian Bach's work from reappearing in the concert halls of the nineteenth century.[10]

The general social change had welded the bourgeoisie, which was previously split into classes and guilds, into a new unit—the free middle class, which now became the bearer of culture. If the broadest classes of the people were excluded at least from the secular music at the courts before, now the rising middle class pressed for its own organizations to satisfy its musical needs. The bourgeoisie now had to espouse the cause of music, because music's bonds to the church had become increasingly slack. On the other hand, the attention paid by the princely courts to the promotion of the arts was flagging; for the Age of Absolutism had had its day. Every retreat in courtly cultivation of music was followed automatically by a blossoming of new musical activity among the bourgeoisie. While the shrinking process which the courts underwent forced many court orchestras out of existence, it liberated many musicians, who had heretofore been in the service of princes, letting them now strive towards new goals.

In Berlin, the fears and deprivations of the Seven Years' War had deeply wounded the music life; and after the Bavarian War of Succession (1778), musical life at court came almost to a standstill. Thus it becomes quite understandable that Johann Friedrich Reichardt, Graun's successor as Director of the Berlin Opera, was able to arrange the first subscription concerts there.[11] At the same time, the King's harpsichordist, Fasch, whose energies were increasingly allowed to lie idle, used them to form from among his private pupils a small chorus, from whose modest beginnings the Berlin *Singakademie* later was to develop. The new bourgeois music life, with its orchestral concerts and singing societies, thus profited from the same musicians who once lent their skills to the musical culture of the courts. The changeover to bourgeois music thus was borne by the servants of the old aristocratic art.

Some facts and dates may briefly be used to illustrate this development. The forerunners of the first bourgeois ensembles with a concert-like character were the old *collegia musica*. The old *Abendmusiken,* which were introduced by Franz Tunder in Lübeck in 1641 and enjoyed such great popularity under his successor Buxtehude, were held after the vesper service as church concerts for the merchants' guild. Similar bourgeois and social functions were also fulfilled by the Collegium Musicum, which Matthias Weckmann had founded in Hamburg in 1668. But even the musical performances of the *House of Frauenstein,* which Telemann directed in Frankfurt from 1713 to 1721,[12] did not yet take the decisive step towards the true public concert. Free concertizing before a socially mixed public is first documented in 1717 by the concerts of Telemann's Collegium Musicum of students in Leipzig, which Bach directed from 1729 until almost 1740.[13] The public aspect of making music in the *Caféhaus* (coffee house) is already quite pronounced here. Although these Leipzig concerts invited an audience, and let skilled instrumentalists appear as soloists, the musicians as a group still remained united among themselves and bound together by social class. Nevertheless, the aspect of keeping up social appearances no longer predominated. Instead, the joy of music was the impetus for this carefree concertizing for its own sake. Again it was Telemann who from 1722 onward—almost simultaneously with the founding of the first *concerts spirituels* by Anne Danican-Philidor in Paris in 1725—gave his Collegium Musicum at Hamburg the format of large public concerts. As regular, paid events, these concerts now became not only an artistic but also a commercial factor in the life of the city.

In Berlin, the development took its own course during the reign of Friedrich Wilhelm I, who was quite inimical to art. Here, the movement was fanned spontaneously by music-loving, middle-class circles, who were not able to depend for support on any existing musical organizations, whether made up of students or others. Moreover, the Prussian capital could also claim the historical honor of having paved the way for the bourgeois singing movement within Germany. As early as 1724, the Berlin Cathedral organist, Gottlieb Hayne, the first music teacher of Frederick the Great, initiated choral sessions with his students and sundry musical amateurs, who made their way to his home for the sheer pleasure of singing.[14] Other amateur concert groups, albeit mostly instrumental, grew out of the bustling activity of several chamber musicians of the Royal Court Chapel in Berlin. These ensembles were founded by J.G. Janitsch, Schale, and J.F. Agricola. Major significance was attained by the *musikübende Gesellschaft* (music-making society), of the organist J. Philipp Sack, which began in 1749, and with the aid of which the first performance of Graun's *Tod Jesu* came about in 1755. The endeavors of this society continued after the Seven Years' War (from 1766 on) in the *Benda-Bachmann Concerts*, which took the premier position among the musical groups that by then were springing up with ever greater frequency. Finally, when Karl Friedrich Fasch, who had become dispensable at the court of Potsdam and had moved to Berlin, gathered a great many students around him for group singing and introduced them week by week to sacred choral music, the cornerstone was laid (in 1791) for the later Berlin Singakademie.

Since people of both sexes from the educated classes first came together in Berlin solely for the pleasure of group singing, the transformation that instituted amateur choruses was completed there. The freedom with which this entire movement became established, at the same time eliminated the obligatory character of the previous school and church choirs. The way by which the middle class, on its own, discovered music to which previously it had had access only in the church, is decisive. Still more important is that the citizen did not hire musicians and singers to perform his new art for him, that he did not distance himself from his art for reasons of class distinction, but that, instead, he made himself the interpreter of his art, that he put himself into the artistic center and thus came to dominate it. Because he did not let music be sung for him but rather sang himself, he transformed vocal music into a bourgeois art form. In the sphere of the new Berlin Singakademie, we are not only concerned with a revival of choral music but also with turning choral singing into a bourgeois activity for massive choirs, which eventually was to steer the Bach movement into totally new directions in the Age of Romanticism. The constantly fading impact of the old choir schools was accompanied by the decline of the art-fiddlers, townpipers and trumpeters. When in 1810 they lost their organizational system and guild protection with the introduction of freedom of occupational choice *(Gewerbefreiheit)* in Prussia, they found shelter, almost unnoticed, in the newly founded concert and opera orchestras, which, like the choral societies, were now headed for an unforeseen rise.

Let us now follow this rise by concentrating on the Berlin Singakademie, which became a model for the entire nineteenth century. The way in which this choral society, which was growing steadily under Fasch's leadership, became representative of middle-class standards was typical of the development of the new organizations that were now springing up all over. The private home, which received these devotees of singing in the first phase of their gatherings, soon became too small. The singers moved to the larger hall of the *Akademie,* whence the name Singakademie. The first venture of a public concert was made in 1794. As in the rehearsals, the first impression was the heavy predominance of women's voices, a fact easily explained in sociological terms and which appears to be characteristic of mixed middle-class choirs. Its correlative in compositional terms is the prominence of the soprano melody in Classical compositions. The noteworthy custom of picking up the ladies in carriages to take them to the rehearsals was first seen in 1797. Here began the change to a feudal system. Over the years the Singakademie gained great fame and a representative power in the cultural life of Berlin. Its name had won such a wide reputation that no visiting celebrity traveling through the city failed to attend one of its evening rehearsals. Persons of rank and nobility joined the audience. The circle of those attending became socially representative. Beethoven attended two rehearsals in 1796; in 1797, the Crown Prince was present. In short, as a member of the Singakademie one was a person of some status. Singing was no longer done only for its own sake, but also for the sake of the importance it was considered to have. By absorbing the many existing smaller choral groups, the Singakademie brought an imperialistic trait into the whole choral movement. When Fasch's eminent successor, Karl Friedrich Zelter, complained about the singing tea parties *(Singe-Thees)* and their "abundance that dissipated their energies" *("kräftezersplitternde Fülle"),* he was clearly expressing the desire to attain sole dominance in Berlin, which because of the high quality of his choir's achievements was in fact both earned and maintained. The Berlin Singakademie thus could become the model for the singing societies that were now blossoming profusely in other cities as well.[15]

At the same time, larger orchestras developed from some of the students' *collegia musica* and middle-class concert societies. The position that the Benda-Bachmann and Reichardt concerts had attained in Berlin was occupied in Hamburg by the admission-charging subscription concerts regularly given by Telemann and later by Carl Philipp Emanuel Bach. In 1743, independently of Sebastian Bach's activities, the *Grosses Konzert,* which later became the Gewandhaus Orchestra in Leipzig, was endowed, in the true sense of the word, by sixteen families of the nobility and bourgeoisie. A part of the audience thus became founder and benefactor of an association that functioned for its own musical enjoyment. Because at first only families rather than individuals became members, the character of a closed society was maintained for a while. In London, Johann Christian Bach, together with Karl Friedrich Abel, the last viol da gamba virtuoso in music history, launched a concert series which consisted of 15 subscription concerts per season. He could, however, look back on a long choral and orchestral tradition, that went back as far as the period before Handel. Instrumental concerts charging admission had already taken place in the Chapel Royal in London from 1672 to 1678 under the direction of John Bannister. While in Germany independent concert halls began to appear only in 1761 in Hamburg[16] and in 1781 in Leipzig,[17] London already owned an independent concert hall in 1713, the *Hickford Room*. The business of public performances of music was English in origin, because there the middle class came to have a voice in cultural life much earlier than in other countries. The founding of the British Museum in 1753 was another accomplishment of the English middle class.

Strivings for Musical Renewal

The Handel Movement. The renaissance of old music in Germany must be seen from this standpoint, especially the magnificent Handel movement. Simultaneously with the Palestrina movement, it took hold in Germany, but much earlier than the more widely spread Bach movement. In Handel's case, however, the word *renaissance* is even less applicable than with Bach, because what was happening with Handel was not a reawakening, a revival, but a first awakening—the discovery, popularization and introduction of his works in Germany. Handel's work could not be transplanted to his native country until the social conditions his art required had arrived. Handel's time could not have come any earlier for the Germans, just as there was a good reason why the master worked far from his native land, in middle-class England, the home he chose for his modern way of thinking. One may call the enthusiam for Handel that was now engulfing Germany a process of *naturalization* in the truest sense of the word. The German Handel movement characteristically began in bourgeois Hamburg, the German city closest to England and Germany's most enlightened city. It started on September 23, 1771 with *Alexander's Feast*.[18] The *Messiah* was first introduced to the Germans by an Englishman, Thomas A. Arne,[19] who presented it at the *Drill-Haus* in Hamburg in 1772, the same year that also brought a performance of one of the coronation anthems.[20] C.P.E. Bach continued the contact once it had been established and repeated the *Messiah*, that mightiest of Handel's oratorios, in 1775 and 1777. C.P.E. Bach thus supported the German Handel movement in his Hamburg concerts long before he did anything for his father's choral works.[21] In Berlin, Handel was again introduced by *Alexander's Feast,* in 1771.[22] In 1774, *Judas Maccabaeus* appeared, with which work the Handel movement began in Vienna in 1779. Meanwhile, the *Messiah* in particular made the rounds of German cities, with first performances, after Hamburg, being given in Mannheim, Schwerin and Weimar. Handel's oratorios gained further acceptance in Reichardt's public concerts in Berlin (1783-84). Blumner[23] used this fact to comment that the "thin, deficient" voices of students (the Singakademie had not yet been founded) would hardly have been commensurate with the ideal Handel style. This statement is important for the early cultivation of Handel's music in Germany, because it was not until 1786 that J.A. Hiller dared to perform the *Messiah* in the Berlin Cathedral, with forces absolutely unknown in Germany before. The orchestra of this performance, which was based quite officially on the model of the centenary performance in London, was 200 strong, while the chorus united all the school choirs of Berlin and Potsdam as well as the Opera chorus and an additional 150 amateurs.[24] This monster performance was soon repeated in Leipzig and Breslau under Hiller's direction and thus defined the countenance of the new oratorio style for Germany. Since the German Handel movement was a choral movement, Handel became from now on a primary task of the new bourgeois singing societies.

The Palestrina Movement. While Handel became the mainstay of German vocal concerts, and composers of large-scale vocal works patterned their choral styles after his, the Palestrina revival pursued a quite different course, more directed towards the church. The enthusiam for the great Italian master did not flare in the open public concert halls, but in the heads of the best German Romanticists. Burney and Reichardt kindled the German Palestrina movement in the 1770s.[25] Reichardt, who was in possession of several works of the master, initiated his friends Tieck and Wackenroder into the mysteries of this art. Soon Hoffmann and Schlegel,[26] Thibaut and Moritz Hauptmann, and later Haberl, who was to make Regensburg the center of the Palestrina movement in the church, became eager adherents of the fanatical Palestrina cult. New printings of Italian choral works were begun in 1812. In 1816, in St. Michael's Church in Munich, Thibaut's friend Kaspar Ett reintroduced a cappella music to the German church, thus making Munich the point of origin for the liturgical a cappella movement. With this, the Palestrina style came to be the model for church music of every kind. Palestrina and serious church music became virtually identical concepts. Intoxicated by this ideal, German church musicians—among them, above all, Ett, the teacher of Franz Lachner—made attempts at imitations. These, however, resulted mostly in a lowering of the standard, containing stylistic elements reminiscent of the style of glee club choruses and the like. This goes to show that a style cannot simply be reproduced under different social conditions. Thus no progress was made beyond a renaissance of Palestrina's music, as no new works of truly sacred nature were created. What the Palestrina movement took over from Rationalism was the preference for the principle of homophony, which was considered obligatory for any genuine church music. No new flowering of the music of the old Netherlands masters occurred that might have paralleled the Palestrina cult. Thus the historical roots that might have nourished a Bach movement in the church were absent; but the esthetic prerequisites were lacking as well, since Bach neither wrote in the homophonic style, nor—except for his motets, which for this reason have always remained in the repertoire—did he write a cappella music. Amid this stylistic prejudice, it was, at least for the time being, impossible to revive Bach's cantatas and Passion music. Despite the good intentions of the Palestrina and Handel movements to revive the art of the past, both movements were under the spell of a stylistic uniformity that was the uniformity of the age, an age that wished to enjoy music without intellectual or esthetic difficulties. The Romantic Bach movement was not rooted in a yearning for direct experience. It was, rather, an outgrowth of a historical perception of old music. This distinguished it from the Palestrina and Handel movements.

While the Palestrina experience had conjured up a new a cappella ideal, all the choral works with orchestra that were now being created were influenced by Handel, who had set an example of such radiance that no composer could escape it. To mention only a few major works: Mozart's *C minor Mass* and his *Requiem*, Haydn's *Creation* and *The Seasons*, Mendelssohn's *Walpurgis-Night, St. Paul* and *Elijah*, and finally the oratorios of Loewe. None of these works is thinkable without Handel. Their creators were influenced by the great London master long before they became acquainted with a choral work by Bach.

Johann Sebastian Bach in the Early Romantic Period

Although Handel and the Italian a cappella composers dominated the scene, even though the Romanticists became intoxicated in Rome by the singing of the Sistine Chapel Choir and thus became esthetically removed from the sturdier church music of Bach, and even though Classical symphonic music in the large concert halls was leading away from the essence of Bach's art, the Bach movement nevertheless did not come to a halt. Bach sought out the musician and friend of music only in other, quieter places that remained hidden from the view of the historian unless he entered into the confines of the home, into the company of musical amateurs, among whom Bach's music continued to live on, far away from the noisy, public business of making music. In the final analysis, however, the Romantic epoch (in contrast to the Rationalistic age) brought about the redemption of the Bach movement from its estrangement from society, from the seclusion in which it was initially left by the first- and second-generation students and enthusiastic friends of the master. At the very beginning of the nineteenth century, the Bach movement laid aside its private character and made its entrance into public music life. We now must review this course, which was to lead from a sectarian Bach cult to a mass movement.

The historian usually failed to see the cultivation of Bach's music in the intimacy of the home. He was not there when the teacher assigned the *Well-Tempered Clavier* to a pupil. Hence the Bach tradition of the late eighteenth century may be judged far too harshly unless the many handwritten copies that were in general circulation are taken into account when ascertaining how widely distributed and how influential the surviving Bach *oeuvre* was. With few exceptions, history has remained silent as to the names of those who studied Bach's works. Only when the teachers and instigators who recommended the study of Bach's music were named Neefe or van Swieten, and when their pupils and friends were named Beethoven, Haydn, or Mozart, does one begin to comprehend how much a matter of course it was at that time to study and play Bach's keyboard works. Yet we learn nothing of what Bach may have meant to all those on whom historical research has lavished its attention less diligently than on the three Viennese Classic composers. None of the amateurs and lesser-known virtuosi who had been Bach's students had anything to say about the master. Nevertheless, it was they who were the anonymous bearers of the Bach tradition. They were the ones who rescued Bach's work and handed it over to a time which was to perpetuate this treasure by publication.

Thus even the narrow-mindedness that caused those around Bach's time to see only his keyboard virtuosity made historical sense. If Bach had not been the masterly performer that he was, and had not attracted and gathered around him a great many important students who were the only ones who felt called upon to carry on his tradition, his work might have been lost to posterity altogether. The remembrance of Bach the keyboard virtuoso led the way to Bach's work and thus to the preservation of his work; and the preservation of his *oeuvre,* along with its popularization, became the primary achievement of the Romantic epoch.

J. S. Bach as Reflected in the Romantic Historiography of Music

In this development, which was destined to liberate Johann Sebastian Bach from the narrow confines of his earlier place in history and introduce him to a wider public, the figure of Johann Nicolaus Forkel played a particularly important role. For Bach historiography in Germany, he represented the turn toward historical mindedness. Forkel was a Thuringian and as such still had access to the centers in which Bach's art survived in central Germany. He began his musical and scholarly career in the tried and true way, as Bach had once done, as a choir boy in Lüneburg. Already there, he may have come into contact with works by Bach. He enrolled at the University of Göttingen in 1769, initially to study law, and was appointed University Music Director in 1778. He received his doctorate, without writing a dissertation, in acknowledgment of the large scale History of Music he had begun to write. As a member of the

Faculty of Scholars in Göttingen, whose lectures the young Romanticists Tieck and Wackenroder attended, Forkel took an active part in the reorientation of human consciousness then occurring. Forkel represented the transformation from a specialized science of music to a history of music conceived as a history of styles.

Forkel's book on Bach, the research for which dated back to the years 1774/75 (as evidenced by his correspondence with C.P.E. Bach), was originally intended to appear as the last volume of his *Allgemeine Geschichte der Musik.* Because he feared that he might not live to see the completion of his life work, his Bach biography was published as an independent book in 1802 by Hoffmeister & Kühnel in Leipzig. Forkel was basically one of the many devotees of Bach's art whose service to the master was performed for the most part in obscurity. History has failed to recognize him as an interpreter of Bach's works, although he was very highly praised as such by Reichardt[27] and played Bach's keyboard works in the Göttingen concerts founded by him.[28] Forkel's activities in behalf of Bach's music belong rather to the anonymous Bach performances of the eighteenth century.

Only when he published his knowledge of Bach in his little book, *Über Johann Sebastian Bachs Leben, Kunst und Kunstwerke,* thereby giving the world its first Bach biography, did Forkel emerge from the ranks of the silent supporters of Bach. He became the champion of a concept of Bach that no longer allowed Bach to be reserved for a few initiates but instead set the master up as an illuminating example, as the everlasting heritage of an entire nation. With Forkel's book thus begins a new phase in the Bach movement. Already by its general tone and its popular language, the work exemplified the new tendency to get away from the limiting confines of the earlier Bach circles by making the master accessible and familiar to a wider public. That the work was dedicated to Baron van Swieten shows that with his book Forkel intended also to win the musical circle of Vienna for the cause of Bach.[29] Forkel also advised his publisher to send the little book to "Livonia and Russia," where, due to Carl Philipp Emanuel's connections with the Baltic states, a lively interest in Bach appears to have existed. For instance, a student of Kittel from Erfurt, Daniel Sperrwitz, served as music teacher at the university in Moscow.[30] This first biography of Johann Sebastian Bach thus tried to find the friends of his art in many a country.

Both the foreword and the conclusion of the book recommend Johann Sebastian Bach to the German people as a supreme legacy, one that imposed obligations. For Forkel, "keeping alive the memory of this great man...[is] not merely an artistic matter—it is a national matter."[31] This is the import of his book "for patriotic admirers of genuine musical art."[32] Its content does, however, not transcend what was then known of Bach. Forkel owed all the material for his book (aside from his private collection of Bach compositions) to his personal contact and his correspondence with Wilhelm Friedemann and Carl Philipp Emanuel Bach. Thus in a time in which historical consciousness began again to play a role, Forkel still had direct access to the world of Sebastian Bach. Yet because he inherited his concept of Bach from Bach's sons, he did not progress beyond their horizon. From him too we learn nothing of the religious Bach, of the Bach of the cantatas and Passions. The question of why Bach was a stranger in his own time still remained unanswered. Only in his introduction, where the enthusiasm of the younger generation breaks through, where he celebrates Bach as an expression of a time and a people, to whose sense of national pride he appeals, did Forkel grow beyond the Rationalism of his age and transcend the bounds of the old science of music.

With this book the way was prepared for Bach to enter public awareness. Forkel's work did not stand alone for long. The first Bach biographer was soon joined by the first Bach esthetician (in the modern sense), which Johann Friedrich Rochlitz can justifiably be called. His name is indissolubly linked with the *Allgemeine Musikalische Zeitung* in Leipzig, which he edited together with Härtel in the first twenty years of its existence (from 1798 to 1818). This musical weekly, which for fifty years (until 1848) faithfully mirrored the complete range of musical life, was another product of the new striving that aimed to make everything connected with music public. The general movement not only encompassed the middle-class concerts and choral societies; it also tore reporting of musical events, heretofore a narrow and specialized guild-like affair, from its moorings. A transformed musical press became accessible to the public, representing the new citizenry it now addressed. Thus not only music but the discussion of music became public, resulting quite naturally in a new form of music criticism. The old posture of all-knowing self-righteousness was replaced by a willingness to follow the artist's intentions faithfully, to identify with his innermost feelings. Technically superior knowledge gave way to the desire to understand.

Accordingly, Rochlitz's reviews are not strict analyses as much as descriptions of his own impressions. Music was judged from the standpoint of the audience, from that of the music lover, that is, no longer from the standpoint of the professional specialist, who scrutinized the master in his studio. What mattered was no longer whether the work was composed well, but what *effect* it created. Only in the nineteenth century did one learn that Bach could be *enjoyed* only if one gave his works their greatest effectiveness. One emphasized in the Romantic period the psychological side of music—and in this Rochlitz was the greatest master before Schumann. The desire to reproduce the feelings inherent in a piece of music caused music criticism to become a wavering, subjective construct. Although, unlike the criticism of the Rationalistic age, it was often capable of entrancing by its imaginative originality, at the same time it could not always be taken as the truth in historical questions.

The language of Romantic music criticism strikes one as astonishingly modern. What Rochlitz and other writers on music had to say about Bach in the *Allgemeine Musikalische Zeitung* resonates with the historical Romantic conception of Bach. That the first volume (1798) of this journal showed Bach's portrait in copper on its title page harmonizes with the sentence we read there on January 14, 1801:[33] "The name of J.S. Bach shines bright and high above all other German composers in the first half of the previous century."[34] The extravagance of language is at first surprising; but it is characteristic of the new generation, for whom J.S. Bach became the Dürer of German music. As Mozart was likened to Raphael, Bach was compared with Michelangelo,[35] and even (and considering the cosmic order in Bach's works, not wrongly) with Newton.[36] The effort to define Bach as an intellectual quantity in music history becomes apparent. By relating him to other heroes in world history, one hoped to gain a certain clarification of his stylistic position.

Rochlitz compared the seriousness of Bach's style with the splendor of Handel's and said:[37] "Handel wanted to be effective through everything he did." And thus his style became popular, "but in the noblest sense of the word... Bach's style was not popular, not even in that refined sense of the word. Only on special occasions (such as in certain numbers in his Passions) did he endeavor with tender care to write in a popular style, to the extent that he was capable of it." Of course such rather amateurish comparisons were not the last word. Above all, an effort was made to give an account of what it was that made the road to the masses so difficult for Bach's art. Bach's style, which the senses alone cannot absorb, was now closely scrutinized. One came to the conclusions that Bach's art provides a satisfaction beyond the satisfaction of an art that merely pleases. Because Bach did not write "for the sake of the approval of the masses,"[38] because he did not seek after "what merely charms, diverts and is then forgotten,"[39] he provided "little for the senses.... For the most part, however, he inspires and occupies the intellect. Thus for one not inclined to reflection, his works have little meaning, and he will neither be able to comprehend their uttermost essence nor enjoy them."[40] The profundity of Bach's mind was interpreted as the product of his sense of artistic responsibility. Herein lies the true meaning of Bach's art, which never supplied what the marketplace asked for and thus tended also to avoid the splendor exhibited by Handel. But one did not yet see the source of Bach's sense of responsibility. The austerity and seriousness of his intellectual posture were recognized but could not be explained. At this time Bach did not yet appear in the role of the master bearing the weight of tradition, explainable only in terms of the ages that preceded him.

Rochlitz alone—who probably had wrestled the hardest to comprehend Bach, precisely because at first, as a young chorister at the Thomas School under Doles, he had not understood him, and even later did not believe Bach to be a man of the masses—pointed toward the future with some fundamental statements. Rochlitz, the first historian to seek the source of Bach's creativity, found this answer: "Without calm tranquility and religious faith in a great soul, *such* works cannot be conceived."[41] Later he elaborated on this magnificent sentence in his commentary to the cantata, *Ein'feste Burg ist unser Gott,* which was published in full score by Breitkopf & Härtel in 1821. After first tracing the steps of Bach's artistry and expressing the highest admiration for the mastery of the whole design, he said:[42] "And all this is by no means artifice, the product of cold calculation, put together with the greatest possible skill; on the contrary, it has quite evidently sprung from a full, profoundly moved heart." *From a full, profoundly moved heart!* One who, like Rochlitz, traced Bach's church music to the religious experience conveyed by the text, had overcome Rationalism in his inmost soul. Bach's omniscience, the substance of his art, if perhaps not completely understood, is at least suggested here. Mention has finally been made of Bach the devout, for whom alone all this was possible. The Bach of Rationalism, who was judged a skilled craftsman without soul, disappeared and made way for Bach whose art bears witness to the religious feeling of the master. Admittedly, this religious feeling was not understood from the standpoint of the Lutheran confession but rather from that of Romantic religiosity.

With his book on Bach, Forkel stood on the borderline between both points of view. Although he recognized the spiritual abundance in Bach's creations, he did not find the way to its origin, the piety of the master. He said,[43] "At best, we can only comprehend and explain his [Bach's] management of the internal mechanism of the art; but how he contrived at the same time to inspire into this mechanic art, which he alone has attained in such high perfection, the living spirit which so powerfully speaks to us even in his smallest works, will probably only be felt and wondered at." Hegel, too, who admired the "magnificent, genuinely Protestant, hearty and yet learned genius"[44] in Bach, saw in his music a contradiction between the warmth of feeling and the austerity of intellect, two principles that make themselves so easily independent of one another.

But the constant factor in all these music-esthetic observations, distinguishing them from Rationalistic views, was the recognition of a component of feeling in Bach's art. In recognizing this, Rochlitz, who was so much reviled by the exact sciences, raised this recognition to the level of the problematical. He dared to pose the question of conscience, whether this Bachian content of feeling could still be effective at all today (that is, in the early nineteenth century). Rochlitz doubted it, but did not give up on the Bach movement. Having gained this insight, Rochlitz showed the Bach movement new vistas of a grandeur of scope that had been hardly suspected before. He said,[45] "It may be that nowadays all these works are no longer suitable for public performance in churches or concert halls." For in "a single hearing, we are often unable to follow the wondrous master at all, and rarely can we listen to him in the proper manner, namely with our minds *and* hearts *together."* Nevertheless, these works must "be saved from perishing and be reproduced in print," if for no other reason, then

> because these works are highly noteworthy examples of a most singular direction taken by the spirit of music itself, and because they are the very apex of their kind. . . . Everything that documents a truly original aspect of the human mind and at the same time constitutes the highest perfection of its kind, must be regarded as a kind of holy legacy, belonging to the entire cultured world. And if nothing else can be done for it, then at least it must be maintained and be made accessible to those who take an interest in it.

With these sentences the scholar Rochlitz truly attains an astonishingly modern level of objectivity. One can almost hear the fervent voice of the great musicologist Otto Jahn, who thirty years later became the conscience of the great *Bach-Gesellschaft* edition. One is almost tempted by these meaningful utterances to trace the beginnings of modern musicology as a historical humanistic discipline, beyond Carl von Winterfeld, back to Rochlitz. He represented, indeed, the beginning of a musicological self-awareness, that recommended entrusting the study of art, not to Romantic feeling, but to scientific analysis.

Performances of Bach's Music in Leipzig during the Early Romantic Period

Among the interpreters of Bach's music August Eberhard Müller, the Thomas Cantor at the time of Forkel and the first new Bach publications, who was also a second generation student of Sebastian Bach, must be mentioned first. While his predecessor as Thomas Cantor from 1789-1800, J.A. Hiller, had championed the choral works of Hasse, Graun and Handel, Müller gave renewed impetus to the study and performances of Bach's music at the Thomas School.[46] As a student of Johann Christoph Friedrich, the Bückeburg Bach, he was still in direct contact with the Bach tradition. He also spent several years in the home of his uncle, the Braunschweig Cathedral organist Müller, in whose house Friedemann Bach had lived during his years of unemployment from 1771 to 1774. Obligated by the hospitality shown him, Friedemann left behind not only several autograph manuscripts of his father but also the portrait of Sebastian that had belonged to him, and that then came into the possession of A.E. Müller. The latter bequeathed it in 1809 to the Thomas School, which preserves the portrait to this day. Thus by the course his life took, Müller, like Forkel, was predestined to assume the stewardship of the Bach legacy within the walls of Leipzig in the new century.[47]

Müller was also the first since Bach's death to concern himself quite consciously with the master's cantata output. Only after one had come to learn to approach Bach from the emotional side could these works, which until then had been rejected, if only for the dogmatic character of their texts, be revived. On the other hand, the discovery of Bach's soul was linked (according to the music reviews of the time) to the rediscovery of his cantatas. At any rate, at the beginning of 1803 the *Allgemeine Musikalische Zeitung* noted the important fact[48] that cantatas by Bach had been "rescued from obscurity" and been heard in the the weekly concerts of the Thomas Choir and in the divine services. The reviewer also commented that Bach was here more than the great mathematician, but also a master of impression and expression that moved the heart. The first performances under Müller of three of these cantatas can be dated. *O Ewigkeit, du Donnerwort* (No. 60) and *Mache dich, mein Geist, bereit* (No. 115) were given at the Thomas Church in late 1802 (since they were reviewed in January 1803 in the *Allgemeine Musikalische Zeitung).* The cantata, *Ach Herr, mich armen Sünder* (No. 135) was first revived on February 10, 1805. The *Allgemeine Musikalische Zeitung* does not mention any other cantatas. Besides repeat performances of these three works, Müller may also have prepared performances of other cantatas that remained unreported by the press. After all, the Thomas School still had in its library over a hundred of Bach's *Sonntagsmusiken* (cantatas)[49] a treasure that a man as conscientious as Müller will hardly have left unused.

At this time, the musical press did not yet review church music with any regularity, particularly not the music offered during worship services. And to the great choral and orchestral concerts that were the primary object of newspaper interest, Bach had not yet gained access. For example, the quite regular Leipzig performances of Bach's motets in the years from 1800 to 1815[50] were mentioned only a single time in the *Allgemeine Musikalische Zeitung.* Yet B. Fr. Richter found evidence of eight motet performances in 1812 alone.[51] Thus the lack of reviews in the press does not allow the conclusion that the Bach movement in Leipzig was faltering. Still less can it be said that interest in Bach was declining, since with the turn of the century the period of the first new Bach publications began; a period in which particularly Leipzig, with its two music publishing houses, Breitkopf & Härtel and Hoffmeister & Kühnel, played a very substantial role.

The Period of the First New Bach Publications

From Bach's death until 1799, the Age of Reason had produced only one single new publication of a Bach work.[52] This was the not even authentic compilation of Bach chorales made by Kirnberger and C.P.E. Bach (see chapter 2, *supra*). However, several pieces by J.S. Bach had also been printed in collections by other authors. For instance, Kirnberger's *Kunst des reinen Satzes,* (1774/79, Part II, Section 3) included a canonic *Christe eleison* for four voices and six instruments by Bach, while Reichardt's *Kunstmagazin* (1782-91, Vol. 1, pp. 198-201) contained a clavier fugue in F minor from the master's hand. Finally, Bach's *Aria con variazioni per il Cembalo* was printed in Hawkins's *History* (Vol. V, p. 256, 1776).[53] Hidden away in anthologies as they were, such printings of Bach works spoke with a very soft voice indeed, as was typical for the rather anonymous cultivation of Bach's music in the late eighteenth century.

The first publication that displayed Bach's name prominently dates from the year 1799. The London organist August Friedrich Christian Kollmann (originally from Hanover) reissued the E-flat major Trio Sonata (No. 1) for organ[54] and in the same year announced an edition of the *Well-Tempered Clavier.*[55] "The primary honor of having introduced Bach to England belongs, however, to the London organist Samuel Wesley, to whom, as he wrote in 1808, Bach's works 'were a musical Bible, incomparable and inimitable.' Above all, Wesley sought to create an understanding for Bach's organ and clavier compositions, but he also devoted attention to the vocal works. With him and some like-minded colleagues, there emerged for the first time in music history a strong partisanship for Bach and against Handel, whom he judged harshly, to the point of injustice."[56] Wesley also founded an English Bach Society, arranged Bach evenings, sponsored a translation of Forkel's Bach book, and even started a subscription for a complete English edition of Bach's works.[57] Thus outside of Germany, and typically in the intellectually most progressive country, England, an early interest in Bach arose that in fact preceded the new movement of Bach publications.[58]

In Germany, Hoffmeister & Kühnel in Leipzig (which later became the Peters publishing house) ventured in about 1800 to announce to the public a plan for a critically correct edition of Bach's works.[59] (Naturally there was as yet no clear idea of the scope of the Bachian *oeuvre,* and especially not of the copiousness of his almost entirely unknown vocal output.) By 1802, however, this plan for a complete edition could already be considered a failure. Hoffmeister & Kühnel now planned to publish only the clavier and organ works of the master over a period of time. A similar fate awaited the first announcements by Simrock in Bonn and Nägeli in Zurich. They too were unable, because of the commerical risk involved, to translate their original intention of producing large-scale Bach editions into practice. Nevertheless, in 1801 a beginning was made in Germany. Simrock, being a cautious publisher, solicited, to begin with, subscriptions to the "celebrated preludes," by which he meant the *Well-Tempered Clavier,* and issued the work in 1801.[60] Nägeli, who besides Pölchau, Zelter and Hauser, was probably the wealthiest in ownership of Bach manuscripts,[61] followed with the *Well-Tempered Clavier* in the same year, as did Hoffmeister & Kühnel. In 1809, Imbault in Paris published only the 48 fugues,[62] while the complete work appeared in London (published by Wesley and Horn) in 1810/13.[63] All this shows the special popularity that the *Well-Tempered Clavier* enjoyed. Its three foreign publications further illustrate the serious cultivation of Bach's music beyond the borders of Germany.

Nägeli, whose edition of the *Well-Tempered Clavier* surpassed that of Hoffmeister in accuracy,[64] published a year later (1802) as the next work the *Art of the Fugue,* in full score and in an edition for clavier, following it by 1804 with the six sonatas for violin and clavier.[65] Nägeli was indeed one of the busiest and most egotistical Bach editors of this period.[66] As early as 1798, at which time he was already the owner of the *Art of the Fugue* and *Clavierübung,* part I, he began collecting Bach's instrumental works and corresponding with Breitkopf & Härtel about sending them to him. He launched his edition of works of the old masters with the aid of Breitkopf & Härtel and the Leipzig *Allgemeine Musikalische Zeitung,* to which he promised an article on Bach. In acting as promoters and manuscript suppliers to the Nägeli enterprise, Breitkopf & Härtel appear initally not to have thought of publishing Bach's music themselves, while Nägeli made extraordinary efforts to get hold of Bach manuscripts, preferably at no cost to himself. Thus he tried to exploit Bach's youngest and impoverished daughter, in whose behalf a campaign for assistance had just been organized, for his own purposes—but without success. Nägeli's collector's zeal extended only to Bach's instrumental works, however, of which he appears to have intended publishing a complete edition. The way was thus clear for Breitkopf & Härtel to publish vocal works by Bach. Nevertheless Nägeli asked them to postpone their publication until he had secured the necessary advance subscribers for his edition of the instrumental works. The race among publishers to produce a first edition of compositions by Bach is almost amusing. On March 21, 1801, the business-minded Nägeli wrote to Breitkopf & Härtel: "If you would rather have Book II of the *Well-Tempered Clavier* follow Book I and then have Handel's Suites follow as the third publication, that is agreeable to me too. However, I must insist that the announcement in this case remain in this particular point as it originally was, so that our competitors will not hurry and we will finish ahead of them.[67] In this case we could deliver the entire *Well-Tempered Clavier* and even the *Art of the Fugue* in a few months. Without announcing it ahead of time, we could outdistance Mr. Hoffmeister in time and undersell him as well."[68] This letter is a fitting forerunner of the attitude of Nägeli's son, who in 1851 refused to make his late father's autograph score of the *B minor Mass* available for the Bach Gesellschaft edition. The friendly and businesslike relations between Nägeli and Breitkopf & Härtel ruptured only later upon Breitkopf's publication of Bach's chorale preludes.

The year 1802-1803 brought the first publication of vocal music by Bach, which naturally took place in the city of the Thomas Choir. The conductor of the Leipzig Gewandhaus concerts, Johann Gottfried Schicht, who was also a collector of Bach manuscripts, oversaw the printing of the master's six motets (in two fascicles) for Breitkopf & Härtel. That the first works of Bach's entire vocal output to draw attention were his only a cappella compositions, is characteristic of the taste of the time. The published edition, however, deviated strongly from the original. Schicht made frequent and substantial changes in the text; and not all six works could withstand later questions as to their authenticity.[69] But this is irrelevant to the singing and performing of the motets in this period. In 1803, Breitkopf & Härtel also issued one of the so-called *"short masses."*[70] By 1804, the interest in Bach's vocal works had grown to such an extent that Breitkopf & Härtel could call attention to the fact that the four complete parts of Bach's chorales (those published earlier by Kirnberger and C.P.E. Bach) were again obtainable from them.[71] Between 1802 and 1806, this energetic Leipzig publishing house also issued Bach's chorale preludes for organ in four books (see above).[72] At the same time, 1801-1806, the rival Leipzig publishing house of Hoffmeister & Kühnel (together with Hoffmeister & Co. in Vienna) published 14 fascicles of Bach's clavier music.[73] Vienna was not involved just indirectly in this wave of new Bach publications through Hoffmeister's editions. The *Musikalienverlag des Kunst- und Industrie-Comptoirs* also took an interest in Bach's music and in 1803 published the *Goldberg Variations*, which Nägeli too appears to have published in 1809,[74] as well as the sonatas for solo violin.[75] In London in 1806, Kollmann released the Chromatic Fantasy, which together with the Fugue did not appear until Peters in Leipzig published it in 1819.[76] This first flood of newly published chamber music by Bach came to an end in 1813 with Kühnel's Leipzig edition of the English Suites for clavier.[77]

In the second phase of new Bach publications (from 1811 to about 1830) some of the great choral and orchestral works were restored to favor. Since the practical pursuit of Bach's music was also increasing steadily in this period, only the most important of the new editions will be listed here. Georg Pölchau, who later became the librarian of the Berlin Singakademie (1833-36), deserves first mention here. By buying up much of the musical estate of C.P.E. Bach, he laid the valuable foundation for his great private collection of Bach manuscripts. In 1811, he edited the *Magnificat* (the E-flat major, rather than the D major version) for Simrock in Bonn, and continued in 1818, again with Simrock as publisher, with the *A Major Mass* (engraved after the autograph score).[78] He was an early promoter of Bach's vocal work, which at that time was practically inaccessible. In 1818, rather curiously at the same time as Nägeli in Zurich, Pölchau announced the publication of the *B minor Mass* as well, for which work he had won many friends in France and England.[79] But neither his nor Nägeli's edition, the latter calling the Mass "the greatest musical artwork of all time and all nations,"[80] was actually published then. Nägeli could not keep his promise until 1833. Among other important Bach editions were the following:[81] the cantata *Ein' feste Burg ist unser Gott*, published in 1821 by Breitkopf & Härtel and edited by Schicht (who had also edited the motet *Lob, Ehr' und Weisheit* in 1819, replacing the motet *Ich lasse dich nicht*, found in the meantime not to be authentic). Furthermore: an eight-part motet *Jauchzet dem Herrn* was published by Kollmann in Leipzig. Its editor, the cantor S. Döring, reported frequent requests for copies of this work. In 1818 plans were made to place a monument on Bach's grave, the location of which was still believed to be known. The expenses were supposed to be covered by the proceeds from Pölchau's *B minor Mass* (see above) and Döring's motet *Jauchzet dem Herrn* (see above).[82] This noble idea, however, came to naught, and Bach's grave fell into neglect. The series of Bach editions that were issued as independent ventures by their publishers, rather than in connection with practical performances, may be said to end with the orchestral Suite in D Major, which appeared before 1815, published by Sieber in Paris.[83] Additional works that found their way onto the market by 1830 turned out to be of relatively little consequence for the Bach movement. It was the revival of Bach's *St. Matthew Passion* by Mendelssohn in 1829 that rekindled a new entrepreneurial spirit among music publishers, and from it the practice and performance of Bach's music was to benefit to a considerable extent.

Romantic Criticism of J.S. Bach

An important characteristic of the Romantic Bach period, found among Bach authors as well as Bach editors, is the distinction they felt had to be made between the master's good and bad works. Both Forkel and Nägeli had the same notion that in his youth Bach had written works that were unworthy of the mature master—and hence unworthy of publication. Forkel said, "Johann Sebastian Bach's first attempts at composition were, like all first attempts, deficient,"[84] and the publishers of the early nineteenth century made it a point to say that they would publish only the "best" works of the master.

Forkel's correspondence with Hoffmeister & Kühnel in Leipzig[85] is one of the most informative sources we have regarding this problem. In his criticism of the complete edition of Bach's instrumental works, which had been begun without his participation, Forkel called the D minor Toccata for organ "a school exercise, an archaic, imperfect piece, . . . one of the earliest works of J.S. Bach and in no way a masterpiece. Like everyone else, Bach had to be at first a blunderer before he could become a master, and his student compositions. . . . do not deserve to be included in a complete edition of his works."[86] One need only compare this pronouncement with Rochlitz's profound comment[87] about the importance—less for practical music making than for scholarship per se—of publishing all the works of a master, to recognize the vast distance separating Forkel from Rochlitz.

In his drastic, uninhibited style, addressed however also to Hoffmeister's edition, which he found equally deficient, Forkel continued, "What connoisseur of music will not find it disgusting to see, instead of the masterpieces he had hoped for, such products of the schoolroom.... A master such as Sebastian Bach should not be subjected to public scandal by botching his works, or by passing off his student compositions [as masterpieces]."[88] A similar statement was made in the same year, 1801, in the *Allgemeine Musikalische Zeitung.*[89] It reads: "J.S. Bach has written not only works that make him immortal, but also others that are nothing but products of scholastic sophistry and fruitless brooding, which lead the growing artist away from his goal rather than towards it." (This pronouncement, reminiscent of Scheibe's old criticism of Bach, was not made by Nägeli but by one of his Leipzig friends, whom Nägeli had authorized to make an advance announcement of his edition of Bach's works. To lay this at the door of Breitkopf & Härtel or Rochlitz as Edgar Refardt has done,[90] seems highly questionable to me. It is certainly out of place in the case of Rochlitz, in view of the serious sense of responsibility expressed in his thoughts quoted above. This statement must have emanated instead from the circle in which Forkel's thoughts prevailed.) Forkel himself, in search of early works of Bach, arrived at some rather strange judgments and discoveries. For instance, he called the marvelous C Major fugue from the *Well-Tempered Clavier* (Book I), with its astonishing and masterly *stretti,* "not a major fugue [*Hauptfuge*], but only an awkward product of his youth."[91] In fact, in contrast to the Second Part of the *Well-Tempered Clavier,* which was thought to be made up of "nothing but masterpieces," there were in the First Part "still some preludes and fugues that bear marks of the immaturity of early youth and have probably been retained by the author only to have the number of four-and-twenty complete."[92] From the autograph corrections that Bach made, not only in the *Well-Tempered Clavier* but above all in the *Inventions* and *Sinfonias,* Forkel deduced that these works were in need of improvement. This caused him "to call the pedantically shortened versions of two preludes of the *Well-Tempered Clavier* authentic."[93] His misunderstandings led so far afield that Forkel believed even cursory, truncated and defective copies made by students to be the products of a final polishing by the mature master. Forkel and his contemporaries were prejudiced. For one, they did not know the works of the young Bach, whose early phase of organ and cantata composition was still totally unexplored; secondly, they overestimated the fact that, after the Mühlhausen cantata of 1708, Bach did not have any of his own works printed and engraved until 1726.[94] As though Bach had not produced any masterpieces until attaining an age at which Mozart and Schubert were already dead![95]

It probably lay in the nature of the entire epoch to interpret the career of a master, aside from general variations in quality of some of his works, as a process of organic development leading to maturity. One was not yet sufficiently trained in history as to know that, in the age of Bach, Music and Man had quite a different syntax at their disposal than in the nineteenth century. Only a later age, one that recognized the pious, retrospective master, could discover the composer who knew no faltering beginnings, who was mature from the outset and who completed his life in innocent unawareness of his genius. The Romanticists did not ask what Bach was as such, but rather what meaning he had for them, what emotional experience he could impart to them. The criticism of Bach in the Romantic period must be understood in this light.

Besides Forkel, who divided Bach's music into early and mature works, Carl Maria von Weber's point of departure was that there was indeed something pedantic and old fashioned about Bach, which his own time had left far behind. In his commentary on twelve Bach chorales, which his teacher, Abbé Vogler[96] had newly harmonized, Bach's chorale settings come off quite badly. Weber, who was familiar with Forkel's Bach book, perceived the singularity of Bach's composing style, despite its severity, as essentially Romantic. However, as a Catholic, he could not fully comprehend and assimilate the spirit of Bach's Protestant art, based on the chorale. As a passionate admirer of the Dresden Court Capellmeister, J.G. Naumann,[97] Weber viewed church music too much from the perspective of Palestrina. For him, Vogler's new system of harmony set the standard for the harmonization of chorales, although Vogler's system had neither the boldness and the strict voice-leading of Bach nor the unpretentious simplicity of Graun. To begin with, the chorales Weber investigated were arbitrarily taken out of the context of Bach's cantatas and Passions and interpreted as pure artifacts, with no consideration of their text or orchestration. Vogler's chorale harmonizations were thoroughly Romantic. His chromaticism enervated and burdened the voice-leading, without giving it tonal firmness. The sense of tonality, which in Bach was still related to the old church modes, began to fluctuate. In Vogler's music there prevailed a sense of delight in a certain lack of tonal definition, in interesting harmonization for its own sake. Vogler's ever surprising change of harmony and avoidance of dissonance, as much as possible, pleased Weber. "Bach always repeats the entire first part, while Vogler varies it each time."[98] Bach's fidelity to the cantus firmus is interpreted by Weber as boring uniformity. Further, "measure 24 in Bach is full of badly sounding passing tones, and in none of the accompaniments [!] by Vogler will one find their like."[99] The adherents of the a cappella ideal could no longer comprehend a vocal style that did not coincide with the ideal of pure song and which for the reinforcement of its bold voice-leading, needed the instruments to double the voices. The Age of Romanticism could not yet see that these were two completely different ideals. It was for this reason that, at a time when denominational boundaries were beginning to blur, the a cappella style was propounded as obligatory also for the Protestant church. E.T.A. Hoffmann was alone in warning against the idea that the revival of the old works compensated for their disappearance from church.[100] He saw two possible forms of existence for old music: the *true* one, belonging to the divine service, and the other, satisfying the longings of nineteenth-century man.

Carl von Winterfeld was the great music historian who, above all, rejected the ways and means by which Bach worked on the emotions of his audience as something unchurchly. In harking back to the pre-Bach a cappella ideal, he discovered in Lasso's pupil, Johann Eccard, the Protestant German Palestrina. He found Eccard's sacred songs to be the more churchly, in comparison with Bach's settings. Since Eccard's settings were less individualistic than those of Bach, to Winterfeld they were closer to the mental capacity of the congregation. Although endowed with more abundant artistic gifts, Bach no longer had the fresh and spontaneous attitude toward his sacred works that Eccard had.[101] Winterfeld made the mistake of perceiving Bach one-sidedly in terms of his relation to congregational singing. He resented that Bach dispensed with the *active* participation of the congregation and subjected the chorale, which long tradition had made familiar to the congregation, to sophisticated elaboration. Generally speaking, Winterfeld took exception to the unpopular element, a quality that is as characteristic of Bach's church music as it is of Gothic cathedrals. In his opinion, Bach's art was a closed book to the layman, thus diverting attention from its content to its form. By being fully comprehensible only to the expert, Bach's art did not belong to the church. In Winterfeld's opinion, Bach had failed to attain the true ideal of church music, because his art was all too heavily burdened by the intellect.

These are Scheibe's old reproaches, which, as demonstrated here, are heard time and again throughout history. Winterfeld was the only one, however, who publicly agreed with Bach's major critic. He said (p. 405), "I believe I am not in error when I assert" that these attacks by Scheibe "expressed frankly the conviction of a great many of Bach's contemporaries." Nonetheless, Winterfeld's and Scheibe's arguments were not effective. They can be evaluated and understood only as expressions of their own time. For in the final analysis, popularity was not of prime concern to Bach. To be generally understood was less important to him than was the sacred structure as such, whose churchly quality did not need to be understood by everyone. Its religious character nevertheless remained untouched, somewhat analogous to the Baroque monastery church, which also loses none of its sacred majesty although one may not grasp the secrets of its proportions.

In contrast to von Winterfeld's ideal of a popular kind of sacred music, Bach represents church music, lifted to the highest possible level of spirituality. The stylistic soil in which Bach was rooted was completely different from the soil that nourished Eccard. Just as various intellectual attitudes exist, various religious attitudes and expressions are equally possible. This the Age of Romanticism could not see, because in terms of church music it oriented itself solely toward the sixteenth century. As much as this epoch differed in practically every respect from Rationalism, in this one point, the prejudice against Bach's style of church music, Romanticism remained indebted to Rationalism. Bach simply cannot be interpreted as deriving from Palestrina. Interrelations are of no help here. After all, it was by no means the goal of the Romantic age to discover Bach *per se*. To the contrary, Bach was to be placed into the mainstream of the intellectual currents of the time. While the Palestrina ideal closed the church to Bach, the Handel movement opened the large concert halls to Bach's sacred music. Nothing could document the crisis in Protestant church music more clearly than the fact that the most valuable musical heritage of the Lutheran church was now entrusted to a new life in a concert setting. With this, Bach was removed from his congregation and declared to be a supra-denominational master.

J.S. Bach in the Concerts of German Orchestral and Choral Societies

The appearance of Bach in the concert hall is indissolubly associated with the Berlin Singakademie. On January 21, 1794, while Fasch was still alive, music by J.S. Bach was rehearsed for the first time.[102] "Today the beginning was made in rehearsing J.S. Bach's Motet No. 1." These were the words Fasch entered into the society's attendance record on that memorable day.[103] Hardly three years had passed since the founding of this new choral society when Bach was introduced with one of his motets. This January day in 1794 that marked the beginning of a Bach revival by the Berlin Singakademie came before the general turning point within the Bach movement. At that time, neither the first new publications of music by Bach nor Forkel's Bach biography had appeared. It was not until four years later that the *Allgemeine Musikalische Zeitung* was founded, while A.E. Müller did not assume the Thomas cantorate until 1800, the year of Fasch's death. With an almost prescient sense of the spirit of the time the Singakademie began its study of Bach, using the master's motets that Fasch had copied. By June, 1794, the motet *Komm, Jesu, komm* had been studied in frequent rehearsals. In the same month, work began on the second motet *(Fürchte dich nicht)*,[104] and by August the challenge of Bach's great 8-part motet, *Singet dem Herrn ein neues Lied*,[105] had been taken on. Rehearsals of these three works continued until the end of the year, and from then on these three works became an essential part of the repertoire of the Singakademie.

Two years later than Bach, Graun found his way into the evening rehearsals of the Society. His *Tod Jesu* was the first work with instrumental accompaniment performed in public by the Singakademie (on April 12, 1796).[106] Thereafter the performance of this Passion-Cantata became the annual Good Friday music of the Berliners. "Ramler's poem may be as it is, and Graun's music, too; enough, their work has created for itself an audience, a trust, that no later work can upset."[107] And so Graun's *Tod Jesu* was able to stay in the repertoire of the Berlin Singakademie without any notable interruptions until 1884.

In 1800, after Fasch's death, Karl Friedrich Zelter (1758-1832) took over the direction of the Singakademie and hence the responsibility for its Bach activities, which he seemed to be called upon to continue like no one else in Berlin at that time. For Zelter was still in close contact with the Bach tradition. He knew personally not only Wilhelm Friedemann and Carl Philipp Emanuel but also Bach's pupils Kirnberger and Agricola. In a letter to Goethe[108] he also named such lesser known Bach interpreters as Ring, Bertuch and Schmalz, who "allowed almost nothing else to be heard than pieces by old Bach," which he himself had been teaching his pupils for a long time. Furthermore, Zelter owned a remarkably extensive and valuable collection of Bach autographs and manuscripts, which had come into his possession from C.P.E. Bach's estate by way of Pölchau and Alexander Mendelssohn (Felix's father).[109] As a former student at the Joachimsthal Gymnasium, he too, like Forkel, must have come into contact with the treasures of that institution's library.[110] This is proven, particularly from 1807 on, by the programs of the instrumental concerts of the Singakademie.

For in this year Zelter founded a small orchestral society, the so-called *Ripienschule*. Initially limited to chamber music, this group was later to become important for the performance of choral works with orchestra. At first, however, the last years of Fasch's life and the first years of Zelter's directorship were devoted to the study of sacred a cappella music. Rehearsed, besides Bach's motets, were above all choruses by Fasch, Reichardt, Vogler, Lotti, Durante, Leo, Naumann, Palestrina (first performed in public in 1801), Handel, Haydn, Graun and Zelter. In 1807, Handel's *Alexander's Feast* was heard for the first time.[111] In that year Zelter began—independently of the Singakademie's choral activities—a new venture. With ten talented members he began to rehearse separately in the *Ripienschule* instrumental compositions by Bach.[112] Although at first more arranging was done than Bach's music could really tolerate, the brave effort on behalf of the old instrumental music eventually outweighs the reservations one may have for historical reasons. All in all, history is greatly indebted to Zelter.

In April 1807 the beginning was made with the E-Major Fugue from the *Well-Tempered Clavier* (Book II), which was presented—and we are immediately reminded of Mozart—in a version arranged for string quartet. From these frequent encounters with arrangements of Bach's works for string quartet (in print, as well; see footnote 83), we may conclude that transferring polyphonic clavier pieces into the sonorous sphere of string instruments was an essential trait of the new concept of Bach. It exemplified the desire to get away from the rigid sound of the harpsichord and to enter the emotion-filled world of the string instruments. This fateful burdening of Bach's instrumental music with emotion had already begun with Mozart (in 1782). Such an excess of emotion is even today found tolerable, indeed indispensable, by the majority of Bach interpreters and audiences alike. The fact that Zelter arranged the *Ricercare* from the *Musical Offering* for strings and practiced this version in 1808 with his instrumentalists,[113] as Edwin Fischer still does today with his chamber orchestra,[114] is typical proof that the pathos with which Bach is played now did not emanate from the Wagner generation, but had already begun with Mozart, although there with much less intensity. Only at the beginning of the twentieth century, when conscience began to bother some music historians, was an attempt made to restore Bach to his rightful place, and with the reintroduction of the harpsichord into chamber music at least a certain part of the Romantic Bach interpretation was cancelled. One had to be well-educated in history in order to know how even to ask questions about Bach. Such training in history was still lacking in the Romantic period, in which historical research was still in its infancy. The style in which Bach's music was performed by the Singakademie was colored, too, by the sentiments and emotions characteristic of the epoch.

The *Ripienschule,* which sought to gain possession of Bach as an instrumental composer, performed the famous D minor Clavier Concerto already in its founding year (1807). From here on, this concerto—though it may go back to an Italian original—has won the particular affection of all Bach devotees. On February 19, 1808, the fifth Brandenburg Concerto was played. Music by Bach was also frequently sung and played in the private weekly music sessions held by Zelter in his home,[115] while the master's motets continued to be sung in the regular choral rehearsals of the Singakademie. Except for the motet *Lobet den Herrn, alle Heiden,* which at that time was still unknown, the other five motets appeared at almost regular intervals, as did the motet *Ich lasse dich nicht,* which was only later revealed to be a work, copied by Sebastian Bach, but composed by his uncle, Johann Christoph.[116] Also a Christmas work, entitled *Kündlich gross ist das gottselige Geheimnis,* which Zelter compiled presumably from choruses by Graun, included two choral movements by Sebastian Bach.[117] Considered to be a work by the Thomas cantor, it enjoyed great popularity in the motet repertoire of the Singakademie.

In the rehearsals of the chorus, Bach as composer of vocal music was until 1811 identical with Bach the composer of the motets. In that year occurred the breakthrough—though nine years after Müller's efforts with his Thomas choristers, but with much greater élan—to Bach's world of cantatas, Masses and Passion music. In October 1811, Zelter presented his singers with Bach's *B minor Mass;* but the study of the difficult work had to be broken off after the *Kyrie.* In September 1813, he rehearsed it with his chorus at least once all the way through (though without orchestra). In the meantime (1812) Zelter had prepared his singers for this task with the short A Major Mass, and in the same year he also worked for the first time on a cantata *(Nimm von uns Herr, du treuer Gott).*

The activities of the *Ripienschule* during the years 1812-13 were of almost equal importance for the revival of Bach's instrumental music. The violin concertos of the master (in A minor and E Major) and the glorious Double Concerto (in D minor) were played, as were parts of the *Art of the Fugue,* arranged for string quartet. Because a good bass singer was available, several bass arias from the cantatas also were heard, among them *Ich will den Kreuzstab gerne tragen.* In 1813 Zelter dared to approach larger orchestral works, such as the D Major and C Major Overtures, the B minor Suite and the fourth and sixth Brandenburg Concertos. The year 1814 brought in addition to repeat performances of already familiar works important new performances: the so-called *Peasant Cantata,* the *Trio* and *Ricercare* from the *Musical Offering* and the first two Trio Sonatas for organ. December of 1814 and the spring of 1815 were taken up by the choir with renewed, energetic rehearsals of the *B minor Mass.* In the summer of 1815, the Passions finally awoke from their hundred year sleep. Parts of the *St. John Passion* were rehearsed at the end of May, and shortly thereafter, the study of the *St. Matthew Passion* began. Fourteen years before Mendelssohn presented the work to the entire musical world, Zelter was acquainting his singers with the choruses of this great Passion music.

However, Zelter did not prepare these works, which he taught his chorus to sing from his place at the piano, for public performance. Throughout his life, he did not believe that Bach's music could possibly exert a widespread effect. He was even skeptical about public performances of the motets, as is implied by his incredulous remark, "Some in the audience acted as if they had really liked it [the motet, *Singet dem Herrn*]."[118] Nevertheless he was proud of this achievement by his Society. On January 7, 1823, he wrote,[119] "The fact that over the last 30 years Sebastian Bach's motets have been appreciated more and more, and that indeed their difficulties are faced intrepidly, is a triumph of the Singakademie. It demonstrates that learning masterpieces, be they pleasing or not, is of indisputable benefit." With this, Zelter meant to say that he cultivated Bach's music for the sake of the vocal mastery his works require, and found his reward in attaining this goal; but he still continued to doubt that the master could become popular, could be understood by the general public. Owning as

he did both scores and performing parts of most of the choral works, Zelter—
had he thought otherwise—would surely have presented Bach's vocal works in
public concerts with his *Ripienschule* and some of his singers. Not even for the
motets, the sole works of Bach that he could perform in their original form, did
Zelter want to take this risk. Yet in his inmost soul he must have understood the
motets, for otherwise he could not have written to Goethe,[120] "If on some
happy day I could let you . . . hear one of Sebastian Bach's motets, you would
think yourself at the center of the world, for a man like you belongs to it."

He was even more mistrustful of the other church compositions. His
attitude toward them was similar to that of Carl von Winterfeld. In these works
he found Bach generally in need of improvement, burdened more than in other
works by the archaic elements of the previous century. If one wanted to make
these works by Bach his own, one had to remove the master's wig, which hid
what was truly masterly in his creations. As Zelter put it:

> Old Bach, with all his originality, is a son of his country and of his age. He could not escape
> French influence, especially that of Couperin. One wants to show one's willingness to oblige,
> and so something is created that does not endure. One can, however, disassociate him from
> this foreign element; it comes off like thin froth, and the shining contents lie immediately
> beneath. Consequently [I] have arranged some of his church compositions, solely for my
> own pleasure, and my heart tells me that old Bach nods approval, just as the worthy Haydn
> used to say, "Yes, yes, that is how I wanted it!" They will probably come and say one should
> not lay hands on something like this, and they are not entirely wrong, because not *everyone*
> may do so; but for me it is a means that leads me to the perception and admiration of what is
> true.[121]

But Goethe's critical mind demanded an accounting from Zelter. He asked,[122]
"I beg you most kindly, to devote a few weighty words to what you call the
French froth, which you feel able to separate from the basic German element,
and in some way to bring this informative relationship before my outer and
inner senses." This clarification, however, eluded Zelter. He could only
answer,[123] "What I called the French froth in Sebastian Bach's art is admittedly
not so easily lifted off that one can seize it. It is like the ether, everywhere
present yet untouchable."

Everyone is steeped in his own time, and Zelter could not transcend the
bounds of his generation. For him, who was the great representative of the
Berlin *Liederschule,* Bach had to be seen in this perspective; that is, he had to be
modernized. Zelter revised Bach's church compositions for himself alone, in
the belief of serving Bach's cause thereby. In doing so, he did not dispute the
seriousness and profundity of Bach's perception. Only what was dated was to
be removed. "Through the orchestra, things have become dressed up too much,
and the style of dress has gone out of fashion."[124] Furthermore, with Bach "the
instrumental style has also found its way into the vocal music, which should be

independent."[125] That Bach made his singers sing "transcribed instrumental music"[126] ran counter to the basic demands that the adherents of the a cappella ideal made of choral music. "In the vocal pieces, often something else is expressed than what the words imply, a fact which has been sufficiently criticized."[127] Bach was held to lack what this period praised as the highest goal: songfulness; and hence also comprehensibility by the senses in the realm of the purely vocal.

One aspect Zelter and his contemporaries could not yet see because they lacked sufficient knowledge of history, namely that Bach had taken over this *modishness* from a long choral tradition, that he inherited his *wig* from the German sixteenth and seventeenth centuries. The archaic legacy of melodic ornamentation *(coloration)*, which had nothing to do with Couperin's nimble-fingered embellishments *(Manieren)*, was not understood by the Romanticists. Since Bach's choral style could not be understood from the perspective of Palestrina or Handel, Bach's music simply had to be bent to fit the ideal of the time. This applied to his texts as well, for Bach was dramatically all too *present* for that time. He offended the religious sensibilities of Pietistically-attuned souls, who preferred to surrender themselves to inward meditation and tranquil self-absorption. Thus Bach was drawn into the Romantic ideology where his works were arranged and adapted to the taste of the time.

In this context the cultivation of Bach by the Berlin Singakademie must be understood. Its director, Zelter, was, with Forkel and Rochlitz, the central personality in the Romantic Bach movement. For Berlin, he was indeed the actual discoverer of Bach's *oeuvre*. Because of its selfless endeavors on behalf of the works of the Thomas cantor, one could well call his Singakademie Germany's first *Bach Society*. That Zelter himself did not dare to take the step of performing Bach's music in public, does not diminish the value of the labors he accomplished for Bach. That he did not always have such a Romantic perception of Bach, in fact, that from time to time he even had direct access to the master's world, some of his statements may demonstrate. He said,[128] "A theme is a just-born inspiration that, like the spark struck from a stone, springs from the first coincidental contact of the foot with the pedal. . . . Even taking into consideration what can be said against him, this Leipzig cantor is a phenomenon of God: plain, yet unexplainable. I could call out to him. You have given me work, I have brought you back to life." Or elsewhere Zelter said, "Of the old Bach, one could say, the pedal is the basic element in the development of his fathomless spirit, and, had he had no feet, he would not have attained his greatness of mind."[129] Zelter understood here the central role which the organ played in Bach's creativity. Bach thus was seen not as the beginning but as the end of a long musical development.

These statements by Zelter were all due to Goethe's inquiring curiosity, to Goethe's desire to come to an understanding of the essence of Bach's art. Yet

Goethe's relationship to Bach cannot be deduced from the intellectual posture of Romanticism. Upon hearing the music of the great Thomas cantor it seemed to Goethe "as though eternal harmony were conversing with itself, as might have happened in God's bosom just before he created the world,"[130] This is in direct contrast to the view of the Romanticist E.T.A. Hoffmann, for whom Bach's "musical number relationships, indeed the *mystical* rules of counterpoint, evoked horror within his heart."[131] Goethe had a sure, albeit incomprehensible, awareness of the great mental currents in Bach's art. This is similar to what Nietzsche, too, could not grasp intellectually but still sensed intuitively. Nietzsche said,[132] "Inasmuch as one hears Bach's music not as an accomplished and experienced expert of counterpoint and all the varieties of the fugal style, and accordingly must do without the actual artistic enjoyment of it, it will seem to us as hearers of his music, (to express ourselves grandly with Goethe's words) as if we were present when God created the world. In other words, we sense that something great is in the process of formation but is not yet actually *there*—namely, our great modern music."

Confronting the purely instrumental music, Goethe was bewildered. He could approach it only with the aid of comparisons from the world of the observable. In his *Wilhelm Meister,* he said, "Melodies, songs and runs without words or sense seem to me to resemble butterflies or those colorful birds that float in the air before our eyes."[133] For that reason he had to value the *Capriccio on the Departure of His Most Beloved Brother,* the sole piece of program music that Bach has given us, so highly. In what he called the "trumpeter's little piece", he could give free rein to his imagination and see Bach for once in a truly pictorial manner.[134] However, Goethe did not remain—as perhaps in this instance—on a merely superficial level, but fought for an understanding of Bach's art. Access to it was, however, not made easy for him, because, even before he became acquainted with Bach, he had heard Handel's *Alexander's Feast* and the *Messiah* in 1780 and had come into contact with Palestrina in 1788 in Italy; that is, he had heard music of the favorites of the Romantic age before he was introduced to Sebastian Bach's art. It was his personal friendship with Zelter that led Goethe toward the spiritual greatness of Bach, while his experience with Bach's clavier music was gained (in 1814) from the organist Schütz, who was also the inspector of the baths in Berka. Schütz had acquired copies of works by Bach from Bach's last pupil, Kittel, in Erfurt and had also bought some from C.P.E. Bach.[135] Goethe particularly asked time and again to have some of the chorales and parts of the *Well-Tempered Clavier,* the music of which both he and Schütz owned, played for him in Weimar and in Berka. "God bless copper, printing and every other means of reproduction, so that something good that once existed cannot perish," exclaimed Goethe[136] when he heard of the fire in Berka which also consumed Schütz's music library. Besides Schütz and Zelter, it was above all the young Felix Mendelssohn who became

Goethe's musical advisor and his interpreter of Bach's art. Mendelssohn was an affectionately-received guest of Goethe's four times,[137] and each time he had to go to the piano and play works by Bach. Thus Goethe heard the Inventions, the *Well-Tempered Clavier* and the D Major Overture.[138] Goethe also had Mendelssohn play compositions of various masters in historical sequence, in order to see "how they had improved matters."[139] He also followed the writings about Bach with eager interest.[140] All these expressions of his wide-ranging mind showed that a history of the Bach movement must not fail to include Goethe's endeavors at coming to terms with Bach.

In the first quarter of the nineteenth century, Zelter and his Berlin Singakademie were the center in which Bach's music was sung and played. The work done there for Bach had a way of overshadowing the Bach activities that were going on at the same time in other German cities. Those cities, however, demonstrated how far the Romantic Bach movement had spread.

In Leipzig, Thomas cantor A.E. Müller left his position in 1810. His place was taken by Johann Gottfried Schicht, the conductor of the Gewandhaus concerts. In this capacity, he had already given a public performance of a Mass for double chorus by Bach on February 7, 1805 and had seen to it that it was printed in 1806. (However, this work, which Rochlitz discussed enthusiastically at the time,[141] was soon proven by Bach scholars not to be authentic).[142] During his time as Thomas cantor (1810-23) Schicht paid only very slight attention to the works of Sebastian Bach. Nevertheless, Schicht deserves a measure of gratitude since, as editor and text arranger of Bach's motets (see above), he at least had these works of the master sung frequently.[143] It was, however, no particular accomplishment to have kept these choral works, which had gradually become a matter of tradition in Leipzig, alive. The revival of Bach cantatas that was begun by Müller was, on the other hand, not continued by Schicht. Only at the end of his life did he fall back on a church work by Bach, namely the cantata *Es erhub sich ein Streit,* which he performed on September 29, 1822 in the Nicolai Church and then repeated the next Sunday in the Thomas Church.[144] Under Schicht's successor, Christian Theodor Weinlig, who was Wagner's first teacher, performances of Bach cantatas seem, despite Weinlig's tenure of twenty years (1823-42), to have come to a complete standstill.[145] The motets, however, retained their traditional place in the Saturday vesper services of the Thomas Choir.[146] During Weinlig's cantorate, the Bach movement in Leipzig seems on the whole to have remained quite stagnant. Even in the press, there were complaints about the noticeable lack of Bach performances. "Especially at times when there is a great influx of visitors, one might wish that works of our J.S. Bach, which many are with good reason eager to hear, be performed more often than appears to be the case just now!"[147] Out of Bach's entire *oeuvre,* the motets were in fact the only compositions of the master that were continuously kept alive in Leipzig. As late as 1830, one did not know what to do with Bach's other works, and that in the city in which Bach had lived and worked. For instance, in 1826 Breitkopf & Härtel still owned unpublished autograph compositions by Bach which they planned only now to publish from time to time.[148]

Bach fared no better in other cities. In Zurich, Nägeli sat on his Bach manuscripts, of which he had thus far published only the tiniest portion.[149] Around 1820 and in several places, the energy seems to have slackened that had been so vigorously expended on behalf of the great Thomas cantor at the beginning of the century. The only event of note in Hamburg in this entire period was a benefit concert in 1808, in which, among other works, a *Gloria* by Bach was performed under the direction of J.F. Hönicke.[150] In Vienna, by contrast, Bach found a home in the private concerts of the music historian R.G. Kiesewetter, where serious efforts were made in behalf of Bach's church music. For the years 1816-20, the following works are known to have been performed in the home of Kiesewetter, who was the owner of a magnificent library of old masterpieces of German and Italian music: the *Kyrie* and *Gloria* from the *B minor Mass*, the motet *Jesu meine Freude*, and the five-part *Magnificat*, which was performed twice with orchestra.[151]

Within Germany itself, the 1820s brought a certain reawakening of enthusiasm for Bach. There Bach's art was cultivated by two just recently founded choral societies. In Heidelberg, it was the great jurist A. Fr. J. Thibaut, who, thoroughly versed in music, from 1825 on championed with his *Singverein* Bach's vocal music,[152] although esthetically he was entirely under the spell of Palestrina. His monograph, *Über Reinheit der Tonkunst*, promoted with the enthusiastic words of a layman the a cappella ideal in the church. With Sebastian Bach he found fault because he was too much inclined toward "bringing the art of figuration to its highest culmination... without taking into consideration what appeals to the pious nature of the people."[153] In Frankfurt, Johann Nepomuk Schelble in 1818 founded the *Cäcilienverein* (St. Cecilia Society), which was later to become so important for the Bach movement. The first phase of this Frankfurt choral society's existence was devoted mainly to Handel and the masters of a cappella music.[154] Yet already in 1823, the *Allgemeine Musikalische Zeitung* noted[155] that music by Bach, Handel and Mozart was continually performed, along with Italian composers. This comment is expressly confirmed by other reports[156] as well as by the public performance of the motet *Fürchte dich nicht* (on December 30, 1825).[157] It is also known that Schelble met the young Felix Mendelssohn in 1822, and that, immediately after a Bach motet had been sung at the *Cäcilienverein*, Mendelssohn improvised on the piano and thereby won Schelble's admiration and friendship.[158] Finally, on March 10, 1828, besides compositions by Mozart and Handel, the *Credo* from Bach's *B minor Mass* was presented, with an array of 172 participants. This was its first performance for the Frankfurt music lovers.[159] In other words, there was a *public* performance of a major choral work with orchestra by Bach, one year before Mendelssohn performed the *St. Matthew Passion* in Berlin.

Also two Berlin Bach performances which preceded Mendelssohn's overwhelmingly successful achievement, and which did not take place in the Singakademie, must still be mentioned. In 1827, the organist August Wilhelm Bach, a pupil of Zelter, performed the *Et incarnatus est* from the *B minor Mass* at the *Marienkirche*.[160] In the next year the Director of the Opera, Gasparo Spontini, inserted the *Credo* from Bach's *B minor Mass* into a program that also included Beethoven's Fifth Symphony, his Overture to *Coriolanus* and parts of the *Missa Solemnis* as well as C.P.E. Bach's *Heilig*.[161] The performance itself (which took place on April 30, 1828) was but faintly praised by the critic (A.B. Marx). Spontini presented the *Credo* only in fragmentary form; the instrumentation had been changed (for instance, clarinets were used in the *Crucifixus!*); and the whole was preceded by an introduction of C.P.E. Bach's composition.[162] Nevertheless, this concert, which was given in the Opera for a charitable purpose, meant that a choral work by Sebastian Bach was for the first time presented to the Berlin public; and for Bach himself it represented the official move from the church to the opera house. On the other hand, the performance of the same *Credo* in the Frankfurt *Cäcilienverein* (two months previously), represented Sebastian Bach's first appearance in a public concert. These surprisingly numerous performances of parts of Bach's *B minor Mass,* which were probably encouraged by Nägeli's announcement of his forthcoming publication of the work, extended to the immediate time of Mendelssohn's revival of the *St. Matthew Passion*. This performance was, besides Paganini's first appearance in Berlin, the main event that awaited Berlin's musical public in 1829. For the historic epoch of Romanticism it signified the final breakthrough of the Bach movement into the public domain.

The Revival of the St. Matthew Passion *by Felix Mendelssohn-Bartholdy*

The conditions which surrounded the revival of the *St. Matthew Passion* had a great deal to do with the phenomenal impact of the work. That the performance was even planned and ventured at all was due to Mendelssohn's obsessive passion for music in general and to his enthusiasm for Bach in particular, as well as to Devrient's fine flair for the practical aspects of the entire undertaking.

For external reasons alone, the Berlin of 1829 was the only place where this spark could be struck and ignite, just as eight years previously, it was only there that *Der Freischütz* could have become *the* German national opera. At that time, a champion was needed who could oppose Spontini, the leader of the Italian party, the ruling head of the Opera and the protégé of the Conservatives, whose opera *Olympia* had just been produced with incredible pomp. This champion would have to be a musician of Romantic passions, one who could represent the German cause. Thus it happened that Weber, whose *Freischütz* expressed in a unique way the Romantic outlook of the time, was chosen by the party of the progressive Germans to lead their fanatic fight against Spontini, the man of the court and the nobility. One need only hear the enthusiastic voice of E.T.A. Hoffmann, who after the experience of the performance of *Der Freischütz* wrote, "In his newest, greatest work, he [Weber] has created a monument that should turn out to be epoch-making in the history of opera.[163] With regard to the music, we must express the opinion, and do so without hesitation, that since Mozart nothing of greater significance for German opera has been written than Beethoven's *Fidelio* and this *Freischütz*."[164] *Der Freischütz* embodied the wish fulfillment of the Romanticists. Here was an opera that no longer exhibited hollow splendor and cold mythology, but one that, with the Romanticists' imaginative sense for the supernatural, unleashed irrational forces,[165] and let them carry on their demonic work. But for the sake of relief, the opera gave also a popular portrayal of the hunter's life, of nature and the forest. It was the representation of the *miraculous* and the demonic, juxtaposed with the representation of piety and nature, that secured the victory for *Freischütz*. This opera, with its Romantic traits, had the good fortune to be born into a Romantic world.

In 1829, the emotional conditions were still the same; the atmosphere of 1821 still prevailed in Berlin. What *Der Freischütz* had offered to the people still expressed the possibilities of artistic experience. Paganini's appearance in Berlin (1829) was yet another powerful reminder of the demonic side of Romanticism.[166] It forced even those with the inner stability of A.B. Marx and Rellstab to lose their emotional balance. Marx confessed, "It was the first time that I have been confronted in the realm of my art with a demonic nature."[167] Still completely overcome by the impression, he admitted that it was impossible for him "to separate the person from the artistic achievement, to separate what is most external from what is most emotional."[168] Zelter, too, said "His personality is thus *more* than music, without being profound music."[169] Beyond the technique, which aroused unlimited admiration, there was something else that Paganini and only Paganini was: the demonic. It radiated from his appearance and with the power of suggestion it made the audience succumb to his spell, virtually electrifying them. Here music was no longer perceived as music, but as sorcery. Paganini knew this. He was conscious of the Romantic glorification of the demonic side of his personality. Such glorification was his conscious goal, which transcended mere interpretation of particular works. He sought this image of himself. He wanted to read in the reviews words such as these: "When he has left the stage, one can no longer understand why they still perform music by Mozart and Beethoven, until he returns." These are the words of A.B. Marx, who was usually so objective.[170] And Rellstab called Paganini the "Orpheus of the violin,"[171] whose musical wonders were the talk of the entire city and who in his entire being seemed akin to Beethoven.[172] So Beethoven too was to be demonized. He too was to be exposed to the distorted light of the artistic atmosphere of Berlin, in which on March 11, 1829, in the midst of the fevered triumphs of Paganini,[173] Bach's *St. Matthew Passion* finally appeared.

Only in terms of this environment can the singularity of the colossal impact of Bach's work and the nature of the approval it evoked at its revival be explained. Zelter had spent years to give Mendelssohn the material that would be needed for a public performance of the *St. Matthew Passion*. Zelter had succeeded early in arousing an interest in Bach in the talented boy, whom he instructed in composition. By the fall of 1820 he could already admit the eleven-year-old Felix and his musical sister Fanny to the Singakademie. Here Felix, who initially sang in the alto section, came to know the world of J.S. Bach. He must soon have become well acquainted with the master's motets, which were still being studied diligently. In the winter of 1822-23, Zelter resumed rehearsing the *St. John Passion*.[174] Experiencing this music must have had a powerful impact on Mendelssohn, although a complete performance never took place, and although again Zelter did not refrain from making changes in the score. On April 4, 1822, Zelter wrote into his copy of the *Passion*, which he had rearranged for practical use, that he had "wanted to make a good deal of it practicable for the abilities of his performers, who were, after all, about a hundred years younger; and if I should ever encounter the good Bach somewhere, I imagine that I would come to terms with him about it."[175] In making his revisions for the sake of performability and easier comprehension, Zelter claimed for his age, that admired the Berlin *Liederstil*, a personal right to Bach. The original form of many of the Bach cantatas in Zelter's possession was altered by him, and they appeared in their new form in the choral rehearsals of the Singakademie. It was in this form that Felix, who also participated regularly in the orchestra rehearsals, became acquainted with them. In the course of time, he learned the entire Bach repertoire of the Singakademie. By 1823, he already knew the *St. Matthew Passion* from choral rehearsals or from private lessons with Zelter, who owned a copy of the score. From here on his thoughts and hopes were directed towards obtaining a copy of the work for himself; and indeed his grandmother asked his violin teacher, Eduard Rietz, to make a copy for him for Christmas 1823. Now began Mendelssohn's study of Bach's mighty Passion music, which five years later was to celebrate its resurrection.

(Besides Schünemann's thorough description [see above], the best material on the performance and the preparations for it are Eduard Devrient's *Erinnerungen an Mendelssohn* and the article by Friedrich Smend, *Zelter oder Mendelssohn?* in the *Monatsschrift für Gottesdienst und Kirchliche Kunst* [vol. 34, No. 7].)

The daring idea of a public performance of the work came to Mendelssohn and his imaginative and energetic friend, Eduard Devrient, during one of the rehearsals that Felix held weekly with a small private choir in his parents' home. Devrient, who in his way seems to have had an affinity with the demonic nature of Paganini, was the driving force here. The first task was to win Zelter, who had little confidence in the effectiveness of Bach's music, for the undertaking. Yet as a man of his generation, Zelter could not comprehend what was happening here. He was unaware of the forces behind this surge of activity. He did not know the demonic side of Devrient, who wanted the deed to be accomplished even at a time when Mendelssohn shrank back in the face of resistance. "Well, if it were only as easy as that!" said Zelter, "But more is needed than we have to offer nowadays."[176] Zelter still had access to the religious world of Sebastian Bach. He sensed the difference between Bach's orthodox piety and the religious sentiments of the Romantic age; hence his misgivings that even the two fanatic youths could not dispel, although in the end they were able to obtain their teacher's acquiescence.

Now the practical preparations could begin. The board of directors of the Singakademie had to be won over; the hall had to be rented; and finally, after the choir had grown from rehearsal to rehearsal, the soloists had to be engaged from the Opera. This point was reached after only nine rehearsals. Given the choir's unheard-of rigorous training and thorough knowledge of Bach, this seems at least understandable. Zelter had actually done a substantial part of the preparation himself by having created the instrument that carried the performance—the choir. Yet it remains Mendelssohn's achievement to have recognized that the time had come for the actual experience of Bach's art.

This was an art that, of course, had but little to do with the essential nature of Bach. For Mendelssohn and Devrient, it "could not be the purpose to give the work, which was influenced in many points by the taste of its time, in its entirety. Yet we had to convey the impression of its outstanding value."[177] This was accomplished not only by making cuts, but also because Mendelssohn, "by clever calculation of his resources," knew how to make "the antiquated masterpiece modern, intelligible and lifelike again."[178] Mendelssohn thus restored and revised the *Passion* music in the spirit of his time. He was allowed to do so, because his contemporaries had given him *carte blanche* for his endeavors. For "there are some old compositions that we cannot reproduce, that we must instead resurrect!"[179] With full consciousness, the Romantic age thus took possession of Bach. Because the question of the authentic Bach was not asked, there arose a Bach designed solely for the Romantic age. By such questionable means as cuts, changes in instrumentation, melodic and textual alterations, one extracted from the

Leipzig master's work whatever Bach, in this Romantic guise, could say to the new age, rather than what he actually had to say.

Thus Romantic life was breathed into the *St. Matthew Passion,* and its essential nature was thereby transformed. Arbitrary revisions in the score altered the picture to a great extent. Zelter's copy of the score of the *St. Matthew Passion,* including his revisions, has been preserved. It may have been similar in some respects to the version produced by Mendelssohn and Devrient. After all, Mendelssohn had learned his Bach from Zelter, and had not been Zelter's pupil in composition in vain. But he did not use Zelter's arrangement. (Devrient's *Erinnerungen* clearly contradict Schünemann's views on this point.)[180] Nevertheless Zelter's revisions may provide some indication of the form of Mendelssohn's score, which can be reconstructed only from the extant program booklet and from the individual reviews that appeared in the press.

Zelter owned a copy of the score that had been made by Kirnberger after an early version of the original. In this copy of Zelter, the chorale "O Mensch, bewein dein Sünde gross" is still lacking, while in the recitatives long, sustained bass notes appear in place of the short notes of the continuo. The revisions in Zelter's handwriting begin with the vocal part of the recitatives. Zelter simplified the vocal part considerably by lowering the high notes (usually by an octave) and by changing difficult intervals.[181] The arias, which were revised in similar fashion, suffered changes in the text as well. Furthermore, difficult vocal figures and syncopations were made to conform to song-like symmetry and simplicity. According to A.B. Marx,[182] who once had the vocal parts in his own hands, "the recitatives and the choral parts, which now and then ended in wondrous and flowery melismas," had been "rewritten" by Zelter, "more or less in the style of Graun." To bring Bach back to life, he had to be made into a Classical master, who could be easily understood by the admirers of the a cappella style as well. To conform to these requirements, Bach naturally was given a completely different appearance. And so his music was rephrased, and the terraced registrations that characterized his time were transformed into the swell-pedal dynamics of Romanticism. Even a fleeting glance at Zelter's score reveals how deeply the alterations, from which at least the chorus was for the most part free, cut into the essence of the work.

Mendelssohn's version, which for the Berliners became an aural experience, and which can be reconstructed to some extent from comments and reviews, was a severely cut, distorted version of Bach's original. Devrient provided a vivid account of how this version came about. He met often with Mendelssohn to discuss how to shorten the score for the performance. The outcome of these deliberations was that "the majority of the arias" were omitted, and of the others, "only the introductions, the so-called

Accompagnements," were retained. The Gospel text, too, was radically shortened, except for the parts belonging to the Passion story itself.[183] Luther's saying, *"Das Wort sie sollen lassen stahn"* ("The Word they shall let stand"), found no echo in the Age of Romanticism. The strength that inheres in fidelity to the biblical word was no longer felt, for the main emphasis was no longer laid on the story of the Passion according to dogma. Thus Devrient could say that what they "had finally determined upon, seems to have been the right thing, for it has been adopted at most of the later performances."[184] Thus the success of the work not only legitimized the changes made in the original work but also flatly declared them obligatory.

This abbreviated version of the *Passion* was by no means performed with its authentic sound. Zelter's full score has already documented how much the dynamics and phrasing, indeed even the text, were made to conform to the ideas of the time, how the recitatives and arias were robbed of their linear freedom of movement and forced into the standardized symmetry of the Berlin *Liederschool* style.

Not only the structure was altered and adapted to the taste of the time. The sound, too, was made to undergo the transformation of a century. By conducting the work from the piano, Mendelssohn introduced into the orchestra an instrument whose sound fell outside the stylistic range of Bach's instrumental forces. Then Mendelssohn not only had the chorale that floats above the opening chorus sung by the eight (!) soloists and individual choral sopranos, but also reinforced it with clarinets and flutes that doubled it an octave higher.[185] The same forces were assigned also to the final chorale of Part I.[186] In Mendelssohn's version the clarinets, which Bach did not yet know, took over the parts of the oboe da caccia and oboe d'amore—that is, the most modern instrument took over the part of those *scholastic* instruments that Bach still carried with him, as *ballast,* from the old Baroque orchestra. Mendelssohn modernized the work by introducing the clarinets and thus coming closer to the Classical ideal of sound. In some passages he even went beyond this, shifting characteristic moments into the sphere of Romantic sound. For instance, and quite in the manner of the demonic parts of *Der Freischütz,* he underlined the words "Und der Vorhang zerriss im Tempel" ("And the veil of the temple was rent") with agitated tremolos in the violins and violas. For this *miracle,* the Romanticist was not to be satisfied with the more straightforward accompaniment by the continuo instruments. That the review[187] should single out for particular praise this musical portrayal of the earthquake, as well as the tranquil feeling of nature in the ensuing aria "Am Abend da es kühle ward," is as remarkable as it is typical. Among the characteristic features of the Romantic conception of Bach were an excessive fondness for detail, a love for the particular moment, in which one thought to discover related traits. The tradition of performing the chorale "Wenn ich einmal soll scheiden" a cappella also dates from this performance by Mendelssohn. With its unhealthy influence up to the present, this tradition demonstrates that even today, in questions regarding Bach's music, one rather seeks Mendelssohn's advice than that of the Thomas cantor himself, who expressly called for the entire orchestra in undiminished strength to double the singing voices. Finally, the figures for realizing the thorough-bass were missing in Mendelssohn's score, a failure that also characterized the edition of the score which Schlesinger published in 1830. The lack of the figuring and the resultant void in the thorough-bass produced such a noticeable gap in the otherwise full sounding harmony that the complaints about the weak and thin sounding accompaniments of the arias are all too easily understandable.

This gap in the sonorities was all the more out of place as in all other respects the work was presented in a colossal performance style reminiscent of Handel. The chorus consisted of 150 singers, while eight members of the Opera were engaged for the solo parts, among whom the spellbinding personality of Devrient, who sang the role of Christ, stood out. The orchestra was composed of the *Philharmonische Gesellschaft* (Philharmonic Society), which the violinist Rietz had founded, and of a number of amateurs, while the first desk players were drawn from the chamber musicians of the Royal Court Chapel. All the participants performed the work, which was presented for a charitable purpose, without remuneration or even any claim to free tickets.

The performance itself was an extraordinary social event for Berlin, and was attended by the King and the entire court. Its success was sensational. There was only one critical voice, namely that of Hegel, who after the second performance under Mendelssohn's direction (on March 21) expressed the opinion that "this is not real music; one had progressed by now beyond it, although the real thing was still far off."[188] Any other reservations that were expressed preceded the performance. Moritz Hauptmann, who later became Thomas cantor, is of particular interest here. Like Zelter, he thought the time for the resurrection of Bach's *Passion* music had not yet come. Such works "have always been too big for the people, and also now their time is not yet here: the Passion music will not be passionate enough for them!—or will seem outdated in form, tasteless and, because of its passing notes, unacceptable."[189] His pronouncement about Bach's *B minor Mass* is also characteristic for his time. Hauptmann said, "The whole work cannot be taken in as a whole, unless one can hear it well performed in its entirety. One shudders when one thinks of a great performance of this work."[190] This fear of the striking effect which a complete performance of a choral work by Bach would make in the Age of Romanticism is typical of those Romanticists who had not yet entirely lost contact with the past. Like Zelter and Hauptmann, they sensed the responsibility of bringing a modernized, Romanticized Bach before the public. Goethe, too, seems to have suspected something of the magnitude of the risk involved when he wrote to Zelter, "The news of the successful performance of the great old masterpiece . . . makes me think. It seems to me as if I heard the ocean roaring from afar. I offer congratulations upon such a complete attainment of the virtually inconceivable."[191]

The younger generation, however, reacted differently. Having been prepared for emotional sensations by the experience of Weber's *Freischütz* and by the demonic appearance of Paganini, it felt itself ready to take the profoundly stirring impact of this *Passion* music, filled with new life, in stride. Initially it was not yet able to do so, as is demonstrated by A.B. Marx's reaction. Though he had been the one who as journalist had prepared the way for the performance, he was still so much under the spell of the experience on the day after the event that he felt incapable of offering an objective review of the work. For "at this time, minds and hearts are still under the influence of the hallowed chant and its afterglow."[192] Only later did Marx join the debate that arose about the work. The question, "whether even in this most sacred work of music, it was proper for Jesus to be portrayed as actually speaking, even uttering the words of the Last Supper,"[193] was answered by Marx with a reference to the immeasurable profundity of Bach's art in setting the text. Religious questions were thus resolved from an artistic point of view. This is important, because with this, criticism becomes the voice of the public that went to concerts to enjoy the music. Bach was thus freed from the denominational. His *Passion* music had turned into a supradenominational religious experience. One was struck by the "wondrous power of the harmony and the original voice-leading"[194] of the chorales. One also admired the arias with their "often strange, though highly affecting instrumentation."[195] Of the religious experience of the *Passion,* we learn, however, nothing. We learn instead that the work had been "a quite extraordinary sensation in the cultured circle of Berlin,"[196] primarily because Bach appeared, particularly in this work, far ahead of his time,[197] in fact, so far ahead that only now could he be understood and performed properly. One thought the large mixed choirs were actually needed to make a performance of the *St. Matthew Passion* possible. The Romantic Age did not comprehend that such massing of sound, while increasing the effectiveness of the work, sacrificed, on the other hand, the intelligibility of the text, and thus the basic churchly character of the work. The fact that the home of polychoral singing, the church, had been abandoned as well, and with it the reliability of the school choirs, that were trained in a true communal environment, was also overlooked. For otherwise, the historian J.G. Droysen could not have said, "Let us be glad . . . that the most solemn expression of genuine Protestant perception and piety should once again become the property of the time, and we hope the property of the congregation."[198] This indicates a complete failure to understand the shifting of the religious foundation—that is, to understand that none of the prerequisites for a Bach movement in the church existed. Zelter alone sensed the danger that Bach's Passion music was being enjoyed by the public purely as music, independently of the text. Therefore Zelter referred in his foreword to the program booklet to the bond between Bach and Lutheranism. Since he no longer assumed that his contemporaries had any knowledge of it, he provided a historical introduction to the genre of Passion music, "the ultimate purpose of which [was] devotion and elevation of the spirit to the certainty of existence and of immortality."[199] Therefore he advised Stümer, who sang the part of the Evangelist, "not to impede the narration by sentimental retards."[200]

But Zelter's efforts were in vain. His time drove Bach toward an international and supradenominational audience that heard the Passion story as occurring in the *"realm of music,"* not in the *"realm of faith."* The *St. Matthew Passion,* as it was conceived by the Romanticists, was the final goal of religious feeling, not the mediator of the Lutheran dogma. It belonged far more to the friend of music than to the friend of the church, both of whom were at home in different camps. Even for Mendelssohn, who perceived the "true church music" in the a cappella pieces of the sixteenth century,[201] the *St. Matthew Passion* did not mean something intrinsically churchly, as is proven by the simple fact that it was he after all who brought the Passion music into the concert hall.

The success of the work proved that Mendelssohn's deed was in harmony with his time. Berlin alone demanded three performances of the work in 1829,[202] and did not allow performances of the Passion music to be taken away from it in later years. The only city that performed the *St. Matthew Passion* independently of Mendelssohn's accomplishment was Frankfurt.[203] The performance which Schelble gave with his *Cäcilienverein* on May 2, 1829 paralleled Mendelssohn's performance in Berlin. It did not copy the performance as it was done in most other cities. But one aspect of it gives pause for thought. As soon as Bach's *Passion* left the soil of Berlin, criticism set in. Undisputed success eluded the work except in Berlin. For Frankfurt, it was even necessary to rewrite Bach's recitatives completely in Graun's style (which was done by Schelble). For Bach's recitatives were said to reflect the "incompetence of the Germans of that time in mastering the recitative style." In his recitatives Bach left "his sure footing, his German territory, and entered as a stranger into another country whose language he did not know."[204] These are the words of Moritz Hauptmann, with which Franz Hauser, Mendelssohn's friend and the owner of the largest private collection of works by Bach, agreed as well.[205] The fact that it was the Evangelist, indeed even Christ himself, "who wrestles so with the notes," went against Hauptmann's sense of propriety. He "would prefer to have it sung in the style of the *collects,* where it goes strictly according to the punctuation—everything sung on one pitch, then at a comma the voice drops a third, and at a period a fifth."[206] To him, the melodies in

Bach's recitatives "are of too wide a range, yet are too minutely detailed in the expression of individual words."[207] Yet something of the "nature of the folk song" should be found in every vocal composition. But "Bach's solo vocal lines cannot extricate themselves from the polyphonic instrumental parts,"[208] they "too often lack the naturalness of song."[209] This may serve as an example of the criticism which Bach encountered outside of Berlin following the Frankfurt performance of the *St. Matthew Passion*.

A summary listing of the next performances of the *St. Matthew Passion* will close this study. From 1830 on, Mosewius, who, with his Singakademie, was the first true champion of Bach's cantatas, and in his intellectual outlook a forerunner of Albert Schweitzer, gave annual Palm Sunday performances of the *St. Matthew Passion* for his fellow citizens of Breslau. The fourth city to venture a public performance of Bach's Passion music was Stettin. There it was Karl Loewe, who, as the first to do so, brought the work back into the Protestant church in April, 1831,[210] although not as a part of the divine service but in the form of a church concert. At the same time, the Thomas Choir was practicing Bach's Passion music for double chorus under Weinlig's direction, but it did not come to a public performance.[211] The city of the Thomas cantor did not experience a public performance until 1841, when Mendelssohn conducted the work. The situation was similar in Hamburg and Vienna, where the work was also studied in those years, but not performed publicly.[212] Two further performances of the work are finally worth mentioning. One of them was a performance in Königsberg on April 17, 1832, which, though severely cut, was for many nevertheless still too long, so that "a part of the audience left the church already during the first half"[213] of the concert. The other performance was a colossal presentation of the work which took place on Palm Sunday, 1833, in the large Opera House in Dresden. One is reminded of Hiller's performances of Handel's *Messiah* when one finds 342 participants listed here,[214] a number that Bach's Passion music in this secular setting may perhaps even have required.[215]

Epilogue

That the present study has focussed almost exclusively on the fate of Bach's *St. Matthew Passion* corresponds to the specialization by the Romantic Bach movement. The other vocal compositions of the master that now attempted to make their way to the public at large faced a difficult battle. None of them was able to create an effect comparable to that made by Mendelssohn's performance of the *St. Matthew Passion* in Berlin, which thus remained a truly unique experience. Because of the breakthrough of this one work, Bach, whose compositions had until then been known only to limited groups and circles, had become the common cultural property of first the German public, and soon thereafter of the European public as well.

Our examination, which was intended to follow Bach's afterlife only up to this turning point, can end here. It has shown that Bach, whose work during his lifetime was not fully understood and recognized as to its true meaning, was equally misunderstood, although in entirely different ways, in the two epochs that followed his death. The more the circles in which his compositions became known widened, the greater was this misunderstanding, which reached its zenith in the Romantic age. The period that followed Romanticism attempted to rediscover the *true* Bach. This attempt, which received its main impetus from *musicology,* claimed the right to be recognized as the sole correct and true method, as compared with the *aberrations* of the previous epochs.

At the conclusion of the present study, which has shown that even during his lifetime Bach was no longer properly recognized, it seems appropriate to raise the question as to whether the premise underlying this method, namely, that the musical artwork has a true and properly recognizable identity, is correct.

Unlike the visual arts which exist in both space and time, music, existing as it does in time alone, attains a transitory existence solely by virtue of the temporal process of *performance.* While a statue leads an enduring and constant existence in time, in the case of a piece of music one cannot speak of such a fixed existence. But in what form, if in any form at all, does the *original* work of music become manifest?

The preceding should have made it clear that on principle, one cannot speak of a *true* existence of a work of music. In the process of creation, during which the composer hears the piece of music take shape within him, the work corresponds perhaps most closely to the intentions of its creator. Yet as with the painter, whose artwork does not yet exist in the image he has conceived in his mind, but becomes existent only in the completed painting, so the musical artwork cannot be recognized as such in what was envisioned during the process of creation, but only in the existence it attains in the external world. Yet there the composition does not achieve a definitive realization either. Even a performance presented by the composer will be able to approach only more or less closely the imagined, but never completely attainable ideal. To this lack of a fixed existence must be ascribed the fact that musical compositions, far more than works in the other arts, are at the mercy of interpretation by later ages. Ages with original, spontaneous creative power will always interpret works of past epochs very much in terms of their own stylistic world, as it happened, in such a drastic manner, with Bach in the Romantic age. In contrast, epochs without a well-defined culture and hence without stong creative impulses tend to be better able to view the art of the past in a more rational and objective manner. For this reason the predominantly intellectual, scientific epoch that followed Romanticism was able to get closer to the *true* Bach—not because it was in some way akin to the time in which Bach was rooted, but because of the lack of strong, original intellectual currents, which would have been distracting. This left its powers available for a more objective recognition of the past. The conviction that one would thereby arrive at an adequate perception of the *true* existence was, however, an illusion. This illusion was perhaps necessary, in order to give the undertaking the strong impetus it needed.

When at the turn of the century (in 1900) Bach's work had been published in its entirety, the closest possible approximation to the *true* Bach may have been achieved. This proximity, however, could be attained only by the inquiring intellect, no longer by sympathetic experience. The *objective* perception of Bach therefore remains reserved for a circle that is primarily dedicated to musical scholarship, while the general public experiences Bach always from the more or less distorted perspective of its time. The public tends therefore to look like an uncomprehending outsider at the so-called fruitless endeavors of scholarship. Even though musical scholarship may be denied a truly profound influence upon the musical life of a period, still for one who finds an intrinsic value in intellectual insight, quite separate from life, scholarship retains a meaning that never loses its validity.

Notes

I am deeply indebted to Jan McLin Clayberg of Washington, D.C. for her excellent draft translation and preparation of the final manuscript of chapter 4.

1. Philipp Spitta, *Zur Musik,* 16 articles. From the article *Die Wiedergabe protestantischer Kirchenmusik auf geschichtlicher Grundlage,* Berlin, 1892, p. 33.

2. As the historian Ranke did.

3. See Hugo Goldschmidt, *Die Musikästhetik des 18. Jahrhunderts,* Zurich and Leipzig 1915, p. 193. (Heinse lived from 1749 to 1803).

4. Ibid.

5. Quoted by Friedrich Strich, *Deutsche Klassik und Romantik,* p. 18.

6. H. Goldschmidt, *Die Musikästhetik,* p. 215.

7. E.T.A. Hoffmann, on *Alte und neue Kirchenmusik,* complete works, vol. VII, p. 153f.

8. E.T.A. Hoffmann, complete works, vol. XV, p. 10. (On Beethoven's Fifth Symphony).

9. Hoffmann, complete works, vol. VI, 1804, p. 242.

10. See the thorough studies by Martin Blumner, Gerhard Pinthus, Caroline Valentin and Josef Sittard. (Exact titles are given in the Bibliography.)

11. The *Concerts spirituels* during Lent 1783-84.

12. Cf. Romain Rolland, *Musikalische Reise ins Land der Vergangenheit,* p. 118.

13. Charles S. Terry, *Johann Sebastian Bach,* p. 322.

14. Cf. Martin Blumner, *Geschichte der Sing-Akademie zu Berlin,* p.2ff.

15. For instance, the Leipzig *Singakademie* which was founded in 1802 by Schicht, the conductor of the Gewandhaus Orchestra and later Thomas cantor. (Here the founder of a bourgeois choral society and the cantor are one and the same person.) In 1818 J.N. Schelble founded the Frankfurt *Cäcilienverein.*

16. The *Konzertsaal auf dem Kappel* (cf. R. Rolland, *Musikalische Reise,* p. 95).

17. The *Musiksaal im Gewandhaus.*

18. See the Jahrbuch *Der Bär* 1929/30, p. 105.

19. 1710-78. He lived, principally as an opera composer, in London.

20. Both works were performed in the original English.

21. Not before 1786 did he perform the *Credo* from the B minor Mass (see above, chapter 2).

22. Cf. Max Seiffert, *Peters Jahrbuch* 1916 (vol. 33), p. 70f.

23. *Geschichte der Singakademie zu Berlin,* p. 4.

24. Ibid.

25. On his trip to Italy, Reichardt met Baini, the papal Chapelmaster of the Sistine Chapel, stronghold of Palestrina's art.

26. Cf. the lectures he gave in 1801 in Berlin.

27. See above, chapter 2.

28. See the *Allgemeine musikalische Zeitung,* Leipzig, vol. XXII (1820), p. 840.

29. Above all, for the complete edition of Bach's works, then planned by Hoffmeister & Kühnel. See Georg Kinsky, *Aus Forkels Briefen an Hoffmeister & Kühnel,* in *Jahrbuch der Musikbibliothek Peters* for the year 1932, p. 55ff. Letter of July 16, 1802.

30. Kinsky, *Jahrbuch der Musikbibliothek.* Forkel's letter of Dec. 23, 1802.

31. See Forkel's Bach book, (reprint of 1925, edited by J.M. Müller-Blattau,) p. 12.

32. Ibid. See its title page.

33. *Leipziger Allgemeine musikalische Zeitung* (from here on abbreviated *LAMZ*), vol. III, p. 279 (Triest).

34. The review of Forkel's Bach book in the *LAMZ,* vol. V, p. 367, states, "He [Bach] has been without doubt the foremost of all German artists."

35. *LAMZ,* vol. II, p. 642 (Rochlitz).

36. *LAMZ,* vol. I, p. 117 (Schubart).

37. Rochlitz, *Für Freunde der Tonkunst,* vol. IV, p. 160f.

38. *LAMZ,* vol. III, p. 260 (Triest).

39. *LAMZ,* vol. XXXIII (1831), p. 267 (Rochlitz).

40. *LAMZ,* vol. V, p. 515, April 1803 (Rochlitz).

41. *LAMZ,* vol. VIII, p. 201 (1806). Besides J.S. Bach, he also means his son C.P.E. Bach, as well as Fasch.

42. *LAMZ,* vol. XXIV, p. 491, (1822).

43. Forkel, p. 14f.

44. G.W.F. Hegel, complete works, vol. 10, *Vorlesungen über Aesthetik,* Part III, p. 208.

45. *LAMZ,* vol. XXIV, p. 485ff, (1822).

46. Regarding what follows, see B. Fr. Richter, *Joh. Seb. Bach im Gottesdienst der Thomaner,* Bach-Jahrbuch 1915, p. 6f.

47. Müller lived from 1767 until 1817. From 1800 to 1810 he was Thomas cantor in Leipzig, but died as court chapelmaster in Weimar. He thus was the only Thomas cantor to leave his position before his death.

48. *LAMZ,* vol. V, p. 247.

49. Ibid.

50. *LAMZ,* vol. IV, p. 506f, (1802).

51. B. Fr. Richter, *Ueber die Motetten Seb. Bachs,* Bach-Jahrbuch 1912, p. 31.

52. Since the *Art of the Fugue* was published in 1752 in accordance with Bach's own last intentions, it cannot be counted as one of the new publications.

53. See Gerber, *Neues Lexikon der Tonkünstler,* vol. I, the entry: Joh. Seb. Bach.

54. Max Schneider, *Verzeichnis von Bachdrucken,* Bach-Jahrbuch 1906, p. 84ff.

55. Gerber (as above, footnote 53).

56. Spitta, *Zur Musik,* 16 articles. From the article, *Händel, Bach und Schütz,* p. 78.

57. See Hermann Kretzschmar's *Bericht* in vol. 46 of the BG edition, p. xxiv.

58. England had already published its Handel edition, begun in 1786 at the order of King George I. It comprises 36 volumes which, however, are not distinguished by great correctness.

59. See above, chapter 2, Beethoven's letter of Jan. 15, 1801, to Hoffmeister.

60. Already in 1790 J.C.F. Rellstab, the father of the well known music critic, had advertised handwritten copies of "zweimal vierundzwanzig Vorspiele[n] und Fugen aus allen Tonarten," adding the remark, "These are announced for advance subscription and, once printed, they will cost only 6 Reichsthaler." (See M. Schneider, op. cit., p. 99). The edition, however, did not materialize.

61. He owned several cantatas, the orchestal Overtures (Suites), Clavier Concertos for 1 to 4 Claviers, the Violin and Flute Sonatas and a good deal more. See *Berliner AMZ,* vol. VI, p. 234.

62. According to H. Kretzschmar (*Bericht,* BG vol. 46) probably edited by Sieber in Paris.

63. Schneider, *Bach-Jahrbuch* 1906, p. 84ff.

64. See *Berliner AMZ,* vol. V, p. 97. The copy Nägeli used (a Leipzig manuscript) was responsible for the errors in his edition.

65. Schneider, *Bach-Jahrbuch* 1906, p. 84ff.

66. Regarding what follows, cf. Edgar Refardt, *Briefe Hans Georg Nägelis an Breitkopf & Härtel,* in *Zeitschrift für Musikwissenschaft,* vol. 13, 1930/1 p. 384ff., particularly pp. 389-98.

67. Refardt, *Briefe,* p. 393.

68. Ibid., p. 395.

69. Schneider, *Bach-Jahrbuch* 1906, p. 84ff.

70. See Richard Hohenemser, *Welche Einflüsse hatte die Wiederbelebung der älteren Musik im 19. Jahrhundert auf die deutschen Komponisten?,* München, 1900, p. 20. The Mass referred to above probably was the Mass for double chorus which Schicht performed in 1805 in one of the Gewandhaus concerts, eliciting most enthusiastic praise from Rochlitz, although the work was not by Bach.

71. See *Intelligenzblatt* No. 20 of the *LAMZ,* vol. VI (August 1804).

72. Max Schneider, *Bach-Jahrbuch* 1906, and (for the 2nd fascicle), *Intelligenzblatt* No. 4 (November 1803) of the *LAMZ,* vol. VI.

73. The Well-Tempered Clavier, the Inventions, Sinfonias, Toccatas, Suites etc. See Max Schneider, *Bach-Jahrbuch* 1906.

74. Ibid.

75. *Zeitung für die elegante Welt,* vol. III, *Intelligenzblatt* No. 50. See also Gerber, *Neues Lexikon,* vol. I, the entry on J.S. Bach. Soon thereafter, three of the Violin Sonatas also were published in Bonn (by Simrock) and in Paris (by Decombe).

76. Max Schneider, *Bach-Jahrbuch* 1906, p. 84ff.

77. *LAMZ*, vol. XV (1813).

78. Max Schneider, *Bach-Jahrbuch* 1906, as well as *LAMZ*, vols. XIII and XIX.

79. *LAMZ*, vol. XX, p. 531.

80. *LAMZ*, vol. XX, *Intelligenzblatt* No. 3, p. 28.

81. See H. Kretzschmar's *Bericht* in BG vol. 46, p. xxxiii.

82. Ibid., p. xxiv, as well as *LAMZ*, vol. XX, *Intelligenzblatt* No. 10.

83. Schneider, *Bach-Jahrbuch* 1906. At the same time transcriptions for string quartet of Preludes and Fugues from the Well-Tempered Clavier were already in circulation. (First in London; cf. Schneider.)

84. Forkel's Bach book, p. 42.

85. Made available only recently by Georg Kinsky in the *Jahrbuch der Musikbibliothek Peters* for the year 1932; see p. 55ff.

86. Kinsky, *Jahrbuch der Musikbibliothek.* Forkel's letter of May 4, 1801; (p. 59).

87. See above, chapter 4.

88. Kinsky, *Jahrbuch der Musikbibliothek.* The same letter of May 4, 1801.

89. *LAMZ*, vol. III, *Intelligenzblatt* No. 6 (Feb. 1801).

90. *Zeitschrift für Musikwissenschaft* 1930/31, p. 392.

91. Kinsky, *Jahrbuch der Musikbibliothek.* Forkel's letter of March 5, 1802.

92. Forkel's Bach book, p. 77.

93. See Müller-Blattau's Afterword to Forkel's Bach book (1925 edition), p. 110.

94. Forkel, (Müller-Blattau ed.), *Über J.S. Bach.*, p. 102.

95. On December 2, 1825, Zelter wrote to Goethe (Correspondence, vol. II, p. 358) what he thought of Forkel. "He has begun to write a history of music and stopped at the point at which for us a history becomes possible.... His hero was Seb. Bach, who nevertheless brought him to despair because he could not bring into accord his aggressiveness, petulances, independence and impudence with a greatness and profundity that cannot be denied." Furthermore (in his letter of April 8, 1827—correspondence with Goethe, vol. II, p. 467) Zelter said, "In his evaluation of the prolific Sebastian Bach, he demands: one should rather dispose of the youthful attempts of such young geniuses than preserve them to the detriment of refined taste."

96. Published by Peters in Leipzig in 1810 together with Weber's commentary. See Max M. von Weber, *C.M. von Weber, ein Lebensbild*, vol. III, p. 14ff.

97. 1741-1801.

98. Max M. von Weber, *Carl Maria von Weber*, p. 13.

99. Ibid., p. 14.

100. In his article of 1814, *Alte und neue Kirchenmusik.* See Heinrich Besseler, *Handbuch der Musikwissenschaft: Die Musik des Mittelalters und der Renaissance*, p. 8.

101. Carl von Winterfeld, *Der evangelische Kirchengesang*, vol. III, p. 310f.

102.   Besides the work by Martin Blumner, see also the extensive article by Georg Schünemann, *Die Bachpflege der Berliner Singakademie,* Bach-Jahrbuch 1928, p. 138ff.

103.   G. Schünemann, *Bach-Jahrbuch* 1928, p. 141.

104.   On June 24, 1794.

105.   On August 26, 1794.

106.   Later it was frequently given (from 1801 on, always in the Opera House) at the request of and together with Frau Bachmann's *Liebhaberkonzert,* which organization was the continuation of the *Benda-Bachmann Konzerte.* Cf. Blumner, *Sing-Akademie,* pp. 16, 35.

107.   Zelter's letter of March 29, 1823, to Goethe. See Correspondence, vol. II, p. 192.

108.   Letter of April 6, 1829. Quoted by Schünemann, *Bach-Jahrbuch* 1928, p. 143.

109.   About 110 cantatas, the Christmas Oratorio, the St. John Passion (partly autograph score), the original parts of the St. Matthew Passion, etc.

110.   Originally they had belonged to Princess Amalia of Prussia, who at her death (in 1787) willed her music collection to the *Gymnasium.*

111.   Blumner, *Sing-Akademie,* p. 38.

112.   Ibid., p. 39.

113.   Schünemann, *Bach-Jahrbuch* 1928, p. 144.

114.   One may also think of W. Gräser's orchestration of the Art of the Fugue.

115.   See Correspondence with Goethe, p. 100.

116.   Spitta, *J.S. Bach,* vol. II, p. 981f. That a motet by this Eisenach town organist who was born in 1642 was thought to be a work by Sebastian Bach, again indicates that J.S. Bach was steeped in the style of an earlier time.

117.   Ibid., p. 821.

118.   Blumner, *Sing-Akademie,* p. 75.

119.   Entry into the rehearsal book of the Singakademie. See Schünemann, *Bach-Jahrbuch* 1928, p. 151.

120.   Zelter's letter of September 7, 1827. Correspondence, vol. II, p. 517.

121.   Zelter's letter of April 5, 1827 to Goethe. Correspondence, vol. II, p. 467f.

122.   In his letter of April 21/22, 1827. Correspondence, vol. II, p. 472.

123.   Letter of June 9, 1827. Correspondence, vol. II, p. 481.

124.   Said Moritz Hauptmann in a letter to Franz Hauser, vol. II, p. 55f.

125.   Ibid.

126.   Ibid.

127.   Zelter's letter of June 9, 1827, to Goethe. Correspondence, vol. II, p. 482.

128.   Ibid., p. 483.

129.   Letter of June 18, 1831. Correspondence with Goethe, vol. III, p. 418.

130. Goethe to Zelter. (Enclosure to the letter of July 17, 1827). Correspondence, vol. II, p. 495.

131. *Kreisleriana,* complete works, vol. I, p. 46.

132. In *Der Wanderer und sein Schatten. Menschliches Allzumenschliches* II, Part 2, p. 149.

133. *Lehrjahre* I, Book 2, II.

134. See Wilhelm Bode, *Die Tonkunst in Goethes Leben,* Berlin 1912, vol. II, p. 133.

135. Ibid., p. 132.

136. In his letter of May 3, 1816 to Zelter. Correspondence, vol. I, p. 462.

137. In 1821, 1822, 1825 and 1830.

138. W. Bode, *Die Tonkunst,* vol. II, p. 268.

139. Hermann Abert, *Goethe und die Musik,* Stuttgart 1922, p. 45.

140. It is known that Goethe had read the articles on Bach in volume 2 of Rochlitz's *Für Freunde der Tonkunst* as well as Thibaut's study *Ueber Reinheit der Tonkunst.* See W. Bode, *Die Tonkunst,* vol. II, p. 313f.

141. *LAMZ,* vol. VIII, p. 200.

142. See Alfred Dörffel, *Geschichte der Gewandhaus Concerte zu Leipzig,* Leipzig 1884, pp. 29, 33-34.

143. Cf. B. Fr. Richter, *"Ueber die Motetten Seb. Bachs," Bach-Jahrbuch,* 1912, p. 31.

144. See B. Fr. Richter, *"Bach im Gottesdienst der Thomaner," Bach-Jahrbuch,* 1915, p. 8.

145. The true revival of Bach cantatas in the Thomas church began during the cantorate of Moritz Hauptmann (1842-68), whose term of office, however, falls outside the time limits of this study.

146. B. Fr. Richter, *"Ueber die Motetten Seb. Bachs," Bach-Jahrbuch,* 1912, p. 31.

147. *LAMZ,* vol. XXX, p. 164, (1828).

148. *LAMZ,* vol. XXVIII, p. 104 and addendum.

149. *Berliner AMZ,* vol. VI, p. 234, (1829).

150. Josef Sittard, *Geschichte der Musik und des Concertwesens in Hamburg,* p. 182.

151. Eduard Hanslick said of these concerts in his *Geschichte des Concertwesens in Wien* (p. 140), "The performances there really were the first *historical concerts* in Vienna." Hanslick's book further proves that, except for the private performances in van Swieten's and Kiesewetter's circles, no music by Bach was presented in Viennese concerts of this time. See also *LAMZ.*

152. A. Schweitzer, *J.S. Bach,* p. 223. (This probably applies only to Bach's motets).

153. Thibaut, *Über Reinheit,* p. 10.

154. Cf. *LAMZ,* vol. XXXXI, p. 57.

155. *LAMZ,* vol. XXV, p. 183.

156. For instance, *Zeitung für die elegante Welt,* vol. 24, p. 8.

157. Oskar Bormann, *Joh. Nep. Schelble,* Frankfurt, 1926.

158. See Eduard Devrient, *Meine Erinnerungen an Felix Mendelssohn-Bartholdy und seine Briefe an mich*, 2d. ed., Leipzig 1872, p. 18.

159. Since 1825 Schelble had owned a copy of Nägeli's autograph score. See Bormann, *Schelble*.

160. Cf. *Berliner AMZ*, vol. IV, p. 423.

161. See *LAMZ*, vol. XXX.

162. *Berliner AMZ*, vol. V, pp. 146, 153f.

163. E.T.A. Hoffmann, complete works, vol. XV, p. 186.

164. Ibid., p. 188f.

165. Which, however, were anticipated by Méhul and Mozart (in his *Magic Flute*).

166. Already in 1828 the *LAMZ* presented Paganini's portrait on the title page of volume XXX.

167. A.B. Marx, *Erinnerungen*, Berlin 1865, vol. II, p. 79.

168. Cf. *Berliner AMZ*, vol. VI, p. 120.

169. Letter of April 30-May 5, 1829, to Goethe. Correspondence, vol. III, p. 138.

170. See *Berliner AMZ*, vol. VI, p. 125.

171. *Zeitung für die elegante Welt*, vol. I, 1829, p. 599.

172. Said Rellstab on March 21, 1829, in the *Vossische Zeitung*.

173. Within nine weeks (from March 4 to May 13, 1829) Paganini gave 12 recitals in Berlin.

174. Which, together with the St. Matthew Passion, he had already begun to rehearse with his chorus in 1815.

175. Schünemann, *Bach-Jahrbuch* 1928, p. 153.

176. Cf. Devrient, *Felix Mendelssohn*, p. 55f.

177. Ibid., p. 60f.

178. Ibid., p. 63.

179. *Berliner AMZ*, vol. VI, p. 100. (A.B. Marx on Bach's St. Matthew Passion.)

180. See Devrient, *Felix Mendelssohn*, p. 60f., and also thereafter. In his article, *Zelter oder Mendelssohn* (in *Monatsschrift für Gottesdienst und kirchliche Kunst*), Friedrich Smend, too, refuted Schünemann's interpretation.

181. Schünemann, *Bach-Jahrbuch* 1928, pp. 148-50.

182. A.B. Marx, *Erinnerungen*, vol. II, p. 86.

183. Omitted from Matthew's Gospel were: verses 58 and 60 of Chapter 26; verses 9, 10, 17, 18, 19, 32-37, 55, 56 and 61 of Chapter 27. Cf. *Berliner AMZ*, vol. VI, 4th review of Bach's Passion music by A.B. Marx.

184. Devrient, *Felix Mendelssohn*, p. 60f. This, too, contradicts Schünemann's speculation that Zelter's arrangement had simply been copied.

185. This was at least true of the 2nd performance on March 21, 1829.

186. See *Berliner AMZ*, vol. VI, 4th review of the St. Matthew Passion by A.B. Marx.

187. See Rellstab's review of March 24, 1829, in the *Vossische Zeitung*.

188. As reported by Zelter. Quoted by Schünemann, *Bach-Jahrbuch* 1928, p. 164.

189. See Moritz Hauptmann's letter of Feb. 3, 1828 to Franz Hauser.

190. Hauptmann's letter to Hauser, dated Nov. 26, 1827.

191. Letter of March 28, 1829. Zelter-Goethe Correspondence, vol. III, p. 127.

192. *Berliner AMZ*, vol. VI. p. 83.

193. Ibid., p. 89.

194. *LAMZ*, vol. XXXI, p. 258.

195. Ibid.

196. Devrient, *Felix Mendelssohn*, p. 67.

197. Cf. *Zeitung für die elegante Welt*, vol. I, 1829, p. 1127.

198. *Konversationsblatt* of the *Berliner AMZ*, vol. VI, p. 99.

199. Quoted by A.B. Marx in the *Berliner AMZ*, vol. VI, p. 81f.

200. See Zelter's letter of Feb. 12, 1829, to Goethe. Correspondence, vol. III, p. 124.

201. See R. Hohenemser, *Welche Einflüsse*, p. 59.

202. The first two performances (on March 11 and 21) were directed by Mendelssohn, the third, on Good Friday, 1829, by Zelter.

203. Plans for a performance go back to 1827. (See Moritz Hauptmann's letter of Feb. 2, 1827, to Franz Hauser.) In the performance Schelble himself sang the part of the Evangelist as well as that of Christ.

204. Hauptmann's letter of April 19, 1833, to Hauser (vol. I, p. 103).

205. Ibid., letter of May 17, 1833 (vol. I, p. 105).

206. Ibid., letter of March 19, 1836 (vol. I, p. 202).

207. Ibid.

208. Ibid., letter of April 11, 1859 (vol. II, p. 167).

209. Ibid., letter of June 18, 1859 (vol. II, p. 172).

210. Karl Anton, *"Zur Geschichte der Bachbewegung,"* Bach-Jahrbuch, 1914, p. 38ff.

211. See *LAMZ*, vol. XXXIII, p. 246 (1831).

212. See H. Kretzschmar, *Bach-Gesellschaft*, p. xxvi, and *LAMZ*, vol. XXXIV, p. 667, (1832).

213. A comment about this performance revealed that the chorale "Wenn ich einmal soll scheiden" was sung without instruments, pianissimo, even *sotto voce*, with a sforzando on the word "aller*bäng*sten" (most frightened).

214. See *LAMZ*, vol. XXXV, 1833.

215. The next performances of Bach's St. Matthew Passion took place: in the year 1836 in Cassel, under Ludwig Spohr, who used Schelble's revision of the recitatives (see M. Hauptmann, *Franz Hauser*, vol. I, p. 200); in 1840 in Paris (in the first concert of the Conservatory of Music, where, however, only certain parts of the Passion music were performed); in 1840 in Halle (only part I of the work); in 1842 in Munich under the leadership of Franz Lachner (with 250 participants).

Bibliography

Abert, Hermann. *W.A. Mozart,* enlarged 5th ed. of O. Jahn, *W.A. Mozart.* Leipzig, 1919-21.
———. *Goethe und die Musik.* Stuttgart, 1922.
Anton, Karl. "Zur Geschichte der Bachbewegung," in: *Bach-Jahrbuch* 1914, p. 38ff.
Bach, C.P.E. "Zwei Briefe an Forkel," ed. by Max Schneider, in *Veröffentlichungen der Neuen Bach-Gesellschaft,* XVII/3.
———. *Versuch über die wahre Art das Clavier zu spielen.* 5th ed. Berlin, 1956.
Benz, Richard. *Die Stunde der deutschen Musik.*
Bernhardt, Reinhold. "Aus der Umwelt der Wiener Klassiker, Freiherr Gottfried van Swieten" in *Der Bär, Jahrbuch von Breitkopf & Härtel 1929-1930.* Leipzig, 1930.
Besseler, Heinrich. *Die Musik des Mittelalters und der Renaissance.* Wildpark-Potsdam, 1931.
Bitter, C.H. *J.S. Bach.* 2 vols., Berlin, 1865.
———. *C.P.E. und Wilhelm Friedemann Bach und deren Brüder.* 2 vols., Berlin, 1868.
Blumner, Martin. *Geschichte der Sing-Akademie zu Berlin.* Berlin, 1891.
Bode, Wilhelm. *Die Tonkunst in Goethes Leben.* 2 vols., Berlin, 1912.
Bormann, Oskar. *Johann Nepomuk Schelble (1789-1837) Sein Leben, sein Wirken und seine Werke.* Frankfurt/Main, 1926.
Borris-Zuckermann, Siegfried. *Kirnbergers Leben und Werk und seine Bedeutung im Berliner Musikkreis um 1750.* Berlin, 1933.
Burney, Charles. *Tagebuch seiner musikalischen Reisen durch Frankreich und Italien. . . . Aus dem Englischen übersetzt von C.D. Ebeling.* Hamburg, 1772.
Cramer, C.F. *Magazin für Musik,* vol. II (1786).
Devrient, Eduard. *Meine Erinnerungen an Felix Mendelssohn-Bartholdy und seine Briefe an mich.* 2d ed., Leipzig, 1872.
Dörffel, Alfred. *Geschichte der Gewandhaus-Concerte zu Leipzig.* Leipzig, 1884.
Ehinger, Hans. *F. Rochlitz als Musikschriftsteller.* Basel, 1928.
Eitner, Robert. "Katalog der Musikaliensammlung des Joachimsthalschen Gymnasiums zu Berlin," in *Monatshefte für Musikgeschichte,* 16 (1884).
Epstein, Peter. *Der Schulchor vom 16. Jahrhundert bis zur Gegenwart. Musikpädagogische Bibliothek.* Leipzig, 1929.
Falck, Martin. *Wilhelm Friedemann Bach, sein Leben und seine Werke.* Leipzig, 1913.
Forkel, Johann N. *Über Johann Sebastian Bachs Leben, Kunst und Kunstwerk,* ed. J.M. Müller-Blattau. Augsburg, 1925.
Gerber, E.L. *Historisch-biographisches Lexikon der Tonkünstler.* Leipzig, 1790-92.
———. *Neues historisch-biographisches Lexikon der Tonkünstler.* Leipzig, 1812-14.
Goldschmidt, Hugo. *Die Musikästhetik des 18. Jahrhunderts und ihre Beziehungen zu seinem Kunstschaffen.* Zurich/Leipzig, 1915.
Graff, Paul. *Geschichte der Auflösung der alten gottesdienstlichen Formen in der evangelischen Kirche Deutschlands bis zum Eintritt der Aufklärung und des Rationalismus.* Göttingen, 1921.

Güttler, Hermann. *Königsbergs Musikkultur im 18. Jahrhundert.* Königsberg, 1925.

Hanslick, Eduard. *Geschichte der Concertwesens in Wien.* Vienna, 1869.

Hashagen, D.F. J.S. *Bach als Sänger und Musiker des Evangeliums und der lutherischen Reformation.* Wismar, 1901.

Hauptmann, Moritz. *Briefe an Franz Hauser.* 2 vols., Leipzig, 1871.

Hegar, Elisabeth. *Die Anfänge der neuen Musikgeschichtsschreibung um 1770 bei Gerbert, Burney, und Hawkins.* Strassburg, 1930.

Hegel, G.W.F. *Werke,* vol. X (Lectures on Aesthetics, part 3). Berlin, 1842.

Hiller, J.A. *Lebensbeschreibungen berühmter Musikgelehrter und Tonkünstler neuerer Zeit.* Leipzig, 1784.

_____. *Wöchentliche Nachrichten und Anmerkungen die Musik betreffend.* Leipzig, 1766-70.

Hirschberg, Walther. "Bach im Wandel der Zeiten," in *Musikblatt der Vossischen Zeitung.* Berlin, March 21, 1925.

Hoffmann, E.T.A. *Sämtliche Werke,* 15 vols, ed. E. Griesebach. Leipzig.

Hohenemser, Richard. *Welche Einflüsse hatte die Wiederbelebung der älteren Musik im 19. Jahrhundert auf die deutschen Komponisten?* Munich, 1900.

Israel, Carl. *Frankfurter Concert-Chronik.* 1876.

Kelletat, Herbert. *Zur Geschichte der deutschen Orgelmusik in der Frühklassik.* Kassel, 1933.

Kemmerling, Franz. *Dis Thomasschule zu Leipzig, eine kurze Geschichte von ihrer Gründung 1212 bis zum Jahre 1927.* Leipzig, 1927.

Kinsky, Georg. "Aus Forkels Briefen an Hoffmeister & Kühnel," in *Jahrbuch der Musikbibliothek Peters,* 39 (1933).

Kretzschmar, Hermann. *Führer durch den Konzertsaal.* 5th ed., Leipzig, 1921.

_____. Report about the Bach-Gesellschaft, in Bach-Gesellschaft edition, vol. 46.

Kümmerle, Salomon. *Enzyklopädie der evangelischen Kirchenmusik.* Gütersloh, 1888-95.

Lewicki, Ernst. "Mozarts Verhältnis zu Sebastian Bach," in *Mitteilungen für die Mozart-Gemeinde in Berlin.* Fasc. 15 (March 1903).

Löffler, H. "J.L. Krebs," in *Bach-Jahrbuch* 1930, p. 124ff.

Löwenthal, S. *Die Musikübende Gesellschaft zu Berlin und ihre Mitglieder J.P. Sack, F.W. Riedt und J.G. Seyffarth.* Basel, 1928.

Lott, Walter. "Zur Geschichte der Passionskomposition von 1650-1800," in *Archiv für Musikwissenschaft,* III/3 (1921).

_____. "Die beiden Uraufführungen des *Tod Jesu* im März 1755," in *Monatsschrift für Gottesdienst und kirchliche Kunst* (May/June 1924).

Marpurg, F.W. Foreword to the *Kunst der Fuge* (1752), reprinted as Foreword to Bach-Gesellschaft edition, vol. 25.

Marx, A.B. *Erinnerungen.* 2 vols, Berlin, 1865.

Mayer-Reinach, Albert. "C.H. Graun als Opernkomponist," in *Sammelbände der Internationalen Musikgesellschaft,* I (1899-1900), p. 446ff.

Mennicke, Carl. *Hasse und die Brüder Graun als Symphoniker,* Leipzig, 1906.

_____. "Zur Biographie der Brüder Graun," in *Neue Zeitschrift für Musik,* 71/8 (1904).

Miesner, Heinrich. *Ph. Em. Bach in Hamburg.* Berlin, 1929.

Nietzsche, Friedrich. *Der Wanderer und sein Schatten, Menschliches Allzumenschliches,* II/2. Leipzig, 1922.

Pietzsch, Gerhard. "Der Wandel des Klangideals in der Musik," in *Acta Musicologica,* IV (1932).

Pinthus, Gerhard. *Die Entwicklungszüge des Konzertwesens in Deutschland bis zum Beginn des 19. Jahrhunderts.* Freiburg/Breisgau, 1932.

Prüfer, Artur. *J.S. Bach und die Tonkunst des 19. Jahrhunderts.* Leipzig, 1902.

Quantz, J.J. *Versuch einer Anweisung die Flöte traversiere zu spielen.* 3rd ed. Breslau, 1789.

Ramler, K.W. *Geistliche Kantaten.* 2d ed., Berlin, 1770.

Refardt, Edgar. "Briefe Hans Georg Nägelis an Breitkopf & Härtel," in *Zeitschrift für Musikwissenschaft,* 13 (1930-31), p. 384ff.

Reichel, Eugen. "Gottsched und J.A. Scheibe," in *Sammelbände der internationalen Musikgesellschaft*, II (1900-01), p. 654ff.

Richter, B.F. "Über die Schicksale der der Thomasschule zu Leipzig angehörenden Kantaten J.S. Bachs," in *Bach-Jahrbuch* 1906, p. 43ff.

———. "Über die Motetten J.S. Bachs," in *Bach-Jahrbuch* 1912, p. 1ff.

———. "Joh. Seb. Bach im Gottesdienst der Thomaner," in *Bach-Jahrbuch* 1915, p. 1ff.

———. "Zur Geschichte der Passionsaufführungen in Leipzig," in *Bach-Jahrbuch* 1911.

Rochlitz, Friedrich. *Für Freunde der Tonkunst*, IV (Leipzig, 1832).

Rolland, Romain. *Musikalische Reise ins Land der Vergangenheit*. Frankfurt/Main, 1923.

Rosenkaimer, Eugen. *J.A. Scheibe als Verfasser seines Critischen Musicus*. Bonn, 1929.

Sachs, Curt. "Musikgeschichte," in *Landeskunde der Provinz Brandenburg*, vol. IV: *Kultur*. Berlin, 1916.

———. "Prinzessin Amalie von Preussen als Musikerin," in *Hohenzollern-Jahrbuch*, XIV (1910), p. 181ff.

Scheibe, J.A. *Critischer Musicus, neue, vermehrte und verbesserte Auflage*. Leipzig, 1745.

Schenk, J.B. *Autobiographische Skizze*, in *Studien zur Musikwissenschaft*, XI (Vienna, 1924), p. 75ff.

Schering, Arnold. *Musikgeschichte Leipzigs*. Vol. II, 1650-1723, Leipzig, 1926.

———. "Die Musikästhetik der deutschen Aufklärung," in *Zeitschrift der Internationalen Musikgesellschaft*, VIII (1906-7).

———. Review of Hugo Goldschmidt's *Die Musikästhetik des 18. Jahrhunderts*, in *Zeitschrift für Musikwissenschaft*, I (1918-19), p. 307ff.

———. "J.P. Kirnberger als Herausgeber Bachscher Choräle," in *Bach-Jahrbuch* 1918.

Schindler, Anton. *Beethoven*. 3rd ed., Münster, 1860.

Schmid, E.F. "Joseph Haydn und Philipp Emanuel Bach," in *Zeitschrift für Musikwissenschaft*, XIV/6 (1932).

Schmidt, F. *Das Musikleben der bürgerlichen Gesellschaft Leipzigs im Vormärz* (1815-48). Leipzig, 1912.

Schneider, Max. "Verzeichnis der bis zum Jahre 1851 gedruckten und der geschriebenen im Handel gewesenen Werke von Bach," in *Bach-Jahrbuch* 1906, p. 84ff.

Schünemann, Georg. "Die Bachpflege der Berliner Singakademie," in *Bach-Jahrbuch* 1928, p. 138ff.

Schwarz, Max. "Johann Christian Bach," in *Sammelbände der internationalen Musikgesellschaft*, II (1900-01).

Schweitzer, Albert. *J.S. Bach*. 4th and 5th eds, Leipzig, 1922.

Seiffert, Max. "Die Mannheimer *Messias* Aufführung 1777," in *Jahrbuch der Musikbibliothek Peters* 1916, vol. 33, p. 61ff.

Sittard, Josef. *Geschichte der Musik und des Concertwesens in Hamburg*. Altona/Leipzig, 1890.

Smend, Friedrich. "Bachs Matthäus-Passion," in *Bach-Jahrbuch* 1928, p. 1ff.

———. "Zelter oder Mendelssohn?" in *Monatsschrift für Gottesdienst und kirchliche Kunst*, XXXIV/7.

Spitta, Philipp. *Johann Sebastian Bach*. 3 vols., Leipzig, 1873, 1880.

———. *Zur Musik* (16 articles). Berlin, 1892.

Storch, K.A. *J.A. Scheibes Anschauungen von der musikalischen Historie, Wissenschaft und Kunst*. Leipzig, 1923.

Terry, Charles Sanford. *Joh. Seb. Bach, eine Biographie*. Leipzig, 1929.

Thayer, Alexander Wheelock. *Ludwig van Beethovens Leben*. German ed. Hermann Deiters. 5 vols., Leipzig, 1907/17.

Thibaut, A.F. Justus. *Über Reinheit der Tonkunst*. New ed. Raimund Heuler. Paderborn, 1907.

Thouret, Georg. *Friedrich der Grosse als Musikfreund und Musiker*. Leipzig, 1898.

Valentin, Caroline. *Geschichte der Musik in Frankfurt am Main.* Frankfurt/Main, 1906.

Walther, Johann G. *Musicalisches Lexicon.* Leipzig, 1732.

Weber, Max M. von. *Carl Maria von Weber, ein Lebensbild.* 3 vols. Leipzig, 1864-66.

Winterfeld, Carl von. *Der evangelische Kirchengesang.* Vol. III (sections on Bach, his sons, Graun, and Telemann). Leipzig, 1843-47.

Zelter, Karl F. *Briefwechsel zwischen Goethe und Zelter in den Jahren 1799-1832,* ed. L. Geiger. 3 vols, Leipzig, 1913.

Journals and Other Reference Works

Allgemeine deutsche Bibliothek, LXXXI (1788), p. 295ff.

Berliner allgemeine musikalische Zeitung, V-VII (1827-29).

Leipziger allgemeine musikalische Zeitung, 50 vols. (1798-1848).

38. Neujahrsstück der allgemeinen Musik-Gesellschaft in Zürich (1850). Article on C.H. Graun.

Vossische Zeitung Berlin (1829).

Zeitung für die elegante Welt (Berlin), III, XXIV (1803, 1824).

Part II

BWV 131
Bach's First Cantata

Cantata 15: *Denn du wirst meine Seele nicht in der Hölle lassen* figured as
Bach's first extant cantata until William Scheide identified it in 1959[1] as one of
18 cantatas composed by Bach's Meiningen cousin, Johann Ludwig Bach.
Johann Sebastian copied them for performances of his own in 1726 at the time
of his first profound disillusionment in his Leipzig position. With the mystery
of Cantata 15 solved, any one of Bach's Mühlhausen cantatas could claim to be
the first among his 194 surviving church cantatas.[2] The following *calendar of
events in Mühlhausen* will place them in context:

1. 1706   December 2: Johann Georg Ahle, organist at St. Blasius's Church,
           dies.
2. 1707   April 24 (Easter): Bach applies for the position and plays before the
           Council.
3.   May 27: The Council agrees on Bach's selection.
4.   May 30: The parish of St. Blasius bears the full fury of a disastrous
           fire that destroys one-fourth of the town (360 houses).
5.   June 14: Bach returns from Arnstadt to state his conditions.
6.   June 15: The certificate of appointment is signed, sealed, and
           accepted by Bach "by a handshake to show his agreement." Three
           of the Councilmen are absent, stating that the recent fire had left
           them even without pen and ink.
7.   June 29: Bach requests his dismissal in Arnstadt, hands in the keys
           to his organ and assigns his salary for the Crucis quarter (June 15—
           September 14) to his cousin Johann Ernst.[3]

Reprinted with permission from *Studies in Eighteenth-Century Music, A Tribute to Karl
Geiringer on His Seventieth Birthday,* edited by H.C. Robbins Landon and Roger E. Chapman
(London, 1970; repr. New York, Dover), pp. 272-91.

8. Undated Arnstadt document: Bach "received his dismissal in July... 1707."
   Items 6-8 indicate that Bach became organist at St. Blasius's in Mühlhausen as early as June 15 and no later than July 1707.
9. August 10: Bach's uncle on his mother's side, Tobias Lämmerhirt, dies childless.
10. September 18: His testament is opened. The four children of Bach's mother receive each 50 Gulden which meant to Bach the equivalent of seven months salary.
11. October 17: Bach, now not only socially but also economically secure, marries in nearby Dornheim his cousin Maria Barbara of Arnstadt. Joh. Lorenz Stauber officiates "without charge."
12. 1708 February 4: Performance at St. Mary's Church of the *Ratswahl* Cantata (BWV 71).
13. June 5: Wedding of Johann Lorenz Stauber to Regina Wedemann, an aunt of Bach's bride.

How do the Mühlhausen cantatas fit into this calendar? If Bach, in addition to showing his mastery of the organ, composed and performed also a cantata at Easter 1707 (item 2 above), BWV 4: *Christ lag in Todesbanden* might well have been Bach's Mühlhausen "Probestück" and thus his earliest extant cantata. This writer has recently posed this question[4] but realizes that, in the form in which *Christ lag* has survived[5], it is a more mature composition than any one of the other four Mühlhausen cantatas.

Gottes Zeit ist die allerbeste Zeit (BWV 106) has been associated with items 9 and 10. Pirro's interpretation of the *actus tragicus* as a mourning cantata for Bach's uncle has recently received new corroborating evidence.[6] (1) The recorders are notated a whole tone higher which is typical of the woodwind parts in Bach's Mühlhausen cantatas. In his Weimar cantatas they are normally notated a minor third higher.[7] (2) The form of the fugue is, in both cantatas 106 and 131, still in a state of flux which, however, points clearly towards a fugue-type that characterizes Bach's vocal music from Cantata 71 (of 1708) onwards well into his Weimar time: the permutation fugue.[8]

The date of *Gott ist mein König* (BWV 71)—item 12—is known through the event proper (the inauguration of a new Town Council), the autograph score "de l'anno 1708" and the title page of the printed text.[9]

Cantata 196 has been assigned by Spitta for cogent reasons to the Stauber wedding (item 13). Spitta's interpretation has remained unquestioned and is still upheld by Frederick Hudson, editor of the *Trauungskantaten* in the NBA (1958).

This leaves only Cantata 131 unassigned or not properly assigned. Terry's supposition that it was composed for the anniversary of the Mühlhausen fire, i.e., for May 30, 1708, is stylistically untenable, as shall be shown.[10]

In contrast to Cantata 106, Bach's autograph score of Cantata 131 has survived. It is, in fact, the earliest autograph of a complete major work by Bach that has come down to us.[11] In 1840 it was in the possession of the Viennese collector Alois Fuchs who added a lovingly adorned title page that includes the date 1707.[12] At such an early time stylistic insight could hardly have caused Fuchs to decide on 1707 in favor of 1708. One wonders whether a document now lost or oral tradition may have been responsible for Fuchs's dating. A generation later, the manuscript is found in the hands of the longtime editor in chief of the Bach Gesellschaft, Wilhelm Rust. His edition of Cantata 131 takes over Fuchs's date of 1707,[13] however, without presenting new evidence. Jealousy of Spitta's Bach biography, completed in 1880 when Spitta was not yet 39 years old, caused Rust to resign his editorship in 1881 after the publication of volume 28. The hard feelings he harbored against Spitta (see Rust's foreword to BG 28!) imply that Spitta, when he described Cantata 131 in volume I of his biography (*i.e.* before 1873), had no access to the autograph score since it was in Rust's possession. Had Spitta known the postscript in which Bach signs himself as "Mühlhausen organist," he would not have misdated this cantata, and consequently neither Cantata 106, as of about 1711.[14]

The watermark in the paper of Cantata 131—the crowned double eagle of the Free and Imperial city of Mühlhausen—is identical with that of Cantata 71 and Bach's other Mühlhausen documents. Also Bach's handwriting shows these cantatas to be neighbors. However, the festive occasion of the *Ratswahl* Cantata prompted Bach to produce a score penned with unusual meticulousness. In contrast, Cantata 131 was written at great speed. Nevertheless its clear writing shows, with two minor exceptions, no corrections. The manuscript is thus a fair copy rather than the composing score. Bar lines are drawn throughout with a ruler. The figuring of the *continuo* part is written out with rare completeness. The same can be said of the many tempo indications and dynamic markings.

Above the three systems that constitute page I of the score—there is no title page—Bach gives the title in old-fashioned German and the instrumentation in amusingly faulty Italian:

Aus der Tieffen ruffe ich Herr zu dir. a una Obboe, una Violino, doi Violae, Fagotto. C.A.T.: B. è Fond. da Gio: Bast: Bach.

The bassoon part is written throughout on the staff above the soprano rather than above the *continuo*.[15] Both oboe and bassoon are notated in true pitch (*i.e.* in A minor, *Kammerton*), a whole note higher than the other instruments and voices. Except for changing meter and tempo indications, the different sections flow one into another as if the cantata were written in one continuous movement.[16]

Below the completed score, at the bottom of the last (the 15th) page appears something unique, an inscription in Bach's hand that reads:

Auff begehren Tit: Herrn D: Georg: Christ: Eilmars in die Music gebracht von Joh: Seb: Bach Org: Molhusin(?).

Georg Christian Eilmar was pastor at the Church of Mary. He represented, as third generation minister in Mühlhausen, the Lutheran orthodoxy, then embattled with the Pietists whose leader was the minister of Bach's church, Johann Adolph Frohne.[17] Eilmar was the author of a book[18] which Mattheson still used to back up his attack on the rigid Pietist stand in matters of church music.

The deceased organist, J.G. Ahle, had been an avowed Pietist, like his pastor Frohne, and as such an enemy of the church cantata. Pastor Eilmar must have looked with profound satisfaction at the election of J.S. Bach, a member of the renowned orthodox Lutheran family of the Bachs, as new organist of his rival's church. The postscript below Cantata 131 shows Eilmar, about 20 years Bach's senior, as instigator of this cantata. It was thus an orthodox Lutheran minister who caused Bach to write his first church cantata. Dürr places Cantata 131 because of stylistic characteristics before Cantatas 106, 71 and 196, *i.e.* before September 1707.[19]

Hence:

at the request of Herrn Dr. Georg Christian Eilmar set to music by Joh. Seb. Bach, organist at Mühlhausen

might mean the following: shortly after the devastating fire, Eilmar offered the use of *his* church (St. Mary), the traditional location of the annual *Ratswahl* cantata, for a special service.[20] According to his writings[21] and his inclination as an orthodox Lutheran, Eilmar promoted the place of the cantata in the service. By furnishing Bach with the most suitable text for such a mourning service—the *De Profundis* (Psalm 130)—he gave the young organist, who had just arrived in town, an opportunity to react as creative musician to the disaster that was still in everyone's mind in the summer of 1707. About a half year later Bach would collaborate again with Eilmar in the *Ratswahl* Cantata. Their friendship outlasted the composer's short stay at Mühlhausen; for Bach asked Eilmar to be Godfather at the birth of his first child, Catharina Dorothea, who was christened on December 29, 1708, in Weimar.

It is, moreover, likely that Bach compiled the texts of his earliest cantatas in collaboration with Eilmar, whose theological influence may be suspected from Bach's preference for Old Testament texts, especially those taken from Psalms. Of the 36 vocal movements in his first 6 cantatas (BWV 131, 106, 71, 196, 4, and 150) almost one-half, or 17, make use of Psalm verses, 12 of hymn stanzas—of which total, however, 7 comprise the text of Cantata 4—4 of scriptural quotations from the Old and only 3 from the New Testament. Five are composed to newly written texts.

Of these cantatas only No. 71 lacks an introductory *Sinfonia.*[22] Independent instrumental opening movements which also occur in six of Bach's Weimar Cantatas—mostly in the earlier ones—thus typify Bach's youthful cantata style. About half of these have two viola parts carrying on the tradition of the five-part texture seventeenth-century composers preferred.

Cantata 131 is based on the complete text of the 130th Psalm, thereby achieving an unusual textual continuity. In movements 2 and 4 two stanzas of Bartholomäus Ringwaldt's Lenten hymn of 1588: *Herr Jesu Christ, du höchstes Gut* are superimposed, with their hymn tune of 1593, on the psalm text. The innate contrast of the *De Profundis,* that of sin and hope for redemption, is softened by the two hymn stanzas. These represent the New Testament's assurance that the sins of the faithful shall be "washed away."

The first task that confronted Bach was the organization of the eight verses of Psalm 130 into a definite number of musical movements. Bach decided on five:

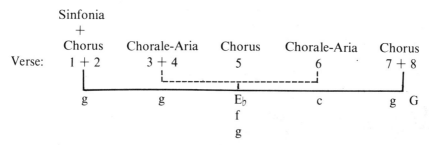

The majority of Bach's early cantatas are conceived symmetrically with a chorus in the center, one at the end and one at the beginning (following the introductory *Sinfonia*).

Rather than fusing a movement into a unified musical whole, as became his ideal later on, Bach is guided in his Mühlhausen and earliest Weimar cantatas by the word. Absorbing himself into his scriptural text, Bach considers it line by line to detect any change of meaning. He does not even shy away from isolating a single word such as the dramatic "aber" in the first chorus of Cantata 21 (bar 38). Having organized his textual material and thus created a blueprint for his composition, Bach sets it, idea by idea, as a series of separate musical sections that vary in speed, meter, key and style according to the implications of the text. The young Bach subscribed to the dictum: "In the beginning was the word," and becomes a master in the description of textual detail. In the motif-creating power of the word he follows the tradition of the seventeenth-century motet. When seven years later, in 1714, he falls under the spell of the operatic aria, the word becomes of necessity the "handmaiden" of music. Yet Bach's habit of seizing upon one word and letting it inspire his musical thought may well have its root in his youthful text-serving approach to composition.

FIRST MOVEMENT (binary)

A: *Sinfonia* (binary)   *Adagio* (above the *continuo* called: *Lente*);
                          3/4; G minor
B: *Vivace*   C; G minor

Among Bach's cantatas, No. 131 is unique insofar as *Sinfonia* and first chorus form one organic whole. Although Bach employs six instruments, the musical "happening" occurs in the outer parts of solo oboe, solo violin and *continuo*, a combination characteristic of Bach's early cantatas.[23] The style seems rooted in Corelli's trio sonatas.[24] The two violas, rhythmically tied to the *continuo*, are harmonically filling parts. The bassoon, when not silent, doubles the *continuo*.

The *Sinfonia* and the following choral portion consist each of three clearly defined cadencing sections. Of these the first two stray happily to the relative major key while the choral portion stays in minor keys underlining the despair of the psalm text. The cadencing sections are composed of a pair of head motifs, *Fortspinnung* (which is once omitted), and closing cadence. The downward plunge of the opening motif a_1:

25

Aus der   Tie-fe

again unique with Bach, seems inspired by the psalm's opening words: "Out of the depth." The second motif a_2 is but an embellished variant of a_1:

that inverts the downward swoop of a fifth, characteristic of a_1, by an upward leap of a fourth. In the choral portion, a_2 is sung unadorned:

and thereby made more singable and more closely related to a_1.

The jarring major second, produced by the overlapping of the motif, set to the second text clause: "rufe[26]ich, Herr, zu dir," (in bars 28, 30, 39-41, 43-44, 50-51) is not an inevitable outgrowth of what precedes it musically. Otherwise it would already have appeared in the *Fortspinnung* of the opening orchestral section. Its entrance at the words: "ruf ich, Herr, zu dir" indicates that the effect was text-inspired. In bars 39-41 the realistic picture of voices crying in anguish out of the depth reaches its dissonant climax. Above the chromatically rising *continuo*, the voices climb by whole tone steps in overlapping imitations thereby spanning the tritone from B-flat to E.

Contrary to his later practice, the young Bach keeps the instruments out of the way of imitations or harmonically complex passages such as this one. He uses the orchestra either antiphonally to strengthen or to echo cadences. In bar 36 the vocal bass descends to the lowest note in the whole cantata on the word "Tie-fe":

Since in Bach's Mühlhausen time this C ("*Chorton*")[27] sounded a whole note higher we should perform this cantata nowadays in A rather than in G minor.

The *Vivace* that leaps out of the final cadence furnishes the earliest vocal instance of Bach's sense of contrast. Bach interprets the text of the second psalm verse as consisting of two parts. "Herr, höre meine Stimme" is treated as a syllabic shout repeated four times. Between the last two shouts Bach inserts a monodic statement that has all the qualifications of a fugal subject, set to the remainder of the text: "lass deine Ohren merken auf die Stimme meines Flehens," Instead of the expected fugal development, however, each solo statement is cut short by the remaining shouts of the chorus. That these show *Stimmtausch* (among all voices but the bass) indicates the young composer's early and as yet inconclusive concern with "total counterpoint."

After the fourth chordal shout, the fugue gets finally under way. Its subject is syllabic except for the graphic portrayal of "Flehen" (supplication). This word inspired Bach not only to the movement's one long, wailing, broken-up melisma which leaps up a diminished seventh, but also to the later echo effects. The rather tentative fugue has paired themes[28] of which the first one does not turn out to be the true fugal subject. It is rather a herald that ushers in the second, the true fugal subject, with seven identical notes. As if this ambiguity were not enough, the two first fugal statements enter, not at the fifth, but at the octave.[29] From the third statement on, the "herald" subject shows its short-lived nature. As it fades away (in bar 78) the true subject is joined, half a bar later in imitation at the octave, by the remainder of the subject. The same canonic double exposure recurs between alto and bass in bars 83-85. After these four fugal statements, of which none follows the grammar of fugal writing, the fifth offers yet further surprises. The (solo) soprano enters without its twin subject. Instead, it inserts two sequences before completing itself, or rather trying to complete itself: for three delicious pairs of echoes—instruments alternating with the voices—prolong its completion. After a repeat of the last four measures Bach continues with yet another echo, a three bar coda in which he seems to take reluctant leave of the sobbing motif he had used as a fitting farewell to the word "Flehen."[30] This movement which refused to begin like a fugue also refuses to end like one. Of its forty-one bars only eighteen "behave" according to fugal terms.

SECOND MOVEMENT (*Bar* form)

Chorale-Aria	*Andante*; C; G minor
Quartet texture:	Oboe, Soprano (*c.f.*: d'—d''), Bass (D—e♭'), *Continuo*

With precocious skill, Bach unifies his musical material. The ceaseless motion of quavers in the *continuo* flows from one movement into the next, though now slowed to *Andante*. With similar continuity, the bass voice takes up the echo motif of the previous movement. The oboe, making it idiomatically its own, gives it a new soothing yet plaintive expression. Above all, the soloistic, personal element enters with the bass voice and the oboe as a sympathetic instrumental companion. Did Bach sense an esthetic conflict between this personal musical prayer and the psalm text, generally more appropriate to choral treatment?

The superimposition of a chorale—complete, unadorned, and in long note values—certainly objectifies the insistent pleading of the solo voice. Here Bach applies for the first time the German Organ Chorale of the seventeenth century to the cantata, and that at a time that witnessed the waning of the influence of Pachelbel, the master of polyphonic integration of the chorale into the musical texture.[31] Bach's adoption of the chorale in this, his second cantata movement, places him still more dramatically outside the trend of *his* time that moved from artistic chorale elaborations to a shallower homophonic concept of the chorale (Telemann). With the incorporation of chorales into Cantatas 131, 71, 106, and 4 Bach became the last master who carried on the Scheidt, Böhm, and Pachelbel tradition that his "progressive" colleagues were to undermine.

The juxtaposition of an aria, which in Bach's early cantatas usually hovers between a declamatory and arioso style, with a vocal *cantus firmus*, appears in 75 percent of his Mühlhausen cantatas but only in 5 percent of his total cantata output.[32] Combining Bible words with suitable hymn verses goes back to Hammerschmidt, even to Bach's two predecessors in Mühlhausen, father and son Ahle, and to Bach's Arnstadt uncle, Johann Christoph. Setting two dissimilar texts simultaneously to music is a dangerous device. It attests to Bach's courage that he tried to master it to a far greater extent than his predecessors.

In Cantata 131 Bach solves it logically by assigning Psalm Verse 3 to the 2 × 2 lines that make up the two *Stollen* of the *cantus firmus*; then by synchronizing Psalm Verse 4 with the three lines of the chorale's *Abgesang*. The Psalm text: "If thou, Lord, shouldest mark iniquities, O Lord, who shall stand?" addresses itself to the God of vengeance of the Old Testament. Ringwaldt's Lenten Hymn (Verse 2) and its tune: "Herr Jesu Christ, du höchstes Gut" that the listeners of Bach's time knew by heart, present the New Testament's way out of such apprehension:

Have pity on me in such distress,
Take this burden from my heart,
Because you have atoned for it
On the cross with pains of death.

Eilmar might have chosen this hymn text, but the musical solution was Bach's alone.

As the chorale tune is the form-giving element in this as well as the fourth movement, neither movement shows traces of *ritornello* or *da capo*. The *c.f.* in both movements is intoned above the solo voice, whose emotions it holds in check. The interludes between the seven chorale phrases belong in 131/2 to the bass voice which either insists, with declamatory repetitions on its text, or enters into dialogue, or is intertwined with the oboe in melismatic semiquavers (bar 44 ff. or end of movement). The note repetitions found in this movement[33] are typical of Bach's youthful vocal style. They are a carryover from the century-old *stile recitativo*. Here (in bars 11-14, 27 f., 37-40, 49 f., and 54-56) they intensify the text. In bars 1-2 and 6-7 of the third movement and bars 13 and 27-28 of the fourth, they vivify musically the text: "I *wait* and "my soul waiteth for the Lord."

In 131/2 it is the word "bestehen" of the question: "If thou, Lord, shouldest mark iniquities, O Lord, who shall *stand?*" that draws from Bach— six times—a long melisma. By letting it glide downwards in syncopated steps that tend to end in a twisting figure, Bach seems to imply that the sinful mortal cannot "stand" firmly before the Lord. In the second part of the movement, set to Psalm Verse 4: "But there is forgiveness with thee, that thou mayest be feared," the first half drives home the message of "forgiveness" by its reiteration of the same note. Again a troubling thought—the word "feared"—is underlined by a long melisma of undulating semiquavers that begin with diminutions of the *continuo* figure repeated three times (bar 44) before drawing the oboe into dialogue.

In spite of much thoughtfulness, Bach's inspiration was hardly burning here at white heat. The melodic and rhythmic inventiveness seems somewhat uninspired, and bars 41 and 44 present even two curious harmonic lapses. The composer's workmanship, however, shows already an unusual, Bachian solidity.

THIRD MOVEMENT

Chorus (binary) A: *Adagio* (short Prelude to) B: *Largo* (Fugue). C; E♭ major—F minor—G minor.

Three homophonic blocks of chords open the *Adagio* and modulate from E♭ to B♭ and finally to C Major. This key in turn serves as dominant to the ensuing fugue in F minor. Already in the solemn opening chords Bach insists on keeping oboe and violin independent from the soprano. Throughout the fugue he gives these two instruments and the two violas true *obbligato* parts.

Bach divides the three clauses that make up the one sentence of Psalm Verse 5 by using the first phrase "Ich harre des Herrn" for the three opening chordal pillars and the two Monteverdian florid melismas (on "*harre*") that keep the E♭, B♭, and C Major tutti blocks neatly separated. The moving from major to major chord, a welcome surprise, is but a moment's relief as the ensuing fugue demonstrates. The second phrase: "meine Seele harret" clings to the principal subject throughout the course of the fugue. The remainder of the text, "und ich hoffe auf sein Wort" is, along with occasional repeats of "meine Seele harret," assigned to the contrapuntal voices.

The fugue is based on a subject that begins with the note repetitions so characteristic of the young Bach. Here they declaim in even rhythm of slow quavers, and a minor third above the tonic, the words "meine Seele." The key word "*harret*" (waits) caught Bach's imagination. A flowing melisma of chromatically descending crotchets and minims that dip down to the leading note below the tonic for cadencing, represents the stoic "waiting" for the "word of the Lord." Of the two countersubjects, the first is exciting, full of leaps, sequential and portrays with its syllabic word repetition of 'ich hoffe' the hope that the text speaks of. This combination of themes of fatalism and active energy shows the textual and musical perception in depth of the young composer.

The first fugal exposition (bars 6-16) is a solid piece of polyphonic architecture—too solid, in fact, to last.

Ob.	5	6	5	6
Vl.		5	6	5
S.				1
A.			1	2
T.		1	2	3
B.	1	2	3	—

The design[34] shows an independent two-part fugue for oboe and violin superimposed upon the opening of a four-part vocal fugue. The latter follows the permutation principle[35] that Bach was to develop soon more fully, though its pattern, overly symmetrical and harmonically confining (tonic-dominant) would not satisfy him for long. That permutation is applied only to the first fugal exposition is an indication of the extremely early time of origin of this cantata. The two remaining expositions retain the principal fugal subject though changing its melodic course and thus its harmonic destination. Condensed or stretched out, depending on the unforseeable length of the subject, this destination turns out to be often quite different from what its initial note seems to imply. Countersubjects 2 and 3 of the opening exposition give way to free counterpoints, and the two-part follow-the-leader game of oboe and violin lapses into a free, though frequently imitative, pattern based on the first phrase of its subject, *i.e.* on our old *Leitmotiv*:   .

The two violas to which Bach had assigned independent filling parts (in "hocket" style) follow the dictates of the figured bass. Twice, however, they are drawn into the imitative game between oboe and violin, causing passages of eight- and even nine-part writing. The unusual fugue without episodes that started in F minor ends in G minor, with a Picardy third 3 bars later.

In the three-bar Handelian coda—*Adagio*—the bassoon takes over the enlivening instrumental work that oboe and violin had engaged in up to this point, and that the oboe seizes upon once more in the last moment for a touching highlight, ending an octave above the sopranos. Throughout this movement the bassoon part was differentiated from the *continuo* by *staccato* treatment. By this modest declaration of independence, Bach prepared the bassoon for its brief moment of eloquence at the solemn (*Adagio*) end of the musical action. Only once more, in the two swift antiphonal surges of the last movement (bars 21-26) will the bassoon be called upon to add to the drama—there, however, as equal partner of oboe and violin.

FOURTH MOVEMENT (*Bar* form)

Chorale-Aria 12/8; C minor
Trio texture: Alto (*c.f.*: g—g′); Tenor (c—a♭′); *Continuo.*

Since Bach employs the same hymn tune here he had used in the second movement, no tempo indication is needed. Playing the quavers 50 percent faster than in 131/2 assures the *c.f.* of its former pace. Bach now had to embed his *c.f.* into music of less apprehensive anxiety. In contrast to the bass voice in the second movement, the tenor in 131/4 moves with greater intervallic freedom and emotional abandon. A true *basso ostinato* opens the movement. Sequential in its melodic profile and gigue-like in rhythm, though flowing more smoothly, the *continuo* starts out like a *Passacaglia*, presenting three statements of a three-measure theme. By what remarkable yet simple sleight-of-hand Bach turns this *ostinato* theme from an insufferable bore, composed of nothing but sequences, into a distinctive melodic and rhythmic entity!

i.e. from:

into:

On the last note of the first *ostinato* theme the voice enters, haltingly, with a monotonous seven-note phrase that for 20 out of 21 beats dwells on one note (g); no doubt, to sustain and thereby illuminate the word "wartet" of the opening text-phrase, "My soul waiteth for the Lord." This vocal opening stands at the beginning like a motto, a favorite device in Bach's arias though rarely found in arias that are twinned with a *c.f.*

The moment the alto chimes in with the fifth stanza of Ringwaldt's hymn, "Herr Jesu Christ, du höchstes Gut," it takes over the form-giving function from the *continuo*. The latter gives up the repetitions of its clearly profiled *Passacaglia* theme in favor of continuous motion. Yet this motion uses, with one three-note exception (bar 20, resp. 42), throughout the *Stollen* the material of the opening *ostinato* theme, *i.e.* x, y and their inversions. Whereas the ceaseless flow of the *continuo* provides only transitory cadences before arriving at a clear cadence at the end of the *Stollen*, the tenor voice, preserving its melodic independence from the *continuo*, tends to create smaller divisions. With the *Abgesang* the procedure changes subtly. Bach emphasizes the new textline, "Von einer Morgenwache bis zu der andern" (more than they that watch for the morning), by giving the voice a new and, on the whole, more syllabic melody. In contrast to the *Stollen*, this melody is taken up by the *continuo* in short *stretto* passages (bars 52-53, 54, 69-70, 79-80). This new relationship of *continuo* to tenor is reinforced by frequent common cadences that Bach had avoided before and that now throw the three remaining *c.f.* phrases into sharper relief (three times C minor—B-flat Major—E flat Major—C minor—E-flat Major, and again three times C minor). During the *Abgesang*, only half of the *continuo* figures derive from the old ostinato theme—and these mostly from bar 59 onwards, when the text of the *Stollen* is repeated. This is further proof of the relative independence of *Abgesang* from *Stollen*.

In 1729 Bach, then twice the age he was when he composed Cantata 131, produced with an instinct of shattering proportions his conceivably most moving superimposition of a *c.f.* upon a chorus. In the opening chorus of the Matthew Passion, Bach intones the German *Agnus Dei*, the chorale "O *Lamm* Gottes unschuldig" as the timeless yet immediate answer to the great cries of the two choruses "sehet—Wen?—den Bräutigam, seht ihn—Wie?—als wie ein *Lamm.*" While light years separate the two chorale arias of Bach's first cantata from this sublime solution of 1729,[36] the principle, *i.e.* the simultaneous setting of two sacred texts, is nevertheless already established in 1707. Though lacking the aptness of the juxtaposition in 131/2, one might even see in 131/4 a forerunner of the opening chorus of the Matthew Passion—the soul waiting for the Lord (tenor), pacified through the confidence expressed by the *c.f.* (alto) which speaks of the sorrowful sinner who would gladly have his sins washed away in Christ's blood.

FIFTH MOVEMENT (binary)

Chorus A: *Adagio—un poc' allegro—adagio—allegro.*
B. Fugue. C; G minor.

As in the two preceding choruses, a predominantly homophonic prelude is followed by a fugue. Again, the prelude adheres to the motet-like principle of interpreting every single textual idea by a different musical setting. In 131/5 four such tempo changing sections compose Psalm Verse 7. Like 131/3, the final chorus opens (*adagio*) with three mighty syllabic shouts, here of "Israel"—

D Major (in first inversion), G minor, D Major. The completion of this first text clause: "hoffe auf den Herrn," marked "*un poc' allegro*," leads from G minor to the relative major and back to the tonic. When the orchestra in this section is not on its own—which it is at the beginning, middle, and end—it doubles the opening phrase of the voices. This syllabic *tutti* phrase is, with slight modifications, heard four times. Twice it is followed by a closely knit imitative melismatic passage on "*hoffe*" and twice by a homophonic echo, marked expressly "*piano.*" These four interludes are accompanied only by the *continuo* (excluding even the bassoon). A final instrumental passage, marked "*pianissimo,*" reduces the second echo to a double echo.

For the two remaining text-phrases of Verse 7, Bach renews the time honoured *adagio-allegro* contrast. In the first, "denn bei dem Herrn ist die Gnade" the chorus extols three times the "mercy of the Lord." In a majestic chordal style and *forte*, this passage moves from C minor (SD) eventually to D Major. While the third statement is an extended version of the first, the middle one uses new material. When the first, quasi *a cappella* statement reaches shining G Major, stimulated by the word "Gnade," Bach floods the senses with an instrumental halo, floating a tender oboe melody above the emotional throb of the remaining instruments. The idea of "mercy" that the text promises here inspired Bach to the most moving harmonies in the whole cantata. Thereafter Bach is carried away by the thought of "plenteous redemption" of the final text clause, "und viel Erlösung bei ihm." He treats it as an *allegro* whirlwind in "hocket" style that whips both the voices and the even more agitated independent instruments (oboe, violin, bassoon) into frenzy. In two breathless imitative waves they move from D Major through B-flat back to G minor.

The concluding fugue, based on the 8th Psalm Verse, begins in bar 27. Did Bach at the age of 22 already employ the number 27 as a symbol of the Trinity, of divine forgiveness?

The cadential motif (ii-V-I) that ushers in this tentative permutation fugue is not its principal subject. Its brevity, its preferred position in the bass and on the dominant, and its lack of physiognomy speak against this. It is rather a fragment, detachable from the second subject,[37] with which it forms a textual rather than musical union: "und er wird Israel/erlösen" (called 2a and 2b on the following chart). The principal subject (I) is set to the final text clause of Verse 8: "aus allen seinen Sünden" (from all its iniquities). It is characteristic of Bach's literal identification with his texts that he portrays not so much redemption from sin but rather the heaviness of stripping off *sin*,[38] the keyword of the German phrase. He does so, slowly, and by a chromatically ascending theme that rises with difficulty and appears to be the counterpart of the stepwise descending fugal subject of 131/3. In 131/5 it is twinned with a counter-subject of the *Fortspinnungs*-type (2b) set to the word "erlösen." Inspired by the thought of "redemption," Bach treats it as he was to do a thousand times hence,

Ob.						Adagio
		3*--(3*)---	-- : -- --2b --(3)	(1)--	:	echo
Vl. I		(3*)1* ---	-- : -- 2b --(3)	-- : -- 1 ---	:	echo
Vla. I		(3*)	-- : -- 2a3 2b 1	(3)--	:	echo
Vla. II		(2b) 3 1	-- : -- 3 --- 1 2b		:	echo
S.	2a-2b 3 (2a)2b	2a 2b (3)	-- 1 2b --(3)	(1)--	:	echo
A.	1 (3)	1 2b	(3)--- 2a 3 2b 1	(3)--	:	echo
T.	2a 2b -- 1	(2b) 3 1	(2b) -- 3 --- 1 2b	(3)--	:	echo
B.	1 2a (2b)1	2a(2b)--- (3)	2a(2b)--1 3 2a 2b-	:	echo
Bn.	2a (2b)1	-- 3	(2a)2b--1 3 2a 2b-	:	echo
Cont.	-- : -- 2a -- : -- 1	-- : --	(2a)-- : -- 2a	:	echo

| | | | | | | G. |

Key: d - g - d - g - c - E: c- g- d- g- d- g- G-

-- means: free counterpoint.
(2a) or (2b) or (1) or (3) means: incomplete, extended or not quite literal statements of the
respective fugal counterpoint.
* designates independent instrumental entrances that do not double the voices.

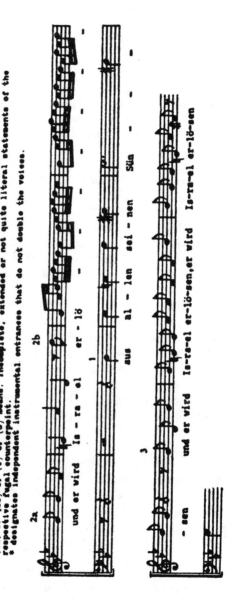

2b
und er wird Is - ra - el er - lö

2a
aus Al - len sei - nen Sün

3
und er wird Is-ra-el er-lö-sen, er wird Is-ra-el er-lö-sen

- sen

- den

by joyous chains of florid melismas that rise in sequences of semiquavers. The juxtaposition of two strongly profiled, contrasted, yet complementary, subjects is typical of concluding movements in Bach's early cantatas. Bach does not, however, help the clear intelligibility of the words—always a problem in choral composition—by introducing his two chief subjects simultaneously from the outset. At the second fugal entrance they are joined by a third subject. Less well defined as to beginning and end, it supplies the welcome concise rhythm of syllabic quavers. While counterpoints 2a and 2b divide the phrase "und er wird Israel/erlösen" between themselves, the last counterpoint (3) not only presents it whole but repeats it as if to compensate for the tendency to divide shown by 2a and 2b.

When the overeager opening motif (2a) appears within the framework of the other three subjects it is heard in the proper key rather than in conflict with its environment (*cf.* bars 57-59). The graph does not indicate that the young composer handles the permutation principle, in spite of all attempted strictness, rather freely. The score alone reveals the frequent abbreviations of the counter-subject (2b) and the many different forms that the third subject (3) assumes. In 131/5 Bach had not yet learned how to organize the counterpoints of a permutation fugue into logical members of a unified whole, i.e. into one successive melody consisting of beginning, *Fortspinnung* and cadence.[39] The jumbling of the counterpoints that begin here with the cadence motif (2a) betrays a lack of sense of continuity typical of a composer still in an experimental stage. Also the order of keys of the twelve fugal statements: G-D-G-D-G-G-C-G-G-D-G-D, all in minor, leaves room for more imaginative treatment.[40] Only the bold final *Adagio* cadence seems to break out of the self-imposed shackles that enclosed Bach in the fugue proper.

After the first fugal exposition (which ought to be sung by solo voices since instrumental support is lacking), the instruments begin (from bar 36 onwards) to double the voices (which therefore ought to be sung *choraliter*). As five instrumental parts—not counting the *continuo*—face four vocal parts, one instrument is always free to add fresh contrapuntal material to the four-part fugue: until bar 52 predominantly the oboe, thereafter the violin. In the final Handelian *adagio* cadence, another characteristic of Bach's early compositions, the composer reverts to the more piercing timbre of the oboe to float a high independent line that begins and ends a sixth above the sopranos and the violin, now doubling.

Only false hero-worship could cause us to call the three fugal movements of this cantata vocally truly effective. It is immaterial whether Bach could not detach himself from the style of the organ, as Spitta believed, or whether he was still grappling with the intricacies of vocal fugal writing, as this writer believes. What matters is Bach's extreme concern with contrapuntal detail, his desire to get maximum usage out of the musical material, once he had chosen it. This, in turn, means: refusal to pad the musical texture for the sake of effect. In this respect Bach differs even at the age of 22 from his contemporaries. Thirty years later, one of them[41] would take Bach to task for darkening the beauty of his compositions by an "excess of art." Finally, Bach's first cantata reveals that the composer had already in 1707 arrived at his artistic credo: the vivification of his text through music.

Notes

1. See *Bach-Jahrbuch*, 1959.

2. In addition to BWV 15, another five cantatas have been wrongly attributed to Bach: cantatas 141 and 160 are by Telemann, 53 and 189 by Melchior Hoffmann and 142 is probably by Kuhnau.

3. Who had substituted for Johann Sebastian during his extended stay at Lübeck one and a half years earlier.

4. Herz, Gerhard, *Bach-Cantata No. 4*, Norton Critical Scores, New York, 1967, p. 94.

5. The autograph score is lost. The surviving performing parts were copied before Easter, 1724 (April 9), except for the cornetto and three trombone parts that were added a year later, before Easter, 1725 (April 1).

6. Dürr, Alfred, *Studien über die frühen Kantaten J.S. Bachs*, Leipzig, 1951, pp. 49, 153.

7. By the same reasoning, Cantata 150, with its bassoon part notated a minor third higher than the other parts, qualifies as a Weimar cantata; but one that on account of its pre-Weimar textform (no recitatives!) was probably composed very early during Bach's Weimar period. Dürr, who finds no reason to question its authenticity, dates it "between 1708 and early 1710." Ibid., p. 210.

8. The permutation fugue follows the scheme of the round. Not only the fugal subject (1) but also all its counter-subjects (2, 3, 4, etc.) are consistently retained and constantly exchanged. No episodes interfere with this rotating process. As in a twentieth century serial composition, practically every note in a permutation fugue is part of a preconceived, kaleidoscopically unrolling structure such as:

$$1 \quad 2 \quad 3 \quad 4 \quad 1 \quad 2 \quad 3, \quad \text{etc.}$$
$$1 \quad 2 \quad 3 \quad 4 \quad 1 \quad 2, \quad \text{etc.}$$
$$1 \quad 2 \quad 3 \quad 4 \quad 1, \quad \text{etc.}$$
$$1 \quad 2 \quad 3 \quad 4, \quad \text{etc.}$$

9. This one and a now lost cantata, composed for the next Town Council election in 1709, are the only cantatas by Bach printed during his lifetime.

10. Dürr, *Studien*, p. 153.

11. It is now owned by the pianist Lilian Kallir-Frank of New York, the wife of pianist Claude Frank. I am indebted to her and to her father, Dr. Rudolf Kallir, the previous owner of the manuscript, for permission to acquire a microfilm for my studies.

12. "Componirt zu Mühlhausen im J. 1707."

13. BG 28, XXI.

14. Spitta, Philipp, *Johann Sebastian Bach*, I, pp. 442, 456.

15. This arrangement is retained in BG 28.

16. The same can be observed in Cantata 106, another bit of corroborating evidence for its similarly early dating.

17. While Frohne was apparently a more soft-spoken person, easy to get along with, the picture of Eilmar, the orthodox zealot, painted by Spitta, *J.S. Bach*, I, p. 359ff., seems overdrawn.

18. *Güldenes Kleinod Evangelischer Kirchen*, 1701. See Mattheson, *Der Musikalische Patriot*, 1728, p. 151.

19. Dürr, *Studien*, p. 157.

20. No cantata performances can be documented for St. Blasius's Church: *Cf.* BWV 106, 71, and 196.

21. In addition to the publication of 1701 (see fn. 18 above): *Entwurf der Andacht bei der Papperoder Brunnensolennité* of 1714.

22. Though the one of Cantata 131 connects with a chorus of the same thematic material.

23. *Cf.* BWV 21.

24. Published between 1681 and 1695.

25. Observe the consistent word-underlay!

26. To suit his purpose, Bach uses both "rufe" and "ruf," a license regarding the scriptural word he shuns in later years.

27. "Choir pitch," *i.e.* the higher pitch of the organs of that time.

28. Like the second movement of the early keyboard Toccata in D minor, BWV 913. *Cf.* Spitta, *J.S. Bach*, I, pp. 450, 439.

29. This again has its counterpart in two early keyboard toccatas: the last movement of the one in D minor (BWV 913), and the second movement of the one in G minor (BWV 915). A cantata by G. Bertuch furnishes the sole known parallel among cantata compositions of this time.

30. A year earlier, in his *Capriccio on the Departure of His Most Beloved Brother*, Bach had used the same motif in order to portray the "Coaxing of the friends to deter him from his journey."

31. Compare the music of the generation of Johann Philipp Krieger, Kuhnau, and Zachow—all Bach's seniors.

32. Besides BWV 131, 106, and 71, in 80a, 60, 158, 49, 58, 156, 159.

33. Also in 131/3 and 4 as well as in 106/3 and 6.

34. Compare Werner Neumann's graphic method of indicating the structure of fugal movements in his *J.S. Bach's Chorfuge*, 3rd ed., Breitkopf und Härtel, Leipzig, 1953.

35. See note 8, above.

36. The vocal version of the *c.f.* belongs, however, to a later revision of the Matthew Passion.

37. See bars 33/4.

38. Compare BWV 28/2; the motif: "hat dir dein 'Sünd' vergeben," with its identical keyword "sin."

39. Compare Dahlhaus, Carl, "*Zer Geschichte der Permutationsfuge*" in *Bach-Jahrbuch*, 1959, p. 95ff.

40. The transcription for organ (BWV 131a), can hardly be blamed on Bach though it attests to the instrumental nature of this fugue. It has come down to us in a copy by Mich. Gotth. Fischer, not by Bach's last pupil Kittel, as was formerly believed. It is included, perhaps wrongly, in BG 38, 217.

41. J.A. Scheibe, in *Der critische Musicus*, May 14, 1737.

Part III

Toward a New Image of Bach

When Johann Sebastian Bach died in 1750 the world did not mourn the death of its greatest composer but rather the passing of its greatest harpsichord and organ virtuoso. The composer, the contrapuntist Bach who wrote his last composition, *The Art of the Fugue*, in the midst of the Rococo or musical *style galant*, was admired by only a few conservative musicians and theorists and dismissed as an anachronism by the progressive majority of his time. The man they called the "old Bach" had died, but Philipp Emanuel was still alive; and *he* was the one they called the "great Bach."

The fact that Johann Sebastian Bach was out of step with the Rationalistic age that surrounded him spelled oblivion for his music during the fifty-year period following his death. At this time the Classical style emerged and all but eclipsed that of the period preceding it. The secular Age of Enlightenment buried Bach. The Romantic Era with its newly awakened sense for history revived him.

Bach was, however, not the first but the third of the giants of the past to be resurrected. Bach reappeared in the wake of a Palestrina cult that embraced the sixteenth-century a cappella style as *the* true ideal of church music and in the wake of a German Handel enthusiasm that was characterized by truly mammoth performances of his oratorios. When, in 1829 with Mendelssohn's performance of Bach's *St. Matthew Passion*, the revival of Bach's church music came, it found the concert halls rather than the churches open to it. The nineteenth-century bourgeois public became the carrier of the new Bach movement.

The period from 1850 to 1900 witnessed the publication of Bach's complete works (the *Bach Gesellschaft* edition) and the appearance of Philipp Spitta's monumental Bach biography (1873, 1880). In spite of these scholarly achievements, Romantic interpretations of Bach's music continued well into the twentieth century with enthusiastic performances of his organ works,

Reprinted by permission from *Bach,* the Quarterly Journal of the Riemenschneider Bach Institute 1/4 (1970), pp. 9-27; and 2/1 (1971), pp. 7-28.

transcribed by Liszt and others for piano, and with large-scale concert performances of the *Matthew Passion* and the *B minor Mass*. This trend of Romantic exuberance lacking in historical concern culminated in America in the 1930s with Stokowski's peformances of such works as Bach's *Organ Toccata in D minor* and the *Chaconne* for unaccompanied violin, transcribed for his 110-piece Philadelphia Orchestra.

But already in the first decade of our century warning voices were heard. Albert Schweitzer considered it "a crime against the style of Bach's music that we perform it with huge orchestras and massed choirs."[1] The young organist Schweitzer also declared war on the factory-built giant organs of the turn of the century and battled valiantly for the preservation of old organs. At the same time Wanda Landowska's playing of the harpsichord opened eyes and ears not only to the applicability but also to the esthetic superiority of the harpsichord over the piano in the execution of Baroque keyboard music. From 1904 on, musicologists used the new *Bach-Jahrbuch* to air their views of Bach as an historical figure and of his music as an historically conditioned phenomenon. Since World War I the gradual revival of practically all the instruments of Bach's time has increasingly undermined the Romantic concept of Bach's music. Since World War II the LP record has brought into our schools and homes the sound of the Baroque orchestra and thereby speeded the unlamented demise of what might be called the "Wagnerian" Bach. Small-scale performances, even of such large choral works as the *B minor Mass*, vie with the old and massive Bethlehem Bach Choir tradition. Robert Shaw's fundamentally different recordings of the *B minor Mass*—the one from the early 1940s, the other from the early 1960s—dramatize to what extent performance practices have been affected and changed by new scholarly insights.

It seems bewildering that the planners of the new Bach edition[2] found in 1950 all the philological and critical problems that the editors of the old *Bach Gesellschaft* and Philipp Spitta had so bravely faced and tried to solve a hundred years earlier. Questions of authenticity and chronology were until twenty-eight years ago still based for the most part on intuition and hypothesis. When Wolfgang Schmieder published his thematic-systematic catalogue of Bach's works in the bicentennial year 1950, the world was aghast at the considerable number of doubtful compositions attributed to Bach and the recurrent *Leitmotif*: "date of origin unknown."

Problems of performance, that is, of the correct historical instruments, of ornamentation, dynamics, and tempo, had been attacked and to an encouraging degree solved. Bach's habit of *parody*—of reusing and revising some of his own music for different later occasions—his use of number and other symbolisms, even his indebtedness to rhetoric have been revealed. Investigations of the social, theological, and musical conditions at

Mühlhausen, Weimar, Cöthen, and Leipzig allow us to see Bach the organist, the *capellmeister*, and the cantor in relation to his environment. The Lutheran orthodoxy, claiming Bach for itself, disclosed its eighteenth-century status. Bach's cantata texts and their authors have been investigated far beyond their artistic merit out of deference to Bach. From all these and more viewpoints, from a hundred years of Bach scholarship, an imposing picture of the composer has emerged—so imposing in fact that Bach and the polyphonic style of his time became once again a living force destined to aid in the breakdown of Romanticism and to contribute to the emergence of the Neo-Classic style to which they gave its solidity of method and form.

The New Bach Chronology

The first part of this article concerns itself with the upheaval in recent Bach research which Friedrich Blume has called an "avalanche"[3] and which Friedrich Smend tried to belittle by calling it "a little breeze."[4] A "little breeze" it certainly is not; for what actually happened is that Spitta's chronology of Bach's compositions, held valid since 1880, has been replaced by a new one which necessitates the redating of two-thirds of Bach's cantatas alone. With the acceptance of this new chronology, a whole world of conjectures and interpretations by Spitta and his countless followers collapses.

It is somewhat disconcerting to observe that music lovers, musicians, and even teachers of music in America are for the most part still barely aware of this break-through in basic Bach research and its profound consequences. I will, therefore, have to concentrate first on the revolutionary findings of Alfred Dürr and Georg von Dadelsen. Twenty-eight years ago these two eminent German Bach scholars published the results and insights they and some of their colleagues had gained from a painstaking analysis of Bach's handwriting, from the various scripts of his many copyists, and from the corroborating evidence supplied by an equally methodical investigation and classification—according to watermarks—of all the paper on which Bach's manuscripts were written.

While Dürr's precise and massive data fill practically the whole *Bach-Jahrbuch* for 1957,[5] von Dadelsen, aiming at greater readability, places his findings into historical context. In the absence of a much needed translation, particularly of von Dadelsen's book,[6] I can do no more nor less than try to touch upon the salient points of Dadelsen's altogether admirable presentation for the sake of those who cannot read his study in its original language. The first part of Dadelsen's book (pp. 15-48) concerns itself with the different methods used for the establishment of a Bach chronology.

The Old Chronology

The sources that aid in ascertaining chronological data which Spitta and his contemporaries interpreted correctly I will only mention. First among them are the originally dated or datable autographs.[7] They are the obvious pillars of any Bach chronology. Yet their reinvestigation has produced new insights. For instance, graphological evidence has recently shown that the "Aria" in *Anna Magdalena Bach's Notebook* of 1725 was entered into the notebook about seventeen years after the title page date, (i.e., at the time *The Goldberg Variations* were written), copied by Anna Magdalena from the printed version or, more likely, from her husband's manuscript.[8] The often expressed doubts regarding Bach's authorship of the "Aria" that begot the variations can thus be laid to rest.

Second in importance for chronological questions are the few compositions that were published during Bach's lifetime.[9] The original printed texts of some of Bach's vocal compositions constitute a third, though a more tricky, source of evidence; for Bach did not always take his cantata texts from already printed text collections, as had heretofore been assumed. Sometimes the poets published them well after Bach had set them to music, a fact which has been disclosed only recently.[10] The liturgical data of the orthodox Lutheran church constitute an obvious fourth source. With their considerable local differences—for instance between Weimar and Leipzig—they frequently become decisive for the dating of Bach's cantatas. Studies of the conditions in certain cities provide further insights. Books such as Smend's *Bach in Köthen* (1951) or Schering's *J.S. Bach und das Musikleben Leipzigs im 18. Jahrhundert* (1941) have shed new light on the music of such periods, their performers, their instruments, their technical abilities, occasions and places of musical performances, and other relevant facts. Also, local variants of chorale melodies as well as of hymn texts (for instance between Weimar and Leipzig usage) can serve as clues to the place of origin of some of Bach's organ and vocal music. Furthermore, exact knowledge of the history of musical instruments and Bach's use of them has produced important results. Dates such as the year of the invention of the *oboe d'amore* (about 1720) become crucial. The gradually increasing compass of the harpsichord and the varying compass of manuals and pedals of Bach's organs, need, in spite of much research that has already been done, the minute attention that has been given to Beethoven's piano. The question of how Bach solved the vexing problem of the difference between the woodwinds which were tuned in true pitch (called *Kammerton*) and the *Chorton* of the organ which was a second or a minor third higher, has from Rust and Spitta to Dürr[11] and Mendel[12] yielded increasingly more precise answers.[13] The same is true of the three different keys that Bach used for the notation of his *oboe d'amore* parts. Here we reach the borderline of the philological: Notation.

Notation has always reflected changing trends in music; and the time of the *Well-Tempered Clavier* is no exception. Remnants of the old church-tone system recede while key signatures and accidentals are used more precisely. Our modern sign for "natural" replaces the sharp, used formerly to cancel a flat. Double sharps and double flats appear. The Dorian notation—D minor without its one flat—begins to disappear, etc. The history of the actual pinpointing of such appearances and disappearances in Bach's autographs begins, as it should, with the chief editor of the old *Bach Gesellschaft (BG)*, Wilhelm Rust. To him belongs the honor of having deduced from these notational differences and changes a quite dependable first order of Bach's undated compositions.

Spitta's Dating Method

Spitta was generations ahead of his time when he went one step further than Rust by declaring the watermarks in the paper of the original manuscripts the most important aid in the dating of Bach's music. By grouping manuscripts with identical watermarks together, he brought for the first time a far more promising order into Bach's artwork; and that already in the 1870s when a total survey of Bach's work was not yet possible. Spitta recognized and arranged— for the most part correctly—the watermarks and corresponding dates of the works of the Weimar, Cöthen, and early Leipzig periods. Spitta proves to be right whenever the dates assigned to a watermark are based on at least one composition that is either dated or otherwise unquestionably datable. When, on the other hand, no dated manuscript for a certain paper exists, or when a watermark has one or several variants with which it could be confused, then two areas of possible error become apparent. These dual possibilities of error, in fact, show precisely where and why Spitta made his crucial mistake in dating the works of Bach's Leipzig period.

Already Spitta's dating of the three principal watermarks of the period is seen to be only partially documented by fact. The watermark of the first Leipzig phase, *IMK*, is found only in datable manuscripts of 1723 and 1724. Spitta's stretching of this phase to the year 1727 is unsupported by evidence. It rather grows out of Spitta's desire to distribute Bach's cantata output evenly throughout his entire Leipzig period. The watermark *MA* appears in several datable manuscripts of the years 1727-35—reason enough for the establishment of a second period. Recent research has learned to differentiate among three different forms and sizes of this watermark. Since these discoveries necessitate the radical redating of only ten cantatas, Spitta's second Leipzig phase is mostly still in accord with truth.

It is the third period, from 1735-44, to which Spitta assigns the chorale cantatas, that turns out to be the misplaced keystone in Spitta's elaborate edifice of a cantata chronology. This period's principal watermark, that of a "Halfmoon," does not appear in a single dated or datable autograph. Except for the *Sanctus* of the *B minor Mass*, it is found only in cantata manuscripts, a fact which of itself should create suspicion as to its use over a full decade. Spitta arrived at his late dating (1735-44) by a number of ingenious hypotheses all of which Dürr and Dadelsen were able to disprove. Let me point out one instance: Spitta considers the simultaneous appearance of the "Halfmoon" and "MA" watermarks in the papers of one and the same composition as proof of a borderline year between these periods. However, in each of the three cases of simultaneous use of two papers[14] only one of the parts[15] shows the "MA" watermark; and as Dürr[16] was able to prove, these single parts were added for later reperformances of the cantatas.

Not only the dates of Spitta's "three Leipzig periods" but also the order of their three principal watermarks must be revised. As we shall presently see, the cantatas with the "Halfmoon" watermark, that is, the chorale cantatas, in which Spitta saw the final form at which Bach arrived at the end of his life, turn out to be the work of Bach's second year in Leipzig. "If one considers," says Dadelsen,[17] "that Spitta's dating of the other watermarks is based far-reachingly on their relation to these principal ones, one can imagine on what uncertain ground the previous chronology rests." Above all, one begins to realize to what extent we will have to revise Spitta's interpretation of the "organic" growth of Bach's cantata style, culminating in the chorale cantatas. Since most style-critical investigations of Bach's music were based on Spitta's chronology, all of them will have to be revised in the light of the new chronology.

Wilhelm Rust, editor of nineteen volumes of the old *BG* edition, was the only one who seems to have perceived the crucial flaw in Spitta's chronology. At least Rust assigns, in the year after the completion of Spitta's biography, to two parts of Cantata 134[18] the Spitta-defying correct order by placing its "Halfmoon"-marked first violin part ahead of the "MA"-marked continuo part. Had Rust only stayed on as editor-in-chief of the *Bach Gesellschaft*, how much closer to truth the interchange of Rust's longer musical and critical editorial experience and Spitta's historical and speculative instincts might have led! It remains one of the true tragedies in the history of Bach scholarship that Spitta's attacks on Rust and finally the completion of his biography hurt and intimidated Rust to such an extent that Rust resigned from the editorship of the *Bach Gesellschaft*. He took this fateful step just at the time when an exchange of ideas might well have prevented some of the cardinal errors that the not yet thirty-nine-year-old Spitta perpetuated without Rust's experienced assistance.

As it was, Spitta's work became law, so to speak. No one dared to question the great biographer's authority. His basic findings and conclusions remained incontestable for seventy-seven years. Necessary corrections concerned only detail and, thus, did not destroy the basic image created by Spitta.

Cantata Texts and Historical Events

Another problem has played havoc with historical truth from Spitta's biography to Whittaker's recent two volumes on Bach cantatas.[19] It concerns the question of whether the texts of some cantatas might not refer to certain historical events. Spitta is still the cautious scholar when he says, "The style of poetry . . . is for the most part too undefined for us to draw any inferences from it, though sometimes it is possible."[20] But later he forgets his own caution and proceeds to utilize textual references to connect two cantatas, BWV 79 and 143, with the war-like conditions of 1735 and Cantata 116[21] with the beginning of the Second Silesian War in 1744. The Bach text specialist, Rudolf Wustmann, encouraged by Spitta, is in 1913 the first of many to see in Cantata 39: *Brich dem Hungrigen dein Brot*, the music for the Sunday service held in 1732 for the Lutheran refugees who had been expelled from their native Salzburg by counter-reformational events. It is touching to read in subsequent accounts of such renowned scholars as Hans Besch and the late Wilibald Gurlitt how the Leipzig citizens opened their doors and their hearts to their Austrian brethren in faith and how Bach, moved by these events, consoled the Salzburg refugees on the following Sunday with his musical sermon: "Break Bread with the Hungry."

Encouraged by Spitta's and Wustmann's conjectures, Arnold Schering goes emotionally overboard in his impassioned description of Bach's "political music" allegedly written during the Polish entanglements of 1734-35 and the Second Silesian War ten years later.[22] To the cantatas already so assigned, Schering adds others. Friedrich Smend, in his studies of Bach's Church Cantatas (1947-49), was already able to refute some of Schering's alleged dates. Dadelsen and Dürr go one step further. They state that not one date of the eight works connected with Spitta, Wustmann, and Schering with events of war and peace can be proven. Six can definitely be disproven, including *Brich dem Hungrigen dein Brot* which belongs to the year 1726. Two cannot be refuted for the simple reason that their autograph scores and original performing parts have not come down to us. The political event, read into certain passages of cantata texts, has certainly proven to be a deceptive source for chronological identification.

Dadelsen cites what is no doubt the choicest among the examples in which Schering lifts Spitta's still carefully worded hypothesis regarding Cantata 116 into the realm of apparently proven fact. The chronological error is thereby less disturbing than Schering's impassioned interpretation of text and music. As an example of the kind of material that fills so many Bach books in our libraries, Schering's passage is quoted in full[23] (the translation is mine):

On the 30th of November 1745 the city [of Leipzig] surrendered to the Count Johann Adolph of Weissenfels. The deputees of the Town Council had to conclude an ignominious treaty and agree to enormous reparations. And on one of these dark November Sundays... Bach tried to console his demoralized congregation with the Cantata *Du Friedefürst, Herr Jesu Christ.*

With high dignity and composure, but also with controlled passion Bach interprets the text. That only one of the four movements is in a minor key while the remaining ones tend towards the bright A Major and E Major, shows Bach's intention not to allow dejection to rise in church. In the first chorus lives a fighting spirit. Only in the errors and carelessness of the continuo part written by the Master himself may we recognize that amidst the booming of Prussian cannons in front of his window, even his heart trembled momentarily.

This is Schering's account. Now for the facts. No guns sounded in front of Bach's window nor anywhere else in Leipzig on the twenty-fifth Sunday after Trinity, November 26, 1724, the true date of the performance which differs from Shering's construed date by twenty-one years. Furthermore, the title page of Cantata 116 states clearly: *"Dom[enica]* 25 *post Trinitatis."* Is it not embarrassing that Schering, this life-long Bach scholar, should have overlooked the fact that the year 1745 for which he claimed the cantata, had only twenty-four Sundays after Trinity? Furthermore, the continuo part is not in Bach's own handwriting but in that of his principal copyist of the early Leipzig years, Johann Andreas Kuhnau, whose youth might account for shaky handwriting and errors. I have quoted this one example in full because the shelves in our libraries bulge with books that relate, with the confidence gained from Spitta, countless similar tales—tales which our newly developed philological tools of handwriting and paper research have proven to be fairy tales.

The Clavierübung Duets

Let me add two additional examples which lie quite outside the realm of Dürr's and Dadelsen's findings. The first concerns the inclusion of the four Duets for harpsichord in *Clavierübung* III, the so-called "Organ Mass." Their interpretation by Gurlitt, Ehmann, and others as communion music seems nullified by their aesthetic irrelevance which already caused Albert Schweitzer to state that they had "got in by mistake."[24] This, however, seems equally unlikely in a work published by Bach at his own expense. Smend has an intriguing theological explanation for the embedding of the twenty-one organ chorales into a composition which—with its opening Prelude and the four Duets, preceding the concluding Fugue—amounts to twenty-seven movements. These Smend[25] compares to the twenty-seven Books of the New Testament of which—true enough—twenty-one are Epistles. Bach may well have observed this coincidence with a knowing smile of satisfaction; but had he planned it that way, the Duets would stand where the four Gospels stand: at the beginning. Rudolf Steglich[26] even goes so far as to compare the Duets to the four elements. However, by drawing on the forces of number symbolism, especially by applying relevant numbers taken from the number alphabet (in which numbers represent the position of each letter in the alphabet) Gerhard Friedemann[27] gives a cunningly appropriate, well-documented, and detailed theological interpretation of the four Duets, representing the Cross, which future musicologists will have to take into serious account.

Since we are not concerned here with the meaning of these Duets but rather with the reason for their inclusion in *Clavierübung* III, let us return to the historical facts. In search of a new position, Bach had tried to make himself more widely known by publishing parts I and II of the *Clavierübung*: the Partitas, the Italian Concerto and the French Overture. Frugal as he was, would Bach have wanted to exclude from the purchase of *Clavierübung* III the many harpsichord players for whom he had written parts I and II and to whom he would appeal again with part IV, the *Goldberg Variations*? Is it not more likely that Bach included the Duets to offset the otherwise one-sided appeal of *Clavierübung* III to the professional organist? Although the eleven small "*manualiter*" versions among the chorale preludes were originally intended for organ, they were also playable on the harpsichord and even on the clavichord. Together with the four Duets, fifteen of the twenty-seven pieces of the *Clavierübung* are, thus, also suitable for harpsichord playing. My admittedly somewhat prosaic guess is that Bach included the Duets in order to retain as purchasers those who, four and eight years earlier, had bought from him parts I and II of the *Clavierübung*.

Bach's Move to Leipzig

My last example will go into the reasons for Bach's move from Cöthen to Leipzig. What we know is considerably less than what historians have read into it. In his letter to his school friend from old Lüneburg days, Georg Erdmann, Bach gives us the facts. Bach tells Erdmann that he had been so content in Cöthen that, had Prince Leopold not married an unmusical Princess (an "*amusa*"), he would have been content to spend the rest of his life in the Prince's service. Bach's first biographer, J.N. Forkel, does not go beyond this simple statement of fact. It is Spitta who embroiders the facts. He speaks of the "narrowness of the musical circle" in Cöthen, "the absence of all development . . . of sacred composition," and of the fact that "it was for this [sacred composition] that Bach must have felt himself especially fitted."[28] With this, Spitta created a theme upon which countless variations were to be written. From Schweitzer who has Bach "lament his virtual severance from church music,"[29] it leads to Gurlitt's moving view of Bach's "fateful decision to place his daily work from now on entirely and once and for all in the service of his church,"[30] and to Fred Hamel who in 1951 spends several pages on the significance of Bach's choice of Leipzig in the name of his "ultimate purpose" to create a well-regulated church music to exalt God's glory.[31] Yet Bach says merely the following, "At first, it did not seem at all proper to me to change my position as Capellmeister for that of Cantor."[32] Forkel was the last one to let Bach leave Cöthen "with regret."[33] The cantorate in Leipzig, Bach would, at least by 1730, have left without any regret. After all, Bach's reason for writing to Erdmann in that year was, that he felt "forced...to seek" his "fortune elsewhere."[34] While asking his old friend to find him a "suitable post" in the city of Danzig where Erdmann lived, Bach does, with no word, indicate a preference for a church position. We can certainly state that, by 1730, Bach was not as interested in a church position as were his biographers for him. This sort of distortion has perhaps been condoned for so long because, from Spitta to the present, it has been perpetuated in the name of Bach's faith.

When Erdmann is unable to comply with Bach's desire for a change, Bach tries in 1733 for a position at the Catholic court in Dresden. In the last sentence of his dedication of the *Kyrie* and *Gloria* of what much later was to become the *B minor Mass*, Bach says:[35]

> I offer myself in most indebted obedience to show at all times...my untiring zeal in the composition of music for the church as well as for the orchestra, and to devote my entire forces to the service of Your Highness.

"For the church" can have only one meaning, namely, that Bach was ready to compose music for the Catholic Church of the Saxon and Polish Court at Dresden. Bach's "humble prayer" for the position he sought was not heard; much to his sorrow, we may assume, but not to that of his biographers who found that fate had saved their subject once more—for the Lutheran cause. To be sure, Bach would never have abandoned his Lutheran faith. About that, there can be no question. But as an artist, knowing his superiority, he was seeking a position—no matter what its denominational affiliation—commensurate with the proportions of his genius. And such a position his church denied him.

The three examples given in the last few pages were cited to help me plead with all possible strength for an historically necessary return to the sources, no matter how disillusioning it may be to leave Romantic interpretation behind and to rediscover the sometimes sobering facts of a science that in German is called *Musikwissenschaft*.

Bach's Calov Bible Rediscovered

That the facts need not be sobering, the following excursion will show. The picture of Bach that has been drawn so far can now be implemented by an all-important source that has recently reappeared. It is nothing less than the

Lutheran Bible with vast commentary by the orthodox Lutheran theologian Abraham Calov (1612-86) that headed the list of books left by Bach at his death: *"Calovii Schrifften. 3. Bände."* This Bible, long believed lost, was exhibited at the 1969 Bach Festival in Heidelberg for which Christoph Trautmann had gathered together the few extant books as well as copies of those books that had once been in Bach's possession. It is almost incredible that the Calov Bible has been in the Library of Concordia Seminary at St. Louis, Missouri, since October 1938, without its identity and provenance being made known beyond the local level. The Calov Bible was returned from its brief sojourn in Germany to St. Louis in October 1969, and I spent the twenty-ninth of December with it at Concordia Seminary. The significance of this spectacular find is obviously the subject for a paper of considerable length.[36] I will relate here only as much as is truly relevant to the up to date picture of Bach I am trying to draw.

Bach acquired the Calov Bible either before or in 1733. Each one of its large, folio-sized volumes, bound in pigskin and in a perfect state of preservation, shows Bach's name with the date 1733 at the bottom right of its three title pages. Beyond countless text corrections and emendations that attest to Bach's intimate knowledge of the Bible text, Bach also added several marginal remarks of which four are of the highest significance as they relate to music.[37] The first is found next to Calov's commentary on Exodus 15: 20-21.

And Miriam . . . took a timbrel in her hands; and all the women went out after her with timbrels and with dances.

And Miriam answered them, "Sing ye to the Lord, for he has triumphed gloriously; the horse and his rider hath he thrown into the sea."

Calov interprets this famous passage as a mighty antiphonal song of Moses and the men of Israel, taken up in response by Miriam and the women. Next to Calov's comment Bach writes—it is unmistakably his handwriting—into the margin:

N.B. Erstes Vorspiel auf 2 Chören zur Ehre Gottes zu musiciren. (*Nota bene.* First Prelude, to be performed with—verbatim: on—2 choirs to God's Glory).

The word *Vorspiel* (Prelude) seems puzzling in this context unless Bach intended to refer to the first number, piece, or movement of a multisectional antiphonal work. If we were to look for such a composition, the opening movement for two four-part choruses of the eight-part motet: *Singet dem Herrn ein neues Lied* comes readily to mind. Its text (Psalm 149: 1-3):

Sing unto the Lord a new song, and his praise in the congregation of saints.
Let Israel rejoice in him that made him: let the children of Zion be joyful in their King.
Let them praise his name in the dance: let them sing praises unto him with the timbrel and harp.

seems almost a paraphrase of the Biblical passage quoted above. Furthermore, Calov's elucidation of this scriptural passage which contains the first words of Bach's motet, *Singet dem Herrn*, uses its next three words, *ein neues Lied.*

Miriam and the other women of Israel did not intone and sing *a new song* but responded like an echo to what Moses and the men of Israel had sung before.

Bach wrote this motet, *Singet dem Herrn ein neues Lied*, either for New Year or, more likely, for the birthday of the Elector of Saxony on May 12, 1727. He inscribed the three title pages of his Calov Bible:

> "J S Bach
> 1733"

The present writer is the owner of an identical signature which perhaps once decorated the flyleaf of the Leipzig copy of the *Organ and Instrument Tablature* by the old St. Thomas organist Elias Nikolaus Ammerbach (Leipzig, 1571). Not only is the date, 1733, the same as that in the Calov Bible but the initial letters, JSB, are intertwined to create precisely the same simple yet beautifully harmonious monogram that appears three times in the Calov Bible.

Whether Bach acquired these books in 1733 or inscribed them in that year after having owned them already for some time, we may never know. The year 1733 as *terminus ad quem* seems more plausible than as *terminus ante quem.* Yet the fact that two out of the six extant titles from Bach's library show not only graphologically identical signatures but also the same year might give pause for reflection. (While none of the other four extant works carries an inscription of the year, Bach signed two of them, one—the Cambridge copy of the Ammerbach *Tablature*—with a very similar monogram, made out of ISB.)

During the years 1731-32 the building that housed St. Thomas School and the living quarters of the rector and cantor was being rebuilt and a new story was added in which Bach received a new room. During the period of construction—from the end of June 1731 to April 21, 1732—Bach and his family found interim living quarters in the house of a Dr. Christoph Donndorf. On April 24, 1732, a horse-drawn coach moved Bach's belongings to his new apartment in the rebuilt St. Thomas School. On June 5, 1732, the new school was solemnly reinaugurated for which event Bach composed a cantata: *Froher Tag, verlangte Stunden* (see Schmieder, *BWV, Anhang, 18*) of which only the text by J.H. Winckler has survived. In spite of the considerable discomfort caused by having to move twice, Bach's duties as cantor and as director of the *Collegium musicum* continued unabated. Into September 1732 falls also Bach's trip and eight-day stay in Cassel where he tested and played the rebuilt organ at St. Martin's. All this activity ceased on February 1, 1733. On that day,

Bach's sovereign, the Elector and King Friedrich August I ("the Strong") died and public mourning was decreed throughout the land from *Estomihi (Quinquagesima* Sunday) to the fourth Sunday after Trinity. During this four-and-one-half month period Bach enjoyed for once a vacation from his performing duties which, in spite of the pause during the Lenten season, would have consisted of about twenty cantatas, the Good Friday Passion music, and the weekly performance of the *Bachische Collegium musicum.* That Bach used this breathing spell to compose a festive *Missa* (the *Kyrie* and *Gloria* of the later *B minor Mass*) as a dedication piece for his new sovereign is, of course, well known. What is less well known is the not particularly noteworthy fact that Bach had for once ample time on his hands.

With this in mind, it seems at least to lie in the realm of possibility that, at some time, less than a year after moving back to the St. Thomas School building, Bach used the sudden cessation of his hectic activities in early 1733 to reassemble and put in order his library and at that time penned his "ex-libris" into his best-loved books. Should, someday, one or the other of the books from Bach's library reemerge and show the same signature and date as that on the Calov Bible and that in the writer's possession, the above hypothesis might be lifted into the realm of probability. For the time being we can only state that Bach's reading of Exodus 15:20-21 and of Calov's subsequent commentary that sparked his own marginal remark, may have been the creative impulse for the composition of the motet, *Singet dem Herrn ein neues Lied.*

Bach's second important entry into the Calov Bible appears at the beginning of the twenty-fifth chapter of the First Book of Chronicles in which the aged King David sets up and, through the casting of lots, provides not only for the music in the Temple but also for the "two hundred fourscore and eight" singers and instrumentalists who are to serve in the house of the Lord. Bach remarks here:

NB. Dieses Capitel ist das wahre Fundament aller gottgefälliger Kirchen Music.
(*Nota bene.* This chapter is the true foundation of all church music pleasing to God.)

The Lutheran scholar Bach sees thus in King David's order the origin of church music as well as that of the profession of the church musician. It is further revealing that Bach selects for a definition of his calling a scriptural passage that not only admits, but even prescribes, instrumental music "with cymbals, psalteries, and harps... for the service of the house of God."

Only a few pages farther on, next to I Chronicles 28:21, Bach notes:

NB. Ein herrlicher Beweis, dass neben anderen Anstalten des Gottesdienstes, besonders auch die Musica von Gottes Geist durch David mit angeordnet worden.
(*Nota bene.* Magnificent proof that, besides other functions of the divine service, music especially has also been ordered into existence by God's spirit through David).

The scriptural words: "and there shall be with thee for all manner and workmanship every willing skillful man, for any manner of service"—might have reminded Bach of the few "willing skillful" men who were put at his disposal in Leipzig "for all the service of the house of God." Bach's dogged and eventually resigned determination to continue his "service of the house of God" under the adverse circumstances at Leipzig may have drawn new faith from Calov's elucidation of this scriptural passage. Calov adds, "[David] did nothing out of his own initiative . . . but followed the model that the Lord through his spirit had placed before him"; and later, "God . . . makes his will clear how he wants to be worshipped by us." Whether or not Bach read something more specific into the meaning of this text and Calov's explanation of it, it seems clear that Bach believed he had found in both texts what he sought: a statement about the God-given, even privileged, position of music in the church service. We know that in Bach's Leipzig years the privileged position of music in the school curriculum, as well as in the church service, was already under attack and that, from September 1725 on, Bach had to fight for rights that, although not revoked, appeared nevertheless outdated to the Leipzig Council. With this in mind, it seems logical but also touching to see Bach looking in his Calov Bible for the help he needed but lacked in life.

II Chronicles 5:13-14 refers to the mystic moment when "it came even to pass, as the trumpeters and singers were as one, to make one sound to be heard in praising and thanking the Lord . . . that then the house was filled with a cloud . . . for the glory of the Lord had filled the house of God." Calov subtitled verses 11 through 14: "How with the beautiful music the glory of the Lord appeared." Bach then underlined *beautiful music* as well as several lines in verses 12 and 13 with red ink. His almost poetic marginal comment, however, is written with black ink—that is, presumably, at a different time. It reads:

> *NB. Bey einer andächtig Musig ist allezeit Gott mit seiner Gnaden Gegenwart.*
> (*Nota bene*. In devotional music, God with his grace is always present).

How did Bach reconcile the comfort he found in the Scriptures with the fights he had to fight in his own professional life? Here a final passage supplies an amazingly relevant answer. After Matthew 5:24-26, which deals with reconciliation with "thy brother" and "thine adversary," Calov adds a commentary that was so personal and significant to Bach that he underlined portions of it. Calov points out:

> NB. As has been said, it is true, that there must be and should be anger. But see to it that it go as it should go and is demanded of you: [namely] that you [must] be angry not when it concerns you but when it concerns your professional service (*Amt*) and God, and that you do not confuse the two: your person and your profession. As for your person, you shall be angry with no one, no matter how greatly you are offended; *but where your service to your*

profession (Amt) demands it, there you must be angry even if *no harm has come,* to you
personally.... *But if your brother has wronged you and made you angry and apologizes to
you for it* ...then the anger shall go away too.

As Bach's underscoring (italicized above) shows, the composer found in this
remarkable passage an answer, even a God-given justification, for his own
pugnacious nature in professional matters.

Bach's comments prove—at least for his use of the Calov Bible—his
particular affinity to the Old Testament and especially to the two Books of
Chronicles with their emphasis on the music of the temple. Bach's desire to seek
and find the origin of church music in the Old Testament, specifically in the
God-inspired concept of temple music by King David, is characteristic of an
orthodox Lutheran who knows the musical history of his church. Above all,
the Calov Bible proves what has always been assumed on the basis of Bach's
church music, namely, that Bach was a profoundly devout person who not only
knew and read his Bible but related his professional life, work, and position to
it.

A Recent Bach View Refuted

When the renowned editor of *MGG*, Friedrich Blume, tried at the Bach
Festival in Mainz in 1962 to use the new Bach chronology for a novel
interpretation of Bach, the man and the artist,[38] the great upheaval in recent
Bach research erupted into open warfare. Blume's picture of a radically
secularized Bach, that of being a cantor and organist against his will, was
certainly overdrawn. Not lacking in sensationalism and occasional disregard of
facts that remain unshaken, this "new look" of Bach gave an unexpected
respectability to the Marxist image of Bach that the Party-faithfuls in East
Germany have tried to evolve. At the same time, Blume's interpretation was all
the more severely attacked by the vested interests of the West German
Lutherans. Led by Friedrich Smend,[39] they retreated all the way to the
formidable line drawn by Spitta some eighty years earlier. They conceded
nothing, not even the results of the great labors of Doctors Dürr and Dadelsen
whose new chronology of Bach's vocal works will, in the conclusion of this
article, be shown as the outstanding achievement of recent Bach research.

Blume's question: "Did Bach have an innermost relation to his churchly
position? Was it for him a necessity of his religious life?" Blume answered in
1962 himself: "Hardly. At least there is no proof of it." But now proof has come
in the form of Bach's entries into his Calov Bible. The spectacular reappearance
of the Bible makes an answer now possible. Bach's relation to his professional
service as organist and cantor was indeed a relation of the heart. In contrast to
Blume, we may now state that there is no split between Bach, the man, and

Bach, the church musician. Bach's recurrent and keen disappointment was not in his faith but in its earthly representatives. With them he fought endless battles; at them he was, as we now can say, "angry" *in nomine Domini.*

Let us finally see how the new Bach chronology was established. Its basic tool is a stupendous catalogue that contains about one hundred different papers and watermarks of all the original manuscripts of Bach's music. They were compiled, carefully described and, in most cases, reproduced in actual size by the paper specialist Wisso Weiss, whose father had already been an avid researcher and collector in this esoteric field. The Bach watermark catalogue has since 1955 been available in typescript to the editors of the *NBA*[40] and has subsequently become a *sine qua non* for all questions regarding authenticity and chronology. Dadelsen sums up its importance by stating that "watermark research is a far more exact means of dating than Spitta dared to hope."[41] Some papers used for a relatively short time allow more than one-half of all manuscripts by Bach to be dated almost to the year on the basis of their watermarks alone.

But it is not so much paper research itself as the combination of watermark and handwriting research that has given Bach scholarship its new solid foundation. Again it was Spitta who first foresaw the importance of Bach's changing handwriting as a tool in questions of chronology. Spitta says:[42]

> Since Bach's manuscripts extend over a period of more than forty years, it would be a by no means impossible task to assign to each period the handwriting that belongs to it by certain distinguishing marks, though in its main features it is curiously constant.

And Spitta even goes on to prophesy that "the difference in the paper would assist in this." Two basic errors prevented Spitta, and thereby the many Bach scholars who followed him almost blindly, from interpreting the organic development of Bach's handwriting correctly: first, the fact that Spitta saw in the chorale contatas, compositions of Bach's late period while in reality they were written from ten to twenty years earlier. This error had to throw any distinct vision drastically out of focus. Secondly, Spitta attributed to Bach many of the manuscripts written by Bach's wife, Bach's sons, and several of his disciples—all of whom imitated the handwriting of their master with some degree of success. As long as these two misconceptions existed, the recognition of the true development of Bach's handwriting remained an unattainable goal.

Handwriting as Evidence for the Dating of Manuscripts

These misconceptions have been cleared up by Georg von Dadelsen. As editor for the *NBA* of the two *Klavierbüchlein für Anna Magdalena Bach*,[43] Dadelsen, in constant close contact with Bach manuscripts, came to realize the importance of handwriting as a primary source for authenticating and dating. Dadelsen's study of the development of the handwriting of Bach himself, as well as that of Bach's family and his circle, became the first of the Tübingen Bach Studies.[44] Dadelsen found obviously early forms of handwriting by both Anna Magdalena and Wilhelm Friedemann Bach in manuscripts with the "Halfmoon" watermark of Bach's chorale cantatas. This discovery undermined the seventy-seven-year-old confidence in Spitta's view of them as the harvest of Bach's cantata output. The appearance in 1956 of Smend's elaborate critical commentary to his *NBA* edition of the *B minor Mass*, with its conclusions still steeped in Spitta's chronology, shocked Dadelsen, Dürr, and some of their collaborators into the realization that the completion and publication of their current investigations of the handwritings in Bach's manuscripts could no longer be delayed. Their systematic and comprehensive comparison of all available dated and undated manuscripts eventually furnished Dürr and Dadelsen with the new tool that Spitta had envisaged but that had eluded him.

Bach's cantatas have usually come down to us in the following form: an autograph score from which a scribe copied one part for each one of the voices and instruments while a second copyist wrote out those parts of which more than one copy was needed. One can imagine how such a combination, often involving even more than one principal copyist as well as several scribes for the duplicate parts, might yield an amazing network of graphological data. These copyists—mostly upperclassmen at St. Thomas School—usually appear for a period of about three years, their youthful handwriting changing and maturing characteristically during this time. These handwritings supply a recurrent rhythmical pattern, particularly welcome in years in which Bach's own handwriting remained rather stable. If we train ourselves to concentrate on such details as the peculiar forms of the three clefs, the accidentals, the rests— especially the quarter rests—the braces, half-notes, single sixteenths, and so forth, clearly distinguishable characteristics will begin to fall into focus.

Let me select from Dadelsen's countless findings a characteristic change which the C-clef undergoes in Bach's autographs. Dadelsen distinguishes between three basic forms that are familiar to those conversant with Bach autographs. One resembles the number "3" and is best known from Bach's Weimar and Cöthen manuscripts. The second C-clef looks like a steep, elongated sinus curve or hook. It characterizes most of Bach's composing scores written in Leipzig. The third form consists of two parts, the "arms" of which make either swinging motions or are rectangular. This form is best known to the layman because Bach used it mostly in calligraphic and fair copies, the esthetic beauty of which made them natural choices for facsimile editions. The professional graphologist might be delighted to learn that Bach's handwriting changed in 1723, the year in which Bach himself changed from capellmeister to cantor, moving from Cöthen to Leipzig where more strenuous composing responsibilities imposing strict deadlines awaited him. The "Number 3" form of the C-clef can be observed in 1723 as giving way to the "hook" form, but not in the most plausible manner. The quantity of Bach's new composing duties in Leipzig would seem to make the unwieldy two-part form of the C-clef unnecessarily time-consuming; yet it is with this form and not with the simpler "Number 3" form that the mutation process begins. Within one year this form develops by recognizable stages into the typical "hook" form that is executed by one simple pen stroke. Once this form is established, the "Number 3" type disappears altogether. (The two-part form continues in calligraphic manuscripts and in its rectangular version characterizes Bach's very last autographs.)

The "hook" form of the C-clef alone allows us to separate the majority of Bach's Leipzig autographs from his earlier manuscripts. In its still transitional forms, the "hook" shape is found in five dated or datable cantatas of 1723.[45] Dadelsen then adds the twenty-four undated manuscripts which show the transitional forms of the C-clef, arranging them according to the earlier and later shapes of the clef as these were documented by the five datable cantatas. This graphological order agreed gratifyingly with the order of these cantatas within the Leipzig church year. Curious gaps in this cantata series began to disappear when Dadelsen added the eight cantatas which have survived only through their performing parts but whose paper and watermarks were found identical to those of the rest of the series. Dadelsen's still tentative list is finally reinforced by:

1. The otherwise inexplicable three-and-three-fourths months gap from *Estomihi* Sunday in February when Bach performed his application piece for the Leipzig position[46] to the first Sunday after Trinity when he entered upon his duties as cantor;

2. The fact that this list includes cantatas for the 25th and even the 26th Sunday after Trinity which did occur in 1723;

3. The correct papers with either the "IMK" or the "MA" (small size) watermarks that belong to the years 1723 and 1724.

Above all, this cantata series proves that Bach created his cantatas week by week, not in a rhythm of one every four weeks, which Dürr had proven in 1951 to be the case for Bach's Weimar cantatas.[47]

This one example, of necessity superficially and all too briefly presented here, will have to serve as a model of Dadelsen's procedure. He shows systematically Bach's changing hand on the basis of all dated and datable autographs. To these facts, supplied by the autographs, he and Dürr then add the powerful corroborating evidence that an equally comprehensive and systematic investigation of the handwriting of all Bach's copyists yielded.

The most startling result of this investigation is the fact that of the three principal copyists[48] whose handwritings are represented in more than three-fourths of the original parts of Bach's Leipzig compositions, not one was found in a datable manuscript after 1727. On the other hand, the handwriting of the copyists of later Bach manuscripts were rarely found in connection with the three principal ones. In the few cases where this happens, the watermarks of the paper used by the later copyists, prove that these parts were added for later reperformances of these compositions.

While the manuscripts began to separate neatly on graphological grounds, the mounting evidence began to show that the bulk of Bach's cantata work was composed before 1727. At the same time Alfred Dürr, whose doctoral dissertation on Bach's early cantatas (see note 11) had already established facts conflicting with Spitta's chronology, came to identical conclusions. From the style-critical method, Dürr was led (as we have seen) to the hard facts of paper and watermark research which sorted out the chief copyists in Bach's manuscripts as neatly as Dadelsen's graphological method did. In the *Bach-Jahrbuch* of 1957 Dürr made known his revolutionary new "time table" for Bach's Leipzig vocal music (see note 5).

Instead of distributing Bach's cantatas evenly throughout his Leipzig years from 1723 to 1745 as Spitta had done, Dürr shows convincingly that Bach—as G.P. Telemann, J.P. Krieger, Christoph Graupner and other composers of his time—composed week after week and holiday for holiday, the music which his new position as cantor at St. Thomas demanded. Although in his first year in Leipzig he frequently reused or remolded earlier Weimar cantatas or revised secular cantatas written in Cöthen, Bach now appears to have labored day by day and week by week for two years to create the basic stock of music needed for his new task. Then . . . he paused.

A Crisis in Bach's Life

When in September 1961, at the first International Musicological Congress held in America, Bach scholars from all over the world pooled their thinking at an unforgettable session at Princeton University, they seemed to converge from ever so many different directions at this impasse of 1725 or some years later. The general question of why Bach's incredible creative energy ceased or slowed down so abruptly was not answered. In retrospect Spitta's spreading of Bach's vocal work over the whole Leipzig period seems more logical and more comforting than the two-year burst of fire, so suddenly calmed. In spite of occasional flames that were to rise again to give birth to the *Matthew Passion*, the *B minor Mass*, the *Christmas Oratorio* (which is mostly parody), and a fair number of cantatas, there seems to have occurred a crisis in Bach's life shortly after Easter, 1725. Unlike the case of Beethoven, there is, in the case of Bach, no nephew, no physical handicap; there are no subsequent dramatic events, no autobiographical outpourings that help to explain the strange reduction of Bach's creative effort. Nevertheless, there must have been a crisis in Bach's life which, some day in the future, will be seen more clearly than I can hope to put it at present.

Bach arrived in Leipzig in 1723, eager to fulfill at last the fifteen-year-old "goal" of his artistic mission—the creation of "a well-regulated church music, to the Glory of God." The first yearly cycle of cantatas shows Bach indulging in an abundance of styles, feeling his way towards the chorale as a sensible method of unifying his weekly composition—though, when he had time in Advent or Lent, he seemed to enjoy working with the freer problems presented by fugal and concerto textures.

The second *Jahrgang* shows the fullest realization of Bach's goal: the chorale cantata. This intensity of production reaches its peak between Christmas, 1724, and *Estomihi* (February 11), 1725, with fourteen imposing works composed in seven weeks, among them the *Sanctus* that some twenty years later became part of the *B minor Mass*.[49] But after Easter the level begins to decline with solo cantatas and adaptations.[50] Then comes *Jahrgang* III. Its motto in Dürr's article, "No performance traceable" punctuates the remainder of 1725. It accounts for the almost unbelievable total of twenty-seven out of thirty-five Sundays and feastdays.

I personally think that we must take the first three complaints that Bach sent to the king late in 1725,[51] and the resultant sharp disillusionment upon receipt of the king's decree,[52] much more seriously than we have done so far. Whether Bach was legally right or wrong in claiming the salary he thought was due him for the music of the Old and the New Service at the University Church, matters as little as whether Beethoven was right, when, fighting for the guardianship of his nephew, he wrote his famous tortured letter to the Appellate Court. What matters is that Bach felt he was being wronged. He felt that he was being treated less fairly than his predecessors Schelle and Kuhnau.[53] He felt that he was being cheated by a bureaucratic university administration out of "fees pertaining to the office."

I think it would be wrong to underestimate the amount of time and nervous energy that it must have cost Bach to answer the lengthy list of rebuttals that the *"Rector, Magistri* und *Doctores"* of the University presented to the king[54] in reply to Bach's accusations. In sixteen pages (220 lines), Bach cites the seven points by which the University defended its "rights" and tries to destroy them in painful detail, point by involved point. It is touching, but at the same time frustrating, to see the master of the fugue struggling in quaint legal language to impart to his and his time's complex sentence structure some of the contrapuntal logic that in music had become child's play for him. The time-consuming and emotional involvement with his superiors had a direct bearing on Bach's creative productivity. We know this for a fact from the cessation of the flow of his Weimar cantatas in 1716. When, after three Advent cantatas, composed with an eye on the vacant post of the chapelmaster, the coveted position bypassed him, Bach wrote no more cantatas in Weimar.

May we not by the same token see in the creative wasteland that stretches[55] from late August to Christmas, 1725, the disastrous effect caused by the "wrong" done to Bach by the University administration? I further believe that, during this time and in the summer of 1725 when the decision to appeal to the king must have ripened in him, Bach simply repeated the Trinity cantatas of *Jahrgang* II (composing Cantata 137 to fill a gap left in that year). The Town Council either did not care or looked purposely the other way, perhaps trying to avoid involvement in Bach's problems with the University. But finally it urged its cantor to begin composing something new again for the Christmas season.

Bach's lack of enthusiasm becomes rather apparent from the modest proportions of the cantatas composed from December 26, 1725, to January 27, 1726, which were written at the time Bach was awaiting his sovereign's reply to his sixteen-page letter of December 31. Did Bach have tongue in cheek when he performed the day before, his cantata 28: *Gottlob! nun geht das Jahr zu Ende* ("Praise God! The Year Comes to an End")? The king's decision (of January 21, 1726) rejecting the principal portion of "the request of said Cantor," must have reached Bach by the end of the month.

How did this bitter news affect him? Did Bach react as man or as artist? All we know is that on February 2—twelve days after the date of the king's decree, or about one week after Bach's receipt of it—Bach began to perpetuate a fraud on his unsuspecting Leipzig congregation. On that day he performed the first of eighteen cantatas composed by his Meiningen cousin, Johann Ludwig Bach (including the Easter Cantata: *Denn du wirst meine Seele nicht in der Hölle lassen*, which William Scheide[56] has proved likewise to be by Johann Ludwig Bach). What an immense decline in quality these cantatas constitute if one compares them with the chorale cantatas of Bach's own *Jahrgang* II! And on Good Friday, Bach's congregation did not hear a new Passion from its cantor's pen, nor a reperformance of his two-year-old *St. John Passion*, but, instead, the Hamburg opera composer Keiser's *St. Mark Passion* that Bach had already copied and performed at Weimar.

Did all these performances constitute a conscious act of artistic cynicism on Bach's part? Were they his "revenge" or his adjustment to the discouraging news that had been handed down to him by the highest authority in the land?

Or did Bach turn to the music of others only after he found his own inspiration wanting?

The fact that Bach must have known better than we do today that the music he performed was vastly inferior to his own compositions makes one wonder whether the "insult" to his congregation and superiors was not deliberate. I cannot help but think that Bach, like any creative artist, wanted recognition; that he was determined to convince the Leipzig Council that he, who in 1723 had been their third choice, was in reality second to none. But after two years of trying to convince his employers and his congregation, Bach came to realize that they remained "deaf."

When he had to fight for certain rights and privileges, the flood of his weekly cantata output dried up. When the king upheld only the minor portion of Bach's request for a redress of grievances, he began to impose the usable but inferior music of his cousin and of Keiser on his congregation.

Then he took up keyboard publication, no doubt in the hope of attracting attention with his six exquisitely wrought Partitas. When this venture had run its modest course, Bach's *"Short but most Necessary Draft for a Well-Appointed Church Music"*[57] seems to indicate a desperate and final attempt to implore the Council (that had just reprimanded him for his indifference to classroom teaching) to treat the subject and practice of music in a more professional and dignified manner. But when the funds sought in 1730 were allocated to the improvement of the building rather than to the music performed in the building, Bach felt that his usefulness to the city of Leipzig had come to an end. Bach's letter to Erdmann,[58] written only nine weeks after his lengthy memorandum to the Town Council, bears this out. It also bears out our reasoning. The financial inadequacy is matched only by his employers' total lack of interest in music and their unawareness of what Bach could do for Leipzig and its music. Bach's own words were:[59]

> But since (1) I find that the post is by no means so lucrative as it had been described to me; (2) I have failed to obtain many of the fees pertaining to the office; (3) the place is very expensive; and (4) the authorities are odd and little interested in music, so that I must live amid almost continual vexation, envy and persecution; accordingly I shall be forced, with God's help, to seek my fortune elsewhere.

When nothing resulted from this attempt to find a new position, Bach applied to the *new* Elector for the position of Court Composer in Dresden with the *Kyrie* and *Gloria* of his later *B minor Mass*. His hopes dashed again, Bach continued with more keyboard publications, this time in the Italian and French manner (the *Italian Concerto* and the *French Overture*). But the irritability of his soul shows in his heated dispute with Rector Ernesti (1736-37). In the midst of this long drawn-out squabble, Bach received from the king, belatedly (on November 19, 1736), the title but not the position he had sought three years earlier.

Soon thereafter the period of festive music, of congratulatory cantatas and other music of homage, comes to an end. Within another few years Bach gives up the *Collegium musicum* that he had directed for a decade. Some time towards the end of the 1730s, Bach seems to have come to the realization that worldly success was not to be his.

Into this time falls Johann Adolph Scheibe's well-known criticism of Bach the composer. Scheibe, who admired Bach's *Italian Concerto*, gives the verdict of the time. Of Bach's compositions, he says that "excess of art darkens their beauty," and that they are "in conflict with nature," that is, in conflict with the Age of Reason, with the progressive trends of his time. This is quite the opposite of the picture that Friedrich Blume had drawn of Bach. If Bach was thought outmoded and out of step with his time, he certainly did nothing to change this impression. On the contrary, according to Bach's devoted friend, Christoph Lorenz Mizler, the third part of the *Clavierübung* was an excellent reply. If we, too, see in this imposing collection (predominantly of organ chorales) an answer to Scheibe's attack, we can only say that Bach was deliberately asking for criticism. That Blume sidesteps this issue, failing also to mention the altogether unique role of the chorale in Bach's music, does not add to the high esteem to which this eminent scholar is otherwise entitled.

Bach and the Palestrina Style

Clavierübung III (the "Organ Mass") is to my way of thinking the beginning of a new style in which Bach turns inward, so to speak. Unlike *Clavierübung* I, II, and IV (the Goldberg Variations that were still to come), this collection of twenty-seven organ pieces, permeated by all kinds of symbolism,[60] was not only written "for Music Lovers"[61] but also "especially for Connoisseurs of such Work."[62] This highlighting of the professional, of form over content, of craftsmanship over musicianly abandon, such as the Partitas or the *Italian Concerto* evoke, has recently been brilliantly illuminated by Christoph Wolff. Wolff shows how at this late stage in life the master, who had taught himself everything he knew, goes once more to school. In his *Der Stile Antico in der Musik Johann Sebastian Bachs—Studien zu Bachs Spätwerk*,[63] Wolff treats for the first time in systematic fashion Bach's hithero underrated study of the Palestrina style. Bach scholarship, generally oriented towards the German roots of Lutheranism, had so far tended to soft-pedal the Catholic-Italian influence on Bach. Wolff's study will go a long way toward eliminating this earlier prejudice.

To the known examples of Latin figural music in Bach's library, mostly copied by Bach himself, Wolff is able to add new ones. Altogether the twenty-four copies—including the spurious BWV 237, 239, 240, 241, and Appendix (*Anhang*) 24-30, 166 and 167—reach from Palestrina's *Missa sine nomine*[64] via

Christoph Bernhard, J.C. Kerll (BWV 241), G.B. Bassani, Joh. Chr. Schmidt, A. Lotti, and A. Caldara to a parody of Pergolesi's *Stabat mater*. Only some of these are strict copies. Others show additions of a short movement (Bassani), of two instrumental upper parts for violins (Caldara), *colla parte* orchestration (Palestrina), retexting and other kinds of revisions. The names of the composers indicate to what extent the Palestrina style survived and was practiced—even by such "modern" composers as Telemann—in the seventeenth and eighteenth centuries. Bach's preoccupation with the *stile antico* is thus by no means unusual for his time.

We know further that Bach owned a copy of Fux's *Gradus ad Parnassum*,[65] that most important theoretical work on the Palestrina style of the eighteenth century. In fact, Bach may well have been the instigator of the first German translation of Fux's treatise since Bach's pupil and admirer, Mizler, was its translator (Leipzig, 1742).

What interests us here above all is that Bach took up the study of this ancient style during the period of his deepest disenchantment with his own time, in the late 1730s and early 1740s.[66] All this would hardly be of prime importance had Bach's preoccupation with the Palestrina style and its continuation in the next two centuries not produced works, written by him, in that style. It is Wolff's chief contribution to have isolated and defined Bach's *stile antico* compositions and deduced their specific style from the principles of composition of the old *prima pratica*.

One look at any one of the ten scores to which Wolff somewhat unnecessarily confines himself shows the large note values and *alla breve* time, so typical of sixteenth-century a cappella compositions. The melodic line, free from accent and ornamentation, returns to monophonic principles and tends to relate to modal *cantus firmi*. Asymetrical prose rhythm replaces periodic bar groupings. The harmony is, for the most part, subordinated to the polyphonic structure. Chordally conceived counterpoint yields to linear texture; expressive harmony (one of the typical Baroque means of moving the listener) to diaphonous polyphony. Structurally, one perceives what might be called total counterpoint—that is, limitation to certain basic contrapuntal formulae and techniques that exclude episodic material and interludes in favor of close and unbroken imitation. In terms of tone color, Bach's *stile antico* compositions reveal themselves either in pure choral sound (with or without *colla parte* instruments) or in the full sound of keyboard instruments. Bach's compositions in *stile antico* are, according to Wolff's perhaps overly restrictive definition (that excludes, for instance, BWV 38/1):

1. The second *Kyrie* (F-sharp minor)   BWV 232/I
   from the *B minor Mass*

2. The three large *Kyries*
   Kyrie, Gott Vater in Ewigkeit   BWV 669
   Christe aller Welt Trost   BWV 670
   Kyrie, Gott heiliger Geist   BWV 671

   The large version of
   Aus tiefer Not schrei ich zu dir   BWV 686
   The first part of the Fugue in E-flat major   BWV 552
   all from *Clavierübung* III

3. *Credo in unum Deum*, F Major, added to
   Mass V by G.B. Bassani

4. Fugue in E Major from   BWV 878
   Well-Tempered Clavier, Book II
5. *Credo in unum Deum*,   BWV 232/II
   Confiteor unum baptisma, both from the
   Credo of the *B minor Mass*

Wolff gives ample evidence that these compositions could only have been written while or after Bach had studied and transcribed music in the style of Palestrina and his adherents in the eighteenth century, such as Lotti and Fux. At the same Wolff shows that Bach's genius was so overpowering that it could make his compositions in *stile antico* also unmistakably his own. Even if we might feel inclined to take a somewhat broader view of Bach's compositions in the old learned style, it is apparent that only a tiny fraction of Bach's compositions are written in his own individual version of the *stile antico*. The second *Kyrie* from the *B minor Mass* is not a pure representative of this style, at least not a much purer one than the *Gratias agimus* from the *Gloria* and similar *alla breve* movements which mix archaic with more contemporary stylistic features.

It seems that Bach's enthusiasm over the conquest of this ageless style expressed itself first in the three giant *stile antico* movements at the beginning of the "Organ Mass." That, however, only one among the six large versions of the catechism chorales is conceived in this style indicates that Bach was in no way about to initiate a new stylistic period. He seems to have been content with adding the results of his studies of the Palestrina style as a new facet to the many styles he had mastered by 1739. The fact that only the first of the three contrasted sections of the concluding Fugue in E-flat Major is written in *stile antico* reinforces this opinion.

The same can be said for the E Major Fugue from the Second Book of the *Well-Tempered Clavier*. Here, too, Bach presents only one example—though one so austere and contrapuntally concentrated that his intention to let it serve as a model of the severe and learned style can hardly be ovelooked. Students such as Krebs, Mizler, Johann Elias Bach, or Kirnberger must have grasped its meaning without fail. In the *Credo in unum Deum* movement, inserted into the Bassani Mass, and in the revision of the *Suscepit Israel* from Caldara's *Magnificat*, we can see the germination of Bach's greatest *stile antico* movement, the *Credo in unum Deum* from the *Symbolum Nicenum* of the *B minor Mass*. The more complex *Confiteor* from the same work is the only case among Bach's *stile antico* compositions notated by Bach in quarter-notes rather than in half-notes. Of the nine movements that comprise the *Credo* of the *B minor Mass*—Bach's last choral work—two represent (different) models of *stile antico* using Gregorian melodies. This is further proof of the decisive yet partial role this style plays in Bach's last creative period.

From the style-critical point of view, Wolff argues in favor of the early 1740s as time of origin for the *Credo* of the *B minor Mass* and consequently also for the movements from the *Osanna* onwards (which are, however, all parodies). This view is not borne out by graphological evidence; on the contrary. This writer sees no reason to question the date of "about 1748"[67] established by Dadelsen and Dürr on sound philological grounds. The different archaic styles of the six-part *Ricercare* from the *Musical Offering* and the opening four *Contrapuncti* from the *Art of the Fugue* do not seem to presuppose the prior existence of the stricter *stile antico* choruses from the *B minor Mass*. Does one style have to be "completed" to make way for another? In the case of Bach, there is ample evidence that he enjoyed composing in different styles simultaneously.

More important than such arguments is the meaning of Bach's *stile antico* compositions. It seems that in his mid-fifties Bach adds to the many styles he had mastered the quasi-timeless style of sixteenth-century vocal polyphony and with it the severe and rather abstract "affect" of *majestas* or *gravitas*—the one furthest removed from the passionate "affects" that had become the *sine qua non* in the Baroque household of emotions. Like the aged Heinrich Schütz (or like Mozart and Beethoven who, however, had Bach and Handel to fall back on), so does Bach towards the end of his creative life return to the very foundations of his art, to the old learned style and to its ageless Latin text. To quote Wolff:[68]

> The reflection upon the music of the old masters, the *ars perfecta* of the sixteenth century, becomes one of the decisive points of origin for the contrapuntal works of the last years of his life. In them, it comes to an unprecedented blending of an historical and contemporary style with that of Bach himself.

To place Bach's concern with the Palestrina style into proper perspective, it should be pointed out that it would take considerably less time to perform the ten movements by Bach assigned by Wolff to the true *stile antico* than it takes to play the *Goldberg Variations*. It is also striking that Bach did not write one single complete composition in *stile antico* but rather reserved this style for certain movements forming parts of larger and stylistically diversified wholes. Yet each one of these compositions, by virtue of the presence of its *stile antico* movements, expands its stylistic horizon beyond that of any work written before 1739.

Bach's Last Compositions

Compared to *Clavierübung* III, *Clavierübung* IV, created three years later, gives the impression that something had given Bach a new lease on life. It seems to have taken no more than the fervent wish—the term "commission" is too strong—from his loyal patron, Count von Keyserlingk, who revered Bach, and the availability of a precocious student as performer[69] to reawaken the old creative powers that were now to generate the *Goldberg Variations*. With their tranquil contemplation or technical fireworks, their moments of expressive profundity, of exhilaration, and even humor, they appear, after the austerity of the "Organ Mass," like a new upsurge of life. Recognition from the Count to whom Bach was indebted for friendship, hospitality, and the ultimate receipt of the title of Court Composer to the Saxon Court, was apparently all Bach needed to ignite in him the spark that was to give to the world his greatest variation work. And for no other composition was Bach ever as royally compensated.[70]

The creative forces, once again released, drew in their wake an even vaster keyboard work: the second book of the *Well-Tempered Clavier*, whose stylistic difference from the first book has not yet found the searching scholarly investigation and interpretation it deserves. It is as though the emphasis on one tonality and one bass, together with the rotation of the three principles of canon, technical display, and character piece that make the *Goldberg Variations* into such a cohesive architectural masterpiece, had freed in Bach forces that had to express themselves once more in all the keys and in the antithetic principles of prelude and fugue. The *Goldberg Variations* and the *Well-Tempered Clavier* II constitute the summit of Bach's art in which he communicates with his fellowmen as friend and as teacher.

What seemed to be a new beginning on a higher plane was but a rich Indian summer. After these two great keyboard works, silence seems to envelop Bach. What is left is no longer an artistic model for his students but his legacy to mankind. From now on we begin to observe a clear tendency on Bach's part to sift what he had written in the past and to give final form to the works he now selects.

During these years, Bach works on the final versions of his Passions, on some of his organ chorales, and on the completion of the *B Minor Mass*. It is touching, for instance, to see the aging master attach meticulously newly written half-pages to the worn marginal borders of the opening movement of the *St. Matthew Passion*,[71] or to see his fingers, stiff from writing cramps or arthritis, revise a passage in the *St. John Passion*.[72] Repeat performances of the Passions, which the adverse conditions in Leipzig made "only a burden"[73] for him, would hardly have prompted Bach to go over the parts and score again with such loving care.

It seems, rather, that at the end of his life, Bach, to whom the world had denied a position befitting his genius, became an autonomous artist, an artist who no longer revised old or created new music with a view toward performance. Such an interpretation is supported by the completion of the *B minor Mass*—consisting of the *Kyrie* and *Gloria* of 1733, the *Sanctus* of Christmas, 1724, the *Symbolum Nicenum* (partly parody, partly freshly composed in the late 1740s) and the newly parodied parts from the *Osanna* onward. The *B minor Mass* was unified and completed characteristically in score form.

The fact that apparently no performing parts were written out is moving evidence of Bach's new concept of music as pure art which addresses itself to posterity rather than to his contemporaries. This seems to be the meaning of the final versions of the *Passions* and the completed *B minor Mass*.

But his church cantatas, the richest part of his oeuvre, were not among the works he selected for survival after his death. Bach seems to have regarded them as *Gebrauchsmusik* for the divine service of his day, composed *ad hoc*, so to speak. That he did not, however, think less highly of the cantatas than of the works he destined for posterity seems proven by the inclusion of the many movements from them that appear in parodied form in the *B minor Mass* and the other late *Missae* (*vide:* the *Crucifixus* from the *B minor Mass*).

Bach's few freshly composed church cantatas, written relatively late in life,[74] may provide a clue here. About half of them[75] represent a new and purer chorale cantata style, based on hymn texts only. Spitta's intuition, which had misled him with regard to the whole second cantata *Jahrgang*, thus turns out to have been a sound intuition after all. Does Bach, by this preference for the more timeless hymn texts, imply that the time of the "madrigal cantata" had passed? Is Bach's subsequent preoccupation with the Latin Mass—not just with the *B minor Mass* but with the short *Missae* in F and g (of ca. 1737) and those in A and G (of the 1740s)—related to the dropping out of favor of the "madrigal cantata"? It seems significant that the direction of the parody moves from German to Latin texts, not vice versa.

The often expressed prejudice against the short Masses that are all or mostly parody tends to overlook that the same is also true of the *B minor Mass* and the *Christmas Oratorio*, neither of which has been downgraded because of abundant parody. Bach's late Mass compositions seem rather to constitute a conscious turning away from the style of the "madrigal cantata" that, because of its inferior German poetry and the stiffness of its stereotyped Italian *da capo* aria form, had outlived its day.

While Bach's interest in vocal music shifted to the Latin Mass, in instrumental music it turned to the organ chorale. In the process of gathering, surveying, revising, and giving finishing touches to his best loved compositions, Bach selected from some of his cantatas[76] six movements in trio or quartet texture with one strict *cantus-firmus* part, arranged them for organ, and had them published by Schübler late in 1746 or in 1747. The final eighteen organ chorales, perhaps also intended for publication (as were—probably—the two parts of the *Well-Tempered Clavier* and the *Inventions and Sinfonias*) constitute Bach's last gathering of organ music intended to survive him.[77] His last organ chorale, *"Vor deinen Thron tret ich hiemit"* ("I Herewith Step Before Thy Throne"), makes the musician or scholar who dares to follow him to such heights almost mystically aware that here Bach is alone with his God.[78]

It is significant that two of Bach's three last compositions owe their existence and publication to external circumstances: the *Canonic Variations on the Christmas Lied, "Vom Himmel hoch da komm' ich her"* and *The Musical Offering*. The set of *Canonic Variations* was the test piece expected from Bach as a new member of Mizler's *Societät der musikalischen Wissenschaften* which he joined as its fourteenth member in June 1747. This scientific society gave Bach the self-taught a welcome occasion to show those who had criticized him[79] that he did not need a university education to be well versed in the sciences.

In his *Canonic Variations*, Bach gave his contrapuntal ingenuity free rein. Let me recall only that almost incredible triumph of mind over matter, those three last *alla stretta* measures[80] in which time and space become as one while Bach telescopes the four chorale phrases and, where space permits, derivations from the first, into a contrapuntal tour de force that allows barely a free note to survive. Through one of these "free" notes, Bach manages even to introduce his name into the final measure. By weaving B-A-C-H (Bb-A-C-B natural) into its middle voices, Bach signs his completed composition. It is as though Bach puts his confident yet subtle seal of approval on what he must have known to be an extraordinary achievement of his genius.

In *The Musical Offering* Bach felt that he had to make some concession to the current taste. At least in the two slow movements of the *Trio Sonata*, Bach demonstrates understandably good decorum by turning—it was to be the last time for him—to the sentimental *style galant* that was fostered at the Court of King Frederick the Great in Potsdam as it was in all European courts of the time. But by surrounding the *Trio Sonata* with ten scholarly canons—some notated as ingenious puzzles—and by crowning the whole work with the archaic six-part *Ricercare*, Bach succeeds in giving the delicate centerpiece of fashionable chamber music a sturdy frame of solidly structured music.

Not tied down by a royal theme or by a traditional hymn tune—that is, totally alone with his genius—Bach writes his monumental *opus ultimum, The Art of the Fugue.* In canonic writing he had said what there was to be said by starting with the amiably flowing nine canons in the *Goldberg Variations* (to which Bach assigns the strategic and symbolic places of Numbers 3, 6, 9 . . . up to 27!) and ending with two different kinds of spectacular canonic skill in the *Canonic Variations* and *The Musical Offering*. In the multifaceted art of the organ chorale, Bach had left *Clavierübung* III, the *Schübler Chorales,* the *Canonic Variations* and the last *Eighteen Chorales,* models of every imaginable kind of style for the "Music Lover," the "Connoisseur," and for posterity. Only in the realm of the fugue had the master who already in his youth "through his own study and reflection alone" had become "a pure and strong fugue writer,"[81] left one possibility unexploited. Now, at the end of his life, years after the completion of the second book of the *Well-Tempered Clavier* with its twenty-four fugues on that many different subjects, Bach was to show the world how one single subject could be made to undergo almost as many varying treatments.

In his very last compositions, Bach's new concept of pure art becomes increasingly abstract, an art full of puzzles and deep symbolism. In this respect, these last compositions—the *Credo* from the *B minor Mass,* the *Canonic Variations, The Musical Offering,* the *Art of the Fugue* and his very last organ chorale, centering on canon, fugue, chorale, even Gregorian chant, though written in the midst of the Rococo era, constitute music's last and crowning link with the Middle Ages. Yet as pure and abstract art they are, unlike Bach's earlier works, ahead of their time, if not timeless. It seems that with the *Art of the Fugue* Bach had explored all that there was for him to explore in music. Had a higher fate not stayed Bach's hand before he could finish the next to the last fugue, Bach's artwork would appear almost too complete for a human being.

In the case of Mozart, it staggers one's imagination to think of what he might yet have produced had a life as long as that of Bach been granted to him. In Bach's case, one comes somewhat reluctantly to the sobering conclusion that there was at the end apparently nothing left for him to compose. Unlike Mozart and Schubert, each of whom seems to have sensed that he could not take his time and, thus, crowded a frenzied amount of composition into the last year of his short life, Bach, by comparison, wrote little during the last decade of his life. In this respect he rather resembles Beethoven with whom he shared not only a somewhat comparable lifespan but, above all, the eventually tragic fate of a composer whose genius had transcended the fashionable style of his day so far that time and fellowmen could no longer follow him.

Bach as a Tragic Figure

Of all those who have reflected on this, only Paul Hindemith has come up with an explanation of the cause underlying Bach's baffling diminishing creative productiveness. Hindemith, who had relinked his own artwork with that of Bach, had as a master craftsman an insight into the creative mind that seems denied to less creative mortals. At the end of his address, given at Hamburg in honor of Bach's bicentennial in 1950, Hindesmith said:[82]

> ...a shadow seems to have fallen upon his [Bach's] creativeness, the shadow of melancholy. With reference to Brahms's compositions, someone [it was Nietzsche] coined the malicious term "melancholy of creative impotence." In Bach's case no incapacity, no artistic impotence is present. ... Yet since the melancholic mood is undeniable, we are justified in calling it the melancholy of capacity, of artistic potency—and with this ... we have found the answer to the riddle....
>
> What can a man do, who technically and spiritually has climbed to the highest rung of artistic production attainable by mankind? He can climb no higher, for he is only a man. Is he serenely to continue his former work, forcing it by mere rearrangement into apparently new forms? In the course of his ascent, he has acquired such a sense of responsibility that this sort of thing must seem to him nothing but primitive reiteration and squandering.... He has arrived at the end, he stands, as the old Persian poem says, before the curtain that nobody will ever draw aside.
>
> For this ultimate attainment he must pay a dear price: melancholy, the grief of having been bereft of all former imperfections and with them the possibility of proceeding further.

Hindemith had the ability to understand that the perfectionist Bach could not bring himself to go over the same ground again and again as Telemann, Vivaldi, and most of the other composers of Bach's time did. Hindemith's beautiful interpretation that Bach's weariness and frustration were of a creative nature reflects not only Bach's but also his own artistic dilemma. Yet there is a great deal, perhaps even the substance, of truth in Hindemith's explanation of these creative low tides which occurred whenever Bach—usually after a short time—had solved the musical problems of his respective positions as organist, chapelmaster, or cantor.

There is, however, another aspect that seems to me, the longer I ponder it, to complement Hindemith's insight in a meaningful way. Edward Lowinsky's article on the concept of musical genius,[83] and subsequent correspondence with him, have convinced me that the prevalent and persistent idea that Bach, being a master craftsman, did not consider himself a genius, is wrong; in fact, not only wrong but a dangerous barrier to our understanding of Bach's overpowering artistic personality. True, Bach did not say: *"Questa è una gran testa!"* as Mozart did, or: *"Beethoven, thank God, can compose, of all else he is incapable."* But although only one truly personal letter by Bach has survived— the one to Erdmann—we do know of Bach that he held Handel not only high in esteem but tried twice to meet him personally. Yet of Hasse's operas Bach spoke somewhat disparagingly as "the lovely Dresden ditties."[84]

Bach, who often needed the stimulus of other composers' music, but then transcended it to reach his own dizzying heights, must have felt his own almost boundless superiority. To cite just one example: the *Harpsichord Concerto in D Major* (BWV 972) after Vivaldi's *Violin Concerto* in the same key. Here we can almost hear Bach chuckle over Vivaldi's harmonic naiveté (first movement) or his childlike melodic and rhythmic simplicity (third movement) as he added harmonic spice to the first and built a crackling fire of Baroque vitality under Vivaldi's "ditty" by adding an exhilarating, jagged bass line to the latter.

How could this same Bach have read or heard music by Telemann, Hasse, Graun, Caldara, and all the other more popular composers of his day without being aware of his own vast superiority? How could Bach help but be shaken to the marrow of his bones when the soaring power of his genius was upon him, when he was engulfed by the creative process that gave birth to music such as the great choruses in the Passions or the *B minor Mass*? What moves us today must have been to its creator, even if he regarded himself as a devout Lutheran, the chosen tool of the Holy Spirit, an ecstatic experience of shattering immediacy.

But while Bach felt his genius, he was also made to feel that his employers and his congregation remained totally unaware of it. His superiors, "odd and little interested in music" as they were, could not see their cantor's hot temper, his intransigence, and stubborn righteousness as a by-product of his genius, as a necessary evil they had to accommodate to and live with. Hence they came to regard these traits as essential and most irritating defects of Bach's character they had not bargained for in 1723.

Throughout Bach's tenure these simple, honest citizens remained earthbound, uncomprehending bourgeois, Papagenos, whom genius either has to tolerate or leave behind. They were aware of a gap that existed between Bach's music and that of their own favorite composers. When Bach was censored for not writing music as these did, they seemed to concur. Bach thus had to live with the knowledge that his music was regarded by the majority as inferior to that of the fashionable composers of his time.

Had Bach's desire to find a new position at Danzig in 1730 or to affiliate himself actively with the Court at Dresden in 1733 been successful, he would, no doubt, have risen to such new artistic occasions, with the result that his disillusionment and nagging frustration would have been postponed. Whether they would, or could have been avoided, had but sufficient and sufficiently varied opportunities come his way, is an unanswerable question.

As it turned out, Bach had to resign himself to his Leipzig position. The gap between him and his superiors that we first observed shortly after Easter, 1725, grew steadily and irrevocably until Bach finally became a tragic figure who fulfilled the mission of his genius—as true genius must—in spite of his environment. Bach's growing realization that the fruits of his genius were increasingly wasted on his contemporaries seems to have been the principal reason for the slackening of his creative productivity and his gradual withdrawal from life. The extent to which Bach felt this tragic, ever widening chasm is the measure of his unhappiness. It drove him eventually into lofty isolation where, undisturbed by external circumstances, he reflected, speculated, and formulated the final masterworks of his earthly existence.

Notes

1.   Here, in *Out of My Life and Thought*, English ed., New York, 1933, p. 83, Schweitzer summarizes observations made in the final chapter of his Bach biography (1905, 1908, 1911, its French, German, and English editions).

2.   *Neue Bach Ausgabe*; from hereon abbreviated *NBA*.

3.   "Outlines of a New Picture of Bach," in *Music and Letters*, XLIV (1963) translated from *Musica*, XVI (1962) pp. 169 ff.

4.   *Was bleibt?* in *Der Kirchenmusiker*, XIII, Berlin, 1962.

5.   Alfred Dürr, *Zur Chronologie der Leipziger Vokalwerke J.S. Bachs*, pp. 5-162.

6.   Georg von Dadelsen, *Beiträge zur Chronologie der Werke Johann Sebastian Bachs (Contributions to the Chronology of Johann Sebastian Bach's Works) Tübinger Bach Studien 4/5*, Trossingen, 1958.

7.   About 40 out of approximately 300 extant autographs.

8.   Compare *Kritischer Bericht (Critical Commentary)* to *NBA* V/4, 1957, p. 94.

9.   Georg Kinsky, *Die Originalausgaben der Werke Johann Sebastian Bachs*, Wien, Leipzig, Zürich, 1937.

10. von Dadelsen, *Chronologie*, p. 25.

11. Dürr, *Studien über die frühen Kantaten J.S. Bachs*, Leipzig, 1951.

12. "On the Pitches in Use in Bach's Time" in *The Musical Quarterly*, XLI (1955), pp. 332-54, and 466-80.

13. In Bach's Weimar scores the string instruments must tune their strings a minor third up to the *Chorton* of the organ while the woodwinds are notated in true pitch, i.e., transposed a minor third higher. In Leipzig Bach notates the organ part in transposition (a whole tone lower) to match the true pitch (*Kammerton*) notation of the other instruments and voices.

14. Cantatas 5, 41, 94. See von Dadelsen, *Chronologie*, p. 41.

15. Once the 1st Vn. and twice the organ part.

16. Dürr, *Chronologie*, pp. 73, 75, 77-78, 112 f., 141.

17. von Dadelsen, *Chronologie*, p. 42.

18. *Ein Herz, das seinen Jesum lebend weiss*, BG 28, p. XXVII.

19. W. Gillies Whittaker, *The Cantatas of Johann Sebastian Bach—Sacred and Secular*, 2 vols., London, 1959.

20. Philipp Spitta, *Johann Sebastian Bach*, vol. I, p. vi.

21. Both score and parts of *BWV* 116, *Du Friedefürst, Herr Jesu Christ*, show the Halfmoon watermark of *Jahrgang* II.

22. *Musikgeschichte Leipzigs*, vol. III (= *J.S. Bach und das Musikleben Leipzigs im 18. Jahrhundert*), Leipzig, 1941.

23. Ibid., p. 296.

24. Schweitzer, *J.S. Bach*, I, p. 322.

25. Smend, *J.S. Bach—Kirchen Kantaten*, 3d ed., Berlin, 1966, IV, p. 12.

26. Steglich, *Johann Sebastian Bach*, Potsdam, 1935, p. 146f.

27. Friedemann, *Bach zeichnet das Kreuz* (Bach signs the Cross), Pinneberg, 1963.

28. Spitta, *J.S. Bach* II, p. 156.

29. Schweitzer, *J.S. Bach,* I, p. 109.

30. Gurlitt, *Johann Sebastian Bach—Der Meister und sein Werk*, 1959, pp. 67-68.

31. Hamel, *J.S. Bach*, Göttingen, 1961, pp. 119ff.

32. H.T. David and A. Mendel, *The Bach Reader*, New York, 1966, p. 125.

33. Ibid., p. 304.

34. Ibid., p. 125.

35. Ibid., pp. 128-29.

36. Christoph Trautmann, who rediscovered the Calov Bible, reported on it in *Musik und Kirche*, July/August 1969, pp. 145-60.

37. They are quoted and reproduced in Trautmann's article.

38. See footnote 3.

39. See footnote 4.

40. Copies can be seen at the *Johann-Sebastian-Bach-Institut* in Göttingen, the *Bach-Archiv* in Leipzig, and in the Music Library at Princeton University.

41. von Dadelsen, *Chronologie*, p. 43.

42. Spitta, *J.S. Bach*, vol. I, p. VI.

43. *Kritischer Bericht* to *NBA*, V/4 (1957).

44. *Bemerkungen zur Handschrift Johann Sebastian Bachs, seiner Familie und seines Kreises*, Trossingen, 1957. It was followed in 1958 by the application of Dadelsen's gathered knowledge in his *Beiträge zur Chronologie der Werke Johann Sebastian Bachs* (Tübinger Bach Studien 4/5) to which this paper is greatly indebted.

45. BWV 23, 22, 76, 119, 194.

46. Feb. 7th: Cantata 22.

47. Dürr, *Studien;* see n. 11.

48. Two of them have in the meantime been identified as Johann Andreas Kuhnau (nephew (?) of the composer) and Christian Gottlob Meissner.

49. The other thirteen are Cantatas 91, 121, 133, 122, 41, 123, 124, 3, 111, 92, 125, 126, 127.

50. Among them are the nine cantatas based on texts by the Leipzig poetess, Mariane von Ziegler.

51. On Sept. 14, Nov. 3, and Dec. 31, 1725.

52. Of Jan. 21, 1726.

53. Compare the two enclosures in his letter of Dec. 31, 1725, that Schelle's and Kuhnau's widows supplied in behalf and at the request of Bach.

54. Oct. 29, 1725.

55. With one documented exception at Reformation: Cantata 79.

56. Compare *Bach-Jahrbuch*, 1959.

57. Aug. 23, 1730.

58. Dated: Leipzig, October 28, 1730.

59. In his letter to Erdmann. Compare David and Mendel, *The Bach Reader*, p. 125.

60. Alluded to on pp. 156-57 above.

61. As stated on the title pages of *Clavierübung* I, II, IV. (See David and Mendel, *The Bach Reader*, pp. 105, 133, 171.)

62. See title page of *Clavierübung* III. (David and Mendel, *The Bach Reader*, p. 164f.)

63. *Beihefte zum Archiv für Musikwissenschaft*, VI, Wiesbaden, 1968.

64. Haberl ed., X, p. 153.

65. Wien, 1725. Bach's signed copy is today in the *Staats-und Universitäts-Bibliothek*, Hamburg.

66. This is proven by up to date watermark and handwriting analysis of Wolff's sources.

67. Cf. Dadelsen, pp. 117, 146f. and Dürr *Chronologie*, p. 116.

68. Wolff, *Stile Antico*, p. 134, translated by G. Herz.

69. J.T. Goldberg (1727-56), who was only 15 years old when Bach wrote the variations that were to immortalize his pupil's name.

70. Bach received "a golden goblet, filled with a hundred *Louis d'or*." (See David and Mendel, *The Bach Reader*, p. 339.)

71. See the recent facsimile edition, Leipzig, 1966.

72. See, for instance, plate 6, opposite p. 295, of Arthur Mendel's article, "Recent Developments in Bach Chronology," in *The Musical Quarterly*, XLVI (1960).

73. See David and Mendel, *The Bach Reader*, p. 162.

74. From about 1731/32 on.

75. BWV 117, 177, 97, 100.

76. BWV 140, 93, 10, 6, 137. Schübler Chorale No. 2 (BWV 646) must be an arrangement of a cantata movement now lost.

77. None of Bach's Preludes, Fugues, Toccatas, etc. for organ were destined for such a higher calling.

78. Smend, *J.S. Bach—Kirchen Kantaten*, III, p. 20.

79. "This great man has not particularly looked into the sciences that are, strictly speaking, demanded of a learned composer" (Scheibe, March 1738. Translated from *Bach-Dokumente II*, 1969, p. 316).

80. Of *Varatio* 5. Cf. *NBA*, IV/2 (1958), p. 211.

81. C.P.E. Bach in a letter of January 13, 1775, to Forkel. (Cf. *The Bach Reader*, p. 278.)

82. Hindemith, *Johann Sebastian Bach—Heritage and Obligation*, 1952, pp. 39-41.

83. "Musical Genius—Evolution and Origin of a Concept," in *The Musical Quarterly*, L, 1964, pp. 321-40 and 476-95.

84. Quoted in *The Bach Reader*, p. 335, which reprints Forkel's Bach biography of 1802 in English translation.

Part IV

The Performance History of Bach's *B Minor Mass*

The recent one hundredth performance of Bach's *B minor Mass* by the Bethlehem Bach Choir, which had introduced this towering choral work to America in 1900—its founding year—offers a welcome challenge to investigate how Bach's great Mass has fared at the hands of history. It will come as a shock to the uninitiated to realize that Bach himself may never have heard the Mass in its entirety.

An early autograph score of the *Sanctus* and its performing parts,[1] which were written at different times and on different paper, attest to the fact that the *Sanctus* was performed as early as Christmas Day, 1724, again in 1726 or 1727, and once more towards the end of Bach's life, with additional performances probable in the intervening years. Since an autograph remark on the first page of the score informs us that Bach lent the original parts of 1724 to Count Sporck of Lissa in Bohemia, a performance there can likewise be assumed. The *Sanctus* is, however, the only part of the *B minor Mass* that has a provable performance history in Bach's lifetime.

Eight and a half years later, when Bach intended to pay homage to his new sovereign, Friedrich August II, he composed a five-part *Missa,* the first and mightiest of his five Lutheran or German Masses that consist of *Kyrie* and *Gloria* only. On July 27, 1733, Bach presented the performing parts of this *Missa* to the Dresden Court, accompanied by the well known dedicatory letter to the new Elector of Saxony. The Dresden Court, however, does not seem to have honored the composer with a performance of his work. Once deprived of the performing parts, which are still in Dresden,[2] Bach could not perform the *Missa* in his own Leipzig unless the parts were copied out anew from the autograph score he had wisely retained. Incredible as it may seem, no new parts appear to have been copied then or later. While the Berlin Bach scholar Friedrich Smend tried to establish that a performance was given by Bach *before* he delivered the parts to the Dresden Court, this assumption is based on wishful thinking rather than proven fact.

Reprinted with permission from the *American Choral Review* XV/1 (1973), pp. 5-21.

When, towards the end of his life, Bach completed the Mass by adding the *Credo* and the sections from the *Osanna* onward, he did so only in score form. The absence of any performing parts of these two sections again suggests that no performance took place. It thus appears that, with the exception of the *Sanctus* and quite in contrast to the cantatas and the Passions, Bach found no occasion in his lifetime for a performance of the other portions of his *B minor Mass.*

The generation that followed Bach's death was preoccupied with the creation of the Classical style. Therefore it considered the learned polyphonic style, of which Bach had been the last and greatest representative, outdated. Although two copies of the *B minor Mass*—again only of the score!—were made in Berlin in the 1760s, we know of only one performance during the period between 1750 and 1800—and this was a performance of the *Credo* only. It was given by Carl Philipp Emanuel Bach, who had inherited the autograph score from his father. The year was 1786, the one in which Mozart's Figaro declared his independence from aristocratic rule and tyranny; the city was C.P.E. Bach's enlightened Hamburg. That this first performance of Johann Sebastian Bach's *Credo* did not take place in church but in a concert hall is prophetically characteristic of the fate that awaited Bach's church music in the bourgeois nineteenth century that was to revive it. The nonliturgical nature of the performance is also stressed by an orchestral introduction, based on the two opening phrases of the chorale *Allein Gott in der Höh' sei Ehr'* that Carl Philipp Emanuel had composed especially for the occasion: a charity concert for the medical institute for the poor. J.S. Bach's *Credo* with his son's orchestral prelude was then followed by the aria "I know that my Redeemer liveth" and the "Hallelujah" chorus from Handel's *Messiah.* The second half of the concert consisted of music by Carl Philipp Emanuel Bach: a symphony, his *Magnificat,* and the popular double chorus *Heilig.* The review lauds "especially the five-part *Credo* of the immortal Sebastian Bach, which is one of the finest pieces that has ever been heard but which must be executed by a sufficient number of voices if it is to produce its full effect."[3] While the anonymous reviewer deplores the apparently small-scale performance of the work that was then still traditional, he does not find fault with dynamic changes, additions of instrumental parts, as well as changes in the orchestration made by Carl Philipp Emanuel Bach.[4] These changes were obviously in tune with the sentimental and *galant* style of his own time.

Four years later, in 1790—the year following the outbreak of the French Revolution—Karl Friedrich Christian Fasch founded the first large-scale bourgeois choral society, the Berlin *Singakademie.* With this a sociologically more favorable climate set in for the revival of the great choral music of the past, that of Palestrina, Handel, and Bach—in this order. On October 25, 1811, Fasch's successor, Carl Friedrich Zelter, who was Goethe's musical mentor, began to rehearse some parts of Bach's *B minor Mass*. By September 30, 1813, all parts of the Mass had been sung and from 1814 on the *B minor Mass* belonged to the basic rehearsal material of the Berlin *Singakademie*.[5] In 1820, Zelter's most gifted pupil, the eleven-year-old Felix Mendelssohn, and his sister Fanny, joined the chorus. Nine years later Mendelssohn was to give the first public performance of Bach's *St. Matthew Passion* with the Berlin *Singakademie*, the performance that was destined to become the watershed of the Bach movement.

Far-off Catholic and Imperial Vienna was no natural haven for the survival of Bach's music. In 1777, Baron van Swieten, who had been Ambassador in Berlin, where he belonged to the Bach circle of Johann Philipp Kirnberger, Princess Amalia of Prussia, Friedrich Wilhelm Marpurg, and Carl Philipp Emanuel Bach, brought the new Berlin Bach enthusiasm to Vienna. There, in van Swieten's hospitable home, Haydn, Mozart, and Beethoven became acquainted with most of the music by Bach and Handel that they were to encounter in their lives. This was, however, by and large, the small portion of Bach's music that was commonly known by that time: the *Well-Tempered Clavier* and other keyboard compositions, the *Art of the Fugue*, and only the Motets from Bach's vocal music. Haydn was the only one who, late in life, owned another major choral work by Bach, namely, a "nicely written...and highly valued" copy of the *B minor Mass*. Of the impact the work made upon the aged composer we, unfortunately, know nothing. Although Beethoven asked Breitkopf and Härtel on October 15, 1810, for a copy of "Bach's great Mass" and quoted the *passacaglia* bass of its *Crucifixus*, his request was apparently not filled. Fourteen years later, on September 9, 1824, Beethoven again requested a copy of the "five-voiced Mass by Sebastian Bach," this time from the Zurich publisher Nägeli, but again apparently to no avail. Van Swieten was by no means the only Bach enthusiast in Vienna. Among those who deserve to be mentioned are the publisher Johann Traeg, the highly musical Prince Karl Lichnowsky, pianist Dorothea von Erdmann, and Wilhelm Karl Rust (uncle of the later editor of most of the cantata volumes in the *Bach-Gesellschaft* edition). Aloys Fuchs and pianist Joseph Fischhof were both ardent collectors of old music—Bach's in particular. The presence of all these Bach lovers in Vienna must have created a favorable atmosphere for private, if not public, performances of Bach's music. Yet few of them can be documented. The private concerts that the music historian and collector Raphael Georg Kiesewetter had been giving at his home since 1815 were the first historical concerts in Vienna. In one of them a *Kyrie e Gloria a 3 voci reali e 4 di ripieno con due orchestre* was performed in 1820 by a chorus of from forty to fifty dilettante singers accompanied by piano and double bass.[6] The "two orchestras" may well point to the spurious eight-part Mass with two orchestras that Breitkopf and Härtel had published as a work by J.S. Bach in 1805 and which was presented in a *Gewandhaus* concert on March 7 of that year.[7] The three solo voices and the four-part chorus, on the other hand, seem to refer to Bach's *Mass in A Major* (BWV 234), the Mass that Simrock had just published in Bonn in 1818, but certainly not to the *B minor Mass*.[8] While Kiesewetter's music collection contained copies of both the short G and A Major Masses, only the *Kyrie* of the *B minor Mass* is listed.

It is not generally known that even before Mendelssohn's history-making performance of the *St. Matthew Passion* in 1829 two additional performances—again only of the *Credo* of the *B minor Mass*—had taken place. The first was given by Johann Nepomuk Schelble (1789-1837), a well known singer who, for reasons of health and because of an aversion to acting, had exchanged a promising operatic career for that of choral conductor. On March 10, 1828, Schelble presented Bach's *Credo* with the *Cäcilien-Verein* of Frankfurt, which he had founded in 1818. Schelble had received a copy of the *B minor Mass* from Hans Georg Nägeli of Zurich who had become the new owner of Bach's autograph score. But the Frankfurt singers developed a "prejudice against the composition" because of its "insuperable difficulties." Schelble either had to give up or surmount "great obstacles." Schelble's love and labors for "the greatest work in the history of art" remained victorious over the "prejudice of loud-mouthed dilettantism." Chaos at the first rehearsal gave way to order, and order to understanding, until friend and foe alike admitted, after the first orchestral rehearsal, "never in their lives to have heard anything more profound and exalted."[9]

The Berlin music critic and Beethoven and Bach expert, Adolf Bernhard Marx, reported in his *Berliner Allgemeine Musikalische Zeitung:*[10]

> Schelble has added to his glory by a performance... of the *Credo* from the 5-part *B minor Mass* by Johann Sebastian Bach. The effect transcended the highest expectations.... The wondrous work made such a powerful impression... that an orchestral society was founded on the spot to prepare itself for a future performance of the whole work.... This success is the more noteworthy since the *Credo* is that portion of the great work which is the most difficult to comprehend. It can produce its effect only by a complete performance when it is preceded by the glowing, enthusiastic *Cum sancto spiritu* and followed by the majestic *Sanctus* and *Osanna.*[11]

One hundred and seventy-two persons participated in this performance which, according to Schelble, went "splendidly." Though he added clarinets and trombones, Schelble did not yet employ the large Romantic orchestra that others would soon use to lend its lavish sound to performances of Bach's Mass and other choral music. Schelble's orchestra consisted of eighteen violins, four violas, four cellos, two double basses,[12] and the usual contingent of wind instruments.

On April 14, 1828, Mendelssohn's sister Fanny wrote to Karl Klingemann,[13] a friend of the Mendelssohn family, about what "is in the air": the forthcoming publication of the *St. Matthew Passion*[14] and Schelble's recent "success in Frankfurt with a part of the Mass." With typical Romantic fervor she continued: "In all corners it stirs, in all branches it rustles; one has to cover one's ears not to hear it...the time is at hand, and we shall witness great things." With "great things" she referred, no doubt, to the planned performance of the *St. Matthew Passion* under her beloved brother's direction (which took place on March 11, 1829). Its overwhelming success must have been most encouraging to Schelble, who had been preparing a performance of the *St. Matthew Passion* on his own; it was given on May 29, 1829, in Frankfurt, and Schelble himself sang the parts of both the Evangelist and of Christ.

On January 5, 1831, Schelble also introduced the *Kyrie* and *Gloria* of the *B minor Mass* to his Frankfurt audience. Three months later, on April 10, he combined a repeat performance of the *Kyrie* and *Gloria* with the *Credo*.[15] This, rather than the much heralded performance by the Berlin *Singakademie* of the same sections of the Mass three years later, is the first performance in history of substantial portions—about four fifths—of Bach's *Mass in B minor*. It took place in the Frankfurt *Domkirche* and was, perhaps because of this, not reported by the press. Neither of the two Frankfurt newspapers took any notice of the event. On the day on which Schelble conducted Bach's *Kyrie, Gloria*, and *Credo*, the Frankfurter *Ober-Postamts-Zeitung* announced the performance on the same evening of Rossini's *Wilhelm Tell*. Though it was by no means the first performance of Rossini's rather recent opera (1829) in Frankfurt, the critic of the other Frankfurt paper, *Didaskalia*, subtitled "Blätter für Geist, Gemüth und Publizität," chose to attend *Wilhelm Tell*. He reviewed it in great detail, apparently because a well known tenor from the Mannheim Court Theater was featured in the role of Melchthal.[16]

In the absence of an eyewitness report of Schelble's pioneering efforts on behalf of Bach's *B minor Mass* on January 5 or April 10, 1831, the twenty-three-year-old Felix Mendelssohn will have to be our witness. In a letter written to Zelter in 1832[17] Mendelssohn speaks rather caustically of Frankfurt as a typical Free City in which music is all too dependent on business interests. But, as if to make up for this,

...there is the *Cäcilien-Verein* for the sake of which alone one must visit Frankfurt. Its members sing with so much fire and together in such a way that it is a joy. The society meets once a week and has two hundred members. Besides this, Schelble assembles a small chorus of about thirty voices on Friday evenings at his home. With himself at the piano he lets them sing and thus gradually prepare his favorite compositions which he does not dare give to his large chorus right away. There I have heard a number of small Sunday musics [i.e., cantatas] by Sebastian Bach, his Magnificat, the great Mass and, besides, other beautiful things.

Mendelssohn continues with enthusiastic praise of the women in both the small and large choruses. "As for the men, a little something is missing; they have business on their minds." Mendelssohn finds the sopranos "magnificent," the altos and basses "very good," but his chief praise is reserved for Schelble: "It is almost incredible what impact a man who knows what he wants can have upon others. Schelble's position here is unique."

This sympathetic picture of Schelble is reinforced by the impression of others. Moritz Hauptmann owed to the *Cäcilien-Verein* his "most beautiful musical impressions";[18] Ferdinand Hiller calls Schelble a "firm and fiery conductor."[19] The *Cäcilien-Verein* is frequently compared with the Berlin *Singakademie* and, after Zelter's death in 1832, often judged to be the better of the two. When anti-Semitism barred the way for Mendelssohn to become Zelter's successor, the leadership of the Berlin *Singakademie* was offered to Schelble. But Schelble chose to remain faithful to his Frankfurt chorus, moving evidence of the deep commitment that bound him to his *Cäcilien-Verein* from 1818, the year in which he had founded it, to his death in 1837. Schelble was to the *Cäcilien-Verein* in Frankfurt what Fasch and Zelter were to the *Singakademie* in Berlin; and after Zelter's death it was the *Cäcilien-Verein* that was regarded as the foremost oratorio society in Germany. The Berlin *Singakademie* had the dubious advantage of larger membership; but in quality the *Cäcilien-Verein* was its equal and, as far as the performance of Bach's works was concerned, even its superior.[20] That Schelble gave up a successful career as operatic tenor (Mozart's Belmonte, Don Ottavio, and Tamino were some of his chief roles) in order to found a choral society that was principally dedicated to the revival of the great choral works of the old masters, makes him sociologically and musically a pioneer in the nineteenth century. Although a composer himself, he rarely performed his own compositions (which have for the most part remained in manuscript form). This too attests to the modesty of the man who gave the first substantially complete performance of Bach's *B minor Mass,* and who prior to the Berlin performances[21] presented the *Sanctus* and *Benedictus* from Beethoven's *Missa Solemnis* less than two months after the composer's death. It is unfortunate that Schelble did not have a gift for promoting his own activities. If he had had the desire to do so, he could have become Zelter's successor in Berlin and a much talked and written about choral director of the press-conscious Prussian capital.

That A.B. Marx did not travel to Frankfurt, as he had done in 1828, and report on the performances of either the *Kyrie* and *Gloria* on January 5 or the *Kyrie, Gloria,* and *Credo* on April 10, 1831, is posterity's loss. That Berlin performances and publications were reviewed, often in great detail, is our gain. While the first performance of Bach's *Kyrie, Gloria,* and *Credo* in Frankfurt left no echo in the press, the opposite is true of the almost simultaneous publication of Bach's *St. John Passion* in Berlin. It drew from Friedrich

Rochlitz's pen a full and detailed evaluation that appeared in three installments totalling thirty-two columns (including musical examples) in the *Allgemeine Musikalische Zeitung* of Leipzig.[22] Of Schelble's city of Frankfurt the same weekly musical journal reported a year later:[23] "The incredible has happened. The Society (i.e., the Frankfurt *Cäcilien-Verein*) has been dissolved as a corporation." This was Frankfurt's gratitude for the selfless efforts of Schelble who, after his guarantors had abandoned him, continued the concerts of the *Cäcilien-Verein* at his own risk. Five years later, Schelble died at the age of forty-eight.

Independently of Schelble's first performance of Bach's *Credo* in 1828, yet less than two months later, on April 30, 1828, the all powerful ruler of the Court Opera at Berlin, Gaspare Spontini, introduced Bach's *Credo* to Berlin. This public ground breaking for Bach's choral music in the Prussian capital took place on Repentance Day during a *concert spirituel* that served a charitable purpose. Spontini, who was one of the first to conduct with a baton, had assembled on the stage of the Royal Opera House: the opera chorus of ninety-six (or 192),[24] celebrated vocal soloists, sixty-eight strings, flutes, oboes, clarinets, bassoons in pairs, and three French horns—the latter in place of Bach's trumpets. Was it this incongruous environment that doomed the beginning of the public revival of Bach's sacred choral music in Berlin? Or was it a combination of this and the curious program? The program consisted of Beethoven's *Fifth Symphony,* the *Kyrie* and *Gloria* from Beethoven's new *Missa Solemnis* (written four years earlier), the Overture to *Coriolan,* the *Credo* from Bach's *B minor Mass* (but only through its sixth movement, the *Et resurrexit*), and finally Carl Philipp Emanuel Bach's *Heilig.* This opera concert amounted to an almost complete Mass, but one written by three composers and introduced at the beginning and after intermission by powerful orchestral compositions by Beethoven.

The mixture of styles provoked the wrath of A.B. Marx. Ever since the advent of German Romantic opera, exemplified by the sensational success of Weber's *Freischütz* in 1821 in Berlin, it was patriotic to be anti-Spontini and stylish to oppose the traditional sway that the Italians held over opera and that Spontini, as King Friedrich Wilhelm III's protégé, represented at the Royal Opera. While the honor of having introduced a vital portion of Bach's Mass to a large Berlin audience admittedly belonged to Spontini, A.B. Marx rightly deplored the stylistic hodgepodge and the presentation of fragments of masterworks that ought to be performed complete.[25] In "unartistic Paris" such a program would do, but not in Germany. Yet, Marx continues, can we reproach Spontini when so many German musicians who have access to such great music do not perform it at all? But why did Spontini use C.P.E. Bach's arrangement of his father's *Credo?* Marx pits Carl Philipp Emanuel's "hurdy-gurdy-like" orchestral introduction against Johann Sebastian's "sturdy" seven-part *Credo* fugue. He considers it "almost ridiculous" that Spontini followed Bach's jubilant *Et resurrexit* (in Latin) immediately with Carl Philipp Emanuel's hollow and pedantic *Heilig* (in German). In the orchestration it is the addition of oboes and clarinets called upon to strengthen the "plaintive sighs" of the flutes in the *Crucifixus* that particularly arouses Marx's ire. Here, in the *Crucifixus*—the inner sanctum of this most sacred Mass—"no part can be altered without damaging and vandalizing the whole."[26] The parts of this performance of the *Credo* have survived. They are full of added dynamic markings. Spontini's *forte* was known to resemble a "hurricane"; his *piano* was as soft as a "breeze"; his *sforzando* "awakened the dead," and so forth. In short, Spontini revived Bach's *Credo* by employing the dynamics of Beethoven's *Missa Solemnis* with which it was so unaccountably paired. Bach's *Credo* was thus introduced to Berlin in the guise of Beethoven's style.

The novelist Ludwig Rellstab, whose polemical and satirical writings against Henriette Sontag (1826) as well as Spontini (1827) had led to his subsequent arrest and imprisonment, found it wiser this time to abstain from polemics. In his review[27] of Spontini's concert of 1828, Rellstab admires the depth of Bach's wondrous work, its artful workmanship, its harmonic daring, and its plaintive and expressive melodic invention. But he also voices a shortcoming that, in his opinion, excludes Bach, "the creator of so many great works," from the "pinnacle of all creative geniuses." Bach lacks the ability to pronounce "his profoundest ideas in simple language." Here is the old criticism of the Rationalists who, since Johann Adolph Scheibe's attack on Bach in 1737, have complained about the complexity of Bach's style. This "excess of art that crowds out beauty" also caused Karl Friedrich Zelter to change Bach's music. By simplifying the vocal line and by removing ornaments—"this layer of foam" that he could not explain to Goethe—Zelter tried to penetrate into the substance of Bach's style and fancied himself doing Bach a service thereby. In reality, Zelter's changes succeeded only in bringing the imaginative Baroque contours of Bach's melodic lines into accord with the simplistic style of the circle of Berlin song composers whose manner of composition Zelter represented.

Only ten and a half months after Spontini's failure to launch a true Berlin Bach revival, Mendelssohn succeeded. He succeeded in the classical hall of the *Singakademie,* which seated no more than nine hundred people, and he succeeded with the performance of a single work—Bach's *St. Matthew Passion*—which he had rehearsed since the winter of 1827.

Though Berlin had become, through Zelter and Mendelssohn rather than through Spontini, the cradle of the Bach revival or "the capital of Sebastian Bach," as Meyerbeer put it,[28] it had to wait three years longer than Frankfurt—until February 20, 1834—for its first performance of substantial portions from Bach's *B minor Mass.* Under Zelter's successor, Karl Friedrich Rungenhagen, the Berlin *Singakademie* presented the *Kyrie, Gloria,* and *Credo* and, a year later, also the *Sanctus* and some but not all of the movements from the *Osanna* onwards. That in these performances the *Qui tollis* and the *Et incarnatus est* were not sung by the chorus but by solo voices indicates that the Berlin *Singakademie*—perhaps through Fasch—still may have preserved a traditional link with Bach's own performance practice. The reviewer stated[29] that the success was "imposing" for a work of such "complexity that is so exceedingly strange to present day audiences." The "colossal artwork," whose details were "so difficult to follow with the ear," found, however, "more admiration than innermost participation." The reporter was relieved that the *Sanctus* and the movements thereafter were omitted since the performance of the rest "already took two hours." A year later when the *Sanctus* was sung and the *Dona nobis pacem* was replaced by the *Osanna* as the concluding movement, the reviewer seemed reconciled to the length of Bach's work.

In the fall of 1833 and apparently in connection with the preparations for the concert by the Berlin *Singakademie,* August Wilhelm Bach (no relative, but the director of the Berlin Institute for Church Music, who had been Mendelssohn's organ teacher) performed the *Christe eleison* and *Gloria*[30] at St. Mary's Church. Shortly *after* Rungenhagen's performance with the *Singakademie* we read again that A.W. Bach presented "the *B minor Mass*"[31] with his "Music Institute" and even with boys' voices. The performance of "the *Gloria*" in 1833 could hardly have been more than its first chorus, because in the same church concert were heard three organ pieces by Pachelbel, Böhm, and Christian Bach, as well as four other choral compositions by Johann Christoph Bach, Handel, Hasse, and Naumann. This is certainly an impressive program for its time, even if only one or two movements from Bach's *Gloria* were actually sung. Scepticism regarding the completeness of the 1834 performance of "the *B minor Mass*" seems likewise indicated. Since church concerts were not reviewed, we simply lack the detailed information we have about public concerts given at the opera house or in concert halls. That the *Et incarnatus est* from Bach's *B minor Mass* had already been sung in 1827 under A.W. Bach's direction speaks highly, however, for his early and conceivably independent promotion of his great namesake's choral music in Berlin.

Friedrich Konrad Griepenkerl, best known in the 1840s as coeditor, with Roitzsch, of Bach's organ compositions, rehearsed and may have given a massive public performance after 1834 of some parts, if not the complete *B minor Mass* with his *Singakademie* in Braunschweig.[32] We hear next of a performance of three choruses from the Mass that Mendelssohn, as conductor of the Leipzig *Gewandhaus* concerts, presented on January 21, 1841, in the first of four historical concerts. In the first half Mendelssohn tried to demonstrate some of the universality and variety of Bach's oeuvre; in the second half, some of that of Handel. The Bach portion consisted of:[33]

1. the *Chromatic Fantasy and Fugue*, played by Mendelssohn on the piano "in his unique and unsurpassable" manner;
2. the eight-part a cappella motet *Ich lasse dich nicht, du segnest mich denn* (formerly attributed to J.S. Bach, but now known to be a composition of his uncle, the Eisenach organist Johann Christoph Bach);
3. the *Chaconne* for solo violin, played "masterfully" by the orchestra's concertmaster Ferdinand David (for whom Mendelssohn was then writing his *Violin Concerto*). In this performance David was accompanied by Mendelssohn, whose addition of a piano part to the "unaccompanied" *Chaconne* belongs, along with that by Schumann to Bach's six Sonatas and Partitas for solo violin, to the curiosities of Romantic Bach interpretation; and
4. *Crucifixus, Resurrexit,* and *Sanctus* from the *B minor Mass.*

The reviewer states[34] that the artistry and feeling shown by Bach in these diverse selections simply lead the idea of progress in the arts *ad absurdum*. Of the *Crucifixus*, particularly of its last four measures that are quoted in print, the reviewer says, "Nowhere in music is there anything more wondrous, more deeply moving." On the other hand, he notes with astonishment Bach's preference for independent obbligato, rather than simply accompanying orchestral parts. That this aspect of Bach's style antedates the "great progress" made since his time in both the improvements and technical mastery of instruments and their unification in much larger orchestras, makes Bach, in the eyes of the reviewer, truly unique. He finally notes that Handel through the frequent performances of his oratorios is better known and therefore far better understood, whereas Bach's choral music is still new and full of unexpected surprises. The festive concert conducted by Mendelssohn on April 23, 1843 at the *Gewandhaus,* as part of the inaugural ceremonies and dedication of the Bach monument in Leipzig, concluded with the *Sanctus* from the *B minor Mass.*

The Swiss music publisher Hans Georg Nägeli had bought the autograph score of the *B minor Mass* in 1805 at an auction of "remnants" from Carl Philipp Emanuel Bach's estate.[35] That this precious manuscript was not among the items bought when Carl Philipp Emanuel's large music collection was offered for sale in 1790 is dramatic proof of the degree of oblivion into which J.S. Bach's vocal music had fallen. Nägeli's purchase, however, indicates that a shrewd businessman sensed in 1805 that the time for the acceptance of Bach's choral music was approaching. But when Nägeli in 1819 announced the publication of the "greatest musical work of art of all times and people" on a subscription basis, Bach's time had not yet come. Lack of subscribers caused postponement of publication until 1833 when the *Missa* was issued and until 1845 when the parts from the *Credo* onward were published (nine years after Nägeli's death). This faulty edition in two installments thus followed in the wake of the enthusiasm for Bach that Mendelssohn's performance of the *St. Matthew Passion* had generated in 1829.

In 1850, the *Bach-Gesellschaft* was founded. It intended to begin its task of a definitive and complete edition of Bach's works with the *Mass in B minor*. But Nägeli's son and heir, Hermann, refused to sell the autograph score or even let it be used by the *Bach-Gesellschaft*, which he regarded as a rival business venture. The *Bach-Gesellschaft* finally issued the *B minor Mass* in 1856 as its volume VI, using the Dresden parts of the *Missa*, the score and parts of the 1724 version of the *Sanctus*, and secondary sources for the rest. A year later, debts forced Hermann Nägeli to part with his score and pawn it to a creditor from whom the Hanover Kapellmeister Arnold Wehner purchased it "for his King."[36] In reality Wehner served as a carefully chosen stand-in for the music historian and Handel biographer, Friedrich Chrysander, who immediately turned his purchase over to the *Bach-Gesellschaft*. With the autograph score finally in hand, the editor of the *B minor Mass*, Julius Rietz, now reedited the work and then had it reprinted from the *Credo* onward. The *Bach-Gesellschaft* redistributed this new volume VI to its subscribers in the same year—1857.[37] This accomplished—again not with sufficient care—the score was sold to the Royal Library in Berlin where it remained until World War II. During the last years of the war it was hidden for safekeeping in Beuron Monastery in Württemberg. After the war's end it found a temporary home in the library of the University of Tübingen. Now the autograph score is among the priceless treasures of the West Berlin *Staatsbibliothek* (in Berlin-Dahlem).

At the time of the publication and revision of the *B minor Mass*, no complete performance of the work had as yet taken place. It remained for the famous *Riedel-Verein* of Leipzig, founded by Karl Riedel in 1854, to present the first performance of the unabridged Mass in 1859, when it was, however, sung in German. Among those present was Franz Liszt, the only member of the Wagner camp who was a subscriber to the *Bach-Gesellschaft* edition. In March 1861, the Frankfurt *Cäcilien-Verein* followed with a performance of the *B minor Mass*, led by its new conductor, Christian Carl Müller.[38] From here on the stream broadened and an enumeration of the increasingly frequent performances of the *B minor Mass* would serve only local interests.[39] The great work now began to become the pride and joy of the large choral societies and orchestras, at first in Germany, then in the rest of Europe—and there mainly in England—and finally in the United States.

The English, traditionally partial to the music of their adopted son Handel, were introduced to Bach's choral music by John Wesley's nephew, Samuel Wesley, who presented Bach's motet *Jesu, meine Freude* as early as

June 3, 1809 in the Hanover Square Rooms in London.[40] Ten years after Schelble and Spontini—on May 1, 1838—the Choral Harmonists' Society of London sang (again only) the *Credo* from the *B minor Mass.* In the same month the Archbishop of York selected the *Gloria, Qui sedes,* and *Quoniam tu solus sanctus,* calling them with Protestant bias "Selections from the Service," for one of Lord Burghersh's Ancient Concerts. Though the attempt to use the original instruments—three trumpets, oboe, bassoon, and French horn—resulted in a dismal failure, at least a beginning had been made. In 1840, the Sacred Harmonic Society began rehearsing Bach's Mass, yet without daring to give a public performance. In 1851, the *Credo,* directed by John Hullah, was heard again.

In 1849—one year before the founding of its more illustrious German counterpart—the English formed their own Bach Society. On April 24, 1860, it presented the *Kyrie* and *Gloria* of the *B minor Mass,* leaving the first documented performance of the *Sanctus* in England to Leslie's Choir in 1868. After a complete and massive performance of the *St. Matthew Passion* at St. James Hall in 1870, a repeat performance in 1871 with boys' voices—also in the soprano and alto solos—appears to have been the first church performance of Bach's Passion music in England. With this "the first step towards the recognition in this country of the highest class of sacred music as a powerful agent in religious worship" was taken *(Musical Times).* In Germany, the well known composer of Romantic ballades, Karl Loewe, had given the first church performance of the *St. Matthew Passion* as early as April, 1831.[41] It took place at St. Jacob's church in Stettin where Loewe was cantor for forty-six years. But this fourth performance of Bach's Passion music—after that by Mendelssohn in Berlin, by Schelble in Frankfurt, and by Mosewius in Breslau—was no trail blazer for additional church performances of Bach's choral compositions in his homeland.

In order to present the *B minor Mass* in England for the first time in its entirety, a new Bach Choir was formed in London in 1875. A year later, on April 26, 1876, it presented the first complete performance of the Mass in England at St. James Hall. It was conducted by its founder, the composer and pianist Otto Goldschmidt, who had been Mendelssohn's pupil at the Leipzig Conservatory, and since 1852 Jenny Lind's husband. Jenny Lind, who had helped train the chorus for the performance of the *B minor Mass,* not only sang the soprano solos but also joined the rest of the sopranos as *prima inter pares* in the chorus. The tenor Coleridge, who by profession was a lawyer, tells us "that no artist of her time rejoiced more in the Bach revival than Lind." He also remembered her saying to him: "To think that an old woman like me (she was then fifty-five) who has lived in music all my life, should have to be told of this by an amateur!" This story reveals the "Swedish Nightingale," who had dazzled audiences throughout Europe and America with her virtuoso singing, as a selfless music lover and a simple and honest musician.

By 1888 the London Bach Choir had given nine unabridged performances of the *B minor Mass* and nine performances were given in Great Britain in 1908 within the short span of four months; five were heard in one single month: two in London, and one each in Leeds, Dublin, and Newcastle on Tyne. There William Gillies Whittaker soon afterwards was to be the first to conduct the whole cycle of Bach's cantatas and even did so twice, anticipating Karl Straube's performance of the complete cantata cycle at St. Thomas's in Leipzig in the 1930s.

By the time France, Italy,[42] and America became acquainted with the great choral works of Bach, the *B minor Mass* had become one of the staples of the religious choral repertory in England. The spectacular growth of choral societies in Great Britain had, by the end of the nineteenth century, transformed the initially tentative Bach revival into a veritable Bach cult.

It was the first American performance of the *St. Matthew Passion,* led by Theodore Thomas at the Fifth Cincinnati Music Festival in 1882 and that of the *St. John Passion,* given by Fred Wolle with his Choral Union in 1888 at the Moravian town of Bethlehem, Pennsylvania,[43] that sent the American revival of Bach's choral music on its way. After he had given a performance of the *St. Matthew Passion* in 1892, Wolle was eager to begin rehearsing the *B minor Mass.* But its staggering difficulties had a dispiriting effect on the members of his choir. Wolle's ultimatum of "all or nothing" led to the disbanding of the Bethlehem Choral Union. It was not until March 27, 1900, that the newly founded Bethlehem Bach Choir, trained and directed by Fred Wolle, gave the first American performance of the unabridged *B minor Mass.* Theodore Thomas had already conducted the *Kyrie* and *Gloria* in 1884 at the Seventh Cincinnati Music Festival. One month after the Bethlehem performance in 1900, the Oratorio Society of New York presented the *B minor Mass,* which was to be followed in the next two years by performances by the choral societies of Boston, Philadelphia, and Cincinnati—all communities with large German populations.

It has been the purpose of this chapter to trace the early performance history of the *B minor Mass.* Having arrived at the twentieth century in our survey, suffice it to add here only the following:[44] The trend of Romantic exuberance in the performance of Bach's music, and hence lacking in historical concern, continued well into the twentieth century in both Europe and America.

But already in the first decade of our century warning voices made themselves heard. Albert Schweitzer considered it "a crime against the style of Bach's music that we perform it with huge orchestras and massed choirs."[45] The young organist also declared war on the giant factory built organs of the turn of the century and battled valiantly for the preservation of old organs. At the same time Wanda Landowska's playing of the harpsichord opened eyes and ears not only to the applicability but also to the esthetic superiority of the harpsichord over the piano in the execution of Baroque keyboard music. From 1904 on, musicologists used the *Bach-Jahrbuch* to air their views of Bach as a historical figure and of his music as a historically conditioned phenomenon. Since World War I, the gradual revival of practically all the instruments of Bach's time had increasingly undermined the Romantic concept of Bach's music. Since World War II the long playing record has brought the sound of the Baroque orchestra and small-scale chorus into our schools and homes and has thereby contributed to the gradual decline of the lush and large-scale concept of Bach. When an artist such as Eugene Ormandy presented the *St. Matthew Passion* in the traditional sumptuous Philadelphia style of his predecessor Stokowski, the critics, by now historically enlightened, pounced upon him as the perpetrator of an esthetic crime. As critics, they have to be up to date. They know that small-scale performances of Bach's cantatas have long replaced the massive Romantic tradition. But the two Passions and the *B minor Mass* have celebrated such decisive victories with large-scale productions in the nineteenth century that it will take a good deal longer to uproot this venerable concert hall tradition. In the case of the *B minor Mass,* this uprooting began with a small-scale performance by Arthur Mendel and his Cantata Singers in 1953, by that of Wilhelm Ehmann and his *Westphalian Kantorei* in 1959, by the performances and recording of the Robert Shaw Chorale in the early 1960s (which are fundamentally different from his interpretation of the mid-1940s), and finally by the recent recording of Nikolaus Harnoncourt and his *Concentus Musicus.* In spite of many artistic differences in these performances—I personally lean towards that of Robert Shaw—theirs and similar present day performances move towards one goal, a goal that was neither sought nor attainable in the nineteenth century. In contrast to their colleagues of the past, today's interpreters do not expect Bach's music to submit to the style of the time of the performers, not to their instruments and choral forces. Instead of asking Bach's music to yield whatever it can to the prevailing taste of the time, they consider it their sacred duty to try to bring Bach's music into accord with the performance practices of *his* time.

Notes

1. Both preserved in the *Staatsbibliothek* in East Berlin.

2. In the former *Bibliotheca Musica Regia,* now the Saxon *Landesbibliothek.*

3. No. 57 (April 1786) of the *Hamburger Correspondent.* Reprinted in Friedrich Smend, *Kritischer Bericht* to the new edition (NBA II/1) of the *B minor Mass,* 1956, p. 398.

4.   In the *Credo in unum Deum*, the *Et in unum Dominum*, the *Et in Spiritum Sanctum*, and the *Confiteor*.

5.   Georg Schünemann, "Die Bachpflege der Berliner Singakademie," in *Bach-Jahrbuch* 1928, pp. 145-48.

6.   *Leipziger Allgemeine Musikalische Zeitung* XXII (Leipzig, 1820), p. 608.

7.   See *Bach-Gesellschaft* edition Vol. 41, p. xxxix.

8.   This writer can find no documentary proof for Smend's assumption (*Kritischer Bach*, pp. 40 and 398) that this was a performance of the *Missa* (the first part of Bach's *B minor Mass*). Smend's source, E. Hanslick's reference in his *Geschichte des Concertwesens in Wien*, p. 140, is general rather than specific.

9.   Martin Geck, *Die Wiederentdeckung der Matthäuspassion im 19. Jahrhundert* (Regensburg, 1967), p. 76.

10. Vol. V, 1828, No. 17, p. 138.

11. Smend, *Kritischer Bach*, p. 398.

12. Geck, *Matthäuspassion*, p. 76.

13. Ibid., p. 23.

14. Which was to be delayed until 1830.

15. Smend, *Kritischer Bericht*, p. 40.

16. *Didaskalia*, Frankfurt a.M., No. 107, Sunday, April 17, 1831.

17. February 15, written from Paris. See Felix Mendelssohn Bartholdy, *Briefe aus den Jahren 1830 bis 1847*, Leipzig, 1882, p. 242.

18. Oskar Bormann, *Johann Nepomuk Schelble (1789-1837). Sein Leben, sein Wirken und seine Werke*, Frankfurt a.M., 1926, p. 28.

19. Ibid., p. 33.

20. See *Beurmanns Telegraph*, Frankfurt a.M., No. 18, October 1837.

21. See the next two paragraphs.

22. April and May, XXXIII, 1831, pp. 265-71; 285-98; 301-13.

23. XXXIV, 1832, p. 864.

24. The ninety-six parts have survived. If two singers sang from one part, which is probable, the chorus may have been twice that size.

25. For Spontini's performance, see Smend, *Kritischer Bericht*, pp. 40, 399-401.

26. Translated from Smend, *Kritischer Bericht*, p. 400.

27. *Vossische Zeitung Berlin*, May 2, 1828.

28. Quoted by Geck, *Matthäuspassion*, p. 25.

29. *LAMZ*, Leipzig, XXXVI, 1834, pp. 226 f.

30. *LAMZ*, Leipzig, XXXV, 1833, p. 717.

31. *LAMZ*, Leipzig, XXXVI, 1834, p. 242.

32. Smend, *Kritischer Bericht*, p. 41.

33. *LAMZ*, XXXXIII, 1841, pp. 174 ff.

34. Ibid., p. 175.

35. C.P.E. Bach's successor in Hamburg, C.F.G. Schwencke, mediated this purchase. See Alfred Dürr, *Nachwort* to the facsimile edition of Bach's *B minor Mass,* Kassel: Bärenreiter-Verlag, 1965, p. 5.

36. Smend, *Kritischer Bericht*, pp. 69 f.

37. This writer's own copy includes both forewords by J. Rietz and clearly shows that the parts from the *Credo* on were newly bound into the old volume.

38. See Friedrich Stichtenoth, *Der Frankfurter Cäcilien-Verein, 1818-68,* Frankfurt a.M., 1968, p. 44.

39. Brahms conducted the *Sanctus* from the *B minor Mass* in Krefeld on January 25, 1881, and the *Osanna* in Cologne (?) on June 18, (?). See *Bach-Jahrbuch* 1971, p. 47.

40. For the following see Percy A. Scholes, *The Mirror of Music*, London 1947, I, pp. 70 ff.

41. Geck, *Matthäuspassion*, pp. 97-99.

42. Paris heard the *St. Matthew Passion* first under Albert Schweitzer's mentor, Charles Marie Widor, in 1885. Rome was introduced to the *B minor Mass* by Alessandro Costa (who founded the Bach Society of Rome six years later). The performance took place in the sacred prayer house, the *Oratorio* of the Via Belsiana, after the Pope had granted special permission for women's voices to be heard there.

43. Raymond Walters, *The Bethlehem Bach Choir*, Boston and New York, 1923, pp. 40 ff.

44. In the preceding article ("Toward a New Image of Bach") I summarized this development which reappears in the next eighteen lines in slightly shortened and revised form.

45. Schweitzer, *Out of My Life and Thought*, p. 83. Here Schweitzer summarizes observations made in the final chapter of his Bach biography (1905, 1908, 1911—its French, German, and English editions).

Part V

Thoughts on the First Movement of Johann Sebastian Bach's Cantata No. 77 "Du sollst Gott, deinen Herren, lieben"

On Sunday, May 30, 1723, Johann Sebastian Bach entered upon his new duties as Cantor of St. Thomas's School in Leipzig. This venerable university town, a stronghold of orthodox Lutheranism, offered Bach the opportunity to fulfill at last his fifteen-year-old "goal" of his artistic mission—the creation of a "well-regulated church music, to the Glory of God." The enthusiasm with which the thirty-eight-year-old composer plunged into his new Leipzig assignment can be gleaned from the lavish proportions and rich orchestration of his first church cantatas. For the first two Sundays after Trinity (May 30 and June 6) Bach created the imposing cantatas Nos. 75 and 76 which, on account of their length alone, must have overwhelmed the Leipzig congregation that was accustomed to Kuhnau's small-scale cantatas. Each one of Bach's cantatas in two parts consisted of the symbolic number of 7 + 7 or 14 movements which to the initiated spelled out the new cantor's name in terms of the then popular number alphabet: B A C H = 2 + 1 + 3 + 8 = 14. A week later Bach performed the longest and most ambitious cantata of his pre-Leipzig period, BWV 21: "Ich hatte viel Bekümmernis" which, with its 11 movements and four extended choruses, seems to have proved too much for performers and listeners alike.

We have no knowledge of what actually happened, whether it came to an open confrontation between Bach and his performers and perhaps even with his authorities. All we know is the startling fact that from June 20, Bach's newly composed cantatas began to average six movements that open with an elaborate chorus and close, after two pairs of recitatives and arias, with a simple four-part chorale harmonization. The cantatas that stand out from this norm by comprising 10 and 11 movements respectively (BWV 147 and 186)

In 1974 the annual meeting of the South-Central Chapter of the A.M.S. was held in Louisville, Kentucky. During this meeting the Louisville Bach Society performed Cantata 77, and for this occasion this article provided the program notes. It is published here for the first time.

turn out to be Advent cantatas of Bach's Weimar period that the composer revised and made suitable for Leipzig usage (on Visitation, July 2, and on the 7th Sunday after Trinity, July 11). It is, of course, also possible that by the end of his third week in Leipzig Bach came simply to the realization that the choral forces put at his disposal were not capable of learning and executing more than one complex chorus per week.

Cantatas 105 and 77 belong to the six-movement type to which Bach resorted after whatever crisis had faced him following June 13, 1723. Cantata 105 was written for July 25, the 9th Sunday after Trinity; Cantata 77 for the 13th Sunday after Trinity, August 22, 1723. While the introductory chorus of Cantata 105, "Herr, gehe nicht ins Gericht mit deinem Knecht" with its Prelude *(Adagio)* and Fugue *(Allegro)* pattern is well worth a separate investigation, the opening chorus of Cantata 77 is the more challenging of the two. It is, in fact, one of the most astounding chorale-choruses in Bach's whole oeuvre.

Can we in any way reconstruct how this cantata, and especially this movement, came into existence? We know that the liturgical calendar determined what the cantata text was to expound and what hymns were to be used on any specific Sunday or holiday. As an integral part of the Lutheran service the cantata performed the liturgical task of interpreting the Gospel (and less frequently the Epistle) for the day in terms of music. We further know and have recently received fresh evidence[1] that the texts of Bach's cantatas were printed and that it was Bach's duty to submit to Superintendent Salomon Deyling beforehand several texts reflecting the Gospel or the Epistle for the day. Each cantata thus begins with the selection of the text. The Gospel for the 13th Sunday after Trinity is Luke 10:23-37, the parable of the good Samaritan. The Epistle for the day is Gal. 3:15-22, while Luther's "Dies sind die heilgen zehn Gebot" is among its *de tempore* pulpit hymns.

The text chosen for the opening chorus of Cantata 77 is Luke 10:27: "Du sollst Gott, deinen Herren, lieben von ganzem Herzen, von ganzer Seele, von allen Kräften und von ganzem Gemüte und deinen Nächsten als dich selbst." (Thou shalt love the Lord thy God with all thy heart, and with all thy soul, and with all thy strength, and with all thy mind; and thy neighbor as thyself.) The following two pairs of recitatives and arias deal, in a free form, paraphrased by a theologically well versed unknown poet, the first with love of God, the second with love of thy neighbor.

Faced in the first movement with the text of the two commandments—the law of love as the foundation of Christian faith—its musical treatment was no longer a matter of free choice for Bach. All passages from the Scriptures that contain or refer to a general commandment are set by Bach, almost without exception, in fugue or canon form. (Compare the foursquare textbook cases of fugal writing, the "Sicut locutus est" from the *Magnificat* or the "Wir haben ein

Gesetz" from the St. John Passion.) In the case of Cantata 77/1 the four-part chorus is treated in a strictly imitative style that could be called fugal if the customary answers at the fifth were not, for the most part, missing. This slight lack of strictness is conceivably caused by the fact that Bach's theological interpretation did not stop with Luke 10:27 on which the choral text is based. Bach remembered the quasi-identical passage in Matthew 22 and its continuation (22:38-39); "This is the first and great commandment. And the second is like unto it, Thou shalt love thy neighbour as thyself" and its all important continuation (22:40): "On these two commandments hang all the law and the prophets."

The theologian in Bach had to enforce this juxtaposition of the old and new law in his music. He did so by the instrumental use of the ten commandment hymn, "Dies sind die heilgen zehn Gebot" (These are the holy ten commandments) which he would never use again in his cantatas, oratorios or motets. This archaic mixolydian pilgrim's song "In Gottes Namen fahren wir" was probably adapted by Johann Walther in 1524 to fit Luther's ten commandment hymn. Bach entrusts this hymn tune to the high trumpet, the *tromba da tirarsi.*[2] Nor is the choice of the trumpet accidental. In choosing the trumpet for the playing of the ten commandment chorale, Bach chose the instrument that he and his time traditionally used to represent the majesty of secular lords and that of the King of Kings. In fact the trumpet may even embody the voice of God itself. At the same time it must have occurred to Bach that this ten commandment chorale could not hover above the musical texture all by itself but that it too had to be treated fugally or canonically. Bach chose the doctrinal and more rigid form of the canon as the proper symbol of law. He therefore assigned the ten commandment hymn as *cantus firmus* also to the continuo, two octaves and a fifth below the trumpet and in note values twice as long as the quarter notes of the latter. As canon in augmentation the ten commandments become now also the foundation of the whole composition. The trumpet anticipates each one of the five *cantus firmus* phrases before the continuo intones them. The symbolic outerparts of the six-part musical texture of this movement are illustrated at the top of the chart. The quicker quarter-note motion of the trumpet chorale allows Bach to let the trumpet repeat the first phrase of the *cantus firmus* (a₁) five times in quasi-rondo fashion and on different key levels (SD, D, and T). By this method he achieves ten clearly articulated entrances of the high-pitched trumpet, one for each one of the commandments. The slow, half-note pace of the continuo (organ) precludes the possibility of ten such symbolic entrances.

The symbolic, canonic outer parts of the musical texture of the first movement of J.S. Bach's Cantata No. 77: "Do sollst Gott, deinen Herren, lieben."

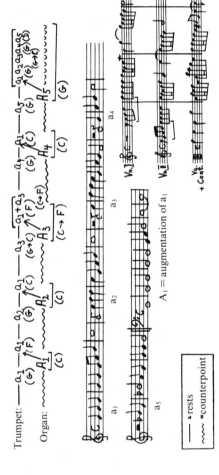

Strings and continuo, later also the four voices—all in diminution—provide the filling between the slow-paced outerlines of the musical texture. Rhythmically they are related to trumpet and organ as 1:2:4, i.e.

Outline of Bach's Cantata No. 77: "Du sollst Gott, deinen Herren, lieben" (mvt. 1)

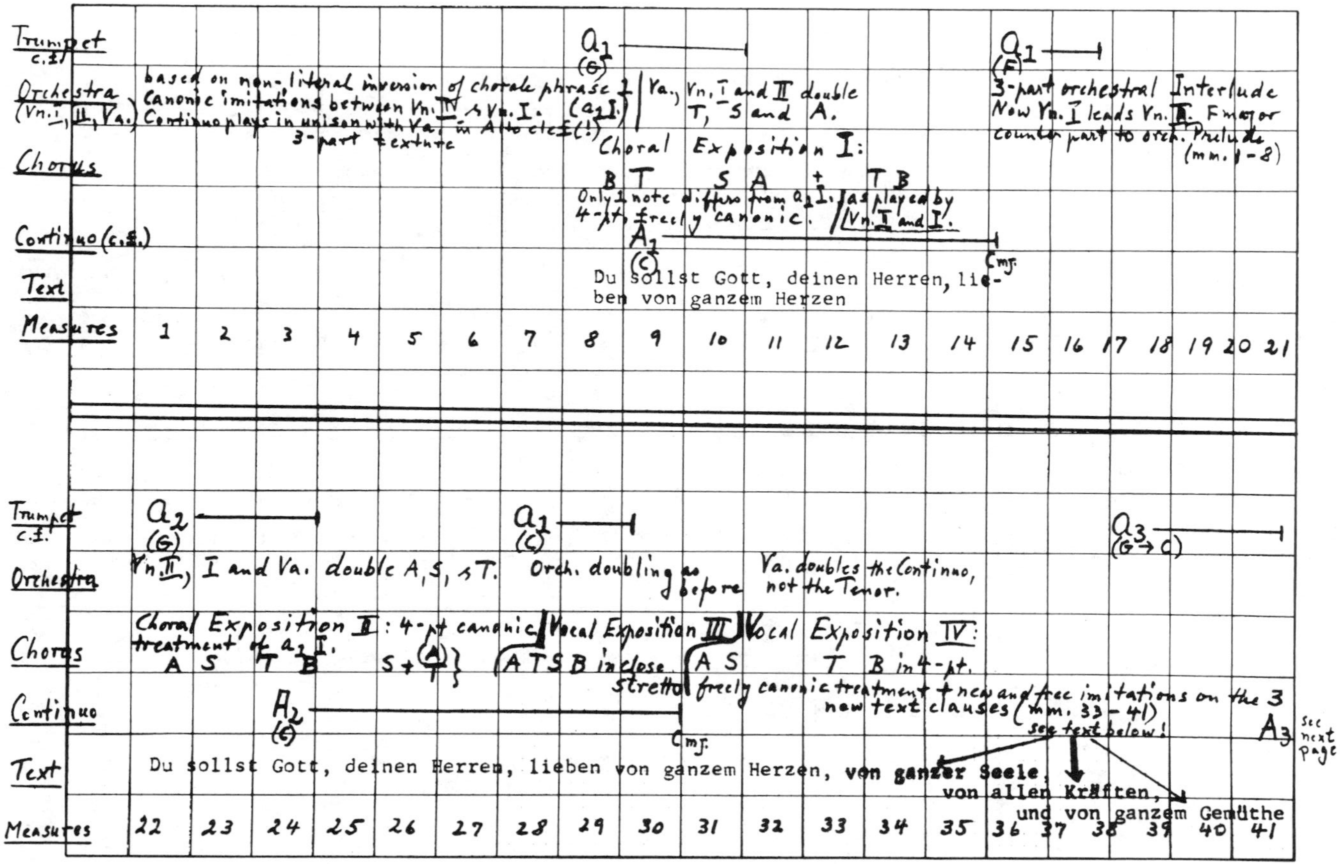

System 1 (mm. 1–21)

Trumpet c.f.: — Q1 (F)

Orchestra (Vn. I, II, Va.): based on non-literal inversion of choral phrase. Canonic imitations between Vn. I, II, Va. I. Continuo plays in unison with Va. in Alto clef (?). 3-part texture — Q1 (G) — Va., Vn. I, and II double T, S and A. (a1) — 3-part orchestral interlude. New Vn. I leads Vn. II Fugato counter part to exp. Prelude (mn. 1–8)

Chorus: Choral Exposition I:
B T S A T B
Only note different from a1) as already by 4-4, freely canonic. Vn. I and II. — A1 (c) — Cmf

Continuo (c.f.):

Text: Du sollst Gott, deinen Herren, lie- / ben von ganzem Herzen

Measures: 1 2 3 4 5 6 7 8 9 10 11 12 13 14 15 16 17 18 19 20 21

System 2 (mm. 22–41)

Trumpet c.f.: — Q3 (G→c)

Orchestra: Q2 (G) — Vn. I, II, I and Va. double A, S, & T. Orch. doubling no... before. — Va. doubles the Continuo, not the Tenor. — Q1 (c)

Chorus: Choral Exposition II: treatment of a1) T, B — A S — A2 (G) — Choral Exposition III: 4-pt canonic S + (A) — (A T S B in close) — Vocal Exposition IV: T B in 4-pt. A S — stretto freely canonic treatment + rearranging text imitations on the 3 new text clauses (mn. 33–41) see text below! — A3 see next page

Continuo: Cmf

Text: Du sollst Gott, deinen Herren, lieben von ganzem Herzen, von ganzer Seele, von allen Kräften, und von ganzem Gemüthe

Measures: 22 23 24 25 26 27 28 29 30 31 32 33 34 35 36 37 38 39 40 41

Trumpet c.f.	a_1 (F) —— + a_3 (C→F) —— (mm. 43–46); a_4 (G) —— (m. 54); a_1 (C) —— (mm. 56–57)
Orchestra	Vn. I, II & Va. mostly double S, A and T. (mm. 41–45); Somewhat less doubling than before (mm. 47–52); as before (mm. 56–58)
Chorus	Vocal Exposition V: 4-pt. imitation of a_1 I. S, A+T (+B), A+S (+T), B (mm. 41–45); Vocal Exposition VI A, S (but varied by new text; the 2 remaining text clauses have their own short motives: b and c; esp. c: A, S, T, A, S, B (mm. 47–53); Vocal Exposition VII B, T, A, S + short imitations on the 3 new text clauses B—A,S—B,T,A,S—T,B+S/A (mm. 54–63)
Continuo (c.f.)	A_3 (C→F) —— (mm. 41–46); Fmj. (m. 47); g- A_4 (C) —— (mm. 54–56)
Text	Du sollst Gott, deinen Herren, von ganzer Seele, lieben von ganzem Herzen, b: von allen Kräften, c: und von ganzem Gemüthe (mm. 41–52); du sollst Gott, deinen Herren, lieben von ganzem Herzen, von ganzer Seele, von allen Kräften, und von ganzem Gemüthe (mm. 54–61)
Measures	41 42 43 44 45 46 47 48 49 50 51 52 53 54 55 56 57 58 59 60 61 62 63

Trumpet c.f.	a_5 (G, mixolydian) —— (mm. 63–65); a_1 (G) + a_2 + a_3 + a_4 + a_5 —— (mm. 67–77)
Orchestra	doubles S, A and T. (mm. 63–66); as before (mm. 68–69); as before (mm. 73–74)
Chorus	Vocal Exposition VIII T, B, S, A based on a_2 I (text line 2) (mm. 63–66); Vocal Exposition IX Final text line: new theme: d T, A, B, S+B, T, A, S (B) (mm. 67–71); Vocal Exposition X B, T, A, S based on a_1 I. | S, A, T, B based on d' (mm. 72–76)
Continuo (c.f.)	A_5 (G) —— organpoint (mm. 64–77)
Text	du sollst Gott, deinen Herren, lieben von ganzem Herzen, (mm. 63–65); d: und deinen Nächsten als dich selbst (mm. 68–70); d: und deinen Nächsten als dich selbst (mm. 72–75)
Measures	63 64 65 66 67 68 69 70 71 72 73 74 75 76 77

Here is perhaps the place to draw the reader's attention to Bach's curious partitioning of the hymn tune into five phrases of which the last two (a_4 and a_5) run counter to the rules of grammar:

a_1 Dies sind die heilgen zehn Gebot	These are the holy ten commandments
a_2 Die uns gab unser Herre Gott	Which gave to us the Lord, our God
a_3 Durch Moses, seinen Diener treu,	Through Moses, his faithful servant,
a_4 Hoch auf dem Berg	High on the mount
a_5 Sinai. Kyrieleis.	Sinai. Kyrieleis.

Is it possible that Bach, who knew the rules of rhetoric as well as any musician of his time, sacrificed them here for the overriding sake of number symbolism? He treated the melody in the same manner in the large version of the ten commandment chorale in *Clavierübung,* part 3 (in which the *cantus firmus* is treated as a canon at the octave in the inner parts). The pattern that Bach designed for the continuo part of Cantata 77/1 is symbolically as illuminating as that of the trumpet part though in an entirely different way. The chart shows that the five statements of the five chorale phrases in the continuo (A_1 through A_5) are preceded by undulating lines. These signify that the continuo, in alto clef (!), participates also in the quarter, eighth- and sixteenth-note movement of the instrumental and, later, vocal ensemble, usually doubling the viola and tenor parts. Bach achieves hereby two astonishing and sharp contrasts: that of fast pace and the slow (half-note) motion of the *cantus firmus,* and that of alto and bass clefs which are often separated by more than two octaves. This fast-slow and high-low quilt pattern of the continuo part produces the apparently desired result of 2 times 5 sections that in Bach's symbolic language might well correspond to the two tables of the law.

In the first two of these contrasted sections Bach's original composing plan of utter contrast between the five sections is maintained and thus esthetically eminently satisfactory. In the three remaining sections the uninterrupted "crowding in" of the choral voices obscures the contrast of the alternating sections and might also drown out the lower lying entrances of the trumpet (in measures 28, 43, and 63). It may seem blasphemous to question Bach, but questions arise: Why did Bach, particularly in those sections that have the *cantus firmus* in the continuo, dwell so exclusively on the first text clause? The remainder of the text is treated more economically, especially the last phrase, "und deinen Nächsten als dich selbst." It seems likely that the design of the canonic outerparts and the contrast between the five sections in which the continuo appears in augmentation in the bass was conceived by Bach from the outset on and that he inserted the vocal parts later into the by then predetermined rigid canonic structure. Any doubts about the twofold symbolic significance of the number 10 in the canonic outerparts of trumpet and continuo should vanish before the evidence of the final organ point which lasts exactly ten measures (while simultaneously the whole hymn tune is heard unbroken as intoned by the trumpet: *"Alpha est et O"*).

Though held in check by the canonic-symbolic vise of the instrumental ten commandment chorale, the orchestra and the four-part chorus are the true moving forces of the movement. The ear assimilates their lively basic pace of eighth notes much more readily than that of the quarter notes of the trumpet and the half notes of the continuo. (The interior of Chartres Cathedral is intended to illustrate this rhythmic relationship of 1:4:2, i.e., of continuo to orchestra and choral voices and to trumpet, or $\flat$: $\downarrow$: $\downarrow$.) That the opening phrase of the two violins and later the—except for one note—identical phrase of the choral voices is derived from the first phrase of the ten commandment chorale has been felt intuitively from the outset. We can now identify the first eight notes of the violins or those of the vocal parts as the retrograde inversion of a_1 in diminution. By this subtle derivation Bach establishes organic unity in all parts of the movement. While the ten commandment chorale imposes its symbolic form (of 10 and 2 times 5) on the two outerparts of the musical texture, the livelier instrumental and vocal parts have a life of their own that creates a subtle contrapuntal friction with the two schemes of the outerparts.

A three-part ritornel, based on canonic imitation between the two violins, opens the movement. The following four-part choral fugal exposition (B,T,S,A,—T,B) shows the quasi-identity of its melodic material as well as the fact that the instrumental parts run parallel with T, S and A. The ritornel returns as the movement's only instrumental interlude (in the key of F). From hereon the instruments double, for the most part, the voices which present one fugal exposition after another. That there are altogether ten of them should no longer surprise us. In the third choral exposition the voices (A,T,S,B) overlap in close stretto. Up to this point only the first line of the text has been used. With the appearance of the three remaining text clauses: "von ganzer Seele" (2), "von allen Kräften" (3), "und von ganzem Gemüte" (4) in choral exposition IV (measures 33-41) new and freer imitations set in. Choral exposition V (measures 41-47) concentrates again on text line 1 but offers for the first time double entrances of the principal subject $(S,A,+\frac{T}{B} - A,+\frac{S}{T}$, B) Exposition VI (measures 47-54) is entirely based on text lines 2, 3 and 4 of which 2/3 are still treated musically as a variant of the principal subject (A,S). But from measure 48 onward text clauses 3 and 4 have musical motifs of their own with (4) playing its own follow the leader game (A,S—T,A,S,B). Its first four notes are not only an inversion of chorale phrase a_4 but constitute also, with their six stretto entrances, a structurally impressive preimitation of a_4 which is sounded by the

Chartres Cathedral—interior

trumpet in measure 53 and the continuo in measure 54. With the return of the complete text in choral exposition VII Bach returns likewise to a four-part fugal exposition of the principal theme (B,T,A,S) and short imitations of the three remaining text clauses (measures 54-63). Exposition VIII is nothing but a four-part fugal exposition (T,B,S,A) based on text line 1. The final two choral expositions coincide with the intoning of the complete ten commandment chorale by the trumpet and the organ point of the continuo. Bach waited for this coda-like moment to introduce his final text line: "und deinen Nächsten als dich selbst" with a distinctive syllabic subject of its own, heard in close imitation nine times (T,A,B,S,B,T,A,(B),S). In the final, the 10th, fugal exposition Bach ties beginning and end together. In measures 72-74 he treats the final text clause as if it were a close relative of the first which theologically it is. In the following measures (74-77) he allows it to conclude the movement with its own theme. These final 2 times 4 imitations rise and fall like an arch high above the sustained low G of the organ (B,T,A,S—S,A,T,B).

If Cantata 77 had failed to come down to us, the story of number symbolism in Bach's music could hardly be told with any degree of conviction as far as the symbolic number 10 is concerned. As it is, this movement has been seized upon eagerly by Arnold Schering[3] and Manfred Bukofzer[4] who in 1925 and in 1939-40 opened the inquiry into number symbolism in Bach's music of which Friedrich Smend has become the leading exponent.

The two organ chorales on "Dies sind die heilgen zehn Gebot" in the third part of Bach's *Clavierübung* tell their own impressive story in regard to the number 10. But their symbolism is not as multilayered as that of Cantata 77/1 in which nine if not ten different kinds of symbolism are woven into one of the most complex tonal tapestries in all music.

1. The first and great commandment "Thou shalt love the Lord thy God" is symbolized by the closely knit imitative pattern of the choral voices proper.
2. The age old hymn tune "These are the holy ten commandments," as sounded on the trumpet, relates the "great commandment" to the Decalogue.
3. The ten commandments are allegorized musically by the form of the canon between trumpet and continuo.
4. The position of this cantus firmus in augmented note values in the bass turns the ten commandments literally into a fundamental law.
5. The *tromba da tirarsi* is called upon to embody the voice of God.
6. There are ten entrances of cantus firmus phrases in the trumpet.
7. The 2 times 5 sections in the continuo likewise symbolize the ten commandments, but in a new and different way.
8. The final organ point is sustained for ten measures.
9. St. Luke's text (10:27) is told by the chorus in ten fugal expositions.
10. Was the momentum of Bach's involvement with the number 10 so great that he could not help but give the recitative that follows ten measures? Bach's treatment of its opening words: "So muss es sein" (Thus it must be) by the correspondingly simple triadic notes c-e-g-c and a look at the bass line that rises through five diatonic whole tones, then falls chromatically, seems to indicate that nothing, even in this short recitative, is left to chance.

Having explored the theologically inspired structure and symbolism of this remarkable movement in detail, I conclude with a brief investigation of the autograph score by which this cantata has survived. Its paper shows the typical watermark of Bach's first year in Leipzig (IMK). Combining this bit of important evidence with the autograph designation of the occasion for which the cantata was written—the 13th Sunday after Trinity—and the ductus of Bach's handwriting (especially that of the curiously scraggly C clefs), the date of its first performance on August 22, 1723 and its actual composition shortly before this date—probably during the week preceding it—can be considered as proven. We are not quite sure whether this score was inherited by Bach's second son, Carl Philipp Emanuel. By the beginning of the nineteenth century it is found in the library of the Berlin *Singakademie* where Goethe's friend and Mendelssohn's teacher Karl Friedrich Zelter may well have rehearsed it since the score shows several annotations in Zelter's hand. In 1854 the Royal Library at Berlin (see stamp at the bottom of the facsimile reproduction) acquired it along with many other manuscripts from the Berlin *Singakademie*. It remained in the Berlin *Staatsbibliothek* (as the Royal Library was called when Germany became a republic at the end of World War I in 1918) until 1943, when it was moved for safekeeping (probably to a monastery in South Germany). After the end of World War II the score found a temporary home in the library of the University of Tübingen and is now in the *Preussische Staatsbibliothek* in West Berlin.

The autograph score contains the bare minimum of information. It lacks the customary title page. It omits the title of the cantata on top of the first page (see its facsimile reproduction). Yet Bach does not forget to begin with a prayer for divine assistance in the act of creation: "J.J." (Jesu juva). This is followed by: "Concerto" (a frequent designation for the weekly "Sunday Music") and: "Doica (Domenica) 13 p. (post) Trinitatis."

Even a superficial glance at the score reveals that this is not a fair copy but a typical composing score written obviously in great haste. The figured bass appears only in a few measures of the first movement (measures 1-8, 15-22). Except for the *tromba da tirarsi* in movements 1 and 5 (where it is simply called *tromba*) Bach failed to indicate any instruments or voices (see facsimile). Since the original performing parts were lost at a very early time, the instrumentation had to be supplied by later copyists or editors. This was, for the most part, not too difficult a task. The different clefs, their order and the compass of the instruments and voices make S,A,T and B, two violins, viola and continuo (organ and cello) not just a matter of conjecture but practically of certainty. Whether a violone (double bass) was meant to play the low-lying *cantus firmus* sections of the continuo remains, however, an open question. The soprano aria (movement 3) has two obbligato instrumental parts both notated in violin clef. Their compass (e' - e''' and c' - b''), their voice-leading, phrasing and predominant parallel motion ask quite unequivocally for two oboes. This choice had already been made by a copyist in the first half of the nineteenth century and was accepted by Wilhelm Rust, who edited the cantata in 1870 for the *Bach-Gesellschaft* (vol. 18). The selection of two oboes has never been questioned since. In the first movement the oboes ought to go along with the two violins rather than strengthen the *tromba da tirarsi*. There was probably also an oboe da caccia *(taille)* part to double the viola part. This conjecture is corroborated by the presence of oboe and oboe da caccia parts in the cantatas immediately preceding and following Cantata 77. We may likewise assume that

Reproduced by kind permission of the Staatsbibliothek
(Preussischer Kulturbesitz) West Berlin

a bassoon part also once existed to strengthen the continuo. Though this completion of a full double reed choir seems to be very plausible, it remains, in the absence of any surviving parts, in the realm of conjecture. The same goes for the text of the concluding chorale. There Rust follows Zelter, who wrote the text of the 8th stanza of David Denicke's hymn of 1659, "Wenn einer alle Ding verstünd" below Bach's textless chorale onto the last page of the autograph score. In his edition for the *Neue Bach Ausgabe*[5] Werner Neumann substitutes the eighth stanza of another hymn by Denicke: "O Gottes Sohn, Herr Jesu Christ."

This essay elucidates some of the problems the editor faces and some of the decisions a conscientious performer has to make. There is perhaps no other cantata by Bach in which the musical and theological weight is concentrated to such an extent in the opening movement. This is to say that the emphasis on the structural design, once Bach had decided on it, is unmatched even by him. The closest parallel is the opening chorus of Cantata 80: "Ein feste Burg ist unser Gott" which, however, has been tampered with and added to by Wilhelm Friedemann Bach who thereby removed it as a reliable basis for comparison.

Apparently forced to create cantatas of a certain length and limited degree of difficulty, Bach seems in Cantata 77 bent on making up in semantic and theological depth what he was forced to renounce in number of movements and richness of orchestration. His theological insight consequently produced a form of supreme logic. But the instrumental canon enveloping the densely imitative four-part chorus whose function was to expound the scriptural text placed unusual melodic and harmonic limitations on the latter. What Bach succeeds in achieving in spite of these restrictions is nothing short of a miracle. That he did not return upon the path of Cantata 77/1 signifies, on the other hand, that even he considered the fetters he had here imposed upon himself too binding. Yet we may well rejoice that the young and still experimenting master gave us this theological sermon in a movement that constitutes a veritable musical tour de force.

Notes

1.   *Bach-Jahrbuch*, 1973, p. 5ff.

2.   This trumpet has a long throated mouthpiece that the player had to "press against his lips with two fingers of the left hand" while drawing "the trumpet out and in like the slide of a trombone." Curt Sachs.

3.   "Bach und das Symbol," *Bach-Jahrbuch*, 1925.

4.   "Allegory in Baroque Music," *Journal of the Warburg Institute* III, 1939-40.

5.   *NBA*, 1/21, 1958-59.

Part VI

Lombard Rhythm in the *Domine Deus* of Bach's
B Minor Mass:
An Old Controversy Resolved

Ever since 1856 scholars have disagreed on the interpretation of the inverted dotted (Lombard) rhythm that appears in the opening measure of the autograph flute part in the duet *Domine Deus* from Bach's *B minor Mass* (Ex. 1).[1]

Julius Rietz, who edited the *B minor Mass* for the *Bach-Gesellschaft,* relied heavily on the original performing parts of the *Kyrie* and *Gloria* that Bach had delivered to the Saxon Court in Dresden on, or about, July 27, 1733. The reason for Rietz's reliance on these parts was that the autograph score of the *B minor Mass* was in 1856 still in Zurich, in the hands of Hermann Nägeli, the son and heir of the Swiss music publisher, Hans Georg Nägeli. Printing measure 1 of the flute part for the first time, Rietz observes:[3]

> The passage is found in this form only this one time, not even in the violin which, imitating the flute, enters one measure later. Therefore, we have given [this passage] everywhere in even sixteenth notes.[4]

How, in the following year, Bach's autograph score was delivered to the *Bach-Gesellschaft* is a detective story of its own.[5] Since Rietz found that in this score

Reprinted with permission from *Bach,* the Quarterly Journal of the Riemenschneider Bach Institute VIII/1 (1977), pp. 3-11.

Bach had not notated the opening measure of the flute part in Lombard rhythm, there was no reason for him to change his mind regarding this measure in his revised edition of the *B minor Mass* of 1857.

Philipp Spitta, quoting the same measure, is in agreement with Rietz when he, too, abstains from applying Lombard rhythm to the corresponding phrases as they occur in the rest of the movement. Spitta says:[6]

> Later on, where the theme recurs, we find in the second half of the bar, simple semiquavers, phrased in pairs; thus the dotted mode of notation only indicates that the first is closely joined to the second, and to be accented, and not that it is of less value than the second. A manual of music by J.G. Walther of 1708, the original autograph of which is in my possession, says on this subject: "*Punctus serpens,* indicates that notes written as follows, should be slurred," e.g.:—

This is, however, no clear parallel to Bach's measure because the notes in Walther's example are not slurred and, hence, need the dot to indicate slurred execution. In Bach's case we have both: slurs above each pair of notes as well as Lombard notation with dots at the end of each pair. Therefore, Bach's dots cannot refer to slurring, since the slurs are already there, but must be understood rhythmically. It is, further, somewhat baffling that Spitta calls on Walther as his chief witness rather than on Carl Philipp Emanuel Bach, who has the following to say about Lombard rhythm:[7]

> Because the phrases are slurred, the first note is not to be executed too briefly [particularly] when the tempo is moderate or slow; for otherwise too much time would be left over. The first note is to be marked by gentle pressure, but by no means by a short jolt or a too sudden push.

Wilhelm Rust, the editor of most of Bach's cantatas for the *Bach-Gesellschaft,* seems to be the first one to have come to grips with this rhythmical problem. As editor of the *Trauungs Kantaten,* he recommends as early as 1864—i.e., long before Spitta—the following mode of execution for the bass aria *Rühmet Gottes Güt und Treu!* from Cantata 195:[8]

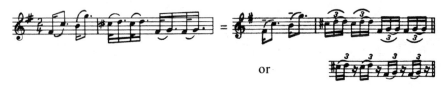

or

Exactly one hundred years after the old *Bach-Gesellschaft* edition, Friedrich Smend, in his vast Critical Report to the *Neue Bach Ausgabe (NBA)* of the *B minor Mass*, fails for some strange reason to mention Bach's peculiar notation of this opening measure in the autograph flute part.[9] For this sin of omission Georg von Dadelsen berates him in his exhaustive review of Smend's new edition of the *B minor Mass*, ending his description of the measure in question with the significant words:[10]

> This type of short-long execution applies, of course, likewise to the ensuing corresponding sixteenth figures of this movement.

By recommending application of Lombard rhythm to the rest of the movement, von Dadelsen concurs with Alfred Dürr, who already in 1955 had taken a similarly written measure from the E-flat major version of the *Magnificat* to be Bach's hint at dotted execution in like and similar passages of the movement.[11] Although in the soprano aria *Quia respexit* from the *Magnificat* Bach indicates regular rather than reversed dotted rhythm, Dürr points to the flute measure from the *B minor Mass* as an applicable parallel to strengthen his advocacy of dotted execution.

This interpretation, based on Quantz,[12] is passionately opposed by Frederick Neumann, who found an ingenious explanation for the Lombard rhythm in the flute part of the *Domine Deus:*[13]

> Several scholars, among them von Dadelsen, Dürr, and, with reservations, Mendel, see in the flute measure an indication that the short-long rhythm was to be used throughout the piece.... That it is in one part *only* compounds the improbability, since it would force us to assume the existence of a convention enjoining all performers to imitate a rhythmic pattern which they hear someone else announce.... The *Domine Deus,* with its stepwise 16th notes in C meter, was a textbook case for the use of the French *Inégales,* and it so happened that the chief flutist in Dresden at the time was M. Buffardin, a Frenchman. Buffardin, or, for that matter, his disciple, Quantz (who was still in Dresden at the time of the presentation in 1733), would have been inclined to play [like this]:

14

Bach's short-longs at the beginning were simply an antidote against the anticipated long-shorts. They were Bach's subtle way of saying, "Do not play it *à la française.*" This would easily explain why this episode is so brief; it was enough to get the idea across and not so long as to produce actual short-longs. It also explains why it appeared in that particular flute part and not in any other part or score, and why Bach never used it anywhere else. If this explanation is correct, it will add another telling point *against* the use of inequality in Bach.

Not this specific case, but F. Neumann's general interpretation of *notes inégales* was subsequently attacked by Robert Donington[15] and taken up again on November 11, 1973, at the meeting of the American Musicological Society in Chicago.

Approximately at the time that F. Neumann's thought-provoking article appeared, Nikolaus Harnoncourt let the flutist in his recording of the *B minor Mass* execute his part in the *Domine Deus* in Lombard rhythm, while asking the violins and viola to play even sixteenth notes throughout. In his extended foreword to the recording,[16] Harnoncourt justifies his interpretation as follows:

> This rhythm is found only in the first bar, and is an important indication that in Bach's music two equal note values are frequently to be played unequally. Now, notes slurred in pairs were very often executed in "Lombardic" rhythm,... without this having to be indicated specially. We believe this rhythmicizing should only appear in the solo part, and not in the analogous passages in the tutti strings, since it is a truly solo articulation, and since the uniformity in principle of analogous passages, frequently demanded today, by no means corresponds to baroque practice.

It can now be documented that Harnoncourt's acceptance of a rhythmic discrepancy between flute and strings is not what Bach intended. Neither does Bach agree with Frederick Neumann's interpretation of the measure as the composer's "short but necessary" antidote to M. Buffardin's natural inclination of playing this phrase as *notes inégales* of long-short values. The reason for Bach's rejection of both Harnoncourt's and Neumann's theses is, that Bach himself notated two further measures in Lombard rhythm.

I discovered this during a side trip from the Leipzig Bachfest 1972 to Dresden where I was permitted to see the original parts of the *Missa*.[17] Since the *Traversiere I* is among the better preserved parts, it was easy enough to verify the reversed dotted rhythm in the opening measure as well as the absence of this type of notation in the remainder of the movement. Hoping perhaps to find in Bach's performing parts the answer to the opposing views held by F. Neumann and N. Harnoncourt, I found that Bach had actually written two further measures in Lombard rhythm. They appear in the particularly well preserved second violin and viola parts:[18]

Viola:

Both parts are unquestionably in Bach's own handwriting. In each one of the two newly found cases, the Lombard rhythm appears in measure 27. This is the only measure in which second violin and viola are called upon to play the opening theme of the movement. The measure is heard in unison with the first violin. The latter, however, gives neither in the autograph part nor in the duplicate part, copied by Wilhelm Friedemann Bach, any indication of Lombard notation:[19]

If the first violin part had also been found to show Lombard rhythm, there would be no question as to its application. But such is not the case. At the same time, the unmistakable (and so far apparently unobserved) appearance of Lombard rhythm in both autograph second violin and viola parts—and that at the only place where its players might have been in doubt as to its proper execution—is certainly a new and strong point in favor of dotted performance.

Yet the old question remains: why does the first violin part lack Lombard notation? It was Bach's habit to write down no more than was absolutely necessary. For example, in his first cantata, *Aus der Tiefe rufe ich, Herr, zu dir* (BWV 131), Bach marked the frequently changing tempi with utmost care and precision. Although the autograph score of the five-movement composition shows twelve separate tempo entries, there is none for the fourth movement. There must be a reason for this apparently strange omission. In this chorale-aria Bach employs the same hymn tune, *Herr Jesu Christ, du höchstes Gut,* he had already used in the second movement, likewise a chorale-aria. If one plays and sings the eighth notes that in the fourth movement proceed in triplets fifty percent faster than in the second movement, the *cantus firmus* will retain the same pace it had in the second movement, which Bach had called *Andante.* Bach apparently took such simple consideration for granted and hence spared himself the trouble of a new tempo indication.

The situation in the *Domine Deus* from the *B minor Mass* is not much different. The first violin follows the flute by only one measure, and that, in literal imitation.

Is it not more than likely that Bach simply relied on the musical ear of the violinist—probably Vivaldi's protégé, Pisendel—whom he could expect to execute this phrase the way he had just heard it played by the flutist and the way the flutist would take it up again in measure 3? This is, after all, primarily a flute piece. Not only had the first violinist just had his exuberant solo in the *Laudamus te,* but also one that is likewise characterized by short-long rhythm. In the *Domine Deus* the first violin is not *primus inter pares.* It is muted and reduced to but occasional partnership, playing rather a game of follow the leader with the reigning flute.

But it is measure 27 that settles the argument in favor of Lombard execution. This measure is to be played in unison by the two violins and the viola:

Since Bach notated this measure in the second violin and viola parts in Lombard rhythm, the first violin could not possibly play even sixteenths against the alternating thirty-second and dotted sixteenth notes that the two other instruments were expressly requested to play. The *violino primo* simply had to fall in line with them.

If this measure, on account of its pairs of slurred descending notes, invites Lombard execution, as Harnoncourt rightly observes, why did Bach take the trouble of writing it out three times in Lombard fashion? Or, looking at it from a more practical angle: if a flutist were told that Bach had notated this meausre in Lombard rhythm, would he not play it quite automatically in the following manner?

Bach may well have sensed that Purcell's, Telemann's, and Vivaldi's infatuation with this fashionable rhythm might lead to a performance that would spread Lombard interpretation also to the first half of the measure. By his precise notation, Bach made it abundantly clear what he wanted and what he wanted to avoid. What mattered to him was the contrast between even flowing note values in the first half of the measure and rhythmical refinement through the four pairs in Lombard rhythm in the second half. This subtle contrast is a stylistic idiosyncrasy of Bach that is essential to the whole movement and, hence, must be understood by the performer and brought out in his interpretation.

The fact that this dotted rhythm appears not, as heretofore had been assumed, in only one, but in three out of the four relevant instrumental parts, and that at the two most strategic points (measures 1 and 27), should solve this old and vexing rhythmic problem which has plagued the performance history of the *B minor Mass* since 1856. If the facts presented here are accepted, future performances of the *B minor Mass* that aspire to historical correctness will have to apply Lombard rhythm—probably best in terms of C.P.E. Bach's definition—to these three measures and all corresponding phrases in the *Domine Deus*.[20]

Later (after 1741) Bach parodied the *Domine Deus* as middle movement of the three-movement Christmas cantata *Gloria in excelsis Deo* (*BWV* 191), setting it there to the words *Gloria Patri et Filio et Spiritui sancto*. Just as the score of the *B minor Mass* from which the *Gloria Patri* was transcribed gives no notational hint of Lombard execution, so, also, does this later score fail to indicate Lombard rhythm. Only the original performing parts of Cantata 191 might have shed light on the way Bach may have felt about the application of Lombard rhythm some eight years after he had penned this rhythm into the parts of the *Domine Deus*. The sources, however, desert us here. The parts of Cantata 191 have not survived. Even if they had survived and shown no trace of Lombard notation, this hypothetical fact would in no way undermine Bach's clear intention as far as the rhythmic interpretation of the *Domine Deus* is concerned. That Bach replaced the solo flute of the *Domine Deus* by two *flauti traversi all'unisono* in the later cantata might be construed as speaking against Lombard performance in the latter. The trill on f-sharp—a note that is difficult to play perfectly in pitch on the Baroque flute—renders Lombard execution of this pair of sixteenth notes practically impossible. But this is precisely the pair that was not meant to be played in the Lombard manner in the *Domine Deus*.

A final question remains. Why did Bach specify Lombard rhythm only in the performing parts of the *Domine Deus* and not in the score? Beyond the fact that Bach's parts generally contain more precise markings and more detail than his scores, the answer here seems even more obvious. Bach delivered the parts of the *Missa* to the Saxon Court in Dresden in the hope that his new sovereign would want to hear the work dedicated to him performed. Bach, thus, had to assume that such a performance, or later performances, might take place in the absence of the composer. To safeguard as correct a performance as possible in Dresden, Bach not only wrote out most of the parts himself—which could be expected in such a work of homage—but also clarified as much detail as possible, including the three strategic measures from the *Domine Deus* notated in Lombard rhythm. Since Bach retained the score, any performances in Leipzig would naturally take place under his own direction. Hence, questions regarding execution could readily be answered by the composer himself.[21]

Notes

1. Except for the two final paragraphs, this report appeared first in German as the major portion of an article in the *Bach-Jahrbuch 1974* that was published in September 1975.

2. Reproduced by kind permission of the Music Division of the *Sächsische Landesbibliothek* in Dresden (D.D.R.).

3. *BG* 6, 1856, p. xx.

4. The translations are by the author (except for those referred to by footnotes 6 and 16).

5. Cf. G. Herz, *The Performance History of Bach's B minor Mass*, in *The American Choral Review*, XV/1 (1973): 16f. and above, p. 197.

6. Spitta, *Johann Sebastian Bach*, vol. III, p. 49, footnote 60.

7. C.P.E. Bach, *Versuch. Das dritte Hauptstück*, par. 24, p. 128.

8. *BG* 13/1, p. xvi.

9. Smend, *Kritischer Bericht* to *NBA*, Serie II, Band 1, 1956, pp. 289ff.

10. Georg von Dadelsen, *Friedrich Smends Ausgabe der h-moll-Messe von J.S. Bach*, in *Die Musikforschung*, XII, 1959, p. 331.

11. *Kritischer Bericht* to *NBA, Magnificat,* Serie II, Band 3, 1955, p. 46f.

12. J. Quantz, *Versuch einer Anleitung die Flöte traversière zu spielen,* Berlin, 1752, Chapter XI, paragraph 12.

13. F. Neumann, *The French Inégales, Quantz, and Bach,* in *Journal of the American Musicological Society,* XVIII (Fall 1965): 355-57.

14. F. Neumann overlooks here that Bach notated also the first of the four pairs of 16th notes at the end of the measure in Lombard rhythm. (Cf. the facsimile of this measure on p. 221).

15. In *Journal of the American Musicological Society,* XIX (Spring 1966): 112-14.

16. Vienna *Concentus Musicus,* Telefunken, SKH—20.

17. They left Dresden only once since 1733, the year in which Bach delivered them to the Court of Saxony. During the last years of World War II, they were removed for safekeeping and, thus, escaped the devastating bombing of Dresden at the end of the war. They were, however, exposed to dampness that caused particularly the outer parts, such as the Clarino I, to deteriorate to a dangerous state of brittleness. The inner parts are fortunately still in fair, some even in good, condition.

18. See the acknowledgment expressed in footnote 2.

19. See footnote 2. The apparently misplaced notes, dots, etc., have bled through from the other side of the page.

20. This was done very convincingly at the Bethlehem, Pa., Bach Festival on May 15 and 22, 1976, under the direction of Alfred Mann, with John Wummer playing the flute part, and repeated at the 51st *Bachfest* of the *Neue Bach Gesellschaft* at Philharmonic Hall in West Berlin on August 26, 1976.

21. However, the handwriting of the famous dedicatory letter that accompanied the *Kyrie* and *Gloria,* as well as that of the title page to the parts of the *Missa,* is that of a Dresden copyist. From this fact and the past tense used on the title page, namely: "bezeigte," that is, "showed" or "expressed with the enclosed *Missa* his most humble devotion the author J.S. Bach," Hans-Joachim Schulze has drawn the sensible conclusion (in *Kongressbericht 1966,* Kassel-Leipzig 1970) that Bach—contrary to former opinion—had apparently had an opportunity to perform the *Missa* in Dresden at the time he delivered the parts to the Saxon Court.

Part VII

Lombard Rhythm in Bach's Vocal Music

In an article in the *Bach-Jahrbuch 1974* (pp. 90-97), the English version of which was published in *BACH,* the quarterly journal of the Riemenschneider Bach Institute, vol. VIII, No. 1, January 1977, I attempted to solve the old controversy about the rhythmic interpretation of the instrumental parts in the *Domine Deus* of Bach's *B minor Mass.*[1] The answer was supplied by two heretofore overlooked measures which Bach had notated unmistakably in Lombard rhythm in the autograph second violin and viola parts of 1733.[2] The present study tries to trace Bach's use of the Lombard manner in the hope of thereby disclosing its meaning. In this quest I have included Bach's equally rare use of short-long rhythms as far as they are systematically employed, and have also touched upon the syncopated style without, however, making any claim to completeness. As far as the history of the Lombard rhythm in music and theory is concerned, the reader is referred to the relevant literature. It reaches from examples given by Ganassi (1535), Caccini (1601), Frescobaldi, Loulié, Muffat, Hotteterre, Heinichen, Couperin, P.F. Tosi, J.G.Walther, Mattheson, Marpurg, Quantz, C.P.E. Bach, Leopold Mozart and Agricola to Charles Burney (1776). This chapter confines itself to the compositions by Johann Sebastian Bach concentrating on the vocal oeuvre of the Master.

The short-long rhythm which usually consists of two thirty-second notes and one sixteenth note and the reversed dotted, the so-called Lombard rhythm, which is characterized by a thirty-second note followed by a dotted sixteenth, are of course different. Yet both of them represent a deviation from the rhythmic norm of Baroque music (in contrast, for instance, to the rhythmic norm of the *ars antiqua*). That, on the other hand, an essential kinship between the short-long and the Lombard rhythm exists—at least in Bach's music—the following example from the bass aria of Bach's wedding cantata BWV 195/3 (measure 43) will demonstrate:

If we disregard the written-out mordent,[3] we come to the conclusion that short-long as well as Lombard rhythms do not occur in Bach's early vocal music, that is, in his Mühlhausen and Weimar cantatas. According to Quantz[4] the Lombard manner owes its name to North-Italian violinists, especially to Vivaldi,[5] and made its appearance as a novel mannerism in about 1722. Still later, in his Memoirs Quantz recalled that Vivaldi created a veritable sensation with his use of Lombard rhythm in his operas, performed in Rome in 1723.[6]

In Bach's vocal music true Lombard rhythm appeared for the first time on October 1, 1724, in the cantata composed for the 17th Sunday after Trinity "Ach, lieben Christen, seid getrost," BWV 114. In its second movement, a tenor aria, Bach wrote for the obbligato transverse flute a number of complex rhythms among which chains of ascending slurred pairs of diatonically descending thirty-second notes and dotted sixteenth notes attract immediate attention. In the ritornel they climb in sequence after sequence to the peak of the long melodic line (measures 9-11):

Later these Lombard figures relieve the tenor voice with the text "Wo wird in diesem Jammertale vor meinen Geist die Zuflucht sein?" (Where in this vale of sorrow, will there be refuge for my soul?). These words tend to give rise to the suspicion that Bach, *le musicien poète*,[7] may have employed Lombard and other bizarre rhythms to illustrate his text. Did Bach try to express man's anxious unfulfilled yearning for salvation by these Lombard phrases which seem particularly "short of breath" when played as here by a woodwind instrument such as the flute? Since BWV 114/2 constitutes a single instance among Bach's earlier Leipzig cantatas, the composer's true intention cannot yet be proven. However, if we compare this movement with others written during Bach's first two years in Leipzig, namely with those which exhibit the almost equally rare short-long rhythm, we may begin to approach an answer to this question.

With the sarabande-like third movement of cantata 75 with which the newly appointed Thomas Cantor introduced himself to his Leipzig audience on May 30, 1723, the insistence on the ♪♪♪ figure reaches the borderline between the ornamental and a more self-conscious short-long rhythm. The text of this tenor aria "Mein Jesus soll mein *al*-les sein" (My Jesus shall be my all) yields, however, no answer. Ten weeks later (on August 8, 1723), in the third movement of Cantata 179 "Siehe zu, dass deine Gottesfurcht nicht Heuchelei sei" (See to it that your fear of God be not hypocrisy) the short-long *Schleifer* belongs to the rhythmic and melodic essence of the tenor and the treble instruments (Oboe I, II and Violino I):

Fal - scher Heuch-ler E - ben-bild

It accentuates the following significant text:

*Fal*scher *Heu*chler *E*benbild
Können Sodomsäpfel heissen,
Die von Unflat angefüllt
Und von aussen herrlich gleissen.

(Likeness of false hypocrites
Sodom's apples could be called,
Though their outside glistens brightly
They are rotten at the core).

With this example the impression begins to grow that the short-long rhythm is employed to emphasize the text, in this case something negative and false, a perversion of truth.

The ornament of two thirty-second notes and one sixteenth note that falls on the upbeat in the oboe and alto parts of BWV 48/4 (of October 3, 1723) might be glossed over if it were not for the dactyllic text which refers again to the sins of Sodom: "Ach, lege das Sodom der sündli-*chen* Glieder, Wofern es dein Wille, zerstöret darnieder!" (Ah, lay down as destroyed the Sodom of your sinful limbs, if it is your will.) That in the central section of this aria in which the text speaks of the purity of the soul, Bach reversed the former rhythmic order of short-long and turned it into the more common long-short ornament of one sixteenth note and two thirty-second notes, might give pause for reflection.

Two weeks later, in BWV 109/5 of October 17, 1723, Bach sharpened the short-long rhythm to the Lombard time relation of 1:3, that is, to two thirty-second notes and one dotted eighth note: ♪♪. Was it the negative thought of helplessness of this minuet-like aria:

Der Heiland kennet ja die Seinen,
Wenn ihre Hoffnung hilflos liegt

(The Savior, yes, he knows his own,
When their hope lies in a helpless state)

that caused Bach to introduce this Lombard figure in all instruments and the alto voice? In the alto aria "Esurientes implevit bonis" (He has filled the hungry with good things) from the Magnificat the short-long rhythm falls consistently on "esurientes," those who are "empty and hungry." We may thus feel inclined to interpret this rhythm as being text-inspired. On Christmas Day, 1723 the Leipzig congregation heard this figure:

Flauto traverso I

Flauto traverso II

still in F Major and played by recorders *(flauti dolci).*[8] At first glance the picture of the notes looks more strongly syncopated than the pastoral sound of the gently flowing flutes—in the later D Major version that of the transverse flutes—transmits it to the ear. Yet it is again the reflection on a sad condition which elicits compassion for the hungry, that appears to have inspired Bach to his only consistent employment of short-long rhythm in the Magnificat.

During Lent of 1724 Bach completed the first version of his *St. John Passion.* The fact that short-long and/or Lombard rhythms appear in only two arias in truly systematic fashion[9] serves as renewed proof of the exceptional role these rhythms play in Bach's creative work, at least up to 1724 and, as shall be shown, beyond. In the tenor aria "Erwäge, wie sein blutgefärbter Rücken" (Behold, how his blood-stained back) the short-long rhythm alternating with the more frequent long-short rhythm represents the melodic peak of the ritornel and accompanies in the first part of the aria and its da capo the realistic words of Jesus' "blood-stained back." Since, however, two of the eight recurrences of this passage underline in the middle section the image of the rainbow which "stands as a token of God's mercy" ("der als Gottes Gnadenzeichen steht"), one might want to question the conclusion that this rhythmic figure was inspired by the image of Christ's "blood-stained back." But such caution vanishes with the subsequent soprano aria which represents the only unambiguous example of text-inspired usage of Lombard and short-long rhythms in the *St. John Passion.* This aria is instrumentally as well as vocally saturated with the following two short-long rhythms:

Zer-flie - ße,— mein Her-ze, in Flu - ten der Zäh - ren,

zer - flie - ße,— mein Her - ze,— in — Flu - ten der—

Bach scored these figures and their countless repetitions not only for the flute and oboe da caccia but let them also be sung consistently by the soprano to the words "Zerfliesse, mein Herze in Fluten der Zähren[10]...dein Jesus ist tot" (Dissolve, my heart, in floods of tears...your Jesus is dead). The poetic German word for tears, "Zähren," reemerged three years later[11] in Picander's text to the Matthew Passion, namely as the key word in the great alto aria which follows Peter's bitter weeping. As "Zerfliesse, mein Herze..." is the clearest manifestation of short-long rhythms in the John Passion, so is the alto aria "Erbarme dich, mein Gott, um meiner Zähren willen!" (Take pity on me, my God, because of my tears) the most eloquent example of these rhythms in the Matthew Passion.

Here we should mention that the tenor aria BWV 114/2 "Wo wird in diesem Jammertale vor meinen Geist die Zuflucht sein?" (Where in this vale of sorrow will there be refuge for my soul?) whose chains of slurred pairs of notes in Lombard rhythm were discussed above (see p. 234) has its chronological place after the *St. John Passion*. Not quite four months after the first performance of BWV 114 on October 1, 1724 the same slurred pairs of descending sixteenth notes in Lombard rhythm reappear. They punctuate the third movement of Cantata 92, the tempestuous tenor aria "Seht, seht! wie reisst, wie bricht, wie fällt, was Gottes starker Arm nicht hält." (See, see, how breaks, how tears, how falls, what God's strong arm does not sustain.)[12] The Lombard articulation of the tenor voice falls on the words "strong" and "invincible." For once—and this is the first time of such usage—Lombard rhythm illustrates God's might while Satan's power is depicted by the dotted rhythm of the French Overture which is customarily associated with the splendor of earthly majesty.

BWV 183/2 composed fifteen weeks later (May 13, 1725) is a tenor aria[13] of tortuous melodic and rhythmic contours. Although the text expressly rejects fear of death, Bach—and this is not uncharacteristic of him—seized upon the word "fear" just the same, literally to shake the melodic line and make it tremble with its vehement accents of two thirty-second notes and one sixteenth note. These accents fall significantly on the syllables shown by italics: "Ich *fürch*-te nicht *des To*-des Schrecken, ich *scheu*-e ganz *kein Un*-ge-mach" (I do not fear the terror of death, I shrink from no calamity).

The short-long rhythm in the serene alto aria "Wohl euch, ihr auserwählten Schafe" (Happy the flock that is chosen), the fifth movement from the wedding cantata BWV 34a of 1726, belongs with its bucolic charm of two flutes and muted violins in the realm of gentle syncopation (to which also the "Esurientes" from the Magnificat could have been assigned). In the opening movement of the solo cantata for soprano "Ich bin vergnügt mit meinem Glücke" (I am content with my good fortune), BWV 84 of 1727, Bach phrases the beginning of the vocal part in apparent Lombard manner:

Ich bin ver - gnügt

while oboe and first violin open the movement with the identical figure,
phrased conventionally:

By this discrepancy of notation Bach seems to have intended a piquant contrast
in phrasing between the instruments and the soprano. The short-long or
syncopated rhythms in measures 4ff. and 15ff. of the ritornelli and in measure
29 of the soprano voice as well as the conclusion of part I of the aria (measures
49-50) furnish additional proof that the above-noted contrast of phrasing is by
no means out of the ordinary in this aria of subtle rhythmic variations.

It can, however, not be sufficiently stressed that Lombard rhythm is found
in Bach's vocal compositions of the 1720s only in a few exceptional instances
and that the short-long rhythm is also still a rarity. This observation is
reinforced by the fact that a work of the scope and magnitude of the Matthew
Passion contains only one movement that is saturated with short-long rhythm,
the aforementioned alto aria "Erbarme dich, mein Gott." This aria for alto,
solo violin, strings and continuo follows immediately upon Peter's remorseful
realization that he had thrice denied his Master: "und ging heraus, und weinete
bitterlich" (and he went out, and wept bitterly) which inspired Bach to one of
the most awe inspiring melismas in the whole history of the recitative.
Although the succeeding aria is given to the alto as a sympathetic and deeply
moved bystander, the following interpretation seems justifiable in view of the
context in which it appears. With the melisma on "and wept bitterly" still in the
listener's ears, what else but the falling of teardrops can Bach have intended by
the reiterative pizzicato pulse of the aria's continuo? The at first calmly
plaintive but then increasingly tortured melody of the solo violin introduces in
measures 5 and 7 two different short-long rhythms. This long, rhythmically
multifaceted melody can only be interpreted as portraying the emotions of an
individual who identifies with Peter. The solo violin's eight-measure ritornel
with its increasing number of notes (11, 11, 15, 11, 24, 27, 32 and 11, the latter
for the final half-measure) illustrates graphically the mounting excitement, in
this case mounting despair. Also the lowest as well as highest notes of the long-
spun melody occur characteristically in the final measure (8 and 7) with their
wealth of notes. When Bach later added the double appoggiatura, the *Schleifer,*
that now opens the ritornel, he created thereby not only an innocent submissive
gesture that ushers in a pleading melody in the Siciliano rhythm so often used

for laments, but made it also the harbinger of the frenzied, now falling, now rising sequences in short-long rhythms that distinguish the second half of the ritornel from the first. This interpretation of the ritornel is further supported by the fact that the short-long figures of the solo violin coincide later (in measures 20-21) with these words of the alto voice: "Erbarme *dich*, mein Gott, um meiner *Zäh*—(four times short-long rhythm during the melisma)—ren willen." Only once does Bach let the alto voice sing a short-long phrase; but this occurs noticeably on the word "*schau-e*" with which the singer seems to point the finger at himself: "*Schau*-e hier, Herz und Auge weint vor dir, weint—(three times short-long rhythm in the solo violin)—vor dir bitterlich." (Look at me, heart and eye cry before Thee, cry before Thee bitterly), (measures 27-30).

To be sure, short-long inflections appear also here and there in other movements of the Matthew Passion. But these rather sporadic cases are with one minor exception[14] not among Bach's original composing ideas. They are afterthoughts added by Bach when he wrote out a new score of the Matthew Passion late in life (about 1740).[15] The copy of the score made by Bach's pupil and later son-in-law, Altnickol, is the earliest extant version of the work.[16] It was in all likelihood copied from Bach's composing score of 1727 which is lost. A comparison of Altnickol's copy and Bach's autograph score reveals several short-long figures to be rhythmic refinements, added by the composer when he gave his work its final form. In the opening movement the flute parts at the words: "Sehet"—"Wen?"—"den Bräutigam" etc. show the ♫ figure in Altnickol's score, an effect Bach throws into sharper relief by changing it in his own score to ♫. In the alto aria "Buss und Reu" (Repentance and rue) (No. 6 [10])[17] Bach replaced even-moving eighth notes (in measure 15) by the familar, rhetorically more pungent figure of two thirty-second notes and one sixteenth note, thus giving greater prominence to the woeful word "Buss" (repentance). In the next aria "Blute nur, du liebes Herz" (Bleed, you loving heart) (No. 8 [12]) the same figure adds to the voice's final melismas (in measures 42 and 44) the resilience of coiling springs on the characteristic words "morden" (to murder) and "Schlange" (snake). The effect hereby achieved is that of two brief moments of shudder in the soprano voice.

In the opening movement of part II of the Matthew Passion Bach revised the heart of the solo alto's melisma "Ach! mein Lamm in Ti-ger-klau-en" (Ah! my lamb in tiger's claws) in a very radical manner. What appeared in the early version as a long-sustained *b* in the bass voice—did Bach still think here of a personification of Peter?:

—is changed into three descending sequences of short-long rhythm, now sung by the alto voice, and a fourth statement of it in the treble instruments:

This short-long articulation not only falls consistently on the strong first beat of each measure but also plunges down three times by the interval of a tritone, the *tonus diabolicus*. Thereby the picture of the "lamb in tiger's claws" is brought into sharper focus, creating an image that is almost too realistic and painful for verbal description.

Among the few other, though considerably less dramatic rhythmic afterthoughts, the three occurrences of ⯑ in the tenor aria (No. 35 [41]) "Geduld, wenn mich falsche Zungen *ste*-chen" (Patience, when false tongues sting me) might be mentioned as well as the appearance of the same rhythmic figure in the aria for bass voice and solo violin (no. 42 [51]) "Gebt mir meinen Jesum wieder" (Give my Jesus back to me). But these two and one or two more instances are not significant enough to affect the conclusion that in the Matthew Passion only the alto aria "Erbarme dich, mein Gott," in which the two short-long rhythms are truly integral parts of the melody, incorporates these rhythms already in the first surviving source and, hence, in all probability already in 1727. The other brief occurrences of short-long ornamentation are thus refinements that Bach added later in life to throw words such as "repentance," "murder," "snake," tiger's "claws" and "stinging" of false tongues into sharpest possible relief.

After the Matthew Passion short-long and Lombard rhythms appear even more rarely which, in view of the general slowing down of Bach's creative activity in the realm of vocal music, should not be surprising. In the rhythmically complex fourth movement of Cantata 188 "Ich habe meine Zuversicht" (I place my trust) of about 1728 both obbligato organ and alto voice incorporate a number of flowingly syncopated and short-long phrases which may owe their invention to the first word of the text:

Unerforschlich ist *die* Weise,	(Unfathomable is the way,
Wie der Herr die *Seinen* führt.	by which the Lord does lead his own).

The *Ratswahl* Cantata BWV 29 of August 27, 1731 became important for Bach during the composition of the *Missa* of the later *B minor Mass*. It supplied Bach with the original version, the opening chorus "Wir danken dir, Gott, wir danken dir" for the "Gratias agimus" of the *Missa*. It also presents finally again, though only for two brief moments, one of those pairs notated in Lombard rhythm that Bach was to apply more fully to the *Domine Deus* of the Mass. Like a hint of what was to come, the Lombard figure appears in the fifth movement of Cantata 29, in measure 3 of the ritornel and in measure 11 of the soprano voice.

With the Ascension Oratorio, BWV 11, an altogether new type of Lombard rhythm makes its appearance, a type in which this rhythm no longer expresses disturbed emotions such as the despair in BWV 114/2 (see p. 234) but on the contrary joy, pomp and splendor. The first movement of the Ascension Oratorio presumably goes back to the opening movement of a cantata the music of which is lost, BWV Anh. 18,[18] which Bach had written for the inauguration ceremonies of the renovated Thomas School Building (June 5, 1732). A year later (August 3, 1733) Bach used the music of this cantata with an appropriately rewritten text again to celebrate the Name Day of his new sovereign, Augustus III. Also of this cantata, BWV App. 12, only the text has come down to us. The music of the first movement of both these cantatas has fortunately survived as the opening chorus of the Ascension Oratorio of the year 1735. There it exhibits the festive, joyous, even dance-like use of Lombard rhythm that was to become a new facet of Bach's composing style in the 1730s. Introduced by short-long rhythm, the subsequent Lombard figures bestow upon the principal theme its dashing élan, at the beginning in the first trumpet and woodwinds:

then in the violins as well as in the soprano and once also in the alto voices which proclaim the joyous text "Lobet Gott in *sei-nen* Reichen" (Praise God in his Kingdom). In the presumed first version (BWV App. 18/1) the text was "Froher Tag, verlangte Stunden" (Joyous Day, desired Hours) and a year later in BWV App. 12/1 "Frohes Volk, vergnügte Sachsen" (Joyous folk, contented Saxons).

Only one month after the performance of the likely Urform of BWV 11/1 Bach composed Cantata 177 "Ich ruf zu dir, Herr Jesu Christ" (I call to Thee, Lord Jesus Christ) for July 6, 1732. In its opening chorus the rhythm:

is heard consistently throughout the movement in the *violino concertante* and as a tutti contrast in the violins of the orchestra. This one and similar short-long figures became by their constantly increasing frequency a characteristic rhythmic spice in Bach's music of this decade.

The St. John's-Day cantata "Freue dich, erlöste Schar" (Redeemed flock, rejoice), BWV 30 of shortly after 1738, is a parody of the secular cantata BWV 30a "Angenehmes Wiederau, freue dich" (Pleasant Wiederau, rejoice) which was first performed on September 28, 1737. It is questionable whether the second bass aria of both cantatas goes back to the ninth movement of the lost cantata, BWV App. 11 of August 3, 1732.[19] The showy and apparently intentionally boastful nature of the Lombard rhythm can hardly be mistaken:

This aria is certainly one of the most willful manifestations of Lombard rhythm in Bach's vocal oeuvre. At the same time it is also one of those cases of the 1730s in which this particular rhythm cannot be explained as growing out of its underlying text; be it the highly questionable Urform, BWV App. 11/9:

Ich will Ihn hegen	(I will cherish him,
Und will Ihn pflegen	I will protect him
Und seiner Seele freundlich tun	and be friendly to his [the king's and elector's] soul)

or the aria from the secular cantata BWV 30a/7 in which "Fortune" promises the new Lord of Wiederau:

Ich will dich halten	(I will keep you
Und mit dir walten	and preside with you,
Wie man ein Auge zärtlich hält	As one protects tenderly an eye)

or the parody in the church cantata BWV 30/8:

Ich will nun hassen	(I now will hate
Und alles lassen,	and abandon all,
Was dir, mein Gott, zuwider ist.	that is offensive to Thee, my God).

Six months after Bach had written what is no longer likely to be the Urform of this movement (BWV App. 11/9) for the Name Day of his sovereign, Augustus II died. During the four-and-one-half-month period of public mourning that was decreed throughout the land Bach composed a *Missa* in homage to his new sovereign, Augustus III. Its *Gloria* contained not only the *Domine Deus,* the Lombard rhythm of which gave this author the reason for his article in the *Bach-Jahrbuch* 1974, but also the aria "Laudamus te" with its sharply profiled short-long rhythms. In this aria Bach contrasts the rhythmically conservative, festive, concerto grosso-like antecedent (measures 1-2) with a more soloistic consequent that is distinguished by two figures of which the first and elegantly syncopated one gives way to pairs of the typical short-long phrase: ♫. The solo violin takes over this short-long figure to climb with it in nine sequences to the melodic peak at the halfway mark of the twelve-measure-long ritornel which constitutes a miniature violin concerto of its own. The short-long figure shows that even the rhythmic reversal of Albert Schweitzer's so-called joy-motif served Bach in the early 1730s for the expression of exalted joy ("lau-*da*-mus te, *a-do-ra-mus* te, *glo-ri*-fi-ca-mus te").

Only one week after he had presented the parts of the *Missa* of the later *B minor Mass* (BWV 232[1]) to Augustus III at the Dresden Court, Bach again sought the favor of his new sovereign, this time with the above-mentioned cantata for his Name Day (on August 3, 1733) "Frohes Volk, vergnügte Sachsen," BWV App. 12 of which only the text has survived. Did Bach intend to characterize, perhaps even to satirize goodnaturedly the "joyous folk," the "contented Saxons" by the exuberance and the somewhat stilted pomposity that the Lombard rhythm lends to its opening chorus which, though lost, was apparently identical with the extant opening chorus of the Ascension Oratorio?

One month later Bach used the occasion of the eleventh birthday of the Saxon crown prince (on September 5, 1733) to furnish renewed proof of his creative abilities and of his esteem for the Electoral House of Saxony. For this purpose he performed with his Collegium Musicum a newly composed cantata "Hercules auf dem Scheidewege" (Hercules at the crossroads), BWV 213. This charming *Dramma per Musica* includes again a movement, the duet between Hercules (alto)—symbolizing the crown prince—and Virtue (tenor) which is permeated with short-long rhythms. The text of this love duet, the cantata's eleventh movement, is again an expression of joy.

Once this cantata or any other secular cantata had been presented at the festive occasion for which it was written, it had fulfilled its social function. However, these secular cantatas had not lost their usefulness for their composer. While Bach adapted some of his secular cantatas to revised or entirely new texts so that they could be performed at other later secular events, he quarried the majority of them for later sacred compositions. Thus the Hercules Cantata and the two secular cantatas BWV 214 and 215 which were to follow in its wake, yielded most of their choruses and arias to the forthcoming Christmas Oratorio, thereby bestowing upon them a new and more enduring life during the annual Christmas season. Except for the recitatives and the final chorus, that Bach had, however, planned to reuse but then rejected, he revised and then did reuse the remaining six movements of the Hercules Cantata in the first four of the six festive cantatas that compose the Christmas Oratorio. BWV 213/11 that was described above became after extensive revision the duet in the third part of the Christmas Oratorio "Herr, dein Mitleid, dein Erbarmen tröstet uns und macht uns frei" (Lord, your mercy, your compassion comforts us and makes us free). But the somewhat frivolous rhythm of the secular cantata is hardly suitable to the new text. The alto aria, BWV 213/9 "Ich will dich nicht hören" (I will not listen to you) in which Hercules renounces Lust, becomes by parody the popular aria "Bereite dich, Zion" (Prepare thyself, Zion) in the first part of the Christmas Oratorio. At about the same time, the seductive soprano aria, sung by Lust (BWV 213/3) "Schlafe, mein Liebster, und pflege der Ruh" (Sleep, my beloved, and cherish the rest) is turned, by a minimum of text change, into Mary's beguiling lullaby for the Christchild in the second cantata of the Christmas Oratorio. What is of interest in the context of the present study is the fact that both these arias from the Hercules Cantata show in their original version no trace of short-long rhythm. In "Bereite dich, Zion" from the Christmas Oratorio, however, Bach embellished the word "prangen" in "deine Wangen müssen heut viel schöner *pran*-gen" (thy cheeks must glow today much more beautifully) with a six-measure outburst of high spirits that culminates in this figure:

BWV 248 I/4

This enlivening coloratura is thus an addition that refines and transforms the much simpler parallel passage in BWV 213/9. A similar, though shorter cadenza-like eruption of melismatic virtuosity, animated by short-long rhythm:

BWV 248 II/10

T. 137 - 139

replaces in the lullaby from the Christmas Oratorio the simple motion of four eighth and two quarter notes that Bach had assigned to the parallel passage in Lust's aria from the Hercules Cantata. In the Christmas Oratorio the new words "unser Herz er-*freu*-en" (to gladden our heart) may have inspired Bach to this sparkling melodic addition to the Virgin's lullaby. These two examples of rhythmic piquancy added to the Christmas Oratorio as well as those that Bach applied to the final version of the Matthew Passion (see pp. 239ff.) indicate that in the 1730s short-long ornaments as a means of rhythmic refinement had become second nature to Bach.

Only three months after the presentation of the Hercules Cantata Bach used the occasion of the birthday of the Electoress of Saxony and Queen of Poland on December 8, 1733, to compose and perform in her honor yet another congratulatory cantata, the *Dramma per Musica,* BWV 214, "Tönet, ihr Pauken! Erschallet, Trompeten! Klingende Saiten, erfüllet die Luft!". Nothing could translate the text "Kettledrums, reverberate! Trumpets, resound! Ringing strings, fill the air with your sound!" more vividly and more literally than Bach's dazzling orchestration with its staggered entrances of kettledrums, trumpets and downward-rushing strings. The later use of the movement as opening chorus of the Christmas Oratorio "Jauchzet, frohlocket, auf, preiset die Tage" (Exult, rejoice and extol the Days) had to sacrifice the perfect union of the musical setting and its original text in BWV 214/1. Bach may well have lent a helping hand to the unknown poet of Cantata 214[20] so as to enable its composer to impress his new electoress and queen with the musical forces he controlled in Leipzig. In the Queen's Cantata it is above all the middle section of the minuet-like fifth movement which assigns to the alto voice the following extraordinarily virtuoso passage, spiced with short-long rhythms and set to the words "Füllt mit Freuden eure Brust" (Fill your breast with joy):

BWV 214/5

Füllt mit Freu - - - - - - den eu-re Brust,
T. 69 - 72

Bach not only retained this vocal tour de force in the extensively revised and parodied tenor aria "Frohe Hirten, eilt, ach eilet" (Hasten, joyous shepherds, hasten) of the Christmas Oratorio (BWV 248^{II}/6) but also enriched the opening ritornel (and its two returns) with an additional bit of short-long articulation as a delightful and technically rewarding ornament for the obbligato flute.

In the year that followed Augustus III's accession to the throne, the Thomas cantor, who was by now thoroughly disenchanted with his Leipzig position, could hardly do enough to court the favor of the new Electoral House of Saxony. On February 19, 1734, Bach observed, although one month *post festum* the coronation of Augustus III as King of Poland, with a performance of Cantata BWV 205a, which was, however, a parody of a congratulatory cantata, BWV 205, which Bach had written in 1725 in honor of a distinguished professor at the University of Leipzig. It seems that Cantata 206 was at least partially composed and prepared as a birthday offering to the king, when Augustus III and his queen announced a surprise visit to Leipzig that coincided with the first anniversary of Augustus' election as King of Poland, an event which preceded his birthday by two days. At incredible speed—apparently within three days—a new cantata, BWV 215, that dealt with the most recent events of the Polish war and Augustus' victory, was readied for the occasion and performed in the presence of the exalted couple on October 5, 1734. The event, sponsored by the students of the University of Leipzig and most lavishly staged, cost almost three hundred thaler of which Bach and his musicians received only fifty and the Leipzig librettist Magister Clauder another twelve.[21] The performance of this cantata was to bring tragedy to a renowned member of Bach's orchestra. On the day after the open air performance that had taken place in front of the king's lodgings and was illuminated by six hundred lighted torches carried by students, Bach's first trumpeter, the sixty-seven-year-old Gottfried Reiche, collapsed and died from a stroke. According to the town chronicler, his death was due to musical exertion and inhalation of smoke.[22] The mighty antiphonal opening chorus of this cantata "Preise dein Glücke, gesegnetes Sachsen" (Praise thy fortune, blessed Saxony) is, with its three trumpets, kettledrums, pairs of flutes and oboes, strings, continuo and with its double chorus of eight voices, the largest setting in Bach's vocal oeuvre. We may assume that Bach did not tell his exalted visitors that he had used this festive chorus already two years earlier in a (now lost) cantata, BWV App. 11/1, for the Name Day of Augustus III's predecessor; and Bach himself was certainly not yet aware that he would use this magnificent double chorus with its rich orchestration still another time. By parody it became the *Osanna* when, in the last decade of his life, Bach was turning Augustus III's *Missa* of 1733 into the complete *Mass in B minor*.

The King's Cantata, BWV 215, is even more richly endowed with syncopations, short-long and Lombard rhythms than BWV 213 and 214, not only in the arias (movements 3, 5 and 7) but even in the first recitative. The soprano aria (BWV 215/7) is the only movement of this cantata that found its way into the *Christmas Oratorio* (BWV 248^V/5) three months later. As in the soprano aria from the Matthew Passion "Aus Liebe will mein Heiland sterben" (Out of love my Savior wants to die) Bach withheld also from BWV 215/7 the solid foundation of the basso continuo. Whether Bach also intended to symbolize an unearthly, superhuman quality here in the King's Cantata, is, in view of the text that praises Augustus III who "repays evil with kindness," at least conceivable:

Aber die Bosheit mit Wohltat vergelten,	(To repay evil with kindness,
Ist nur der Helden,	is the perogative of heroes,
Ist Augustens Eigentum.	of Augustus alone.)

The familar Lombard ornament $\overset{\frown}{\text{♪♪♪}}$ is usually heard in two or three rising sequences, at first in the melody-carrying flutes and, in the aria's middle section, also in the soprano and the strings. It becomes particularly noteworthy in measures 104-110 with the text as cited above:

It is interesting that at the word "*Bos*-heit" (evil) Bach turned the direction of the Lombard figures that, with one exception, had consistently ascended, twice downward. For the Christmas Oratorio (BWV 248^V/5) Bach rewrote this B minor soprano aria without continuo as an F-sharp minor bass aria with continuo. He retained, however, the Lombard ornaments throughout the parodied movement although the new text "Er-*leuch*-te mein Herze, erleucht auch meine *fin*-stre Sinnen" (Illumine my heart, illumine also my dark mind) is obviously less well suited to the melodic and rhythmic capriciousness of the original cantata movement.

Still another two movements from the *Christmas Oratorio,* which do not seem to be parodies, show short-long rhythm. In BWV 248^V/9 it appears in the solo violin as written-out *Schleifer;* in the soprano aria BWV 248^{VI}/4 the ornament in Lombard rhythm falls (in measure 45) perhaps intentionally on the word "Stolz" (pride) in the passage "seiner Feinde Stolz zu enden" (to end the pride of his enemies). The composition of these two movements and that of the above-cited vocal flourishes in "Bereite dich, Zion" and "Schlafe, mein Liebster" which proved to be additions to these arias, must therefore have taken place during Advent 1734 when Bach wrote the score of the Christmas Oratorio.

Also the rhythmically tortuous aria for tenor, solo violin and continuo, BWV 97/4, with its short-long figures and syncopations was written— according to the autograph date at the end of the score—in the year 1734.

Cantata 206, planned and, as mentioned above, perhaps already partially composed for Augustus III's birthday in 1734, was in all probability performed for his sovereign's birthday two years later on October 7, 1736. Also this cantata boasts of a movement, the ninth, which belongs to the category of modish display of Lombard rhythm. Did Bach perhaps allude with this vocal Gavotte to a then current vogue of the Lombard manner in Leipzig? At any rate, Bach displayed this rhythm prominently in the cantata's final aria in which, as is fitting, harmony is restored. Bach may have intended to make a fine point when he let this aria with its Lombard articulation be sung by the soprano, the voice which represents in this cantata of four rivers Leipzig's own river, the Pleisse: "Hört doch! der sanften Flöten Chor" (Hear now, the choir of soft flutes):

It is not surprising that the Coffee Cantata, which was probably written in the second half of 1734, again contains a movement, BWV 211/8, which is permeated by the characteristic short-long *Schleifer* upbeat [23]:

The constantly repeated, in the literal sense of the word breathtaking *Schleifer* is in this charming as well as humorous soprano aria of daughter Liesgen an apt and ironic reflection of the girl's anticipation of the "heute noch" (still today) promised state of matrimony. Picander's for the time quite daring text[24] was lifted by Bach's musical setting with its waltz-like lilt and exciting short-long upbeats to an artistically as well as psychologically unsurpassable level.

We do not know whether the dotted rhythm toward the end of the ritornel in the final movement of the solo cantata "Non sa che sia dolore," BWV 209, was perhaps also intended to be executed in reversed short-long rhythm. Since neither the autograph score nor the original performing parts have come down to us, Bach scholars face a tricky problem which does not only concern questions of rhythm but also the customary dating of the cantata as "approximately 1729." Should clues develop in the course of further investigations regarding this rather poorly documented cantata that might indicate a somewhat later date of origin (perhaps in the early 1730s), the above-pronounced assumption that short-long rhythmic execution was intended would receive considerable, though still indirect support.

The Ascension Oratorio contains beyond its opening chorus with its short-long and Lombard rhythms still another movement in which short-long figures play an essential role. Like the opening chorus so does the fourth movement presumably go back to a lost source, namely to a wedding cantata of November 27, 1725; "Auf! süss entzückende Gewalt" (Come! sweetly captivating power) of which only Gottsched's text has survived. That the familiar ornament consisting of two thirty-second notes and one sixteenth note formed already a part of the music set to Gottsched's original text: "Entfernet *euch,* ihr *kal*-ten Herzen" (Cold hearts, depart from here), is improbable for the following two reasons. Not only is this figure in Bach's vocal music around 1725 extremely rare, but it is also absent from its second parody, the *Agnus Dei* of the *B minor Mass,* which probably was derived from the movement's first version of 1725. Be this as it may, in the Ascension Oratorio of 1735 the short-long ornament appears to be a rhythmic refinement that Bach added, probably for rhetorical reasons, to stress the plaintive text. Following upon Christ's farewell, the alto pleads with Jesus:

Ach, Bleibe *doch,* mein *lieb*-stes Leben,   (Ah, stay with me, my dearest life,
Ach, fliehe nicht so bald von mir!   ah, do not flee from me so soon).

Over a decade later, when he shaped the *Agnus Dei* of the *B minor Mass,* Bach tightened this movement resolutely and left the eloquent melody pure and unornamented. What Bach regarded in 1735 as a desirable text-serving expressive figure no longer satisfied him in the 1740s when he completed the *B minor Mass.* It was probably the spiritual Latin text that induced the composer not to burden the melody with ornamentation.

The most ostentatious manifestations of Lombard rhythm encountered so far occurred in the opening movement of the Ascension Oratorio and in the bass aria from "Angenehmes Wiederau" (BWV 30a/7) and the latter's sacred parody in the St. John-Day cantata (BWV 30/8). Again it is a bass aria and, as in the earlier cases, a composition in $\frac{2}{4}$ time, that shows Lombard rhythm at its most willful and most pronounced: the third movement of the wedding cantata BWV 195. It seems as though in this, perhaps his last vocal composition employing the Lombard manner, Bach intended to exhibit the rhythm in all its variety:

As pointed out at the beginning of this article[25] this movement contains passages in which Lombard rhythm and short-long figures are heard simultaneously. The text "Rühmet Gottes Güt und Treu, rühmet ihn mit reger Freude" (Praise the grace and faith of God, praise Him too with lively gladness) may have contributed to Bach's choice of Lombard rhythm, but it can hardly have engendered its extravagance and ostentatiousness. Perhaps the occasion for which this cantata was composed may have called for the unusual showiness of the Lombard manner. This cantata was not intended for a regularly recurring Sunday or holiday of the church year. It was composed for a very special occasion: either the church wedding of an aristocratic couple, as the text-clause "Hochedles Paar" might indicate, or the church wedding of the mayor of the town of Naumburg on September 11, 1741 and the daughter of the late pastor of the Thomas Church, a great-grandniece of Heinrich Schütz.[26] One will hardly go too far in assuming that Bach knew the latter pair personally; but also in the other case, that of an aristocratic couple, it seems quite conceivable that Bach was told or learned indirectly that one or even both of the future marriage partners were special devotees of the Lombard manner which was then apparently the latest fashion in Leipzig. As will be shown with regard to the secular cantata BWV App. 13 (see pp. 254ff.), Bach knew, when it mattered, perfectly well, how to adapt his music to the musical taste of his listeners.

The present study has disclosed Bach's use of short-long and Lombard rhythms in his vocal music in two different ways and at two different stages of his life. The few and rather weak traces of short-long rhythm that preceded Bach's arrival in Leipzig can for all practical purposes be disregarded. It is in 1723 that the short-long rhythm—though not yet conspicuous—made its appearance in Bach's vocal music while Lombard rhythm—at first, however, only in a single instance[27]—is found sixteen months later on October 1, 1724 (in BWV 114/2). From 1723 to 1728[28] Bach used short-long rhythms in most of the still infrequent cases for word painting, just as he did in the one instance of

Lombard rhythm. Words of grief, pain, dismay, disgust or abnormal emotions, exaggerated or distorted gestures, became the motivation for Bach's choice of short-long emphasis (and once also of true Lombard rhythm). The words interpreted in such fashion reached from "false hypocrites" and the "Sodom" of man's "sinful limbs," the "hungry," the "shackles" of sin, Christ's "bloodstained" back, the "vale of sorrow" of human existence (Lombard rhythm!) to the "sting" of false tongues. Short-long rhythm lent its peculiarly pungent accentuation to phrases such as "Thy Jesus is dead," "dissolve, my heart, in floods of tears," "have pity on me, my God, because of my tears" that "cry before Thee bitterly." Short-long ornaments gave prominence also to the words "unfathomable," "repentance," "murder," "snake" and tiger's "claws." Stunning as this word-inspired use of short-long rhythm is in most cases, it is merely an occasional stylistic phenomenon.

From 1732 on this changed abruptly. A new type that preferred Lombard to short-long rhythm emerged. As a positive manifestation of joy, pomp and power, it was encountered in at least one movement of about one half of Bach's remaining thirty-odd vocal compositions. Especially significant was, that from June 1732 to October 1734 in not a single newly-written vocal composition was one of these two rhythms found missing. During the next three years, on the other hand, new vocal works containing movements with short-long and Lombard rhythms began to give way to new vocal compositions lacking these two rhythms. In the last decade of Bach's creative life (from about 1738 to about 1748) Lombard rhythm vanished from his vocal music, with the possible exceptions of the wedding cantata BWV 195, should its third movement have been written between 1738 and 1741, and the two parodies BWV 30/8 (see p. 243) and BWV 191/2, the shortened version of the *Domine Deus* from the *B minor Mass* with its new text *Gloria Patri et Filio et Spiritui sancto*. Another nine vocal compositions, among them parodies, are completely free from this rhythmic idiosyncrasy, though not from movements with syncopation. Bach's predilection for the Lombard manner appears to have been a relatively short-lived phase which reached its peak between the years 1732 and 1735 though lasting apparently until 1741.

The sudden showy appearance of Lombard rhythm in 1732 seems at first bewildering. However, it begins to make sense when the occasions for which these compositions were written are reviewed in chronological order.

	BWV	DATE	OCCASION
1.	29/5	8-27-1731	Inauguration of a new Town Council
2.	App. 18/1	6-5-1732	Rededication of the renovated and enlarged Thomas School Building

3.	177/1	7-6-1732	4th Sunday after Trinity
4.	App. 11/1	8-3-1732	Name Day of Augustus II
5.	232[1]	before 7-27-1733	Tribute to the new sovereign, Augustus III
(6.)	App. 12/1	8-3-1733	Name Day of Augustus III (Parody of App. 18/1)
7.	213	9-5-1733	Birthday of Electoral Crown Prince
8.	214	12-8-1733	Birthday of Electoress of Saxony, Queen of Poland
9.	215	10-5-1734	Anniversary of Augustus III's election as King of Poland
10.	97/4	1734	Special occasion unknown
11.	248[I-VI]	12-25-1734 to 1-6-1735	The Holidays (and one Sunday) of the Christmas season
12.	211/8	end of 1734 or early 1735	Performance by the Collegium Musicum
(13a.)	11/1	5-19-1735	Ascension Day (Parody of App. 18/1 and App. 12/1)
(13b.)	11/4	5-19-1735	Ascension Day (Perhaps parody of the Hohenthal/Mencke wedding cantata; without BWV number)
14.	206/9	10-7-1736 probably already partly written in October 1734	Birthday of Augustus III
15.	30a/7	9-28-1737	Homage to J.C. von Hennicke, Lord of the Manor at Wiederau
(16.)	30/8	after 1738	St. John's Day (Parody of 30a/7)
17.	195/3	after 1737, perhaps 9-11-1741	Church wedding of a distinguished couple

In an attempt to evaluate this list, later adaptations, i.e. the parodies (placed above in parentheses) will have to be excluded from consideration. With the one possible exception of BWV 11/4, it can be assumed that the occasions for which Bach wrote the original versions of these compositions prompted him to employ short-long and/or Lombard rhythms. It then appears that close to one-half of these works—six out of fourteen—were composed in celebration of festive days in the lives of members of the ruling house of Saxony: four for Bach's sovereigns Augustus II and Augustus III and one each for the queen and the crown prince. Of the remaining eight compositions, two were written for festive municipal events in Leipzig: one for the inauguration of a new Town Council (No. 1), the other for an especially joyous day in the life of the Thomas School Building (No. 2). Whether in the case of the Coffee Cantata (No. 12) a specific event had occurred or an occasion had arisen that gave the concert of the Collegium Musicum in the "Zimmermannischen Kaffee-Haus" a special meaning, is unfortunately not known. Even though the wedding cantata (No. 17) was not necessarily intended for an aristocratic couple ("hochedles Paar"), it was in any case written for two socially prominent citizens. Only BWV 177/1 (No. 3) and BWV 97/4 (No. 10) could, as far as their short-long rhythms are concerned, fit stylistically and liturgically also into the time from 1723 to 1728. Finally, one of the four parodies (No. 6) was used by Bach for the Name Day of Augustus III.

What all these examples have in common is their festive character. The purpose for which Bach wrote the majority of these compositions was to pay homage to his rulers and also to create music as a tribute to the Town Council and the Thomas School. It seems quite obvious that Bach intended to present himself with these compositions in the most favorable light, first with the city authorities, and then, especially, with his sovereign and his family. Within the incredibly short time of fourteen-and-a-half months, from the end of July 1733 until October 1734, Bach dedicated the *Missa* of the later *B minor Mass* to Augustus III and then performed no less than six cantatas in honor of the elector and his family: BWV App. 12, BWV 213, 214, 205a, still another cantata that is no longer known, and 215. Of these seven works the composition that was performed on August 3, 1734 in honor of Augustus III's Name Day is lost. Among the other six compositions only BWV 205a, the cantata celebrating the coronation of Augustus III, lacks Lombard or distinct short-long rhythms. The fact that this cantata is a parody of a bourgeois congratulatory cantata of the year 1725 may well be the reason for the lack of these modish rhythms.

That trumpets and kettledrums symbolize not only God's majesty but also the glory of secular rulers is well known. They furnish brilliant color and sonorous beat also to the above-cited festive works, with the characteristic exception of the birthday cantata for the sickly eleven-year-old crown prince.

To the symbolic use of these festive instruments we may now add as stylistic components of Bach's compositions of homage which were written in the 1730s, also the presence of Lombard and short-long rhythms and that of syncopation.

What may have been the reason for Bach's use of these rhythms? 1730 was the year in which Bach was not only accused of negligence in his classroom instruction but in which also his general attitude was called "incorrigible" by a member of the Council. It was the year in which Bach made a last attempt at a satisfactory solution of the musical conditions in the Leipzig churches. When this "Most Necessary Draft for a Well-Appointed Church Music" fell upon deaf ears, Bach began to look for a position elsewhere. The letter to his former school friend Erdmann and, two years and nine months later, his application for a title and position at the Court in Dresden constitute the extant evidence of Bach's unmistakable desire to leave Leipzig.

What did Bach try to convey to the Saxon Court by his use of Lombard and short-long rhythms as well as syncopation? He probably wanted to show that he, who as master of the polyphonic style had gained the reputation of a conservative composer, was therefore by no means adverse to modern trends such as the Lombard manner, and knew perfectly well how to make successful use of it. In short, he intended to prove that as a composer he was very much *au courant* and thus could be counted among his time's progressives.[29] But why did he employ these rhythms only in one or two movements of these compositions? Did Bach perhaps try to show with these isolated movements, particularly with those featuring Lombard rhythm, that in his case the Lombard manner was not allowed to take over and become a mannerism, as it had become in the works of his then more illustrious colleagues Telemann and Vivaldi, to say nothing of the "Scotch Snap" of the English masters such as Henry Purcell?

Should this modish display of Lombard rhythm in Bach's vocal music of the 1730s really have been a means to an end? Is it warranted to make such an assumption about a genius such as Bach? It does not lie in the character of genius to isolate itself artificially from all outside influences. Moreover, we are at the moment considering not Bach, the otherworldly visionary, but the profoundly disillusioned artist who after seven years as Thomas Cantor was desperately seeking a change of position. We are considering Bach the man, indeed Bach the politician. Seen in this light, the suspicion that Bach used the Lombard style for diplomatic reasons begins to make sense. It becomes even more convincing upon rereading Bach's petitions and letters of complaint from 1725 to 1737 and thereby observing style and manner in which the great artist tried, at times in a dogmatic and stubborn way, to deal with legal, social, financial and often petty human affairs.

What history has handed down to us about Bach's cantata BWV App. 13 will, in spite of the fact that its music is lost, not only reinforce the previous reasoning but raise its conclusions to the point of near-certainty. Less known than Johann Adolph Scheibe's notorious attack upon Bach the composer which, with its rebuttals and rerebuttals, lasted from May 1737 to April 1739, is a passage in a communication Scheibe sent to Mattheson in January 1738.[30] It reads: "Bach's church compositions are always more artificial and laborious but by no means of such effect, conviction and reasonable reflection as the works of Telemann and Graun." Bach's friend Lorenz Christoph Mizler came to the Leipzig cantor's defense and tried to refute Scheibe's opinion of Bach's cantata style in a manner that is highly relevant to our line of reasoning. Mizler wrote,[31] "Herr Telemann and Herr Graun are excellent composers, and Herr Bach has written works of just the same quality. If Herr Bach, however, at times writes the inner parts more fully than other composers, he has taken as his model the music of twenty or twenty-five years ago. But he can also write otherwise, when he wishes to. Anyone who heard the music that was performed by the students at the Easter Fair in Leipzig last year [that is, in 1738] in the Most High Presence of his Royal Majesty in Poland which was composed by Capellmeister Bach, will have to admit that it was done entirely in accordance with the latest taste, and was approved by everyone. So well does the Herr Capellmeister know how to adapt himself to his audience." Magister Birnbaum, Bach's self-appointed and somewhat righteous and longwinded defender in the two-year-long controversy with Scheibe, also used this cantata as his counter-argument to Scheibe's criticism, made in the latter's note to Mattheson.[32] That both Mizler and Birnbaum chose this cantata as the most recent and most convincing example of Bach's vocal music in their efforts to refute Scheibe's criticism, makes the loss of its music particularly deplorable. When Mizler states that this cantata was "written entirely in accordance with the latest taste and was approved by everyone," he made both a stylistic and a sociological observation. By adding: "So well does the Herr Capellmeister know how to adapt himself to his listeners," Mizler gave the all important reason for Bach's employment of the fashionable modern style. Here, then, is irrefutable evidence of what has been presented in this study so far as a carefully developed assumption. What Mizler spelled out is that BWV App. 13 was written in accordance with "the latest taste" for a reason, namely because Bach addressed himself with this cantata to his elector and king.

On November 19, 1736, after a three-year period of waiting, Bach finally received the title of "Composer to the Royal Court Capelle." Seventeen months later, an official visit to the city of Leipzig by Augustus III and his family was announced. This visit gave Bach the first official opportunity to express personally in terms of music his gratitude for the honor bestowed upon him.

On April 10, 1738 the Thomas Cantor received the commission for a composition from the sponsors of the lavishly planned event. Bach had thus for once ample time to set the libretto which was by Gottsched[33] to music. This "evening serenade" was presented by the students of the University of Leipzig[34] on April 28, 1738 "to the sound of trumpets and drums"[35] in celebration of the forthcoming marriage of the elector's and king's oldest daughter, Princess Maria Amalia to "His Majesty the King of the Two Sicilies." The presence of two generations of the Royal House of Saxony that included in addition to the king, his consort and two princesses, may well have inspired Bach to converse with his illustrious guests in the most up to date and fashionable style of the time. But since the music of this cantata is lost, do we have any right to assume that Lombard rhythm played a role in it?

Its closest extant neighbor, written seven months earlier, and therefore perhaps best suited for comparison, was the cantata for the Lord of the Manor at Wiederau, BWV 30a, which can conceivably be called the most modern among Bach's surviving cantatas. Its opening chorus, which is to be repeated at the end of the work, belongs to the syncopated style of which Mattheson had said "which nowadays is the highest fashion."[36] The fifth movement, an alto aria, is similarly saturated with syncopations[37] which are later joined by Lombard figures. The seventh movement, the bass aria (discussed on pp. 243f.) presented us with one of the most conspicuous examples of Lombard rhythm encountered in this study. The chronological proximity of the Wiederau Cantata to the lost cantata of 1738 and the fact that both Mizler and Birnbaum[38] did not make use of it in their attempts to refute Scheibe's critical arguments, should allow us to deduce that Cantata BWV App. 13 was even more up to date, more lavish in its use of short-long and Lombard rhythms and syncopation than the Wiederau Cantata, BWV 30a.

The dactyllic meter of the first and last stanzas of Gottsched's text[39] is, with the exception of the opening "upbeat," also found in the opening and concluding stanzas of Cantatas 214, 215 and 206 which were composed (see pp. 246-49) for altogether comparable courtly functions. To judge by these secular "precursors" which were written just a few years earlier,[40] BWV App. 13/1 and 9 should likewise have been festive movements in 3/8 time (which can only be assumed) with "trumpets and drums" (which is known).[41] The arias, the third and fifth movements of BWV App. 13, are written in trochaic meter,[42] the meter that characterizes also the opening chorus of the Ascension Oratorio (with its jubilant and festive Lombard figures), the bass aria BWV 195/3 (with its deluge of Lombard and short-long rhythms) and the syncopated opening movement of the Wiederau Cantata. The supposition that at least in movements 3 and 5 of the lost Cantata BWV App. 13 these rhythms were distinctly present is supported by the trochaic meter common to all of them, and by the fact they were created during the heyday of Bach's use of these rhythms. That BWV App. 13 is Bach's last composition for the Court of Saxony deserves a final moment of attention. Once Bach had (in November 1736) received the title of court composer but not the position he had so fervently sought in 1733, there no longer seemed to be any practical reason to continue to strive for Augustus III's favor by creating new compositions in his and his family's honor. While cantata performances for the Name Day of his sovereign are documented for the years 1740 and 1742, they turn out to be no more than repeat performances of Cantata 206 and of his first secular cantata, the Hunting Cantata BWV 208 of 1713, the latter refitted with new texts for two out of its fifteen short movements.

A cursory survey of Bach's instrumental music—the one artistic realm not yet called upon—should either confirm or challenge the conclusions drawn from our investigation of his vocal music. The following survey will reveal that Bach was attracted similarly to short-long rhythms and the Lombard manner in his instrumental works, namely from 1726 to the Goldberg Variations of 1742-45. Needless to say, touches of short-long rhythm can already be found in Bach's chamber and orchestral music of the Cöthen period. However, outspoken cases of this rhythm are extremely rare also there. The few that can be found show the familiar three-note figure ♫♪. Bach used this figure either as an ornament, as a *Schleifer*-upbeat or for rhythmic emphasis, but usually only in a few measures. The opening movement of the Violin Concerto in A minor and the last movement of the Sonata in B minor for Violin and Clavier serve as good examples, to which the fourth movement of the Sonata No. 6 for Violin and Clavier or the second movement of the Sonata in D Major for Viol da Gamba and Clavier could be added. Compared to the almost inexhaustible wealth of chamber music composed at Cöthen, these sporadic appearances of the short-long rhythm are even rarer than they were in the vocal works of Bach's early years in Leipzig. They are thus of little consequence.

A change can be noted from 1726 onward. Bach's disagreements with the Administration of the University of Leipzig had begun towards the end of 1725. Since the composer's painfully relevant and detailed letters to the Elector failed to produce (in January 1726) a decision that satisfied the Thomas Cantor, Bach's disappointment with the general situation in Leipzig may already have set in at that time. Already after May 27, 1725 his steady flow of cantata compositions had come to a sudden halt. In the following year Bach wrote and published the first of his six Partitas for clavier with which he addressed himself for the first time to a larger public. He obviously intended to introduce himself by an easily accessible work that capable amateurs would find quite playable and that would spread his reputation as composer beyond the limiting confines of Leipzig. In the next few years five more Partitas appeared as single (although not exactly annual) publications. Collected together in one volume, the six Partitas were published in 1731 as Bach's Opus 1 (Part I of his *Clavierübung*).

On the other hand, nothing of Bach's ample output of clavier compositions and chamber music, written in Cöthen, had been published. Since Bach was apparently content as Capellmeister in Cöthen, he saw no reason to publish his music. In Leipzig, however, reasons arose. Is it just coincidence that the first Partita opens with a *Praeludium* in which short-long and syncopated figures flow gently along as if the composer was eager to convey to the musical world that Bach the composer was quite aware of the most recent trends in music (see above p. 254)? It does indeed seem to be more than coincidence that each one of the six Partitas includes at least one movement showing either traces or outspoken manifestations of short-long or syncopated rhythms.[43] The almost complete absence of these rhythms in the English and French Suites[44] and in the vast remainder of Bach's Cöthen compositions for harpsichord or clavichord as well as their total absence in the unaccompanied Sonatas, Partitas and Suites for Violin or Cello, for example, should go a long way to support the thesis that the six Partitas hold a special place in the Master's clavier style. They also stand apart in their use of $\frac{2}{4}$ meter, which can be observed in Bach's music from here on and which, as shown above (pp. 243, 248, 250-51) lent its dance-like beat to Bach's most outspoken vocal movements in Lombard rhythm.

Bach's organ music follows a similar pattern. The vast amount of organ compositions, written in Weimar, is practically free of short-long rhythms. Lombard rhythm does not appear at all. Not until Bach wrote his six Trio Sonatas for organ, supposedly "after 1727" and probably for his precocious son Wilhelm Friedemann, does the short-long rhythm manifest itself in Bach's organ music. In the final movement of the third Sonata the three-note figure ♫♩ belongs as upbeat and as rhythmic double accent to the substance of the principal theme. Less essential are the short-long beginnings of the themes in the opening movement of the same Sonata or in the second movement of the fourth Sonata and the short-long figure which appears towards the end of the theme in the middle movement of the fifth Sonata. The second movement of the Sixth Sonata begins as a Siciliano, introduces in measure 2 the short-long, three-note ornament and continues with more complex syncopated phrases:

T. 3

In the final movement of the same Sonata Bach used the short-long, three-note figure to give the principal as well as the secondary themes of the movement rhythmically sharper profiles. If Bach composed these Trio Sonatas in the order of their autograph numbering, one would be justified in considering the increasing use of short-long phrases indicative of Bach's composing style of these years.

Not only the Clavier Partitas but also the remaining three parts of the *Clavierübung* contain movements that distinguish themselves at first by the use of short-long, but later also by that of Lombard rhythm. This seems logical inasmuch as these four published collections of keyboard music address themselves expressly to musical amateurs and *Clavierübung* III also to professionals, i.e. to the music-buying public. *Clavierübung* II, published in 1735, harbors only traces of short-long rhythm, namely in the first and second movements of the Italian Concerto and in *Passepied* II, in the *Gigue* and the *Echo* of the Overture after the French Manner. On the other hand, *Clavierübung* III, the Organ Mass, published in 1739, contains the most radical example of Lombard rhythm in Bach's whole instrumental oeuvre, the large five-part version of the organ chorale "Vater unser im Himmelreich" (Our Father in Heaven).[45] In this complex double-canonic movement Bach left the modish nature of Lombard rhythm far behind, sublimating and lifting it to the highest level of spiritualized art. The symbolism of this movement has evoked from scholars as many different interpretations as there have been scholars to investigate this composition. Instead of adding still another view, I may suggest that an explanation of the symbolism of the Lombard rhythm in this movement be sought in Rhetoric, that is, in the rhetorical doctrine of musical figures.

Shortly before this time Bach wrote his great B minor Sonata for Flute and Clavier.[46] In its first two movements, particularly in the first, short-long rhythm plays an essential role. The transverse flute has already frequently been noted in our study of vocal music as an instrument that Bach favored especially with short-long and Lombard phrases and ornaments. The Polonaise, No. 19 in Anna Magdalena Bach's second Notebook (begun in 1725), would be one of Bach's most persistent, but also one of his most naive examples of the use of the short-long, three-note figure, if it were not for the fact that the composer of this stylish little dance is not Johann Sebastian but his son Carl Philipp Emanuel Bach. If we accept Georg von Dadelsen's date as between 1730 and 1734,[47] we may deduce from C.P.E. Bach's persistent application of this figure that the latter was not only a striking stylistic feature in J.S. Bach's music during these years, but that it was also in the literal sense of the word at home in Bach's household. Already in the 1720s the Polonaise had entered upon its successful conquest and established itself as one of the most fashionable dances in European countries. As late as 1772 Charles Burney spoke of a "Polonaise fad in Saxony."[48]

In the fourth part of the *Clavierübung,* the Goldberg Variations, published in 1742/45 (?), Lombard rhythm is used at its most elegant in the Aria that begets the variations.[49] Earlier widespread opinion that the Aria was not by Bach and was written into Anna Magdalena's Notebook of 1725 shortly after the date of its title page has been refuted by Georg von Dadelsen. In the

Kritische Bericht to the NBA edition[50] he proved by graphological means that Anna Magdalena entered the Aria into her Notebook in a late phase of her handwriting. From this fact von Dadelsen deduced that Bach's wife copied this Aria from her husband's manuscript at (or shortly after) the time Johann Sebastian started the composition of the variations.

The time span 1726-42/45 during which Bach employed at first short-long rhythm and syncopation, then Lombard rhythm with a certain regularity in his instrumental music, coincides roughly with the period 1723-41 during which these rhythms appear also in the composer's vocal music. But the most convincing examples of Lombard rhythm in Bach's instrumental music, the large version of the "Vater unser" organ chorale, the Aria of the *Goldberg Variations* (if Bach is its composer) and the measures from the slow movement of the E Major Violin Concerto, as they appear in Bach's transcription in the D Major Harpsichord Concerto (BWV 1054),[51] are chronological neighbors of the most conspicuous compositions in the Lombard manner in Bach's vocal oeuvre, the bass aria from Cantata 195 (see above, pp. 250-51). The present study has concentrated less on Bach's instrumental music because it is not as easily datable (unless it has come down to us in autograph manuscripts or has appeared in print) as Bach's vocal music, most of which was composed *ad hoc* for specific Sundays or holidays of the church year and the vast majority of which has survived in autograph form.

A return to the *Domine Deus* from the *B minor Mass* which I discussed in the preceding article seems warranted. Its Lombard rhythm differs in one basic aspect from the examples that have so far been explored. If it were not for the three measures notated by Bach in Lombard rhythm in three of the autograph parts, the Lombard rhythm in the *Domine Deus* would be invisible, so to speak. I interpreted these three measures as Bach's calculated invitation to identical execution in all corresponding phrases. In the course of the present study, slurred pairs of alternating thirty-second notes and dotted sixteenth notes descending diatonically were encountered in relatively few compositions. They were first observed in convincing form in 1724, in the second movement of Cantata 114. Less consistently notated, they then appeared in 1725 in BWV 92/3, more than six years later, in 1731, in BWV 29/5, but from there on more frequently up to BWV 195/3 and to *Clavierübung* III and IV.

In the third part of the *Clavierübung*, in the manualiter version of the organ chorale "Wir glauben all an einen Gott" (We all believe in one God) which thrives on the majestic dotted rhythm of the French Overture, Bach inserted three descending pairs in Lombard rhythm to rein the mighty forward thrust of the movement to a halt. In the Aria of the *Goldberg Variations* Bach spelled out such pairs in Lombard rhythm only in measures 7, 8 and 22. However, the ear hears a good number of additional Lombard and short-long figures if the various grace notes and appoggiaturas of the Aria are properly executed. Measures 23-24 and 48-49 in the second movement of the Harpsichord Concerto in D Major raise the question[52] as to why Bach notated the corresponding measures in the Violin Concerto in E Major in even sixteenth notes while notating them in the above later transcription for harpsichord as thirty-second and dotted sixteenth notes, (applying slurs each time to two of these diatonically descending Lombard pairs). As numerous cases of the present study have shown, it was an integral part of Bach's creative instinct to add rhythmic refinements to his compositions when he parodied or transcribed them, particularly in the 1730s, during which decade he recast the Violin Concerto as a Harpsichord concerto. The relative inability of the harpsichord to articulate rhythmically and dynamically as readily and as subtly as the violin may have motivated Bach to notate the two passages in the Harpsichord Concerto unmistakably in Lombard rhythm. If a violinist executes these measures today with Lombard articulation, he interprets them in the "modern style" of the 1730s and thus possibly not in the style that Bach envisaged in his Cöthen years. It is not my intention to solve this question, but rather to present it for further thought and discussion. But why did Bach not notate another short passage in the slow movement of the D Major Harpsichord Concerto in Lombard rhythm? The answer to this might be that in this 35th measure the slurred pairs of sixteenth notes do not descend but ascend diatonically.

Insofar as our observations have revealed mostly descending pairs notated in Lombard rhythm, the following conclusion seems sufficiently well documented, namely that, above all, slurred pairs of diatonically descending sixteenth notes not only permit but also ask for Lombard execution. The examples of Lombard figures that are given in the theoretical works by Quantz, C.P.E. Bach and Leopold Mozart show a comparable preponderance of stepwise descending slurred pairs of notes. On the other hand, the majority of the slurred pairs in Lombard rhythm that appear in Vivaldi's instrumental compositions move by larger intervals.[53]

The large version of the organ chorale "Vater unser..." is particularly instructive in this connection. What in the *Domine Deus* from the *B minor Mass*—except for the three measures notated in Lombard rhythm—was implied, Bach wrote out meticulously throughout the long movement of the "Vater unser" chorale. But why? The organ chorales from *Clavierübung* III were published as models of their kind for the benefit "of Music Lovers and especially for Connoisseurs of such Work." Therefore Bach could not afford to have his intentions misunderstood and consequently misinterpreted. Unlike his vocal music, which was rehearsed and performed under his direction but was not published, the four parts of the *Clavierübung* were sent out into the world to be played and performed by others. Hence they had to be notated and printed as precisely as possible.

It should no longer come as a surprise that in the organ chorale "Vater unser" the overwhelming majority of slurred pairs of alternating thirty-second and dotted sixteenth notes descend diatonically: 229 out of 254. A mere 6 ascend. Of the 19 remaining pairs that do not proceed stepwise, twice as many leap downwards as upwards, preferring in doing so the interval of a third. The numerical proportions in the *Domine Deus* from the *B minor Mass* are of startling similarity. Of the slightly more than 200 slurred pairs of sixteenth notes 187 descend by diatonic steps; only 16 pairs ascend diatonically and a mere 3 descend by thirds. In the bass aria from Cantata 195, perhaps the last and certainly the most radical case of Bach's use of Lombard rhythm in his vocal music, the numerical relations are, however, quite different. That 152 pairs move diatonically and 38 by larger intervals still fits, though more roughly, the expected pattern. What is, on the other hand, unusual is that almost as many of the stepwise moving pairs ascend (74) as descend (78). The same relation can be observed among the pairs that proceed by larger intervals; 20 of them leap downwards and 18 upwards. Bach employed yet another, a slower but higher leaping Lombard figure ♪♪. which avoids the third and prefers larger intervals, especially the octave. This Lombard figure jumps only 5 times downwards but 53 times upwards. Frequently it is answered by the descending Lombard figure ♫♩·, with which it also appears simultaneously. This bizarre movement is, because of its relatively large number of disjunct pairs and its vast number of diatonically ascending pairs in Lombard rhythm, unique in Bach's oeuvre. All other instances of slurred pairs in Lombard rhythm which we encountered (in BWV 114/2, 92/3, 29/5, the Aria of the *Goldberg Variations,* etc.) are, on the other hand, classic examples of the stepwise descending Bachian norm.

However, before anyone draws the obvious conclusion from what has been pointed out above, he will have to ascertain that the following conditions are met: the composition by Bach to whose slurred pairs of descending sixteenth notes he might feel inclined to apply Lombard articulation must show numerical relations that are proportionate to those cited above (save BWV 195/3). Furthermore, this piece of music should have been composed between 1724 and the early 1740s, because it must comply with the time span of Bach's own predilection for the Lombard manner.

The purpose of this study has been to isolate and thus to identify the short-long rhythm and, above all, the Lombard manner, as related valid idiosyncrasies of Bach's composing style and to show that Bach's partiality to these rhythms became most plainly evident in the early 1730s, at a time when the composer had serious reasons to present himself as a friend and connoisseur of the latest fashionable trends. But the fashionable aspects of these rhythms dissolved at the time of the *Christmas Oratorio,* the B minor Flute Sonata, the D Major Harpsichord Concerto and the large version of the

"Vater unser" organ chorale so naturally in his composing style that these rhythms eventually became genuine stylistic facets of Bach's music of the 1730s.

It is truly remarkable that the most modern stylistic trend, the Lombard manner, and the time-honored *stile antico* to which Bach also turned late in life,[54] should have lived side by side and approximately simultaneously in Bach's work. In fact, their creator considered each one of them worthy of being passed on to his fellowmen and to posterity as "models of their kind" by publishing examples of both styles in the third part of the *Clavierübung*. Only geniuses of the magnitude of a Bach, Monteverdi, or Mozart could embrace both the old and the new and make each of them their own by transforming them into artworks reflecting their own personalities. To reveal the new, the Lombard manner, as a time-conditioned phase in Johann Sebastian Bach's work has been the purpose of this study.

ABBREVIATIONS

BG	= Gesamtausgabe der Bach-Gesellschaft, Leipzig 1851-1899
BJ	= Bach-Jahrbuch, Leipzig 1904 ff.
BWV	= Wolfgang Schmieder, Thematisch-systematisches Verzeichnis der musikalischen Werke von Johann Sebastian Bach. Bach-Werke-Verzeichnis, Leipzig 1950
Bach-Dok. II	= Bach-Dokumente, herausgegeben vom Bach-Archiv Leipzig, Supplement zu Johann Sebastian Bach, Neue Ausgabe sämtlicher Werke. Band II: Fremdschriftliche und gedruckte Dokumente zur Lebensgeschichte Johann Sebastian Bachs 1685-1750. Vorgelegt und erläutert von Werner Neumann und Hans-Joachim Schulze, Leipzig, Kassel 1969
Krit. Ber.	= Kritischer Bericht
NBA	= Neue Bach-Ausgabe. Johann Sebastian Bach. Neue Ausgabe sämtlicher Werke. Herausgegeben vom Johann-Sebastian-Bach-Institut Göttingen und vom Bach-Archiv Leipzig, Kassel 1954 ff.

Notes

1. Translated freely by the author, this article is published here for the first time in English. It was originally published in the *Bach-Jahrbuch* in 1978.

2. See Part VI above.

3. It appears for the first time before 1716, namely in the third movement, a soprano/bass duet from Bach's Weimar Christmas cantata "Christen, ätzet diesen Tag" (BWV 63), set to the text "Gott, du hast es wohl *ge*-füget." In the eighth movement of the cantata "Ich hatte viel Bekümmernis" of 1713 (BWV 21), but notated first in the form of written-out mordents in the

autograph Cöthen parts of 1720, this embellishment not only falls again on the upbeat but occurs also again in a duet for soprano (the Soul) and bass (Christ). Here it is set to the metrically identical words "Komm, mein Jesu, und *er*-quicke—Ja, ich komme und *er*-quicke." In both cases the written-out mordent functions as springboard to the following accented syllable which falls on a strong beat of the measure. (See further BWV 66a/4 of 1718, again a duet, which—parodied—survives in the church cantata BWV 66/5.)

4. Quantz, *Versuch einer Anweisung die Flöte traversière zu spielen,* Berlin, 1752, XVIII. Hauptstück (main chapter), paragraph 58. See also V. Hauptstück, paragraph 23 as well as Tabelle (Table) II, Figure 8.

5. Quantz does not mention Vivaldi by name but leaves little room for doubt whom he meant by a "famous violinist."

6. Compare the English edition of Quantz's *Versuch,* London, 1966, footnote 5 as well as M. Pincherle's *Vivaldi,* New York, 1957, p. 47.

7. This is the subtitle of the first, the French edition (1905) of Albert Schweitzer's Bach biography.

8. Cf. NBA II/3 (A. Dürr), p. 48.

9. The two purely ornamental occurrences of the three-note figure ⌐♫ in the soprano aria "Ich folge dir gleichfalls mit freudigen Schritten" (I follow you likewise with joyful footsteps) can be left out of consideration. The short-long ornament in the alto's opening measure, measure 9 of the aria "Von *den* Stricken meiner Sünden mich zu entbinden" (From the shackles of my sins to unbind me) is a rhythmic twist that belongs to a later version of the *John Passion.* On the other hand, Bach had used the figure ♪♩♪ six times already in the early version of 1724, though set to different words while retaining it only three times in the later autograph score of about 1739.

10. As shown in the music example above, Bach declaims this text to both rhythms, for instance to (a) in measures 41-45, to (b) in measures 119-21. The phrase "Mein Jesus ist tot!" however, is heard only to the rhythm of (b). (See measures 69 and 79.)

11. I follow here Joshua Rifkin's new dating of the first version of the *Matthew Passion:* Good Friday 1727. Compare *The Musical Quarterly* 61, 1975, p. 360ff.

12. However, true Lombard notation alternates in identical sequences which are doubtlessly intended to be executed in the same Lombard manner, with the simpler notation of two slurred sixteenth notes. This is a time saving device that characterizes also the score of BWV 114/2 and most of the relevant measures in the *Domine Deus* from the *B minor Mass* etc.

13. This is the third time since the *St. John Passion* that a tenor aria (BWV 114/2, 92/3 and 183/2) features Lombard or short-long rhythm.

14. The bass aria "Komm, süsses Kreuz" (Come, sweet cross). (NBA II/5, No. 57; BG 4, No. 66; see measures 12, 43).

15. See the facsimile edition, VEB Deutscher Verlag für Musik, Leipzig 1974.

16. Cf. NBA II/5a (A. Dürr).

17. The new numbering used in NBA II/5 precedes the old numbering of the BG edition which is placed here in brackets.

18. From hereon abbreviated App. (for Appendix).

19. According to BJ 1972, pp. 80f. and 88f. (Werner Neumann), Bach had planned such a parody but then decided to compose a new movement (BVW 30a/7). The 14th movement of the Peasant Cantata (BWV 212) is apparently the one which goes back to BWV App. 11/9.

20. As Spitta already suspected. Spitta, *Johann Sebastian Bach,* vol. II, p. 630.

21. Terry, *Bach,* p. 219.

22. Arnold Schering, *Johann Sebastian Bach und das Musikleben Leipzigs im 18. Jahrhundert,* Leipzig, 1941, p. 144.

23. In BG 29, p. 158, this three-note figure is printed in the manner in which Bach had notated it in the score: 𝄇, in spite of the fact that he notated it in the autograph first violin and soprano parts consistently in the reversed, the short-long manner. The parts which were written by Bach shortly after he had completed the score, thus represent a new version, namely one that tightened the rhythm's forward thrust in a manner altogether typical of this time and which ought to be understood as Bach's second and final decision. Werner Neumann printed the short-long, three-note figure of the original parts for the first time in 1970 (in NBA I/40, p. 212) as corresponding to Bach's proper performance wishes. See also Neumann's *Krit. Ber.,* NBA I/40, p. 199.

24. "Heute noch.   (Today, still today,
     Lieber Vater, tut es doch!   Dear father, by all means do it!
     Ach, ein Mann!   Ah, a husband!
     Wahrlich, dieser steht mir an!   Indeed, he'd suit me!

     Wenn es sich doch balde fügte,   If it only soon would happen,
     Dass ich endlich vor Coffee,   That even before I have my coffee
     Eh ich noch zu Bette geh,   And before I go to bed
     Einen wackern Liebsten kriegte!"   I'd finally get a stouthearted lover!)

25. See the measure printed on p. 233.

26. Alfred Dürr, *Die Kantaten von Johann Sebastian Bach,* Kassel, 1971, p. 609.

27. If we disregard its brief appearance in BWV 92/3 (see above, p. 237).

28. Even beyond 1728, that is, including the short-long figures added later to the Matthew Passion (see above, p. 239).

29. See Robert L. Marshall, "Bach The Progressive: Observations on His Later Works," in *The Musical Quarterly,* 62, 1976, p. 313ff.

30. Bach-Dok. II, p. 307.

31. Ibid., p. 336.

32. Ibid., p. 332 (in Birnbaum's lengthy argument of March 1739).

33. Cf. Werner Neumann, *Sämtliche von Johann Sebastian Bach vertonte Texte,* VEB Deutscher Verlag für Musik, Leipzig, 1974, pp. 418-19.

34. The staging of the event was apparently as formidable as that which had celebrated the King's visit to Leipzig during which Cantata 215 was performed (see above, p. 247 as well as Bach-Dok. II, p. 327f.).

35. Bach-Dok. II, p. 327.

36. *Der vollkommene Capellmeister,* Hamburg 1739, Part II, Chapter 6, paragraph 32, "Amphibrachys." (See the facsimile edition, Kassel and Basel 1954, p. 168.)

37. Regarding the syncopated style in Bach's vocal music see also BWV 51/5, 100/4, 214/7 ($=248^{I}/8$), 206/3 (for instance measure 41ff.), 206/7, $248^{II}/21$, $248^{III}/31$ and $248^{V}/51$, all of which are compositions of the 1730s.

38. Of course it is possible that these two good friends of the Thomas Cantor did not know the Wiederau Cantata.

39. "Willkommen! Ihr herrschenden Götter der Erden!" (Be welcome! You ruling Gods of the Earth!) = movement 1.
    "Auf! theureste Enkelinn mächtigster Kaiser!"
    (Hail! Dearest granddaughter of mightiest Emperors)
    = final movement.

40. In 1733, 1734 and 1734-36.

41. See Bach-Dok. II, p. 327.

42. "Fürsten sind die Lust der Erden;   (Princes are the Earth's pleasure,
    Wenn sie Hirten ihrer Heerden"   when they are shepherds of their flock)
          (movement 3)   (= movement 3)

    "Sanfte Stille! Süsse Fülle!   (Gentle quiet! Sweet abundance!
    Die der Friede, Künsten schenkt"   Is what peace gives to the arts)
          (movement 5)   (= movement 5)

43. See the Sarabande from Partita IV (1728), The Passepied from Partita V (1730), the syncopated Courante and Gavotte from Partita VI (which appeared already in Anna Magdalena's Notebook of 1725, but which by no means had to be composed in the year shown on its title page) and, though just for a fleeting moment, the Andante middle section of the opening movement of Partita II (1727) and finally a mere touch of short-long rhythm in the Scherzo from Partita III of the same year.

44. The six English Suites are completely free of this rhythm (though the written-out *agréments* of the Sarabande from the second Suite show understandably four short-long figures). In the second French Suite the short-long upbeat belongs to the peculiarity of the dotted (3/8) rhythm of the Gigue. In the Gigue of the next Suite the familiar short-long three-note figure appears twice. In the Gavotte of the sixth Suite Bach gives to three phrases the rhythmically droll half-close of a sixteenth note and a dotted eighth note and ends the charming little dance with the short-long three-note figure appearing twice. This figure lives on in the beginnings of the diverse themes in the following Polonaise.

45. Also the first of the Four Duets is characterized by short-long and syncopated rhythms.

46. In the afterword to the facsimile edition (*Faksimile-Reihe Bachscher Werke und Schriftstücke,* vol. 4, Leipzig, n.d.) W. Neumann placed this Sonata into Bach's middle period in Leipzig.

47. *Krit. Ber.,* NBA V/4, p. 70.

48. Burney, *Tagebuch einer musikalischen Reise,* Hamburg 1772/73, p. 38f. of vol 3 (which was written in Dresden towards the end of 1772): "The musical pieces that are known by the name

"Polonoisen" [sic] are not only in Dresden but also in many other regions of Saxony very much in vogue. It is easy to understand that they [the Polonaises] entered the country through the manifold associations of the Poles and the Saxons during the reigns of Augustus II and III."

49.   See measures 7-8 and 22. Bach employed short-long figures and syncopations also in variation 25.

50.   *Krit. Ber.*, NBA V/4, p. 94.

51.   G. Herz in *Bach-Jahrbuch,* 1974, p. 97.

52.   I did not address this question in the preceding article.

53.   S. Babitz, "A Problem of Rhythm in Baroque Music," in *The Musical Quarterly* 38, 1952, p. 548.

54.   See Christoph Wolff, *Der stile antico in der Musik Johann Sebastian Bachs* = Beihefte zum *Archiv für Musikwissenschaft,* vol. 6, Wiesbaden, 1968.

Index